STUDY GUIDE

Psychological Science

THIRD CANADIAN EDITION

STUDY GUIDE

Psychological Science

THIRD CANADIAN EDITION

Michael S. Gazzaniga • Todd F. Heatherton •
Diane F. Halpern • Steven J. Heine

Anna K. Tirovolas
McGILL UNIVERSITY

Georgina Archbold
McGILL UNIVERSITY

WITH CONTRIBUTIONS BY:

Gary W. Lewandowski Jr.
MONMOUTII UNIVERSITY

Brett L. Beck and Eileen Astor-Stetson
BLOOMSBURG UNIVERSITY

W • W • NORTON & COMPANY • NEW YORK • LONDON

Printed in the United States of America

Third Canadian Edition

Ancillary Editor: Matthew A. Freeman

Composition and layout by R. Flechner Graphics

ISBN 978-0-393-91242-5

W. W. Norton & Company, Inc., 500 Fifth Avenue, New York, NY 10110
www.wwnorton.com

W. W. Norton & Company Ltd., Castle House, 75/76 Wells Street, London W1T 3QT

2 3 4 5 6 7 8 9 0

CONTENTS

TO THE STUDENTS

PSYCHOLOGY IS IMPORTANT AND RELEVANT TO YOUR LIFE

You are living in a world where knowledge is accumulating at an unprecedented rate. The best preparation for an unknown future is to build a solid foundation for learning that emphasizes the twin abilities of knowing how to learn and how to think critically about the myriad issues you will face. You will need to know the major principles of psychological science if you intend to tackle the many challenges that await you, from global issues such as pollution, hunger, racism, poverty, and terrorism to personal questions about being a good parent, making wise decisions about money and health, and finding and keeping love and happiness.

LONG-TERM LEARNING AND UNDERSTANDING

With knowledge accumulating at an exponential rate, you can expect to be a lifelong learner. Good study habits are difficult to learn; reading your textbook and painting the pages with a bright highlighter isn't evidence of good learning. If all you do to study is read and highlight, then, when the information is complex, you will find that it all goes in one eye and out the other. There are better ways to make learning stick. There are powerful learning strategies that produce durable learning—learning that lasts well into the future.

In a rapidly changing world, you'll need to learn how to use information that was learned in one context (in this example from your class and textbook) in another context (for example, at work or at home). After all, the reason you are in school is to acquire knowledge and skills that will be useful sometime later in life, in settings that are very different from school. Everyone can become a better learner by consistently applying a few general principles that promote learning that lasts and the transfer of learning to new contexts.

HOW TO SUCCEED IN SCHOOL AND LIFE

Durable learning is effortful, but with sufficient effort, everyone can become a better learner. We are talking about changing your personal epistemology: the way you think about learning and knowledge. For example, some people believe that they "cannot do" math or science or some other subject. What this means is that it is difficult for them to learn these subject areas, which they interpret as meaning that they are not good at learning. If you work hard at learning, subsequent learning becomes much easier. But, also know that your hard work is important for your future and that a quality education pays a lifetime of dividends.

Here are five strategies or tools for better learning. Like any powerful tool, they can have significant positive effects when used consistently, wisely, and well.

1. Practice with Effortful Retrieval

Psychologists who study learning and memory have demonstrated the importance of response. As you read each chapter, notice that every major heading is in the form of a question. When you finish reading each section, stop and write out an answer. Use your own words. One technique is to write out the answer in the wide margins in your text so that when you go back to study you have your own notes and the text next to each other. Be sure that you answer the questions without looking at the book, and then check the accuracy and completeness of what you wrote.

Every time you learn something you create "memory traces" in your brain. By retrieving the information that was learned, you strengthen the memory trace and make that memory more likely to be recalled in the future. There is a saying in psychology: "The head remembers what it does." If you want your studying to pay off in durable learning, you need to practice remembering what you read and what you learn in class. We also end each section with a few questions about the material you just read. Answer the end of section and end of chapter questions (without looking at the text). Write out the answers as a way of confirming that you understand the material well enough to write about it, and use the questions and your answers when you review your learning. Be sure to check your answer with the information in the text.

2. Space Your Study Sessions: Cramming Is a Crummy Way to Learn

You have a busy life. It might be some combination of sports; a killer course load; a part-time or even full-time job; family responsibilities, which may include caring for children, parents, or other family members; volunteer activities; and much more. It is easy to postpone studying until the night or two before an exam, but there is too much to learn in every chapter to cram the learning into a few days or late nights. You might be able to remember some information learned by cramming long enough to do well on an exam, but cramming does not produce learning that lasts. Space out your study sessions over the semester and build in plenty of time for active review. A good-sized chunk of learning might be one or two main sections within a chapter at a single sitting—the actual best "chunk" of information will depend on your prior knowledge. Space your study sessions as you go through school, and you will be rewarded with long-term knowledge retention.

3. Use Multiple Representations

People process information in two channels—visuospatial and verbal. Use both of these information formats. Take notes in words and supplement your words with concept maps and other types of diagrams, including graphs, which are called visuospatial displays. Diagrammed concept maps show the main idea at the centre and the most important points branching out from the main idea. Examples appear throughout your study guide.

4. Explain for Good Retention (Memory)

As you learn, keep in mind the classic journalists' questions —what, why, when, and how. You should be able to explain and describe even the most complicated topics to anyone by organizing your thoughts around these questions. A deep level of learning organized around the journalists' questions would allow you to hypothesize and use a more holistic understanding to reason out answers.

5. Develop the Habits and Skills of a Critical Thinker

Every chapter presents two critical thinking skills that will help you recognize faulty reasoning designed to get you to buy or believe something. The underlying rationale for a skills approach to teaching critical thinking is that there are critical thinking skills that can be learned and, if you learn them and apply them appropriately, you will become a better thinker. There is ample evidence, scattered through the book, that this is true. For example, in a recent study, adults who could recognize and use seven basic critical thinking skills reported fewer negative life events; they are less likely to run out of checks when they are needed, less likely to rent and return a movie without watching it, and less likely to engage in risky behaviours such as unprotected intercourse (de Bruin, Parker, & Fischhoff, 2007). In other words, you really can become a better critical thinker if you learn and use the critical thinking skills presented throughout this book—so dig in and learn the skills of critical thinking.

There are many more important rules for learning, but these five are a good start toward making you an efficient learner. *25 Principles of Learning* can be found at the Web site for the Association for Psychological Science's task force on lifelong learning (http://psyc.memphis.edu/learning). It is likely that this list will continue to grow.

As you start your adventure in psychology, we wish you a happy and productive journey. Remember that learning is not a spectator sport, so get involved and enjoy your trip into the world of psychological science.

STUDY GUIDE

Psychological Science

THIRD CANADIAN EDITION

CHAPTER 1 Introduction to Psychological Science

CONCEPT MAP

I. Introduction to Psychological Science
  A. Goal of Psychologists
    1. Role of Brain Imaging
  B. Psychological Science
    1. Mind
    2. Brain
    3. Behaviour

II. Themes of Psychological Science
  A. Psychology Is an Empirical Science
    1. Being a Good Consumer of Research
  B. Nature and Nurture Are Inextricably Entwined
    1. Nature/Nurture Debate
  C. The Brain and Mind Are Inseparable
    1. Mind/Body Problem
      a. Dualism
  D. A New Biological Revolution Is Energizing Research
    1. Three Main Developments
      a. Brain Chemistry
      b. Human Genome
      c. Watching the Working Brain
        1. Localization
  E. The Mind Is Adaptive
    1. Evolutionary Theory
      a. Natural Selection
      b. Survival of the Fittest
      c. Adaptations
        1. Modern Minds
    2. Culture
  F. Psychological Science Crosses Levels of Analysis
    1. Biological
    2. Individual
    3. Social
    4. Cultural
  G. We Are Often Unaware of the Multiple Influences on How We Think, Feel, and Act
    1. Automaticity of Behaviour

III. The Development of Psychology's Foundations
  A. Early Influences
    1. Non-European Influences
    2. John Stuart Mill
  B. Schools of Thought
    1. Structuralism
      a. Key Figures
        1. Wilhelm Wundt
          A. Introspection
        2. Edward Titchener
    2. Functionalism
      a. Key Figures
        1. William James
        2. John Dewey
        3. Rights of Women
          A. Mary Whiton Calkins
          B. Mary Salter Ainsworth
          C. Margaret Floy Washburn
          D. Emma S. Baker
      b. Stream of Consciousness
      c. Application of Psychology
    3. Gestalt Psychology
      a. Phenomenological Approach
    4. Freud and the Power of the Unconscious
      a. Unconscious
      b. Psychoanalysis
    5. Behaviourism
      a. Key Figures
        1. John B. Watson
        2. B. F. Skinner

6. Cognition's Role in Behaviour
    a. Key Figures
        1. Wolfgang Köhler
        2. Edward Tolman
        3. George A. Miller
            A. Cognitive Psychology
    b. Information Processing
7. The Role of Social Situations in Behaviour
    a. Key Figures
        1. Kurt Lewin
            A. Field Theory
8. Psychological Therapy Is Based on Science

IV. Applying Psychological Science
    A. Psychological Knowledge Is Used in Many Professions
        1. Career Outlook
    B. People Are Intuitive Psychological Scientists
    C. Psychological Sciences Require Critical Thinking
        1. Critical Thinking
    D. Psychologists Adhere to a Code of Ethics
    E. Psychology Is Relevant to Every Person's Life

CHAPTER SUMMARY

What Are the Seven Themes of Psychological Science?

• Psychology Is an Empirical Science: Psychological science relies on empirical evidence as a way of knowing about how we think, feel, and behave.

• Nature and Nurture Are Inextricably Entwined: Nature and nurture depend on each other, and their influences cannot be separated.

• The Brain and Mind Are Inseparable: Older dualist notions about the separation of the brain and mind have been replaced with the idea that the (physical) brain enables the mind; brain and mind cannot be separated.

• A New Biological Revolution Is Energizing Research: The scientific knowledge of brain activity has been enhanced by the discovery of more neurotransmitters. Mapping of the human genome has furthered genetics' role in analyzing both disease and behaviour. Tremendous advances in brain imaging have revealed the working brain. These advances are changing how we think about psychology.

• The Mind Is Adaptive: The brain has evolved to solve survival problems and adapt to environments. Many modern behaviours are by-products of adaptation.

• Psychological Science Crosses Levels of Analysis: Psychological scientists examine behaviour from various analytical levels: biological (brain systems, neurochemistry, and genetics), individual (personality as well as perception and cognition), social (interpersonal behaviour), and cultural (within a single culture and across several cultures).

• We Often Are Unaware of the Multiple Influences on How We Think, Feel, and Act: Hundreds of studies show that subtle events in the environment can change how we think, feel, and act without our awareness of the way they influence us.

How Did the Scientific Foundations of Psychology Develop?

• Experimental Psychology Begins with Structuralism: Although psychology's intellectual history dates back thousands of years, psychology began as a formal discipline in 1879, in Wilhelm Wundt's laboratory in Germany. Using techniques of introspection, scientists attempted to understand conscious experience by reducing it to its basic elements—its structure.

• Functionalism Addresses the Purpose of Behaviour: According to functionalists, the mind is best understood by examining its functions, not its structure.

• Gestalt Psychology Emphasizes Patterns and Context in Learning: The assertion that the whole experience (the gestalt) is greater than the sum of its parts led to an approach emphasizing the subjective experience of perception.

• Women Made Pioneering Contributions to Psychology: Women's early contributions to psychological science, such as the achievements of Mary Calkins, Mary Salter Ainsworth, Margaret Washburn, and Emma S. Baker have gone underacknowledged.

• Freud Emphasized the Power of the Unconscious: The psychoanalytic assumption that unconscious processes are not readily available to our awareness but influence our behaviour had an enormous impact on psychology.

• Most Behaviour Can Be Modified by Reward and Punishment: Discoveries that behaviour is changed by its consequences caused behaviourism to dominate psychology until the 1960s.

• Cognition Affects Behaviour: The computer analogy of the brain and the cognitive revolution led to the information processing perspective.

• Social Situations Shape Behaviour: Work in social psychology has highlighted how situations and other people are powerful forces in shaping behaviour.

• Psychological Therapy Is Based on Science: Scientific research over the course of the twentieth century taught psychological scientists that there is no universal treatment for psychological disorders. Instead, different treatments are effective for different disorders.

How Can We Apply Psychological Science?

• Psychological Knowledge Is Used in Many Professions: Because psychology focuses on human behaviour, it is of interest to many students and professionals and is used in virtually every profession.

• People Are Intuitive Psychological Scientists: Humans naturally explain and predict others' behaviour, but biases and prejudices often lead to wrong conclusions, so we need to use scientific methods and critical thinking.

• Psychological Science Requires Critical Thinking: The use of critical thinking skills will improve how we think. Skepticism, an important element of science, requires the use of critical thinking skills, including a careful examination of how well evidence supports a conclusion. Using critical thinking skills and understanding the methods of psychological science are important for evaluating research reported in the popular media.

• Psychologists Adhere to a Code of Ethics: In most countries, psychologists are governed by a code of ethics. These codes require psychologists to treat people with respect and dignity and to show utmost concern for people's safety.

• Psychology Is Relevant to Every Person's Life: The popular press regularly reports psychological findings, so educated adults need to know how to think about research reports and how to apply psychological knowledge. Psychology can help us be better students, parents, employees and employers, team members, peacemakers, and more. The field is broad with applications to all areas of life.

COMPETENCY MODEL

Introduction to Psychological Science

Psychological Science

1. Distinguish between mind, brain, and behaviour.

Themes of Psychological Science

2. List and explain the seven themes of psychological science.

Nature and Nurture Are Inextricably Entwined

3. Identify the differences between nature and nurture.

The Brain and Mind Are Inseparable

4. Understand Descartes's theory of dualism.

A New Biological Revolution Is Energizing Research

5. Identify the three main developments in the biological revolution.
6. Distinguish between characteristics associated with brain chemistry, human genome, and watching the working brain.

The Mind Is Adaptive

7. Explain evolutionary theory.
8. How do the concepts of natural selection and survival of the fittest differ?
9. How do the concepts of modern minds and culture relate to adaptations?

Psychological Science Crosses Levels of Analysis

10. Distinguish between the levels of analysis.

We Are Often Unaware of the Multiple Influences on How We Think, Feel, and Act

11. How does automaticity influence behaviour?

The Development of Psychology's Foundations

Early Influences

12. Identify psychology's non-European influences.
13. Identify John Stuart Mill's contribution to psychological science.

Schools of Thought

14. Describe structuralism.
15. Identify the contributions of Wilhelm Wundt and Edward Titchener to structuralism.
16. Describe how functionalism was a reaction to structuralism.
17. Identify the contributions of William James and John Dewey to functionalism.
18. Identify the contributions of Mary Whiton Calkins and Margaret Floy Washburn to functionalism.
19. Describe Gestalt psychology.
20. Describe Freud's contributions to psychological thought.
21. Describe behaviourism.
22. Identify the contributions of John B. Watson and B. F. Skinner to behaviourism.
23. Describe how the cognitive school of thought was a reaction to behaviourism.
24. Identify the contributions of Wolfgang Köhler, Edward Tolman, and George A. Miller to cognitive psychology.
25. Identify the historical event that helped give rise to social psychology.

26. Describe the contributions of Kurt Lewin to social psychology.

27. Describe the role of science in psychological therapy.

Applying Psychological Science

Psychological Knowledge Is Used in Many Professions

28. Describe how psychology is used in other professions.

People Are Intuitive Psychological Scientists

29. Describe how people are intuitive psychological scientists.

Psychological Sciences Require Critical Thinking

30. Describe the principles in critical thinking.

Psychologists Adhere to a Code of Ethics

31. List four features of the ethical code of the CPA.

KNOWLEDGE CHECK

1. Janice is interested in studying thoughts and feelings. The aspect of psychological science that she should focus on is:
   a. the mind
   b. the brain
   c. behaviour
   d. the nonconcious

Concept: I. B   Competency: 1
Question Type: *Applied*

2. List the seven themes of psychological science.
   1. ______________________________
   2. ______________________________
   3. ______________________________
   4. ______________________________
   5. ______________________________
   6. ______________________________
   7. ______________________________

Concept: II   Competency: 2
Question Type: *Factual*

3. Sy believes that if people are bad it's because they were born that way. June disagrees; she feels that it is treatment that makes someone turn out bad. Their disagreement reflects:
   a. James's ideas about stream of consciousness
   b. ideas based on structuralism
   c. the mind/body problem
   d. the nature/nurture debate

Concept: II. B   Competency: 3
Question Type: *Applied*

4. Carol believes that you can study bodily processes but you cannot study the mind. Her view reflects:
   a. monism
   b. dualism
   c. the nature/nurture debate
   d. ideas based on structuralism

Concept: II. C   Competency: 4
Question Type: *Applied*

5. Concept: II. D. 1   Competency: 5
Question Type: *Factual*

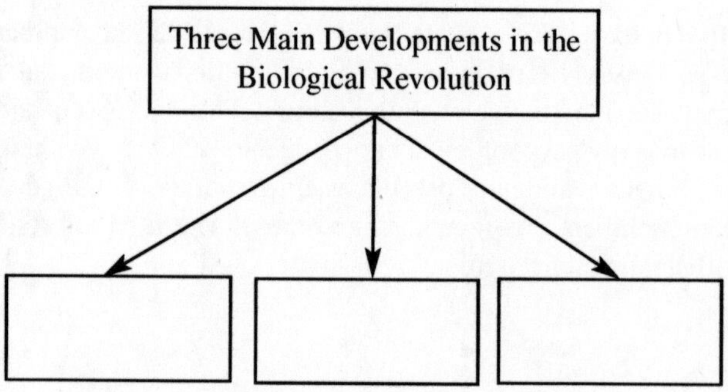

6. For each of the following, please match the characteristics with the development in the biological revolution.

____ Examine how brain regions interact
____ Identifies the basic genetic code or blueprint for the human body
____ Focuses on neurotransmitters
____ Directly helps the development of genetic therapy
____ Focuses on studying localization

a) Brain chemistry
b) Human genome
c) Watching the working brain

Concept: II. D. 1   Competency: 6
Question Type: *Factual*

7. According to evolutionary theory, our brains have evolved to solve which two problems?

____

and ___________________________________.

Concept: II. E Competency: 7
Question Type: *Factual*

8. Dr. Linus recently discovered that certain ants were particularly suited for carrying large pebbles, and that offspring of these ants also had this ability. This concept is known as ________________________.
This ability also led to the production of more offspring (compared to those ants without the profound pebble-lifting ability). This concept is known as ______________________________.

Concept: II. E Competency: 8
Question Type: *Applied*

9. Joe loves his sweets; candy, cookies, and the like are his favourite foods. Unfortunately, Joe is starting to put on weight. Based on the information on adaptive behaviour, Joe's overeating of high-calorie foods may indicate that:
   a. a human trait that was once adaptive is no longer adaptive
   b. Joe is an example of where evolution did not work
   c. psychological science cannot predict this kind of behaviour
   d. cultural variables do not influence adaptation

Concept: II. E. c Competency: 9
Question Type: *Applied*

10. Research by the social psychologist Richard Nisbett has demonstrated that people from most Asian countries have a view of the world that is quite different from the worldview of people from most European and North American countries. Which of the following statements support his findings?
   a. Easterners focus on individual levels of analysis.
   b. Westerners tend to focus on single elements in the forefront.
   c. Westerners better appreciate the "big picture."
   d. Westerners see the inherently complicated whole, with all elements affecting all other elements.

Concept: II. E. c Competency: 9
Question Type: *Factual*

11. A researcher who studies differences in dopamine levels in depressed and nondepressed individuals is working from the __________ level, while a researcher who observes how parents teach their children to behave in restaurants is working from the ___________ level.
   a. individual; social
   b. individual; cultural
   c. biological; individual
   d. biological; cultural

Concept: II. F Competency: 10
Question Type: *Applied*

12. Give two examples of how automaticity has been shown to influence behaviour.

____

____

____

____

Concept: II. G Competency: 11
Question Type: *Conceptual*

13. Which of the following statements about non-European influences on psychology is FALSE?
   a. Muslim scholar Al-Kindi produced hundreds of writings about sorrow and grief, and identified treatments that are similar to behavioural therapy used today.
   b. During the Han Dynasty the Chinese used multiple tests to select candidates for jobs with the government.
   c. Confucius emphasized human development, education, and interpersonal relations.
   d. During the Ming Dynasty national multi-stage testing was used to determine service in public office.

Concept: III. A. 2 Competency: 12
Question Type: *Factual*

14. John Stuart Mill proposed that psychology should become distinct from philosophy by focusing on:
   a. observation and experimentation
   b. the functioning of nerve energies
   c. theory and speculation
   d. functionalism and structuralism

Concept: III. A. 2 Competency: 13
Question Type: *Factual*

15. If you were from the structuralism school of thought, how would you look at an impressionist painting (such as those by Monet)? What is a potential problem with this?

____

____

____

____

Concept: III. B. 1 Competency: 14
Question Type: *Conceptual*

16. Which researcher is credited with opening the first psychological laboratory? Which researcher broke down musical tones into their elements?
    a. Wundt; James
    b. Wundt; Titchener
    c. Titchener; Wundt
    d. Titchener; James

Concept: III. B. 1. a Competency: 15
Question Type: *Factual*

17. A researcher from the __________ school of thought would look at a car and want to know about each individual part, while a researcher from the __________ school of thought would want to know how the parts work together.
    a. behaviourism; functionalism
    b. functionalism; behaviourism
    c. structuralism; functionalism
    d. functionalism; structuralism

Concept: III. B. 2 Competency: 16
Question Type: *Conceptual*

18. Whose contribution included a progressive approach to education that valued divergent thinking over memorization? Who was the first person to give a lecture on psychology?
    a. Dewey; James
    b. James; Dewey
    c. Dewey; Wundt
    d. Skinner; James

Concept: III. B. 2 Competency: 17
Question Type: *Factual*

19. Which of the following is TRUE of Mary Whiton Calkins, one of America's early psychologists?
    a. She never worked as a professor, but instead helped her husband earn his degree.
    b. She was denied a degree by Harvard despite her outstanding performance.
    c. She was the first American to earn a Ph.D. in psychology.
    d. She was asked to leave the practice of psychology by the American Psychological Association.

Concept: III. B. 2. a. 3 Competency: 18
Question Type: *Factual*

20. Which school of thought suggests "the whole is different from the sum of the parts"?
    a. structuralism
    b. Gestalt psychology
    c. functionalism
    d. cognitive

Concept: III. B. 3 Competency: 19
Question Type: *Factual*

21. Tony had a dream about a duck flying away with his penis. Tony's therapist believes the dream is not really about ducks, but is about some conflict in Tony's mind of which he is not aware. Tony's therapist is taking an approach similar to:
    a. James
    b. Watson
    c. Freud
    d. Titchener

Concept: III. B. 4 Competency: 20
Question Type: *Applied*

22. Dr. Cohen believes that the study of psychology should be limited to stimuli that can be measured and responses that can be observed. This approach is:
    a. psychoanalysis
    b. structuralism
    c. behaviourism
    d. cognitivism

Concept: III. B. 5 Competency: 21
Question Type: *Applied*

23. Rita watches her dog drool every time he sees food. Rita believes this is due to environmental influences and that trying to understand the dog's mental processes is not necessary. Her view is most similar to which psychologist?
    a. Dewey
    b. James
    c. Skinner
    d. Watson

Concept: III. B. 5. a Competency: 22
Question Type: *Applied*

24. How was the cognitive school of thought a reaction to behaviourism?

____

____

____

____

Concept: III. B. 6 Competency: 23
Question Type: *Conceptual*

25. Identify the contributions of each of the following to cognitive psychology:

____ showed that animals could learn by observation	a) Wolfgang Köhler
____ found that chimpanzees achieved insight when problem solving	b) Edward Tolman
____ developed cognitive psychology	c) George A. Miller

Concept: III. B. 6. a Competency: 24
Question Type: *Factual*

26. Which of the following historical events was most responsible for the rise of social psychology?
   a. World War I
   b. World War II
   c. the Great Depression
   d. the Vietnam War

Concept: III. B. 7 Competency: 25
Question Type: *Applied*

27. Caryl is observing people's behaviour while they wait in line at a food court in the mall. She believes that people's actions are the result of the combination of their biology, habits, and the social nature of the situation. Which psychologist had ideas most similar to this?
   a. Lewin
   b. James
   c. Skinner
   d. Watson

Concept: III. B. 7. a Competency: 26
Question Type: *Applied*

28. Which of the following is most true of the relationship between psychological science and psychological practice today?
   a. Psychological scientists and psychological practitioners have little in common.
   b. Psychological science has little relevance for practice.
   c. Psychological therapy is increasingly based on psychological science.
   d. Psychological scientists and psychological practitioners are generally interested in unrelated areas.

Concept: II. B. 8 Competency: 27
Question Type: *Factual*

29. Which of the following statements about how psychology is used in other professions is FALSE?
   a. In order to persuade jurors, lawyers need to know how groups make decisions.
   b. Psychological scientists make major contributions to research on mental health, but few contributions to human physical health.
   c. Politicians use psychological techniques of impression management to make themselves attractive to voters.
   d. Psychology can help physicians relate to their patients.

Concept: IV. A Competency: 28
Question Type: *Factual*

30. Provide your own example of a time when you were an intuitive psychological scientist.

____

____

____

____

Concept: IV. B Competency: 29
Question Type: *Applied*

31. Psychological science is based on critical thinking. This means that psychological scientists:
   a. accept without question any information that is given to them by an authority
   b. are very critical of any statement of fact, and try to find fault with it
   c. do not believe anything that they did not discover themselves
   d. evaluate information before they accept it

Concept: IV. C Competency: 30
Question Type: *Factual*

32. The ethical code includes ____________________, ____________________________, and ______________________________.

Concept: IV. D Competency: 31
Question Type: *Factual*

Psychology and Society

Imagine you are hired to serve as a peer academic advisor for incoming first-year university students. One of your advisees comes to you in hopes you can help him decide whether introductory psychology would be a good course for him. Compose an email to this student explaining why you would or would not recommend a psychology course. Be sure to support your position with ideas from the chapter. (Of course, this question is asking you to provide advice based on exposure to just one chapter from the text; your answer may or may not look very different at the end of the course.)

ANSWER KEY

Item **Answer**

1. a
2. 1. Psychology is an empirical science. 2. Nature and nurture are inextricably entwined. 3. The brain and mind are inseparable. 4. A new biological evolution is energizing research. 5. The mind is adaptive. 6. Psychological science crosses levels of analysis. 7. We are often unaware of the multiple influences on how we think, feel, and act.
3. d
4. b
5. brain chemistry; human genome; watching the working brain
6. c, b, a, b, c
7. survival and reproduction
8. natural selection; survival of the fittest
9. a
10. b
11. d
12. People in a study were shown words related to kindness, then subsequently rated a new acquaintance as kinder compared to another group that didn't see kind words. Second, those who held a hot cup of coffee for a busy person rated another person as "warmer," compared to another group that held a cold cup of coffee.
13. a
14. a
15. Rather than view the painting as an overall picture of a nature scene, you would break down the component processes through introspection and would focus on the individual dots of paint, the perception of the colour, and the nature of the light waves reaching the eye. A potential problem is that an individual's perception is subjective and may vary from person to person. For example, what I perceive as pink, you may perceive as mauve, or rose.
16. b
17. c
18. b
19. b
20. b
21. c
22. c
23. d
24. Behaviourism set forth the notion that mental processes were irrelevant, and not necessary to understand behaviour. Instead, behaviour consisted of simple stimulus-response pairings. In contrast, the cognitive school of thought emphasized the role of the mental processes such that behaviour was the result of thinking first and then acting.
25. b, a, c
26. b
27. a
28. c
29. b
30. Answers can vary, but any time you tried to predict someone else's behaviour (e.g., will that person make a good relationship partner?), tried to understand why someone engaged in a certain behaviour (e.g., why did my roommate eat all of my food?), or developed a hypothesis about psychological outcomes (e.g., I bet that if I look at the top of a tree on campus, others will also look to see what I'm looking at), you were acting as an intuitive psychological scientist.
31. d
32. respecting the dignity of all people, caring for them with competence, maintaining proper relationships with them, and acting in ways that are responsible to society.

Psychology and Society Answer:

You can elect to either recommend a psychology course or not. That said, you will probably recommend the course, noting the relevance of psychology to daily interactions, a multitude of professions, and the ability to understand research as reported in media. You should also highlight the opportunity to develop critical thinking skills and a deeper understanding of ethical dilemmas.

KEY TERM EXERCISES

adaptations

Textbook Definition:
Your Own Definition:
Your Own Example:

critical thinking

Textbook Definition:
Your Own Definition:
Your Own Example:

behaviourism

Textbook Definition:
Your Own Definition:
Your Own Example:

culture

Textbook Definition:
Your Own Definition:
Your Own Example:

cognitive neuroscience

Textbook Definition:
Your Own Definition:
Your Own Example:

evolutionary theory

Textbook Definition:
Your Own Definition:
Your Own Example:

cognitive psychology

Textbook Definition:
Your Own Definition:
Your Own Example:

functionalism

Textbook Definition:
Your Own Definition:
Your Own Example:

Gestalt theory

Textbook Definition:
Your Own Definition:
Your Own Example:

nature/nurture debate

Textbook Definition:
Your Own Definition:
Your Own Example:

introspection

Textbook Definition:
Your Own Definition:
Your Own Example:

psychoanalysis

Textbook Definition:
Your Own Definition:
Your Own Example:

mind/body problem

Textbook Definition:
Your Own Definition:
Your Own Example:

psychological science

Textbook Definition:
Your Own Definition:
Your Own Example:

natural selection

Textbook Definition:
Your Own Definition:
Your Own Example:

social psychology

Textbook Definition:
Your Own Definition:
Your Own Example:

stream of consciousness

Textbook Definition:
Your Own Definition:
Your Own Example:

unconscious

Textbook Definition:
Your Own Definition:
Your Own Example:

structuralism

Textbook Definition:
Your Own Definition:
Your Own Example:

CHAPTER 2 Research Methodology

CONCEPT MAP

I. Scientific Inquiry
   A. Introduction
      1. Amiable Skepticism
   B. Scientific Method
      1. Four Goals
      2. Essential Elements
         a. Theory
            1. Testable
         b. Hypotheses
         c. Research
            1. Data
      3. Cyclical Nature of Research
         a. Replication
      4. Unexpected Findings
         a. Serendipity

II. Types of Psychological Research
   A. Common Characteristics of All Types
      1. Variables
      2. Operational Definitions
   B. Three Main Types of Psychological Research
      1. Descriptive
         a. Naturalistic Observation
         b. Participant Observation
         c. Use of Descriptive Methods
            1. Early in Research Process
            2. Developmental Designs
               A. Longitudinal Studies
               B. Cross-sectional Studies
         d. Issues
            1. Observer Bias
               A. Experimenter Expectancy Effect
            2. Solution
               A. Use of "Blind" Experimenters
      2. Correlational
         a. The Role of Ethics
         b. Issues
            1. Correlation Does Not Equal Causality
               A. Directionality
               B. Third Variable Problem
      3. Experimental
         a. Establishing Causality
            1. Independent vs. Dependent Variables
            2. Control Group vs. Experimental Group
            3. Rule Out Alternative Explanations
               A. Confounds
            4. Need to Generalize
               A. Random Sampling vs. Convenience Sampling
            5. Establish Equivalent Groups
               A. Avoid Selection Bias
               B. Random Assignment
         b. Issues
            1. Artificial
            2. Sample Size
               A. Meta-analysis

III. Methods of Data Collection in Psychological Research
   A. Level of Analysis
      1. Biological
      2. Individual

- 3. Social
- 4. Cultural
  - a. Culturally Sensitive Research
- B. Methods
  - 1. Observational Techniques
    - a. Setting: Lab or Natural Environment?
    - b. How Should the Data Be Collected?
    - c. Should the Observer be Visible?
      - 1. Reactivity
      - 2. Hawthorne Effect
  - 2. Case Study
    - a. Issues
  - 3. Asking People about Themselves
    - a. Methods for Asking Questions
    - b. Open-ended vs. Closed-ended Questions
    - c. Experience Sampling
    - d. Issues
      - 1. Self-report Bias
        - A. Socially Desirable Responses
        - B. Better-Than-Average Effect
  - 4. Response Performance
    - a. Reaction Time
    - b. Response Accuracy
    - c. Stimulus Judgments
  - 5. Psychophysiological Assessment: Body/Brain Activity
    - a. Electrophysiology
      - 1. Electroencephalograph (EEG)
    - b. Brain Imaging
      - 1. Positron Emission Tomography (PET)
      - 2. Magnetic Resonance Imaging (MRI)
        - A. Functional Magnetic Resonance Imaging (fMRI)
      - 3. Transcranial Magnetic Stimulation (TMS)
  - 6. Animal Research
    - a. Genetic Research

- IV. Ethics in Psychological Research
  - A. Ethical Concerns
    - 1. Privacy
    - 2. Confidentiality
    - 3. Anonymity
  - B. Methods for Ensuring Ethical Treatment
    - 1. Research Ethics Boards
    - 2. Informed Consent
      - a. Deception
      - b. Debriefing
      - c. Relative Risk
      - d. Risk/Benefit Ratio
  - C. Ethics and the Nuremberg Code

- V. Data Analysis and Evaluation
  - A. Data Quality
    - 1. Validity
    - 2. Reliability
    - 3. Accuracy
  - B. Data Analysis
    - 1. Descriptive Statistics
      - a. Measures of Central Tendency
        - 1. Mean
        - 2. Median
        - 3. Mode
      - b. Variability
        - 1. Standard Deviation
        - 2. Range
      - c. Correlation
        - 1. Scatterplot
        - 2. Correlation Coefficient
          - A. Positive Correlation
          - B. Negative Correlation
    - 2. Inferential Statistics
      - a. Comparing Groups
      - b. Statistical Significance

CHAPTER SUMMARY

What Is Scientific Inquiry?

• The Scientific Method Depends on Theories, Hypotheses, and Research: Scientific inquiry relies on objective methods and empirical evidence to answer testable questions. Interconnected ideas or models of behaviour (theories) yield testable predictions (hypotheses), which are tested in a systematic way (research) by collecting and evaluating evidence (data).

• Unexpected Findings Can Be Valuable: Unexpected (serendipitous) discoveries sometimes occur, but only researchers who are prepared to recognize their importance will benefit from them.

What Are the Types of Studies in Psychological Research?

• Descriptive Studies Involve Observing and Classifying Behaviour: Researchers observe and describe naturally occurring behaviours to provide a systematic and objective analysis.

• Correlational Designs Examine How Variables Are Related: Correlational studies are used to examine how variables are naturally related in the real world, but cannot be used to establish causality or the direction of a relationship (which variable caused changes in another variable). Correlational reasoning occurs in many contexts, so readers need to be able to recognize correlational designs in everyday contexts, not just when reading research reports.

• An Experiment Involves Manipulating Conditions: In an experiment, researchers control the variations in the conditions that the participant experiences (independent variables) and measure the outcomes (dependent variables) to gain an understanding of causality. Researchers need a control group to know if the experiment had an effect.

• Random Assignment Is Used to Establish Equivalent Groups: Researchers sample participants from the population they want to study (e.g., all women who work). They use random sampling when everyone in the population is equally likely to participate in the study, a condition that rarely occurs. To establish causality between an intervention and an outcome, all participants must be equally likely to be in the experimental group or the control group, to control for pre-existing group differences.

What Are the Data Collection Methods of Psychological Science?

• Observing Is an Unobtrusive Strategy: Data collected by observation must be defined clearly and collected systematically. Bias may occur in the data because the participants are aware they are being observed or because of the observer's expectations.

• Case Studies Examine Individual Lives and Organizations: A case study, one kind of descriptive study, examines an individual or an organization. An intensive study of an individual or organization can be useful for examining an unusual participant or unusual research question. Interpretation of a case study, however, can be subjective.

• Asking Takes a More Active Approach: Surveys, questionnaires, and interviews can be used to directly ask people about their thoughts and behaviours. Self-report data may be biased by the respondents' desire to present themselves in a particular way (e.g., smart, honest). Culturally sensitive research recognizes the differences among people from different cultural groups and from different language backgrounds.

• Response Performance Measures Information Processing: Measuring reaction times and reaction accuracy and asking people to make stimulus judgments are methods used to examine how people respond to psychological tasks.

• Body/Brain Activity Can Be Measured Directly: Electrophysiology (often using an electroencephalograph, or EEG) measures the brain's electrical activity. Brain imaging is done using positron emission tomography (PET), magnetic resonance imaging (MRI), and functional magnetic resonance imaging (fMRI). Transcranial magnetic stimulation (TMS) disrupts normal brain activity, allowing researchers to infer the brain processing involved in particular thoughts, feelings, and behaviours.

• Research with Animals Provides Important Data: Research involving nonhuman animals provides useful, although simpler, models of behaviour and of genetics. The purpose of such research may be to learn about animals' behaviour or to make inferences about human behaviour.

• There Are Ethical Issues to Consider: Ethical research is governed by a variety of principles that ensure fair and informed treatment of participants.

How Are Data Analyzed and Evaluated?

• Good Research Requires Valid, Reliable, and Accurate Data: Data must be meaningful (valid) and their measurements reliable (i.e., consistent and stable) and accurate.

• Descriptive Statistics Provide a Summary of the Data: Measures of central tendency and variability are used to describe data.

• Correlations Describe the Relationships between Variables: A correlation is a descriptive statistic that describes the strength and direction of the relationship between two variables. Correlations close to zero signify weak relationships; correlations near +1 or –1 signify strong relationships.

• Inferential Statistics Permit Generalizations: Inferential statistics allow us to decide whether differences between two or more groups are probably just chance variations (suggesting that the populations the groups were drawn from are the same) or whether they reflect true differences in the populations being compared.

COMPETENCY MODEL

Scientific Inquiry

1. What is amiable skepticism? How does it differ from being cynical?

Scientific Method

2. What are the four main goals of the scientific method?
3. Explain the differences and interaction among theories, hypotheses, and research.
4. Be able to identify a good theory.

5. What is meant by the cyclical nature of research? What is the role of replication in this?
6. Identify the use of unexpected findings.

Types of Psychological Research

7. List the advantages and disadvantages of different research methods.

Common Characteristics

8. How are variables and operational definitions used in the different types of research?
9. What are the three main types of research?

Psychological Research—Descriptive

10. Distinguish between naturalistic and participant observation.
11. How are descriptive methods used in the beginning stages of the research process?
12. Distinguish between longitudinal and cross-sectional studies.
13. How can observer bias influence a study's findings?
14. How can researchers counteract observer bias?

Psychological Research—Correlational

15. Describe why some research needs to be correlational due to ethical concerns.
16. Be able to explain why correlation does not equal causation.
17. Be able to identify potential third variables when reading about correlational associations.

Psychological Research—Experimental

18. Distinguish between independent and dependent variables.
19. Distinguish between control and experimental groups.
20. Be able to identify alternative explanations when reading about causal relationships.
21. How does a sample relate to a population?
22. Distinguish between random sampling and convenience sampling.
23. Why do we need equivalent groups when designing an experiment?
24. Why is selection bias problematic?
25. Explain why random assignment is important when designing experiments.
26. A problem with experiments is that they can be artificial. Explain.
27. Why is sample size important?
28. What does a meta-analysis do? What are the benefits?

Methods of Data Collection in Psychological Research

29. Provide examples of data collection methods that are appropriate for different research questions.
30. What ultimately dictates the appropriate data collection method?

Level of Analysis

31. What are the levels of analysis we can use in psychological research?
32. Describe what it means to engage in culturally sensitive research.

Observational Techniques

33. Describe the purpose of observational techniques, and how researchers use them.
34. Be able to identify the three main decisions observational techniques require.
35. Identify issues associated with having the observer visible.

Case Study

36. Describe the purpose of case studies, and how researchers use them.
37. Identify issues associated with case studies.

Asking People about Themselves

38. What are the methods of asking participants questions?
39. What are the pros and cons of self-report techniques such as surveys and interviews?
40. Distinguish between open-ended and closed-ended questions.
41. Distinguish between socially desirable and the better-than-average effect.

Response Performance

42. Identify and explain the three main types of response performance.

Psychophysiological Assessment: Body/Brain Activity

43. How is psychophysiological assessment different from the other data collection techniques?

44. What is electrophysiological information? How do researchers measure this?

45. Identify and distinguish between the four main types of brain imaging.

Animal Research

46. What are the benefits of animal research?

Ethics in Psychological Research

Ethical Concerns

47. Identify ethical issues and explain their importance.

Methods for Ensuring Ethical Treatment

48. What is the purpose of REBs?

49. What is the purpose of informed consent? What does informed consent provide?

Data Analysis and Evaluation

Data Quality

50. What are the three indicators of data quality?

Data Analysis—Descriptive Statistics

51. Describe measures of central tendency and variability.

52. Distinguish between positive and negative correlations.

Data Analysis—Inferential Statistics

53. Discuss the rationale for inferential statistics.

54. What does it mean when something is "statistically significant"?

KNOWLEDGE CHECK

1. Adam is in charge of recruitment for his fraternity and relies on his "gut feeling" when deciding on whether to accept a new pledge. Larry, however, relies on the pledge's interview, observes sociability, and solicits information from multiple sources. Which of the following characteristics best demonstrates Larry's approach?
   a. validity
   b. amiable skepticism
   c. scientific method
   d. cynicism

   Concept: I. A. 1 Competency: 1
   Question Type: *Applied*

2. Sonya is looking around the mall for her friend. Because this is a visual search task, Sonya will have the easiest time finding her friend among the distractors based on all of the following features EXCEPT:
   a. colour
   b. shape
   c. size
   d. movement

   Concept: I. B Learning Objective: 2
   Question Type: *Applied*

3. All of the following are goals of the scientific method, EXCEPT:
   a. proving that intuitions are correct
   b. predicting when a phenomenon will happen
   c. controlling what causes a phenomenon to happen
   d. explaining why a phenomenon happens

   Concept: I. B. 1 Competency: 2
   Question Type: *Factual*

4. Theories, research, and hypotheses are all part of the scientific method. Which of the following best describes how these three elements are related?
   a. After conducting research, a theory is created to support the hypotheses.
   b. Research tests theories, the results of which generate hypotheses.
   c. Theories are most general and help create hypotheses that are tested via research.
   d. Hypotheses help generate theories, that are tested via research.

   Concept: I. B. 2 Competency: 3
   Question Type: *Conceptual*

5. What is a theory? What makes a theory a "good" theory? Why was Freud's theory not a good theory?

   ____

   ____

   ____

   ____

   Concept: I. B. 2. a Competency: 4
   Question Type: *Conceptual*

6. Jenna reads about a study where caring for plants helps the elderly and wants to test the same procedure. This process is known as __________. However, Jenna decides to test this same procedure among children with cancer. This change reflects Jenna's desire to __________.

   a. replication; test a different hypothesis
   b. replication; generate a new theory
   c. control; test a different hypothesis
   d. control; generate a new theory

   Concept: I. B. 3. a Competency: 5
   Question Type: *Applied*

7. A researcher who obtains data that show an association between variables that was unexpected should:

   a. ignore it since it was not hypothesized
   b. ignore it because the findings are incorrect
   c. ignore it because the scientific method should be neat and orderly
   d. consider it a case of serendipity, and report the findings

   Concept: I. B. 4. a Competency: 6
   Question Type: *Factual*

8. Which type of psychological research is the best?

   ____

   ____

   ____

   ____

   Concept: II Competency: 7
   Question Type: *Conceptual*

9. Britney is conducting a study on relationship infidelity and needs to create an operational definition. Which of the following is the best operational definition?

   a. hooking up with someone other than your current partner
   b. any physically intimate act with a potential romantic partner that your current partner does not condone
   c. kissing another person and not telling your current partner
   d. anything past "first base" with a person who isn't your partner

   Concept: II. A. 2 Competency: 8
   Question Type: *Applied*

10. Concept: II. B. Competency: 9
    Question Type: *Factual*

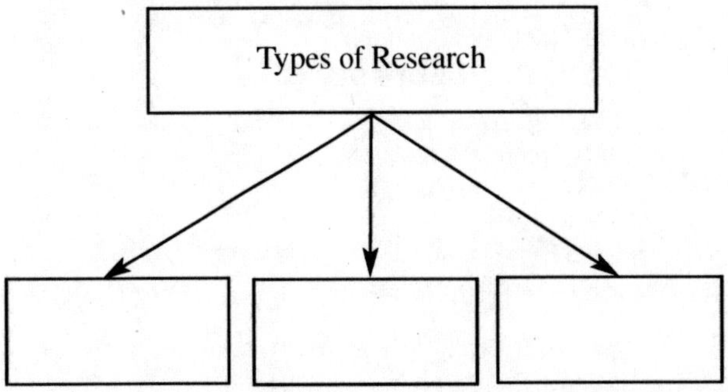

11. Jay and Marshall both want to learn more about gangs by observing them. Marshall uses __________ observation and decides to join a gang, while Jay uses __________ observation by being in areas where gangs frequently hang out.

    a. incognito; naturalistic
    b. naturalistic; incognito
    c. participant; naturalistic
    d. naturalistic; participant

    Concept: II. B. 1. a-b Competency: 10
    Question Type: *Applied*

12. Skyler wants to do research on cheating on the SAT. What should she do first?

    a. descriptive research
    b. correlational research
    c. an experiment
    d. a longitudinal study

    Concept: II. B. 1. c. 1 Competency: 11
    Question Type: *Applied*

13. For each of the following, please indicate which it describes:

    ____ Measures the same group of people several times
    ____ Is generally less expensive and faster to administer
    ____ Has a greater possibility that unidentified third variables explain the differences
    ____ Can be jeopardized by participants dropping out
    ____ Measures different groups of people

    a) Longitudinal
    b) Cross-sectional studies

    Concept: II. B. 1. c. 2 Competency: 12
    Question Type: *Factual*

14. Chip is studying flirting behaviour at a local coffee shop. Because he believes that women flirt more, he notices women flirting more than men. This demonstrates what concept?
    a. correlational research
    b. observer bias
    c. participant observation
    d. blind experimentation

    Concept: II. B. 1. d. 1 Competency: 13
    Question Type: *Applied*

15. In order to solve Chip's problem from the previous item, Chip should engage in what?
    a. correlational research
    b. observer bias
    c. participant observation
    d. blind experimentation

    Concept: II. B. 1. d. 2 Competency: 14
    Question Type: *Applied*

16. A researcher wants to determine if parental divorce during elementary school influences promiscuity in high school. What type of psychological research should be used? Why?

    ____

    ____

    ____

    ____

    Concept: II. B. 2. a Competency: 15
    Question Type: *Conceptual*

17. Dr. Spezio has conducted extensive research showing that socioeconomic status positively correlates with being materialistic. Based on this research we can conclude:
    a. that the two variables are related, and that greater materialism causes higher socioeconomic status
    b. that the two variables are related, and that higher socioeconomic status causes greater materialism
    c. that the two variables are related, but can not determine causation
    d. that the two variables are probably not actually related

    Concept: II. B. 2. b. 1 Competency: 16
    Question Type: *Applied*

18. Joe, who works in urban planning, found that the more dogs there were in a city, the more fire hydrants there were, too. He knew he could not conclude that having more dogs caused an increase in fire hydrants. Rather, some other factor probably caused both the increase in dogs and the increase in hydrants. This reflects:
    a. the third variable problem
    b. the limitations of an experiment
    c. the ability to make a causal statement from a correlational study
    d. the limits of random assignment

    Concept: II. B. 2. b. 1 Competency: 17
    Question Type: *Applied*

19. The variable that is manipulated is the ____________, and the variable that is measured is the ____________.
    a. experimenter; dependent
    b. control; experimental
    c. dependent; independent
    d. independent; dependent

    Concept: II. B. 3. a. 1 Competency: 18
    Question Type: *Factual*

20. Dr. Todd did an experiment where he gave one group of students a caffeinated energy drink and another group no energy drink. He then compared how quickly they did a puzzle. What was the dependent variable in this experiment?
    a. the amount of caffeine
    b. the age of the students
    c. the time it took to complete the puzzle
    d. the energy drink

    Concept: II. B. 3. a. 1 Competency: 18
    Question Type: *Applied*

21. Dr. Hernandez did an experiment where she gave half of her participants alcohol and half of her participants no alcohol. She then measured how long each participant could balance on one leg. The participants who received no alcohol are:
    a. irrelevant to the experiment
    b. the experimental group
    c. the independent variable
    d. the control group

    Concept: II. B. 3. a. 2 Competency: 19
    Question Type: *Applied*

22. Anything that affects a dependent variable that may unintentionally vary between the different experimental conditions of a study is a

    ______________________________.

    Concept: II. B. 3. a. 3 Competency: 20
    Question Type: *Factual*

23. If pollsters want to determine how the entire population of the country feels about a political issue, what do they need to do?
    a. Collect data from the population and then generalize to the sample.
    b. Collect data from a sample and then generalize to the population.
    c. Collect data from every person in the sample.
    d. Collect data from every person in the population.

    Concept: II. B. 3. a. 4 Competency: 21
    Question Type: *Applied*

24. When sampling from the population it is ideal to use ________________ sampling. Most of the research done in psychology uses ________________ sampling, or those willing to participate for course credit or payment.

    Concept: II. B. 3. a. 4. A Competency: 22
    Question Type: *Factual*

25. A senior thesis student wants to determine the impact of required study hours and has decided to compare students in fraternities and sororities who typically have study hours, to those who are not in those organizations. The thesis student's advisor points out that there will be selection bias. What does this mean? How is this avoided in an ideal experiment? Why are non-equivalent groups a problem for the study?

    ____

    ____

    ____

    ____

    Concept: II. B. 3. a. 5 Competency: 23, 24, 25
    Question Type: *Conceptual*

26. Random assignment accomplishes all of the following EXCEPT:
    a. random assignment balances out known factors
    b. random assignment balances out unknown factors
    c. random assignment eliminates the influence of individual differences
    d. random assignment helps create equivalent groups

    Concept: II. B. 3. a. 5. B Competency: 25
    Question Type: *Factual*

27. In order to manipulate variables in an experiment we often have to create an artificial situation. Why? What is the potential problem with this?

    ____

    ____

    ____

    ____

    Concept: II. B. 3. b Competency: 26
    Question Type: *Conceptual*

28. As consumers of research, we need to understand that studies which are junk science have a greater tendency to have a ________________ number of participants in their sample.

    Concept: II. B. 3. b Competency: 27
    Question Type: *Factual*

29. A ________________ is an analysis of multiple analyses, or studies that have already been conducted. It has the benefit of ________________.

    Concept: II. B. 3. b. 2 Competency: 28
    Question Type: *Factual*

30. For each of the following, please match the research question with the most appropriate data collection method:

____ What is the influence of obsessive-compulsive disorder on all aspects of a person's life?	a) Observational
____ How do attractive pictures influence arousal?	b) Case study
____ How do peers influence deviant behaviour at shopping malls?	c) Asking people about themselves
____ What is your attitude toward canned laughter on television shows?	d) Response performance
____ How quickly can a person hit the brake pedal while driving and talking on their cellphone?	e) Psycho-physiological assessment

    Concept: II. B. 1. c. 2 Competency: 29
    Question Type: *Applied*

31. A fundamental principle of psychological research is that ________________ dictates the appropriate data collection method.

    Concept: III Competency: 30
    Question Type: *Factual*

32. Concept: III. A Competency: 31
Question Type: *Factual*

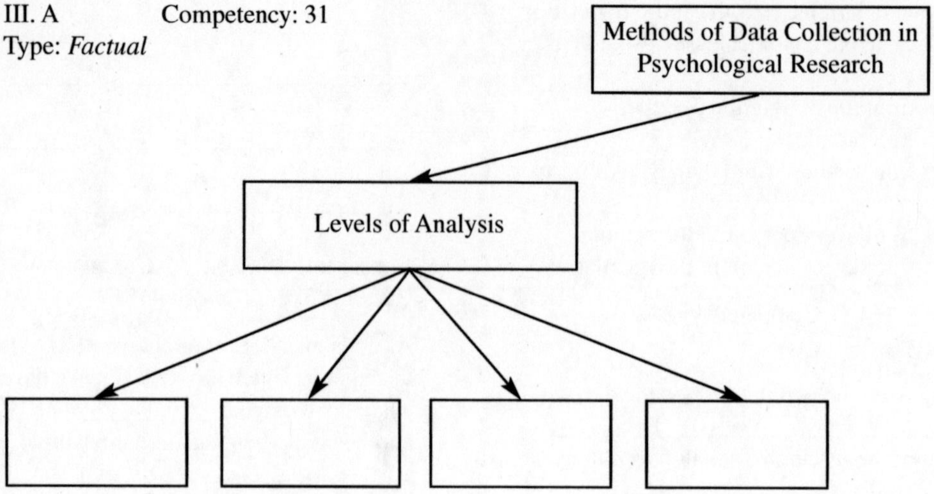

33. If a researcher wants to study the meaning of love, and wants to be culturally sensitive, what types of things should be considered?

____

____

____

____

Concept: III. A. 4. a Competency: 32
Question Type: *Conceptual*

34. Researchers use observational techniques to ______________________________________.

Concept: III. B. 1 Competency: 33
Question Type: *Factual*

35. Concept: III. B. 1 Competency: 34
Question Type: *Factual*

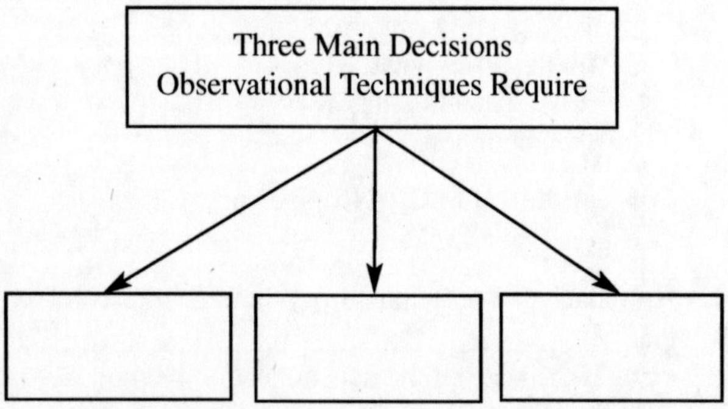

36. Dr. Bert tried to do an observational study of how students act at parties. However, he noticed that when he attended a party, the students tended to act unnaturally by being very quiet and staring at him. The fact that the students were not acting naturally demonstrates the:
a. the third variable problem
b. Hawthorne effect
c. experimenter expectancy effect
d. observer bias

Concept: III. B. 1. c. 2 Competency: 35
Question Type: *Applied*

37. Dr. Ramirez did research that involved a detailed examination of a patient who suffered brain damage from a car accident. Dr. Ramirez's study is an example of a:
a. response performance study
b. reaction time study
c. case study
d. correlational study

Concept: III. B. 2 Competency: 36
Question Type: *Applied*

38. Dr. Ramirez's study from the previous item also revealed that the patient experienced dramatic recovery and watched 18 hours of reality television each day. Should all brain damage victims start watching reality TV?

____

____

____

____

Concept: III. B. 2. a Competency: 37
Question Type: *Conceptual*

39. Concept: III. B. 3. a Competency: 38
Question Type: *Factual*

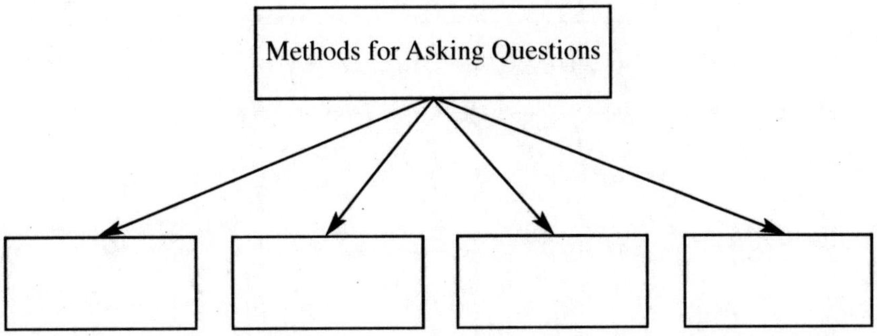

40. All of the following are strengths of self-report methods EXCEPT:
    a. interviews can be used very successfully with groups that cannot be studied through surveys, such as young children
    b. questionnaires can be used to gather data from a large number of people
    c. questionnaires are easy to administer and cost-efficient
    d. researchers who use questionnaires can collect a great deal of data but it takes a very long time

    Concept: III. B. 3. a Competency: 39
    Question Type: *Factual*

41. "How do you feel about global warming?" is an example of:
    a. an experience-sampling technique
    b. an open-ended question
    c. a closed-ended question
    d. a feeling question

    Concept: III. B. 3. b Competency: 40
    Question Type: *Applied*

42. What is the difference between a socially desirable response and the better-than-average effect?

    ____
    ____
    ____
    ____

    Concept: III. B. 3. d. 1 Competency: 41
    Question Type: *Conceptual*

43. Sarah was in a study where the experimenter measured how quickly she could judge whether a group of letters made up a word. What was the experimenter measuring?
    a. reaction time
    b. response accuracy
    c. reliability
    d. electrophysiology

    Concept: III. B. 4 Competency: 42
    Question Type: *Applied*

44. Raul is doing a study of humour and wants a form of assessment that uses the biological level of analysis, is free from self-report bias, and is a direct assessment. Which type of assessment should he use?
    a. observation
    b. asking people about themselves
    c. response performance
    d. psychophysiological assessment

    Concept: III. B. 5 Competency: 43
    Question Type: *Applied*

45. ______________________________ is a data collection method that measures electrical activity through the use of electrodes placed onto the participant's scalp. The device that measures brain activity is an ______________________________.

    Concept: III. B. 5. a Competency: 44
    Question Type: *Factual*

46. Of the main types of brain imaging, which is least like the other three? Why?

    ____
    ____
    ____
    ____

    Concept: III. B. 5 Competency: 45
    Question Type: *Conceptual*

47. Concept: III. B. 5 Competency: 45
Question Type: *Factual*

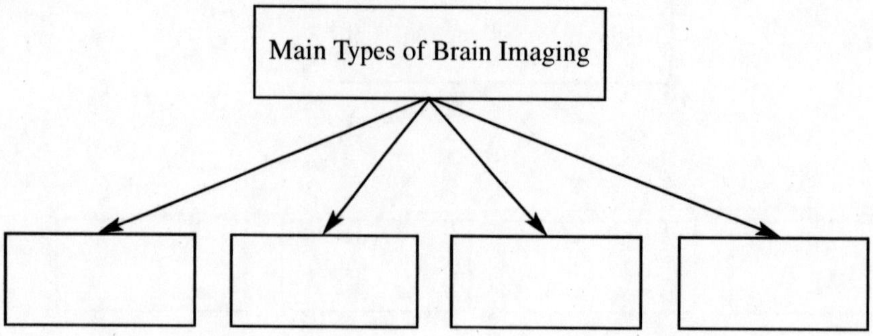

48. Which of the following statements about animal research is FALSE?
    a. Many of the most important research findings have been obtained by studying nonhuman animals' behaviour.
    b. Manipulating genes in mice can help inform us about the human genome.
    c. There are very few other species that can tell us anything about humans.
    d. The forces that control the behaviours of rats, dogs, and humans are in many ways the same.

Concept: III. B. 6 Competency: 46
Question Type: *Factual*

49. For each of the following, please match the statement with the most applicable ethical concern:

____ the researcher tells friends about the participant's answers	a) privacy
____ secretly listening in on cellphone conversations	b) confidentiality
____ the researcher has participants place their names on the study materials	c) anonymity

Concept: IV. A Competency: 47
Question Type: *Applied*

50. Concept: IV. A Competency: 34
Question Type: *Factual*

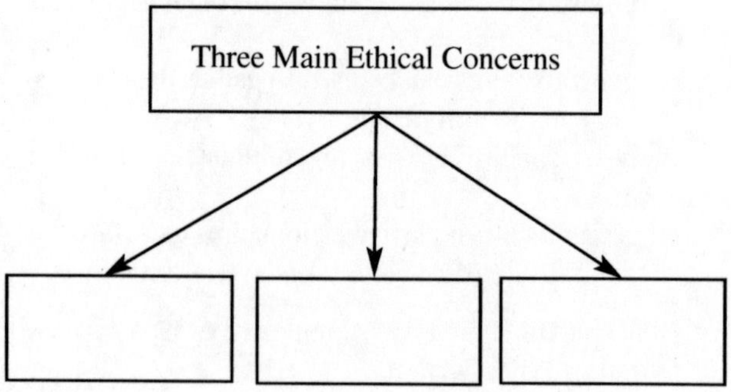

51. Dr. Smith designed a study to investigate memory in university students. Before she could do the study she first had to get approval from which group?
    a. the school board
    b. the Research Ethics Board
    c. the Canadian Psychological Association
    d. the American Psychological Society

Concept: IV. B. 1 Competency: 48
Question Type: *Factual*

52. Concept: IV. B. 2 Competency: 49
Question Type: *Factual*

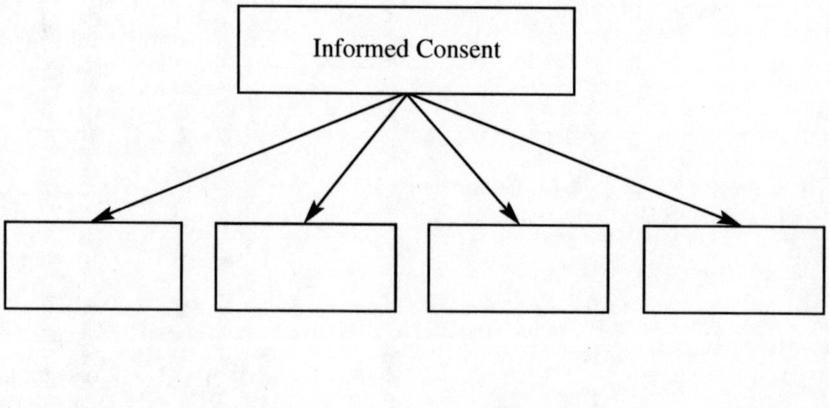

53. Concept: V. A Competency: 50
Question Type: *Factual*

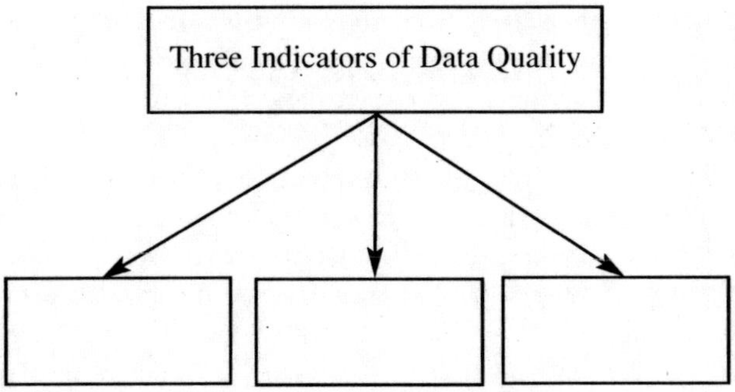

54. When looking at central tendency, the ________________ is the most common response, the ________________ is the arithmetic average, and the ________________ is the middle score.
    a. mean; median; mode
    b. median; mode; mean
    c. mean; mode; median
    d. mode; mean; median

    Concept: V. B. 1. a. 1-3 Competency: 51
    Question Type: *Factual*

55. ______________ generally indicates how spread out scores are around the mean; ______________ is a type of this where the highest and lowest values are given.
    a. Variability; standard deviation
    b. Variability; range
    c. Central tendency; variability
    d. Central tendency; standard deviation

    Concept: V. B. 1. b. 1-2 Competency: 51
    Question Type: *Factual*

56. If a study found a high positive correlation between the amount of pop people drink and their weight, this means that:
    a. people who drink more pop weigh more
    b. people who drink more pop weigh less
    c. pop drinking is unrelated to weight
    d. sometimes pop drinking causes weight gain and sometimes it does not

    Concept: V. B. 1. c. 2 Competency: 52
    Question Type: *Applied*

57. What is the difference in the kind of information provided by descriptive statistics, correlations, and inferential statistics?

    ____

    ____

    ____

    ____

    Concept: V. B. 1-2 Competency: 51; 53
    Question Type: *Conceptual*

58. Findings are said to be ____________________ when there are differences found between groups that actually exist and did not happen by chance.

    Concept: V. B. 2. b Competency: 54
    Question Type: *Factual*

SUMMING UP AND MEASURING UP

What Are the Types of Studies in Psychological Research?

There are three main types of studies in psychological research: descriptive, correlational, and experimental. In descriptive and correlational designs, researchers examine behaviour as it naturally occurs. These types of studies are useful for describing and predicting behaviour, but they do not allow researchers to assess causality. Correlational designs have limitations, including directionality problems (knowing whether variable A caused variable B or the reverse) and the third variable problem (the possibility that a third variable is responsible for variables A and B). In an experiment, a researcher manipulates the independent variable to study how it affects the dependent variable. An experiment allows a researcher to establish a causal relationship between the independent and dependent variables and to avoid the directionality problem when trying to understand how one variable might affect another. An experiment gives the researcher the greatest control, so that the only thing that changes is the independent variable. The researcher must assign participants at random to different experimental groups to make the groups as equal as possible (on average) on all variables except the one being studied. The group the researcher wants to know about is the population, but because it is usually impossible for everyone in the population to be a research participant, the researcher uses a representative sample of the population and then generalizes the findings to the population. Random sampling, in which everyone in the population has an equal chance of being a research participant, is the best way to sample, but since this is usually not possible, most researchers use a convenience sample. Among the most important factors in whether the results from a particular sample can be generalized back to the population is sample size. In general, large samples provide more accurate results than small ones.

Read the following (hypothetical) example of a psychological study. Identify the dependent variable, independent variable, and type of study.

Researchers wanted to know if men who had been punished harshly as children were more likely to be violent as adults than were men who had not been punished harshly as children. The researchers interviewed men who had committed either violent crimes (e.g., domestic violence, assault) or nonviolent crimes (e.g., parking violations, embezzlement, credit card fraud), asking them about the punishment they received when they were children. They found that, as predicted, the men who had committed violent crimes were more likely to have been punished harshly as children than were those who had committed nonviolent crimes.

Write "DV" next to the hypothesized dependent variable, "IV" next to the hypothesized independent variable; write "NA" (for "not applicable") if the item is neither a DV nor an IV.

___ Crime—violent or nonviolent
___ Age of participant when the crime was committed
___ Punishment received as a child—harsh or not harsh
___ Sex of participant (men or women)
___ Population from which the men were selected

What type of study is this? Check one:
___ Observation
___ Correlation
___ Experiment

What Are the Data Collection Methods of Psychological Science?

In psychological science, there are five basic data collection methods, which operate at different levels of analysis; the choice of which to use is generally dictated by the research question. First, researchers can observe behaviours as they take place and either write down general descriptions of the behaviours or check off a tally sheet of prespecified behaviour categories. Second, researchers can ask people for information about their thoughts, feelings, and preferences by using surveys, questionnaires, interviews, and self-reports. Third, researchers can measure how quickly and accurately people respond to a stimulus. Fourth, researchers can directly measure the brain's electrical activity and blood flow, and they can disrupt ongoing brain processes; these techniques are increasingly being combined with the other three methods. Finally, researchers can use animal models in which genes, chemicals involved in the way neurons function, or brain structures are altered to study the effects on behaviour. Regardless of the method chosen, researchers must consider the ethical consequences of their data collection; they must weigh the study's relative risks against its potential benefits.

Suppose you want to study the effect of socioeconomic status (meaning, roughly, financial status and education) on weight. You theorize that wealthier people tend to be thinner than poorer people because wealthier people can afford to buy healthier food. You plan to gather data by having observers rate the weight of each person who enters a nearby supermarket, using a rating scale that ranges from very thin to obese. The observers will also rate as healthy or unhealthy each food a person purchases. Finally, observers will follow the shoppers into the parking lot and, as an indicator of socioeconomic status, record the type of car each person drives. All of the observers' evaluations will take place without the participants' knowledge. Which of the following ethical concerns are likely to be considered by the REB that has been asked to review this research proposal? Check all that apply:

___ informed consent
___ privacy
___ risk to participants
___ confidentiality
___ protection of human participants

How Are Data Analyzed and Evaluated?

Data analysis begins with descriptive statistics, which summarize the data. Measures of central tendency indicate statistical averages across sets of numbers, whereas the standard deviation indicates how widely numbers are distributed about an average. Correlations describe the relationship between two variables: positive, negative, or none. Inferential statistics show whether the results of a study were due to the effect of one variable on another or whether the results were more likely due to chance.

How does variability affect our confidence in the mean?

a. The more variable the data, the more confidence we can have that we would get a similar mean value if we repeated the experiment.
b. The more variable the data, the less confidence we can have that we would get a similar mean value if we repeated the experiment.
c. Variability in the data is unrelated to what we can say about the mean.
d. Variability in the data is a natural consequence of the fact that people are different, so it should give us more confidence in the mean we get.

ANSWER KEY

Item **Answer**

1. b
2. a
3. c
4. c
5. A theory is a model or set of interconnected ideas that explains how something works. The theory is based on observation and makes predictions about future events. A good theory produces testable hypotheses, or specific predictions of what should occur. Freud's theory was not a good theory because it did not generate testable hypotheses. There is no way to test whether his ideas are correct.
6. a
7. d
8. No one type is superior in all ways. Each type of research has advantages and disadvantages. Descriptive research is a useful first step if you want to determine if a phenomenon exists, or want to study a phenomenon in its natural setting. The drawback is the observer might not be 100 percent accurate in their report. Correlational research is useful if you want to study sensitive topics that do not lend themselves ethically to an experiment or observation. The disadvantage is that you can not definitively determine causality. Experiments can determine causality, but can be limited due to their artificial nature.
9. b
10. Descriptive; Correlational; Experiment
11. c
12. a
13. a, b, b, a, b
14. b
15. d
16. The researcher would need to use correlational research due to ethical concerns. That is, even though you believe divorce causes promiscuity we can not ethically conduct an experiment where one group is randomly assigned to have their parents get divorced while the control group's parents stay married.
17. c
18. a
19. d
20. c
21. d
22. confound
23. b
24. random; convenience
25. Selection bias basically means the two groups are not the same at the start of the experiment. Ideally, this would be avoided by randomly assigning participants to conditions. Since this is not feasible for this research question, it creates a confound such that any findings may be due to the difference in groups (i.e., non-equivalent groups) that existed and not to participation in required study hours. If groups do not start out the same, it is impossible to be certain if a manipulation actually caused the outcome.
26. c
27. An artificial situation is a situation over which the experimenter has more influence (most likely in a laboratory), and as a result, can have more control over possible confounds. This makes the influence of the independent variable on the dependent variable more definite. However, because the situation is artificial, we can not be 100 percent sure the participant is acting naturally, or would act similarly outside of the laboratory in a more natural setting.
28. low
29. meta-analysis; factoring in the size of the sample by giving more weight to larger samples
30. b, e, a, c, d
31. the question the researcher wants to answer
32. biological; individual; social; cultural
33. Fundamentally, the researcher should realize that participants' culture will influence how they think about love, how they feel and experience love, and how they express their love. The researcher should be aware that these features of love are not universal and are culturally dependent.
34. systematically code or assess behaviours that can be seen.
35. Setting: Lab or Natural Environment?; How Should the Data Be Collected?; Should the Observer Be Visible?
36. b
37. c
38. This can not be determined unless there is substantial further study. Because this finding was from a case study of only one participant it is very subjective. This makes it difficult to know what pre-existing conditions may have contributed to the outcome, or what unique characteristics of this one individual could have played a role. For example, it could be that this particular patient was going to get better regardless of the type of TV watched.
39. surveys; interviews; questionnaires; self-reports
40. d
41. b
42. Social desirability involves a knowing and purposeful attempt to make yourself look good while the better-than-average effect is a natural tendency to describe yourself in an overly positive way unintentionally.
43. a
44. d

45. electrophysiology; electroencephalograph (EEG)
46. Transcranial magnetic stimulation. It is the only type of brain imaging that actively introduces stimulation. The other three types record ongoing activity.
47. Positron Emission Tomography (PET); Magnetic Resonance Imaging (MRI); Functional Magnetic Resonance Imaging (fMRI); Transcranial Magnetic Stimulation (TMS)
48. c
49. b, a, c
50. privacy; confidentiality; anonymity
51. b
52. deception; debriefing; relative risk; risk/benefit ratio
53. Validity; Reliability; Accuracy
54. d
55. b
56. a
57. Descriptive statistics summarize basic patterns. For example, descriptive statistics indicate what response is most typical (i.e., central tendency). One way to define "typicality" is the arithmetic average, or mean. Another way to define what is typical is by looking at what is most common, or the mode. A third way to define typicality is to determine the middle score, or median. Correlations provide a numerical value that describes the strength of the relationship between two variables. When two variables are strongly related, one can be predicted from the other. Sometimes researchers have two sets of numbers and need to determine whether there are real differences between them. This is done with inferential statistics.
58. statistically significant

Summing Up and Measuring Up

What Are the Types of Studies in Psychological Research?

DV; NA; IV; NA—all participants were men; NA; Correlation

What Are the Data Collection Methods of Psychological Research?

An REB would be concerned about privacy because people are being watched and followed. It would also be concerned about the protection of human participants because people might feel threatened if they sense they are being followed, especially to their cars. Confidentiality would not be an issue, since no identifying data are being collected that could be traced to any particular shopper, and there would be no need for informed consent, since all the behaviours are occurring in public places. Even so, many people would not be comfortable if they knew other people were judging their weight and watching what they purchased. An REB would likely not pass this study as it is described and would require a revised, less intrusive method.

How Are Data Analyzed and Evaluated?

b.

KEY TERM EXERCISES

accuracy

Textbook Definition:
Your Own Definition:
Your Own Example:

case study

Textbook Definition:
Your Own Definition:
Your Own Example:

brain imaging

Textbook Definition:
Your Own Definition:
Your Own Example:

central tendency

Textbook Definition:
Your Own Definition:
Your Own Example:

confound

Textbook Definition:
Your Own Definition:
Your Own Example:

control (or comparison) group

Textbook Definition:
Your Own Definition:
Your Own Example:

correlational study

Textbook Definition:
Your Own Definition:
Your Own Example:

cross-sectional study

Textbook Definition:
Your Own Definition:
Your Own Example:

culturally sensitive research

Textbook Definition:
Your Own Definition:
Your Own Example:

data

Textbook Definition:
Your Own Definition:
Your Own Example:

dependent variable

Textbook Definition:
Your Own Definition:
Your Own Example:

descriptive statistics

Textbook Definition:
Your Own Definition:
Your Own Example:

descriptive studies

Textbook Definition:
Your Own Definition:
Your Own Example:

directionality problem

Textbook Definition:
Your Own Definition:
Your Own Example:

electroencephalograph (EEG)

Textbook Definition:
Your Own Definition:
Your Own Example:

experiment

Textbook Definition:
Your Own Definition:
Your Own Example:

experimental (or treatment) group

Textbook Definition:
Your Own Definition:
Your Own Example:

experimenter expectancy effect

Textbook Definition:
Your Own Definition:
Your Own Example:

functional magnetic resonance imaging (fMRI)

Textbook Definition:
Your Own Definition:
Your Own Example:

hypothesis

Textbook Definition:
Your Own Definition:
Your Own Example:

independent variable

Textbook Definition:
Your Own Definition:
Your Own Example:

inferential statistics

Textbook Definition:
Your Own Definition:
Your Own Example:

longitudinal studies

Textbook Definition:
Your Own Definition:
Your Own Example:

magnetic resonance imaging (MRI)

Textbook Definition:
Your Own Definition:
Your Own Example:

mean

Textbook Definition:

Your Own Definition:

Your Own Example:

median

Textbook Definition:

Your Own Definition:

Your Own Example:

meta-analysis

Textbook Definition:

Your Own Definition:

Your Own Example:

mode

Textbook Definition:

Your Own Definition:

Your Own Example:

naturalistic observation

Textbook Definition:

Your Own Definition:

Your Own Example:

observational technique

Textbook Definition:

Your Own Definition:

Your Own Example:

observer bias

Textbook Definition:

Your Own Definition:

Your Own Example:

participant observation

Textbook Definition:

Your Own Definition:

Your Own Example:

population

Textbook Definition:

Your Own Definition:

Your Own Example:

positron emission tomography (PET)

Textbook Definition:

Your Own Definition:

Your Own Example:

random assignment

Textbook Definition:
Your Own Definition:
Your Own Example:

research

Textbook Definition:
Your Own Definition:
Your Own Example:

reactivity

Textbook Definition:
Your Own Definition:
Your Own Example:

research ethics boards (REB)

Textbook Definition:
Your Own Definition:
Your Own Example:

reliability

Textbook Definition:
Your Own Definition:
Your Own Example:

response performance

Textbook Definition:
Your Own Definition:
Your Own Example:

replication

Textbook Definition:
Your Own Definition:
Your Own Example:

sample

Textbook Definition:
Your Own Definition:
Your Own Example:

scatterplot

Textbook Definition:
Your Own Definition:
Your Own Example:

scientific method

Textbook Definition:
Your Own Definition:
Your Own Example:

selection bias

Textbook Definition:
Your Own Definition:
Your Own Example:

self-report method

Textbook Definition:
Your Own Definition:
Your Own Example:

standard deviation

Textbook Definition:
Your Own Definition:
Your Own Example:

theory

Textbook Definition:
Your Own Definition:
Your Own Example:

third variable problem

Textbook Definition:
Your Own Definition:
Your Own Example:

transcranial magnetic stimulation (TMS)

Textbook Definition:
Your Own Definition:
Your Own Example:

validity

Textbook Definition:
Your Own Definition:
Your Own Example:

variable

Textbook Definition:
Your Own Definition:
Your Own Example:

variability

Textbook Definition:
Your Own Definition:
Your Own Example:

CHAPTER 3 Biological Foundations

CONCEPT MAP

I. What Is the Genetic Basis of Psychological Science?
 A. Genetics
  1. Chromosomes
   a. Genes
    1. DNA (deoxyribonucleic acid)
 B. Heredity Involves Passing Along Genes through Reproduction
  1. Mendelian Genetics
   a. Dominant and Recessive Genes
   b. Genotype vs. Phenotype
    1. Phenylketonuria (PKU)
   c. Polygenic Effects
 C. Genotypic Variation Is Created by Sexual Reproduction
  1. 23 Pairs of Chromosomes
  2. Gametes
  3. Zygote
   a. Cell Division
   b. Mutations
    1. Sickle-Cell Disease
  4. On Ethics: Genetic Testing
 D. Genes Affect Behaviour
  1. Behavioural Genetics Methods
   a. Twin Studies
    1. Monozygotic Twins
    2. Dizygotic Twins
   b. Adoption Studies
    1. Raised Together
    2. Raised Apart
  2. Understanding Heritability
   a. Heredity vs. Heritability
 E. Social and Environmental Contexts Influence Genetic Expression
 F. Genetic Expression Can Be Modified
  1. Knockouts

II. How Does the Nervous System Operate?
 A. Neurons Are Specialized for Communication
  1. Types of Neurons
   a. Sensory Neurons
    1. Somatosensory
   b. Motor Neurons
    1. Efferent Neurons
    2. Interneurons
  2. Neuron Structure
   a. Dendrites
   b. Cell Body
   c. Axon
    1. Myelin Sheath
     A. Glial Cells
    2. Nodes of Ranvier
   d. Terminal Buttons
   e. Synapse (Synaptic Cleft)
  3. Resting Membrane Potential
   a. Polarization
  4. The Roles of Sodium and Potassium Ions
   a. Ion Channel
  5. Action Potentials Cause Neural Communication
   a. Changes in Electrical Potential
    1. Excitatory Signal
    2. Inhibitory Signal
   b. Action Potentials Spread along the Axon
    1. Propagation
    2. Multiple Sclerosis
     A. Demyelination
   c. All-or-None Principle
  6. Pre- vs. Postsynaptic Neurons

B. Neurotransmitters Bind to Receptors across the Synapse
  1. Neurotransmitters Bind with Specific Receptors
    a. Reuptake
    b. Enzyme Deactivation
    c. Autoreception
  2. Neurotransmitters' Effects
    a. Agonists vs. Antagonists
  3. Types of Neurotransmitters
    a. Acetylcholine (ACh)
    b. Serotonin
      1. Selective Serotonin Reuptake Inhibitors (SSRIs)
    c. Dopamine
      1. Parkinson's Disease
    d. GABA
    e. Glutamate
    f. Endorphins
    g. Substance P

III. What Are the Basic Brain Structures and Their Functions?
  A. Functional Units of the Nervous System
    1. Central Nervous System (CNS)
    2. Peripheral Nervous System (PNS)
  B. History of Understanding Brain Functions
    1. Phineas Gage
    2. Phrenology
    3. Autopsy
      a. Broca's Area
  C. The Brain Stem
    1. Spinal Cord
      a. White vs. Grey Matter
    2. Structures
    3. Functions
    4. Reticular Formation
  D. Cerebellum
  E. Subcortical Structures
    1. Limbic System
    2. Hypothalamus
    3. Thalamus
    4. Hippocampus
    5. Amygdala
    6. Basal Ganglia
      a. Nucleus Accumbens
  F. Cerebral Cortex
    1. Occipital Lobe
      a. Primary Visual Cortex
    2. Parietal Lobe
      a. Somatosensory Homunculus
    3. Temporal Lobe
      a. Primary Auditory Cortex
      b. Fusiform Face Areas
    4. Frontal Lobe
      a. Primary Motor Cortex
      b. Prefrontal Cortex
      c. Lobotomy
    5. Corpus Callosum

IV. How Are Neural Messages Integrated into Communication Systems?
  A. Peripheral Nervous System
    1. Somatic Nervous System
    2. Autonomic Nervous System (ANS)
      a. Sympathetic Division
      b. Parasympathetic Division
  B. Endocrine System
    1. Hormones
      a. Gonads
        1. Androgens vs. Estrogens
  C. Actions of the Nervous and Endocrine System Are Coordinated
    1. Pituitary Gland
      a. Growth Hormone

V. How Does the Brain Change?
  A. Plasticity
  B. Interplay of Genes and Environment Wire the Brain
    1. Cell Identity Becomes Fixed over Time
    2. Experience Fine-Tunes Neural Connections
      a. Critical Periods
  C. Culture Affects the Brain
    1. Cultural Neuroscience
  D. The Brain Rewires Itself throughout Life
    1. Change in Strength of Connections Underlies Learning
      a. Neurogenesis
    2. Changes in the Brain
      a. Phantom Limb
    3. Synesthesia
  E. Females' and Males' Brains Are Similar and Different
    1. Sexual Dimorphism
    2. Size
    3. Lateralization
  F. The Brain Can Recover from Injury
    1. Radical Hemispherectomy
    2. Stem Cells

CHAPTER SUMMARY

What Is the Genetic Basis of Psychological Science?

• Heredity Involves Passing Along Genes through Reproduction: The Human Genome Project has mapped the genes that make up humans' 23 chromosomal pairs. Genes' variations are either dominant or recessive. The genome represents the genotype, and the observable characteristics are the phenotype. Many characteristics are polygenic.

• Genotypic Variation Is Created by Sexual Reproduction: Because half of each chromosome comes from each parent and the two halves are joined randomly, there is enormous potential variation in the resulting zygote's genome. Mutations also give rise to variations.

• Genes Affect Behaviour: Behavioural geneticists can quantify the similarity and variation in a population's shared characteristics. Twin studies, research on adoptees, and other investigations of hereditary and genetic influence provide insight into heritability.

• Social and Environmental Contexts Influence Genetic Expression: Gene expression is a complex interaction between genetic makeup and environmental context.

• Genetic Expression Can Be Modified: Genetic manipulation has been achieved in mammals such as mice, but has proved difficult in humans. However, animal studies using the technique of "knocking out" genes to determine their effects on behaviours and on disease are a valuable tool for understanding genetic influences.

How Does the Nervous System Operate?

• Neurons Are Specialized for Communication: Neurons are the basic building blocks of the nervous system. They receive and send chemical messages. All neurons have the same basic structure, but neurons vary by function and by location in the nervous system.

• Action Potentials Cause Neural Communication: Changes in a neuron's electrical charge are the basis of an action potential, or neural firing. Firing is the means of communication within networks of neurons.

• Neurotransmitters Bind to Receptors across the Synapse: Neurons do not touch; they release chemicals (neurotransmitters) into the synapse, a small gap between the neurons. Neurotransmitters bind with the receptors of postsynaptic neurons, thus changing the charge in those neurons. Neurotransmitters' effects are halted by reuptake of the neurotransmitters into the presynaptic neurons, enzyme deactivation, or autoreception.

• Neurotransmitters Influence Mind and Behaviour: Neurotransmitters have been identified that influence aspects of the mind and of behaviour in humans, including emotions, motor skills, sleep, learning and memory, pain control, and pain perception. Drugs and toxins mimic neurotransmitters' actions or reduce neurotransmitters' availability.

What Are the Basic Brain Structures and Their Functions?

• The Brain Stem Houses the Basic Programs of Survival: The top of the spinal cord forms the brain stem, which is involved in basic functions such as breathing and walking as well as general arousal.

• The Cerebellum Is Essential for Movement: The cerebellum ("little brain"), the bulging structure connected to the back of the brain stem, controls balance and is essential for movement.

• Subcortical Structures Control Emotions and Basic Drives: The subcortical structures play a key part in psychological functions because they control vital functions (the hypothalamus), sensory relay (the thalamus), memories (the hippocampus), emotions (the amygdala), and the planning and producing of movement (the basal ganglia).

• The Cerebral Cortex Underlies Complex Mental Activity: The lobes of the cortex play specific roles in controlling vision (occipital), touch (parietal), hearing and speech comprehension (temporal), and planning and movement (frontal).

How Are Neural Messages Integrated into Communication Systems?

• The Peripheral Nervous System Includes the Somatic and Autonomic Systems: The body's internal environment is regulated by the autonomic system, which is divided into the alarm response (sympathetic) and the return-to-normal response (parasympathetic).The somatic system relays sensory information.

• The Endocrine System Communicates through Hormones: Both endocrine glands and organs produce and release chemical substances, which travel to body tissues through the bloodstream and influence a variety of processes, including sexual behaviour.

• Actions of the Nervous System and Endocrine System Are Coordinated: Most of the central control of the endocrine system occurs through the actions of both the hypothalamus and the pituitary gland; the latter controls the release of hormones from the rest of the endocrine glands.

How Does the Brain Change?

• The Interplay of Genes and the Environment Wires the Brain: Chemical signals influence cells' growth and function. Environmental experiences, especially during critical periods, are necessary for cells to develop properly and for them to make more detailed connections.

• Culture Affects the Brain: Daily social interactions, which vary among cultures (and subcultures and individuals), are reflected in each brain's unique organization.

• The Brain Rewires Itself throughout Life: Although plasticity decreases with age, the brain retains the ability to rewire itself throughout life. This ability is learning's biological basis.

• Females' and Males' Brains Are Similar and Different: Although males' and females' brains are predominantly similar, males' brains are larger than females' (on average), and females' verbal abilities are organized more bilaterally (more equally in both hemispheres).There are sex differences in the rate of development for some areas of the brain.

• The Brain Can Recover from Injury: The brain can reorganize its functions in response to brain damage, although this capacity decreases with age. Anomalies in sensation and in perception, such as synesthesia, are attributed to cross-wiring connections in the brain.

COMPETENCY MODEL

What Is the Genetic Basis of Psychological Science?

Genetics

1. Describe the relationship of chromosomes to genes to DNA.
2. What determines what a cell ultimately becomes? Does DNA vary from cell to cell in the same organism?
3. Be aware of the Human Genome Project's major findings.

Heredity Involves Passing Along Genes through Reproduction

4. Describe how dominant and recessive genes combine.
5. Distinguish between genotype and phenotype.
6. Identify characteristics of phenylketonuria (PKU).
7. What are polygenic effects?

Genotypic Variation Is Created by Sexual Reproduction

8. What is the importance of cell mutations?
9. Identify the ethical issues related to genetic testing.

Genes Affect Behaviour

10. Distinguish between monozygotic and dizygotic twins.
11. What do twin studies tell us about behavioural genetics?
12. What do adoption studies tell us about behavioural genetics?
13. Distinguish between heredity and heritability.

Social and Environmental Contexts Influence Genetic Expression

14. Explain the importance of social and environmental contexts on genetic expression.

Genetic Expression Can Be Modified

15. Understand the significance of knockouts.

How Does the Nervous System Operate?

Neurons Are Specialized for Communication

16. Identify the two main types of neurons.
17. Distinguish the roles of efferent neurons and interneurons.
18. Describe how motor and sensory neurons work together.
19. Identify the structures and their functions of a neuron.
20. What does a myelin sheath help with?
21. Identify the electrical charge of the resting potential.
22. What influences flow through the ion channel?
23. Where do the excitatory and inhibitory signals arrive? How are they different?
24. What is demyelination? What disease results from this?
25. Explain the all-or-none principle.

Neurotransmitters Bind to Receptors across the Synapse

26. What are receptors? Where are they located?
27. What three events stop the influence of neurotransmitters in the synaptic cleft?
28. Distinguish the effects of agonists and antagonists.
29. List the major neurotransmitters and what they do.
30. Which neurotransmitter is most closely associated with Parkinson's Disease?

What Are the Basic Brain Structures and Their Functions?

Functional Units of the Nervous System

31. Identify the two functional units of the nervous system.

History of Understanding Brain Functions

32. What was the role of Phineas Gage in helping us to understand brain functions?
33. Describe the process and goal of phrenology.
34. What was the role of autopsies in helping us understand brain functions?

The Brain Stem

35. Distinguish between white and grey matter.

36. Identify the main structures in the brain stem.

37. What functions is the brain stem responsible for?

38. Know the function of the reticular formation.

Cerebellum

39. Know the function of the cerebellum.

Subcortical Structures

40. Know the functions of the limbic system.

41. Identify the functions of the structures in the subcortical area.

Cerebral Cortex

42. Identify the functions of the lobes in the cerebral cortex.

43. What brain area makes humans unique in the animal kingdom?

How Are Neural Messages Integrated into Communication Systems?

Peripheral Nervous System

44. Identify the divisions of the peripheral nervous system.

45. Distinguish the sympathetic from the parasympathetic division of the nervous system.

Endocrine System

46. Explain how the endocrine system influences behaviour.

Actions of the Nervous and Endocrine Systems Are Coordinated

47. How does the pituitary gland coordinate the nervous and endocrine systems?

How Does the Brain Change?

Plasticity

48. Explain plasticity.

Interplay of Genes and Environment Wire the Brain

49. How does an enriched environment influence brain development?

Culture Affects the Brain

50. Describe the role of culture on the brain.

The Brain Rewires Itself throughout Life

51. Understand how learning influences the brain.

52. Describe phantom limb.

53. What is synesthesia?

Females' and Males' Brains Are Similar and Different

54. Explain how female and male brains are similar and different.

The Brain Can Recover from Injury

55. Describe ways a brain can recover from injury.

KNOWLEDGE CHECK

1. Which of the following represents the relationship of chromosomes, DNA, and genes?
   a. Chromosomes contain DNA which is a segment of genes.
   b. Chromosomes contain genes which are segments of DNA.
   c. Genes contain chromosomes which are segments of DNA.
   d. Genes contain DNA which is a segment of chromosomes.

   Concept: I. A. 1 Competency: 1
   Question Type: *Factual*

2. Penny is collecting cells from mice. When she extracts cells from the brain, and cells from the heart, what should she find? Penny knows that the genes varied in their expression due to what?
   a. the DNA is the same in each; the influence of environmental factors
   b. the DNA is different in each; difference in their DNA
   c. the DNA is the same in each; difference in their DNA
   d. the DNA is different in each; the influence of environmental factors

   Concept: I. A Competency: 2
   Question Type: *Factual, Conceptual*

3. One of the most striking findings from the Human Genome Project is that there are only about ______________ genes in a human being.
   a. 23 pairs of
   b. 30,000
   c. 15–20 million
   d. 1 billion

   Concept: I. A Competency: 3
   Question Type: *Factual*

4. Shannon and Kevin are having a baby and want to know if their baby will be able to curl his tongue (a recessive trait). Shannon is able to curl her tongue, while Kevin cannot. If their baby can curl his tongue, what do we know about Kevin's dominant and recessive genes?
   a. Kevin must have two dominant genes.
   b. Kevin must have two recessive genes.
   c. Kevin must have one dominant and one recessive gene.
   d. It isn't related to Kevin's genes; the baby can curl his tongue because Shannon has two recessive genes.

   Concept: I. B. 1. a Competency: 4
   Question Type: *Applied*

5. Steve plants two tomato seeds from the same plant in the ground. A few weeks later, both plants look identical. Based on this, what do we know about their genotype and phenotype?
   a. The plants have the same phenotype, but may have similar or different genotypes.
   b. The plants have the same phenotype, and have the same genotype.
   c. The plants have the same genotype, but may have similar or different phenotypes.
   d. The plants have the same phenotype, but have different genotypes.

   Concept: I. B. 1. b Competency: 5
   Question Type: *Applied*

6. George has to be careful about drinking sodas or ingesting certain dairy products. He has a genetic disorder in which he is unable to break down an enzyme (phenylalanine) contained in these products. For him, ingesting these substances could lead to severe brain damage. George's disorder is known as:
   a. Down syndrome
   b. La Vache Folle disorder
   c. General Genetic Syndrome
   d. Phenylketonuria

   Concept: I. B. 1. b. 1 Competency: 6
   Question Type: *Applied*

7. Most human characteristics (such as height and weight) are considered polygenic, which means ____________________.

   Concept: I. B. 1. c Competency: 7
   Question Type: *Factual*

8. During cell division mutations can occur. Which of the following statements about mutations is FALSE?
   a. Mutations result in physical or mental abnormalities.
   b. Most mutations have little, if any, influence on the organism.
   c. Mutations are often adaptive and can help the organism.
   d. Sickle-cell disease is the result of genetic mutations.

   Concept: I. C. 3. b Competency: 8
   Question Type: *Factual*

9. What is genetic testing? What are the ethical arguments for and against it?

   ____

   ____

   ____

   ____

   Concept: I. C. 4 Competency: 9
   Question Type: *Conceptual*

10. Bennell and Burnell are identical twins. They look alike, act alike, and often have a great time fooling their teacher about who they are. Their similarity is the result of one zygote dividing into two, each having the same chromosomes and the genes they contain. Bennell and Burnell are also known as:
    a. dizygotic twins
    b. fraternal twins
    c. matching twins
    d. monozygotic twins

    Concept: I. D. 1. a Competency: 10
    Question Type: *Applied*

11. What do twin studies tell us about behavioural genetics?

    ____

    ____

    ____

    ____

    Concept: I. D. 1. a Competency: 11
    Question Type: *Conceptual*

12. What do adoption studies tell us about behavioural genetics?

____

____

____

____

Concept: I. D. 1. b Competency: 12
Question Type: *Conceptual*

13. ______________________________ is the transmission of characteristics from parents to offspring by means of genes. A term that is often confused with this is ______________________, which is a statistical estimate of the genetic portion of the variation in some specific trait.

Concept: I. D. 2 Competency: 13
Question Type: *Factual*

14. Caspi and colleagues' study of New Zealanders founds that those with low-level MAO who had a history of maltreatment were responsible for most of the violent crime. This study is important because it suggests:
   a. MAO is a key gene activity for determining violent behaviour
   b. a history of maltreatment is key for determining violent behaviour
   c. the combination of genetic factors and environmental factors are key for determining violent behaviour
   d. from the cultural level, New Zealanders are more prone to violent behaviour

Concept: I. E Competency: 14
Question Type: *Conceptual*

15. Vincent is working with transgenic mice and wants to find the gene that leads some mice to have longer tails. Following the principle of knockouts, what should he do?
   a. Disturb the activity of the genes he believes determine the longer tails and see if that leads to longer tails in the next generation.
   b. Disturb the activity of the genes he believes determine the longer tails and see if that leads to shorter tails in the next generation.
   c. Stimulate the genes he believes determine the longer tails and see if that leads to longer tails in the next generation of mice.
   d. Disturb the activity of the genes that surround the gene he believes determines the longer tails and see if knocking out the surrounding genes leads to longer tails in the next generation.

Concept: I. F Competency: 15
Question Type: *Applied*

16. Concept: II. B Competency: 16
Question Type: *Factual*

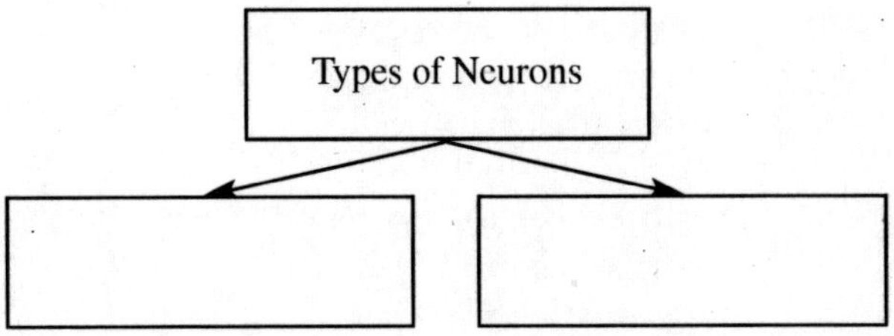

17. ______________________________ neurons transmit signals from the brain to the muscles throughout the body, whereas ______________________________ communicate within local or short-distance circuits.

Concept: II. A. 1. b Competency: 17
Question Type: *Factual*

18. Motor and sensory neurons work together. If you didn't have any sensory neurons, what would happen if you picked up an egg?

____

____

____

____

Concept: II. A. 1 Competency: 18
Question Type: *Conceptual*

19. Tony was riding his bicycle at the X-Games when he fell on the half-pipe and broke his arm. Which of the following types of neurons sent pain signals from his broken arm to his brain?
   a. sensory neurons
   b. motor neurons
   c. interneurons
   d. efferent neurons

Concept: II. A. 1 Competency: 18
Question Type: *Applied*

20. Please match each of the following structures with its function:

____ Increases the neuron's receptive field	a) Dendrite
____ Transmits neural signals from one end of the neuron to the other	b) Cell body
____ Information received from thousands of other neurons is collected and integrated	c) Axon
____ The site of chemical communication between neurons	d) Terminal buttons
____ Releases chemical signals from the neuron	e) Synapse
____ Detects chemical signals from neighboring neurons	

Concept: II. A. 2 Competency: 19
Question Type: *Factual*

21. Wire is to rubber insulation as axon is to:
    a. nodes of Ranvier
    b. terminal button
    c. myelin sheath
    d. synapse

Concept: II. A. 2. c. 1 Competency: 20
Question Type: *Applied*

22. The electrical charge of the resting potential is ____________________.

Concept: II. A. 3 Competency: 21
Question Type: *Factual*

23. Two types of ions that contribute to a neuron's resting membrane potential are ______________________________ and ______________________________. These ions pass through the cell membrane at ______________________________, specialized pores located at the nodes of Ranvier.

Concept: II. A. 4 Competency: 22
Question Type: *Factual*

24. Excitatory and inhibitory signals arrive at the ______________________________. ______________________________ signals decrease the chance of firing, while ______________________________ signals increase the chance of firing.

Concept: II. A. 5 Competency: 23
Question Type: *Factual*

25. Richard is experiencing numbness in his limbs and blurry vision. After visiting his physician, he is told that he has a neurological disorder resulting from the decay of the myelin sheath surrounding his axons. Richard is suffering from:
    a. muscular dystrophy
    b. multiple sclerosis
    c. Down syndrome
    d. Huntington's disease

Concept: II. A. 5. b. 2 Competency: 24
Question Type: *Applied*

26. The characteristic that a neuron fires with the same potency each time is known as the:
    a. absolute refractory period
    b. relative refractory period
    c. consistent velocity phenomenon
    d. all-or-none principle

Concept: II. A. 5. c Competency: 25
Question Type: *Applied*

27. Receptors are located in the ______________ neuron and are the location where ______________ bind to create excitatory or inhibitory signals.
    a. presynaptic; sodium ions
    b. presynaptic; potassium ions
    c. postsynaptic; neurotransmitters
    d. postsynaptic; potassium ions

Concept: II. B Competency: 26
Question Type: *Factual*

28. Concept: II. B. 1 Competency: 27
Question Type: *Factual*

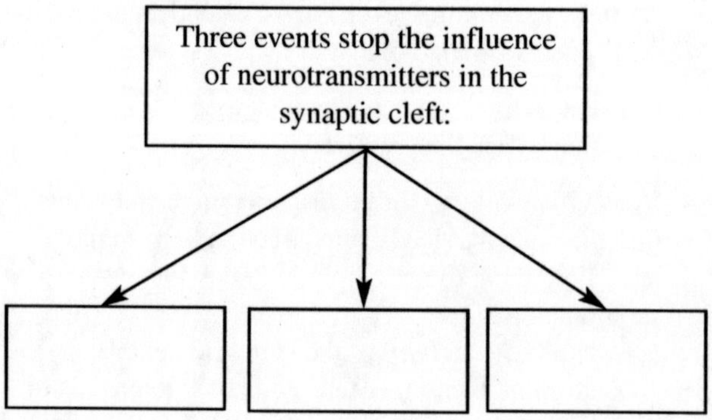

Three events stop the influence of neurotransmitters in the synaptic cleft:

29. Prozac is an antidepressant medication that works by preventing the neurotransmitter serotonin from being taken back into the presynaptic terminal button. Thus, it works by inhibiting the process of:
    a. enzyme deactivation
    b. depolarization
    c. reuptake
    d. autoreception

    Concept: II. B. 1 Competency: 27
    Question Type: *Applied*

30. Sara and Dopey are chemicals that hang out in the vesicles of the nervous system. When they receive an action potential, they spill out into the synapse to facilitate communication among the other neurons. Sara and Dopey are part of a family of chemicals known as:
    a. antagonists
    b. agonists
    c. dendrites
    d. neurotransmitters

    Concept: II. B. 2. a Competency: 28
    Question Type: *Applied*

31. Indiana is searching for treasures in a South American cave. Just as he is about to find the Lost Ark, he is shot with an arrow containing curare on the tip. The curare enters his bloodstream and binds to receptors, thus inhibiting the mechanisms that produce muscle movement. Curare competes with the mechanisms of which neurotransmitter?
    a. acetylcholine
    b. serotonin
    c. dopamine
    d. GABA

    Concept: II. B. 2. a Competency: 29
    Question Type: *Applied*

32. Shannon suffers from a number of nonspecific anxiety disorders. Her physician prescribes a benzodiazepine medication to deal with this. The medication works because it assists with the binding of which neurotransmitter?
    a. acetylcholine
    b. serotonin
    c. dopamine
    d. GABA

    Concept: II. B. 2. a Competency: 29
    Question Type: *Applied*

33. For each of the following, please match the function with the most appropriate neurotransmitter.

____ Pain reduction; Reward	a) Acetylcholine (ACh)
____ Emotional states and impulsiveness; Dreaming	b) Serotonin
____ Pain perception	c) Dopamine
____ Inhibition of action potentials; Anxiety and intoxication	d) GABA
____ Motor control over muscles; Learning, memory, sleeping, and dreaming	e) Glutamate
____ Enhancement of action potentials; Learning and memory	f) Endorphins
____ Reward and motivation; Motor control over voluntary movement	g) Substance P

    Concept: II. B. 2. a Competency: 29
    Question Type: *Factual*

34. Cassius suffers from Parkinson's disease, a neurological disorder marked by muscular rigidity, tremors, and difficulty initiating voluntary action. This disease is most likely due to a depletion in which of the following neurotransmitters?
    a. epinephrine
    b. serotonin
    c. dopamine
    d. GABA

    Concept: II. B. 2. a Competency: 30
    Question Type: *Applied*

35. Concept: III. A Competency: 31
    Question Type: *Factual*

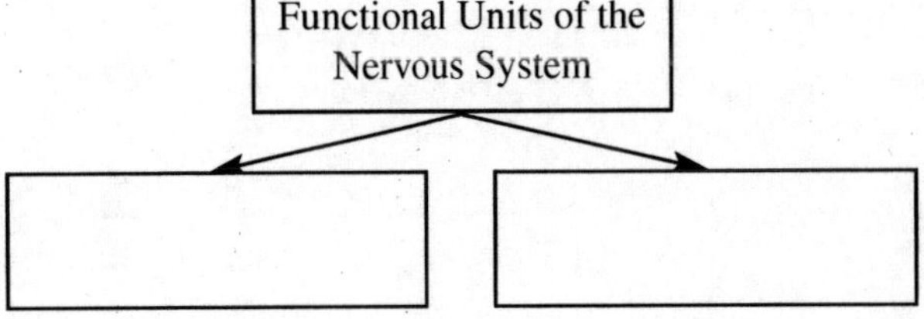

36. Phineas Gage is important to the history of understanding brain function because he:
    a. discovered a way to stimulate the brain with electric pulses
    b. was the first person to use phrenology
    c. experienced a major brain trauma resulting in an altered personality
    d. invented MRI technology

    Concept: III. B Competency: 32
    Question Type: *Applied*

37. Frank works at a carnival where he tells people their personality by feeling the bumps on their heads. Frank is practicing:
    a. a craniotomy
    b. a structural introspection
    c. phrenology
    d. psychoanalysis

    Concept: III. B. 2 Competency: 33
    Question Type: *Applied*

38. What was the role of autopsies in helping us understand brain functions?

    Concept: III. C. 3. a Competency: 34
    Question Type: *Factual*

39. ________________ matter consists mainly of cell bodies, while ________________ matter consists mainly of axons.

    Concept: III. C. 1. a Competency: 35
    Question Type: *Factual*

40. Concept: III. C. 2 Competency: 36
    Question Type: *Factual*

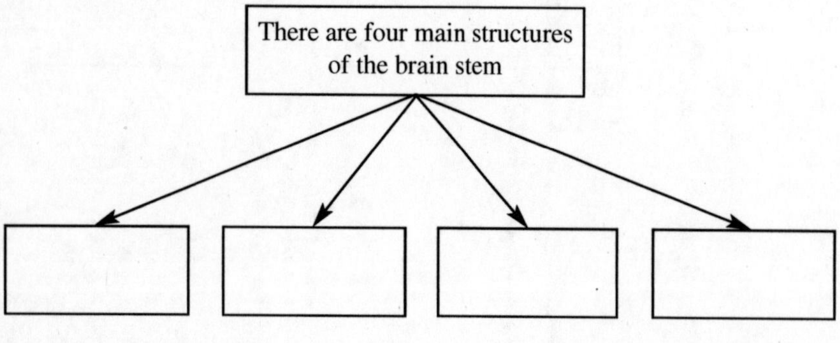
There are four main structures of the brain stem

41. In terms of our ability to survive, which area of the brain could we least afford to lose?

    Concept: III. C. 3 Competency: 37
    Question Type: *Conceptual*

42. Casey has a problem staying alert, and experiences problems regulating her sleep cycle. What brain structure is most likely to blame?
    a. medulla oblongata
    b. the pons
    c. the midbrain
    d. reticular formation

    Concept: III. C. 4 Competency: 38
    Question Type: *Applied*

43. Timmy has trouble coordinating his muscle movements, and experiences a slight head tilt. What brain structure is most likely to blame?
    a. medulla oblongata
    b. cerebellum
    c. cerebral cortex
    d. reticular formation

    Concept: III. D Competency: 39
    Question Type: *Applied*

44. Which of the following is controlled by the limbic system?
    a. motivation to eat or drink
    b. sleep
    c. motor coordination
    d. most of the major senses with the exception of smell

    Concept: III. E. 1 Competency: 40
    Question Type: *Applied*

45. For each of the following, please match the function with the most appropriate structure in the subcortical area.

____ Serves a vital role in our learning to associate things in the world with emotional responses
____ Important for experiencing reward
____ Regulates body temperature, body rhythms, blood pressure, and blood glucose levels
____ Crucial for planning and producing movement
____ All incoming sensory information, except smell, goes through here before reaching the cortex
____ Plays an important role in the storage of new memories

a) Hypothalamus
b) Thalamus
c) Hippocampus
d) Amygdala
e) Basal ganglia
f) Nucleus accumbens

Concept: III. E Competency: 41
Question Type: *Factual*

46. For each of the following, please match the function with the most appropriate lobe in the cerebral cortex.

____ Primarily responsible for hearing
____ Directing and maintaining attention, keeping ideas in mind while distractions bombard us from the outside world
____ Devoted partially to touch
____ Contains somatosensory homunculus
____ Devoted almost exclusively to vision
____ Essential for planning and movement

a) Frontal
b) Parietal
c) Occipital
d) Temporal

Concept: III. F Competency: 42
Question Type: *Factual*

47. Which brain area is the one, according to scientists, that makes humans unique in the animal kingdom?

____

Concept: III. F. 4 Competency: 43
Question Type: *Factual*

48. Concept: IV. A Competency: 44
Question Type: *Factual*

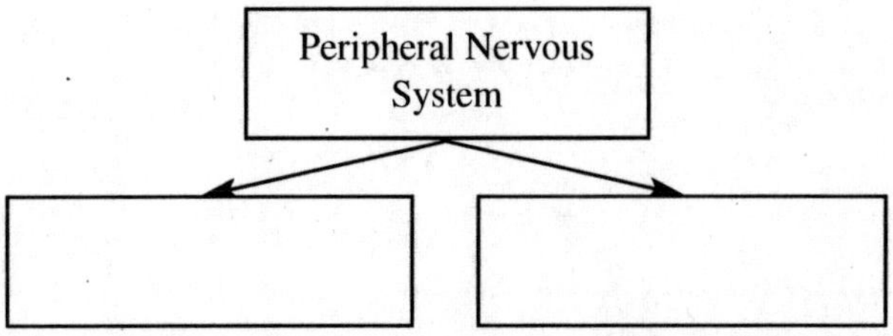

49. Amarillis is a chronic worrier and cannot deal with the stressors in her life. Her chronic state of agitation has been going on for many years and her friends' attempts to be of help have mostly failed. Because of her worries, Amarillis suffers from ulcers and heart disease. These diseases are likely associated with chronic activation of which nervous system?
a. the parasympathetic division of the autonomic nervous system
b. the parasympathetic division of the peripheral nervous system
c. the sympathetic division of the central nervous system
d. the sympathetic division of the autonomic nervous system

Concept: IV. A. 2 Competency: 45
Question Type: *Applied*

50. While in the remote jungle, Reuben nearly steps on a poisonous snake. After the poisonous snake disappears into the jungle, Reuben finally calms down. Which part of his nervous system allows this to occur?
a. the parasympathetic division of the autonomic nervous system
b. the parasympathetic division of the peripheral nervous system
c. the sympathetic division of the central nervous system
d. the sympathetic division of the autonomic nervous system

Concept: IV. A. 2 Competency: 45
Question Type: *Applied*

51. The nervous system is to electrochemical signals as the endocrine system is to:
a. adrenaline
b. neurons
c. hormones
d. neurotransmitters

Concept: IV. B Competency: 46
Question Type: *Factual*

52. The ____________ is located at the base of the hypothalamus and sends hormonal signals that control the release of hormones from endocrine glands.
   a. thalamus
   b. pituitary gland
   c. gonadal gland
   d. release factor

   Concept: IV. C. 1 Competency: 47
   Question Type: *Factual*

53. Charlotte experienced a brain injury as a young child resulting in an inability to speak. However, over time, her brain compensated for the damaged area by reorganizing itself. This demonstrates which concept?
   a. plasticity
   b. localization
   c. electrochemical signaling
   d. propagation

   Concept: V. A Competency: 48
   Question Type: *Applied*

54. Based on the findings from the research on rats raised in deprived rather than enriched environments, what would be a good idea for raising your own kids?
   a. Provide them with just the basic needs, and allow their creativity to take over.
   b. Provide an environment with lots of different activities, including things to play with and puzzles to solve.
   c. Provide an environment that focuses heavily on problem solving without an emphasis on physical activities.
   d. Provide an environment that focuses heavily on physical activities without an emphasis on mental activities.

   Concept: V. B. 2 Competency: 49
   Question Type: *Applied*

55. What do findings from cultural neuroscience suggest about culture's influence on the brain?

   ____

   ____

   ____

   ____

   Concept: V. C. 1 Competency: 50
   Question Type: *Factual*

56. After reading this chapter on the brain, and learning about all the information it contains, how will your brain change?

   ____

   ____

   ____

   ____

   Concept: V. D. 1 Competency: 51
   Question Type: *Applied*

57. Sergeant Sullivan has returned from the war in Afghanistan without his left leg. Even though he no longer has the leg, he feels like it is still there, and often experiences pain in the leg. This is due to what phenomenon?
   a. neurogenesis
   b. sensory dementia
   c. synesthesia
   d. phantom limb

   Concept: V. D. 2 Competency: 52
   Question Type: *Applied*

58. Pete is an accomplished chef who tends to experience tastes when he reads words. For example, if Pete saw the word "magnanimous" he would immediately experience the taste of coconuts and mangos. This is due to what phenomenon?
   a. neurogenesis
   b. sensory dementia
   c. synesthesia
   d. phantom limb

   Concept: V. D. 3 Competency: 53
   Question Type: *Applied*

59. For each of the following, please match the description of brain function with the most appropriate sex.

   ____ Greater use of spatial-related brain regions — a) Females
   ____ Have brains that are more bilaterally organized for language — b) Males
   ____ Greater use of language-related brain regions
   ____ Generally have larger brains
   ____ Less impaired following a stroke

   Concept: V. E Competency: 54
   Question Type: *Factual*

60. If a person is suffering from epilepsy, they can possibly recover by having an entire hemisphere of their brain removed. This process is known as ________________________________.

Concept: V. F Competency: 55
Question Type: *Factual*

SUMMING UP AND MEASURING UP

What Is the Genetic Basis of Psychological Science?

Human behaviour is influenced by genetic processes. People inherit both physical characteristics and personality traits from their parents. Only recently have scientists developed the tools to measure genetic processes and the roles that various genes play in psychological activity. The Human Genome Project has mapped DNA's basic sequence, information that eventually will be translated into medical treatments and a greater understanding of individual differences among people. Researchers increasingly are studying how and when genes are expressed, in addition to particular traits' heritability. Among the genetic research tools are methods that enhance or interrupt gene expression by selectively knocking out specific genes to reveal which behaviours are affected.

Complete the following sentences by filling in each blank with one word: "identical," "similar," or "different."

a. For monozygotic twins reared together, heredity will be ________________ and environment will be ________________.

b. For monozygotic twins reared apart, heredity will be ________________ and environment will be ________________.

c. For dizygotic twins reared together, heredity will be ________________ and environment will be ________________.

d. For dizygotic twins reared apart, heredity will be ________________ and environment will be ________________.

e. For nonbiological adopted siblings reared together, heredity will be ________________ and environment will be ________________.

f. For biological siblings reared together, heredity will be ________________ and environment will be ________________.

g. For any two people selected at random, heredity will be ________________ and environment will be ________________.

ANSWER KEY

Item **Answer**

1. b
2. a
3. b
4. c
5. a
6. d
7. They are influenced by more than one gene.
8. d
9. Genetic testing involves procedures aimed at identifying genetic diseases or determining the sex of an unborn child. Using this information parents can decide whether to continue with the pregnancy or not. The ethics of this involve a person's right to choose about pregnancy outcomes. In the case of avoiding diseases these procedures might seem more justified, but using them to pick the sex of one's baby may seem less justified. The counterargument is that it is the parents' right, and their ultimate decision.
10. d
11. Twin studies focus on the influence of genetics while keeping the environment relatively controlled. Monozygotic twins have the same genetics, while dizygotics are like any other pair of siblings. To the extent that monozygotic twins are more similar than dizygotic twins, the increased similarity is considered most likely due to genetic influence.
12. Adoption studies focus on the combined influence of genetics and environment because they allow you to compare twins or siblings raised together (same environment) to twins raised apart (different environment). This can provide more information about the role of genetics, and the role that the environment plays in the expression of traits.
13. Heredity; heritability
14. c
15. b
16. Sensory; Motor
17. Efferent; interneurons
18. Most likely you would crush the egg because you would have no way of knowing the correct amount of pressure to exert in picking it up. The good news is that you also wouldn't be able to sense the resulting mess!
19. a
20. a, c, b, e, d, a
21. c
22. negative
23. sodium and potassium; ion channels
24. dendrite; excitatory; inhibitory
25. b
26. d

27. c
28. reuptake; enzyme deactivation; autoreception
29. c
30. b
31. b
32. d
33. f, b, g, d, a, e, c
34. c
35. Central and Peripheral Nervous Systems
36. c
37. c
38. An autopsy of a person with a specific problem (e.g., inability to speak) allowed early physicians like Broca to identify areas of the brain that had damage, resulting in the conclusion that the area with damage was responsible for language production. Generally speaking, it aided in localization of function in the brain.
39. Grey; white
40. medulla oblongata; the pons; the midbrain; and the reticular formation
41. The brain stem because it is responsible for our most basic functions: breathing, making our heart pump, digestion, and sleep.
42. d
43. b
44. a
45. d, f, a, e, b, c
46. d, a, b, b, c, a
47. prefrontal cortex
48. somatic; autonomic
49. d
50. a
51. c
52. b
53. a
54. b
55. The culture a person is in changes the way the brain perceives background from foreground, how it pays attention to certain elements of lines, and how it processes emotion.
56. The brain will undergo an actual physical change such that existing connections in the brain will be stronger. It is also possible that new connections will grow through neurogenesis.
57. d
58. c
59. b, a, a, b, a
60. radical hemispherectomy

Summing Up and Measuring Up

a. identical, similar; b. identical, different; c. different, similar; d. different, different; e. different, similar; f. similar, similar; g. different, different

KEY TERM EXERCISES

acetylcholine (ACh)

Textbook Definition:
Your Own Definition:
Your Own Example:

agonist

Textbook Definition:
Your Own Definition:
Your Own Example:

action potential

Textbook Definition:
Your Own Definition:
Your Own Example:

all-or-none principle

Textbook Definition:
Your Own Definition:
Your Own Example:

amygdala

Textbook Definition:
Your Own Definition:
Your Own Example:

antagonist

Textbook Definition:
Your Own Definition:
Your Own Example:

autonomic nervous system (ANS)

Textbook Definition:
Your Own Definition:
Your Own Example:

axon

Textbook Definition:
Your Own Definition:
Your Own Example:

basal ganglia

Textbook Definition:
Your Own Definition:
Your Own Example:

brain stem

Textbook Definition:
Your Own Definition:
Your Own Example:

Broca's area

Textbook Definition:
Your Own Definition:
Your Own Example:

cell body

Textbook Definition:
Your Own Definition:
Your Own Example:

central nervous system (CNS)

Textbook Definition:
Your Own Definition:
Your Own Example:

cerebellum

Textbook Definition:
Your Own Definition:
Your Own Example:

cerebral cortex

Textbook Definition:
Your Own Definition:
Your Own Example:

chromosomes

Textbook Definition:
Your Own Definition:
Your Own Example:

dendrites

Textbook Definition:
Your Own Definition:
Your Own Example:

dizygotic twins

Textbook Definition:
Your Own Definition:
Your Own Example:

dominant gene

Textbook Definition:
Your Own Definition:
Your Own Example:

dopamine

Textbook Definition:
Your Own Definition:
Your Own Example:

endocrine system

Textbook Definition:
Your Own Definition:
Your Own Example:

endorphins

Textbook Definition:
Your Own Definition:
Your Own Example:

epinephrine

Textbook Definition:
Your Own Definition:
Your Own Example:

frontal lobes

Textbook Definition:
Your Own Definition:
Your Own Example:

GABA

Textbook Definition:
Your Own Definition:
Your Own Example:

gene

Textbook Definition:
Your Own Definition:
Your Own Example:

genotype

Textbook Definition:
Your Own Definition:
Your Own Example:

glutamate

Textbook Definition:
Your Own Definition:
Your Own Example:

gonads

Textbook Definition:
Your Own Definition:
Your Own Example:

heritability

Textbook Definition:
Your Own Definition:
Your Own Example:

hippocampus

Textbook Definition:
Your Own Definition:
Your Own Example:

hormones

Textbook Definition:
Your Own Definition:
Your Own Example:

hypothalamus

Textbook Definition:
Your Own Definition:
Your Own Example:

interneurons

Textbook Definition:
Your Own Definition:
Your Own Example:

monozygotic twins

Textbook Definition:
Your Own Definition:
Your Own Example:

motor neurons

Textbook Definition:
Your Own Definition:
Your Own Example:

myelin sheath

Textbook Definition:
Your Own Definition:
Your Own Example:

neuron

Textbook Definition:
Your Own Definition:
Your Own Example:

neurotransmitter

Textbook Definition:
Your Own Definition:
Your Own Example:

nodes of Ranvier

Textbook Definition:
Your Own Definition:
Your Own Example:

norepinephrine

Textbook Definition:
Your Own Definition:
Your Own Example:

occipital lobes

Textbook Definition:
Your Own Definition:
Your Own Example:

parasympathetic division of ANS

Textbook Definition:
Your Own Definition:
Your Own Example:

parietal lobes

Textbook Definition:
Your Own Definition:
Your Own Example:

Parkinson's disease (PD)

Textbook Definition:
Your Own Definition:
Your Own Example:

peripheral nervous system (PNS)

Textbook Definition:
Your Own Definition:
Your Own Example:

phenotype

Textbook Definition:
Your Own Definition:
Your Own Example:

pituitary gland

Textbook Definition:
Your Own Definition:
Your Own Example:

plasticity

Textbook Definition:
Your Own Definition:
Your Own Example:

prefrontal cortex

Textbook Definition:
Your Own Definition:
Your Own Example:

receptors

Textbook Definition:
Your Own Definition:
Your Own Example:

recessive gene

Textbook Definition:
Your Own Definition:
Your Own Example:

resting membrane potential

Textbook Definition:
Your Own Definition:
Your Own Example:

reuptake

Textbook Definition:
Your Own Definition:
Your Own Example:

sensory neurons

Textbook Definition:
Your Own Definition:
Your Own Example:

synapse, or synaptic cleft

Textbook Definition:
Your Own Definition:
Your Own Example:

serotonin

Textbook Definition:
Your Own Definition:
Your Own Example:

synesthesia

Textbook Definition:
Your Own Definition:
Your Own Example:

somatic nervous system

Textbook Definition:
Your Own Definition:
Your Own Example:

temporal lobes

Textbook Definition:
Your Own Definition:
Your Own Example:

substance P

Textbook Definition:
Your Own Definition:
Your Own Example:

terminal buttons

Textbook Definition:
Your Own Definition:
Your Own Example:

sympathetic division of ANS

Textbook Definition:
Your Own Definition:
Your Own Example:

thalamus

Textbook Definition:
Your Own Definition:
Your Own Example:

Special Note: In this chapter, many of the concepts represent structures in the brain. This may make it more difficult to apply your own example. However, I have included those places in case you wanted to note a structure's location, or provide additional information that might be helpful to you as you study.

CHAPTER 4 The Mind and Consciousness

CONCEPT MAP

I. How Is the Conscious Mind Experienced?
  A. Consciousness
    1. Content
    2. Level
  B. Dualism

II. The Subjective Nature of Consciousness
  A. Qualia
    1. Role of Brain Imaging
  B. Variability of Consciousness
    1. Influences
      a. Automatic vs. Controlled Processes
  C. Consciousness and Coma
    1. Varied States
  D. Consciousness and the Split Brain
    1. Split Brain
      a. Left Hemisphere
        1. Interpreter
          A. Speculative Interpreter
            a. Right Hemisphere
  E. Unconscious Processing Influences Behaviour
    1. Subliminal Perception
    2. Freudian Slips
    3. Priming
  F. The Smart Unconscious
    1. Thinking vs. Not Thinking
      a. Verbal Overshadowing
  G. Brain Activity and Consciousness
    1. Blindsight
    2. Global Workspace

III. Sleep
  A. Stages of Sleep
    1. Before Sleep
      a. Beta Waves
      b. Alpha Waves
    2. Stage 1
      a. Theta Waves
    3. Stage 2
      a. Sleep Spindles
      b. K-Complexes
    4. Stage 3 and 4
      a. Delta Waves (Slow-wave Sleep)
    5. REM Sleep
      a. Rapid Eye Movements
      b. Paradoxical Sleep
      c. General Characteristics
  B. Sleep Disorders
    1. Insomnia
    2. Sleep Apnea
    3. Narcolepsy
    4. REM Behaviour Disorder
    5. Somnambulism (Sleepwalking)
  C. Sleep is Adaptive Behaviour
    1. Why Do We Sleep?
      a. Unihemispherical Sleep
      b. Restorative Theory
        1. Sleep Deprivation
        2. Microsleeps
      c. Circadian Rhythms
      d. Sleep and Learning
  D. Sleep, Wakefulness, and Neural Mechanisms
    1. Brain Stem and Arousal

E. Dreams
   1. When Dreams Occur
   2. Content of REM vs. Non-REM Dreams
   3. The Meaning of Dreams
      a. Freud
         1. Manifest Content
         2. Latent Content
      b. Activation-Synthesis Hypothesis
      c. Evolved Threat-Rehearsal Strategies

IV. Altered States of Consciousness
   A. Hypnosis
      1. Post-hypnotic Suggestions
      2. Not Everyone Can Be Hypnotized
      3. Theories of Hypnosis
         a. Sociocognitive Theory
         b. Dissociation Theory
      4. Hypnosis and Pain Management
         a. Hypnotic Analgesia
   B. Meditation
      1. Concentrative Meditation
      2. Mindfulness Meditation
      3. Transcendental Meditation
         a. Health Benefits
         b. Cognitive Benefits
   C. Losing Yourself in an Activity
      1. Exercise
      2. Religious Ecstasy
      3. Flow
      4. Escaping the Self

V. People Use—and Abuse—Many Psychoactive Drugs
   A. Psychoactive Drugs
      1. Marijuana
      2. Stimulants
         a. Cocaine
         b. Amphetamines
      3. Ecstasy (MDMA)
      4. Opiates
      5. Ethics: Consciousness and End-of-Life Medical Treatment
   B. Alcohol
      1. Gender Differences in Alcohol Consumption across Cultures
         a. Body Volume
         b. Under-reporting
         c. Psychosocial
            1. Power
            2. Sex
            3. Risks
            4. Responsibilities
      2. Expectations of Alcohol Use
      3. Physical Effects of Alcohol Use
   C. Addiction
      1. Physical Dependence (Addiction)
         a. Withdrawal
         b. Tolerance
         c. Insula
      2. Psychological Dependence
         a. Social Level of Analysis
            1. Social-Learning Processes
         b. Individual Level of Analysis
      3. Context of Addiction

CHAPTER SUMMARY

How Is the Conscious Mind Experienced?

• Consciousness Is a Subjective Experience: Consciousness is difficult to study because of the subjective nature of our experience of the world. Brain imaging research has shown that particular brain regions are activated by particular types of sensory information.

• There Are Variations in Conscious Experience: Consciousness is each person's unified and coherent experience of the world around him or her. At any one time, each person can be conscious of a limited number of things. A person's level of consciousness varies throughout the day and depends on the task at hand. Whereas some people in comas show no brain activity (a persistent vegetative state), people in minimally conscious states show brain activity indicating some awareness of external stimuli.

• Splitting the Brain Splits the Conscious Mind: The corpus callosum connects the brain's two sides; cutting it in half results in two independently functioning hemispheres. The left hemisphere is responsible primarily for language, and the right hemisphere is responsible primarily for images and spatial relations. The left hemisphere strives to make sense of experiences, and its interpretations influence the way a person views and remembers the world.

• Unconscious Processing Influences Behaviour: Research findings indicate that much of a person's behaviour occurs automatically, without that person's constant awareness. Thought and behaviour can be influenced by stimuli that are not experienced consciously.

• Brain Activity Produces Consciousness: Blindsight demonstrates visual ability without awareness. The global workspace model of consciousness demonstrates how awareness depends on activity in various different cortical areas.

What Is Sleep?

• Sleep Is an Altered State of Consciousness: Sleep occurs in stages, which vary according to levels of brain activity and of respiration. REM sleep activates the brain and produces both body paralysis and genital stimulation. Sleep disorders include insomnia, sleep apnea, and narcolepsy.

• Sleep Is an Adaptive Behaviour: Sleep restores the body, and circadian rhythms control changes in body function and in sleep. Learning is consolidated during sleep.

• Sleep and Wakefulness Are Regulated by Multiple Neural Mechanisms: Brain stem structures are involved in arousal and REM sleep.

• People Dream while Sleeping: REM dreams activate different brain areas than do non-REM dreams. Sigmund Freud thought dreams revealed unconscious conflicts. The activation-synthesis hypothesis posits that dreams are side effects of brain activity. Antti Revonsuo has theorized that dreaming is adaptive.

What Is Altered Consciousness?

• Hypnosis Is Induced through Suggestion: Scientists debate whether hypnosis is an altered state of consciousness or whether hypnotized people merely play the role they expect (and are expected) to play. Brain imaging research suggests that hypnotized subjects undergo changes in their brain activity.

• Meditation Produces Relaxation: The goal of meditation, especially as practiced in the West, is to bring about a state of deep relaxation. Studies have shown that meditation can have multiple benefits for people's physical and mental health.

• People Can Lose Themselves in Activities: Exercise, certain religious practices, and other engaging activities can produce a state of altered consciousness called flow, in which people become completely absorbed in what they are doing. Flow is a positive experience, but escapist activities can be harmful if people use them for avoidance rather than for fulfillment.

How Do Drugs Affect Consciousness?

• People Use—and Abuse—Many Psychoactive Drugs: Stimulants increase behavioural and mental activity. MDMA (ecstasy) produces energizing and hallucinogenic effects. THC (the active ingredient in marijuana) alters perception. All drugs, including opiates, provide high reward value by increasing dopamine activation.

• Alcohol Is the Most Widely Abused Drug: Though believed to reduce anxiety, alcohol consumption can increase anxiety and negative mood. A drinker's expectation can significantly affect his or her behaviour while under the influence of alcohol.

• Addiction Has Psychological and Physical Aspects: Physical addiction involves the body's responses to and tolerance toward a substance. Psychological dependence involves both habitual use and compulsion to use, despite consequences.

COMPETENCY MODEL

How Is the Conscious Mind Experienced?

Consciousness

1. What is consciousness?
2. Distinguish between the two components of consciousness.

Dualism

3. What is dualism? How does it relate to consciousness?

The Subjective Nature of Consciousness

Qualia

4. Explain the role of qualia in consciousness.

Variability of Consciousness

5. Identify factors that influence the variability of our consciousness.
6. Distinguish between automatic and controlled processes.

Consciousness and Coma

7. Distinguish between a persistent vegetative state and a minimally conscious state.

Consciousness and the Split Brain

8. Explain how the brain can be "split" and what disorder this helps.
9. Identify the functions of the left hemisphere.
10. Explain the left hemisphere's role of "interpreter." Explain how this can be a speculative process.
11. Understand the speculative nature of the interpreter.

Unconscious Processing Influences Behaviour

12. Identify the three types of unconscious processing that influence behaviour.
13. Distinguish between subliminal perception, Freudian slips, and priming.

The Smart Unconscious

14. Identify the influence of thinking versus not thinking.

Brain Activity and Consciousness

15. Distinguish between blindsight and global workspace.
16. What is the importance of the global workspace model?

Sleep

Stages of Sleep

17. Explain the characteristics of the stages of sleep.
18. Distinguish between the different types of brain waves associated with sleep.
19. Explain why REM sleep is considered paradoxical.
20. Describe several general characteristics about REM sleep.

Sleep Disorders

21. Identify the different types of sleep disorders.
22. What can bring about insomnia?
23. Distinguish between narcolepsy and REM behaviour disorder.
24. Identify a common misconception about sleepwalking.

Sleep Is Adaptive Behaviour

25. Identify reasons that we sleep less now compared to the early twentieth century.
26. Identify characteristics associated with unihemispherical sleep.
27. Explain why we need to sleep, according to restorative theory.
28. Identify the effects of sleep deprivation on physical and cognitive performance.
29. What are microsleeps? Are they generally beneficial or harmful?
30. Explain the circadian rhythm theory of sleep.
31. Explain the sleep and learning theory of sleep.

Sleep, Wakefulness, and Neural Mechanisms

32. How does the brain stem influence arousal?

Dreams

33. Identify when dreams occur.
34. Distinguish between the content of REM and non-REM dreams.
35. Distinguish between manifest and latent content.
36. According to the activation-synthesis hypothesis, what is the meaning of dreams?
37. According to the idea of evolved threat-rehearsal strategies, what is the meaning of dreams?

Altered States of Consciousness

38. Identify three altered states of consciousness.

Hypnosis

39. What are posthypnotic suggestions?
40. Why are some people more susceptible to hypnosis than others?
41. Explain the sociocognitive and dissociation theories of whether hypnosis is an altered state of consciousness.
42. What is the role of hypnosis in pain management?

Meditation

43. Distinguish between concentrative, mindfulness, and transcendental meditation.
44. Identify the health and cognitive benefits of transcendental meditation.

Losing Yourself in an Activity

45. Identify four main ways you can lose yourself in an activity.
46. Distinguish between flow and the concept of escaping the self.

People Use—and Abuse—Many Psychoactive Drugs

Psychoactive Drugs

47. Identify the types of psychoactive drugs.
48. Identify outcomes and associated brain areas for the types of psychoactive drugs.

Alcohol

49. Identify the three main reasons for gender differences in alcohol consumption.
50. Identify four psychosocial factors that account for gender differences in alcohol consumption.
51. How do expectations influence alcohol use?
52. Describe the physical effects of alcohol consumption.

Addiction

53. Distinguish between various aspects of physical dependence.
54. Explain psychological dependence at the social level of analysis.
55. Explain addiction using the individual level of analysis.
56. How does context help us understand addiction?

KNOWLEDGE CHECK

1. ______________________ refers to moment-to-moment subjective experiences, such as being able to reflect on your current thoughts or pay attention to your immediate surroundings.

   Concept: I. A Competency: 1
   Question Type: *Factual*

2. Following a bad motorcycle accident in which he was not wearing a helmet, Bobby is in a coma. However, visitors to the hospital are sure he knows when people are there and can distinguish family and friends from hospital workers. Bobby's coma is an example of the ____________ of consciousness, while his awareness of people is an example of the ____________ of consciousness.
   a. level; content
   b. substance; level
   c. level; substance
   d. content; level

   Concept: I. A Competency: 2
   Question Type: *Applied*

3. Carol believes that you can study bodily processes but you cannot study the mind. Her view reflects:
   a. monism
   b. dualism
   c. the nature/nurture debate
   d. the limitations of adaptation

   Concept: I. B Competency: 3
   Question Type: *Applied*

4. When Monica tastes a glass of chardonnay, she describes it as fruity. However, when Rachel tastes the same glass she describes it as slightly bitter, and nutty. This describes:
   a. dualism
   b. qualia
   c. unconscious experience
   d. different levels of consciousness

   Concept: II. A Competency: 4
   Question Type: *Applied*

5. According to William James, our consciousness is a unified and coherent experience. What implication does this have if you try to text message during class?

   ____

   ____

   ____

   ____

   Concept: II. B Competency: 5
   Question Type: *Applied*

6. Michael is a superstar basketball player and the best free-throw shooter ever to play the game. Skip has never played basketball. For Michael, shooting free-throws is a(n) ____________ process, for Skip they are a(n) ____________ process.
   a. controlled; controlled
   b. automatic; controlled
   c. controlled; automatic
   d. automatic; automatic

   Concept: II. B. 1. a Competency: 6
   Question Type: *Applied*

7. Palo has been in a coma for weeks, and does not respond to his surroundings. However, he does seem to have sleep/wake cycles. This state of consciousness is known as:
   a. an unconscious state
   b. a persistent vegetative state
   c. a minimally conscious state
   d. a mild coma state

   Concept: II. C. 1 Competency: 7
   Question Type: *Applied*

8. The two hemispheres of the brain can become "split" by ____________. This procedure is helpful in the treatment of ____________.
   a. cutting the cerebellum; multiple personality disorder
   b. cutting the corpus callosum; multiple personality disorder
   c. cutting the cerebellum; epilepsy
   d. cutting the corpus callosum; epilepsy

   Concept: II. D. 1 Competency: 8
   Question Type: *Factual*

9. All of the following are functions of the left hemisphere, except it does NOT control:
   a. spatial abilities
   b. language
   c. speech
   d. the right hand

   Concept: II. D. 1. a Competency: 9
   Question Type: *Factual*

10. Hugh is a split brain patient. He is shown a dollar sign in his right visual field and a nude pinup photo in his left visual field. When asked what he sees, his left hemisphere answers, "A dollar sign." However, he is flustered and embarrassed. When asked why, he says, "This is some wild machine you have!" This left hemispheric propensity to construct a world that makes sense is called the:
    a. combiner
    b. reality language device
    c. split conscious phenomenon
    d. interpreter

    Concept: II. D. 1. a. 1 Competency: 10
    Question Type: *Applied*

11. Assume you go to play roulette and your friend is working the wheel. Your friend has given you some inside information by telling you that this wheel hits on red 67 percent of the time. What is the smartest way to place bets over the next 100 spins? How would the speculative nature of the interpreter influence how we bet?

    ____

    ____

    ____

    ____

    Concept: II. D. 1. a. 1 Competency: 11
    Question Type: *Conceptual*

12. Concept: II. E Competency: 12
    Question Type: *Factual*

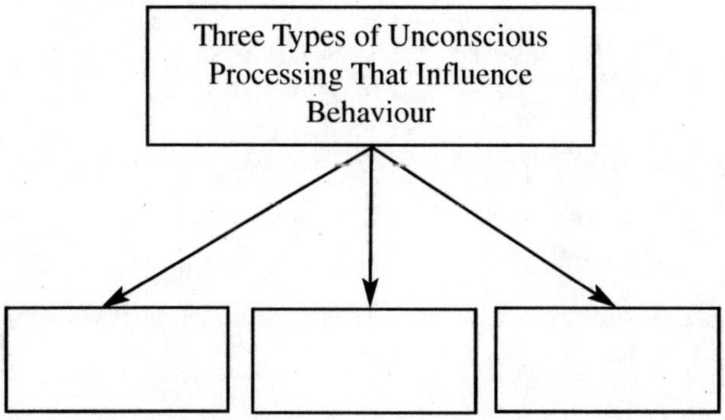

13. Larry has lost his vision following a couple of strokes. However, when he takes his kids to the mall he amazes them by guessing fairly accurately the expressions of people without actually seeing them. This phenomenon of visual processing without visual awareness is known as:
    a. qualia
    b. subliminal perception
    c. unconscious awareness
    d. blindsight

    Concept: II. E Competency: 13
    Question Type: *Applied*

14. Provide your own example of when you or someone you know experienced a Freudian slip.

    ____

    ____

    ____

    ____

    Concept: II. E Competency: 13
    Question Type: *Applied*

15. Mike is making cookies from a special recipe for his roommate Tina's birthday. When he asks his other roommate Sergio to eat a cookie and describe how it tastes, what will Sergio likely find according to the research?
    a. Describing the tastes is easy and enhances his enjoyment of the cookie.
    b. Describing the tastes allows him to identify many more subtle flavours.
    c. Describing the tastes is very difficult but enhances his enjoyment of the cookie.
    d. Describing the taste is very difficult and alters how subsequent cookies taste.

    Concept: II. F Competency: 14
    Question Type: *Applied*

16. A condition in which people suffer blindness due to damage in the visual cortex, but continue to have some visual capacities in the absence of any visual awareness is known as ____.

    Concept: II. G Competency: 15
    Question Type: *Factual*

17. The importance of the global workspace model is that it ____.

    Concept: II. G. 2 Competency: 16
    Question Type: *Factual*

18. As you enter stage 2 sleep, there are occasional bursts of activity known as sleep spindles and large waves called:
    a. alpha waves
    b. beta waves
    c. k-complexes
    d. REM

Concept: III. A Competency: 17
Question Type: *Factual*

19. Joe wants to put shaving cream on his roommate's face and write "STUPID" on his forehead. Which sleep stage should he pick for his roommate to be least likely to detect this?
    a. stage 1
    b. stage 2
    c. REM
    d. stage 4

Concept: III. A Competency: 17
Question Type: *Factual*

20. For each of the following, please match the type of brain waves with the stage of sleep where it is most likely to occur.

____ Sleep spindles	a) Relaxed but awake
____ Theta waves	b) Stage 1
____ Delta waves	c) Stage 2
____ Alpha waves	d) Stage 3/4
____ Beta waves	e) REM

Concept: III. A Competency: 18
Question Type: *Factual*

21. REM is often referred to as paradoxical sleep. Why?

____

____

____

____

Concept: II. E Competency: 19
Question Type: *Applied*

22. Which of the following is NOT characteristic of REM sleep?
    a. dreaming
    b. slow-wave sleep
    c. muscle paralysis
    d. genital arousal

Concept: III. A. 5. c Competency: 20
Question Type: *Factual*

23. William often has difficulty getting to sleep. He tosses and turns and thinks about all his problems from the day. William's inability to sleep is known as:
    a. insomnia
    b. hypersomnia
    c. narcolepsy
    d. REM behaviour disorder

Concept: III. B Competency: 21
Question Type: *Applied*

24. Your housemate is experiencing symptoms of insomnia. Based on what you know about insomnia, what might you suggest?

____

____

____

____

Concept: II. E Competency: 22
Question Type: *Applied*

25. While watching a play on Broadway, you notice that one of the actors falls asleep in the middle of his monologue. What sleep disorder is this most indicative of?
    a. insomnia
    b. sleep apnea
    c. narcolepsy
    d. REM behaviour disorder

Concept: III. B Competency: 23
Question Type: *Applied*

26. Debbie acts out the activities in her dreams. She beats on her husband while dreaming of playing the drums and jumps around the bedroom while dreaming of dancing. This acting out of dreams that comes from the lack of the normal muscle paralysis is known as:
    a. insomnia
    b. sleep apnea
    c. narcolepsy
    d. REM behaviour disorder

Concept: III. B Competency: 23
Question Type: *Applied*

27. If you find someone sleepwalking, you should do what?

____

____

____

____

Concept: III. B Competency: 24
Question Type: *Factual*

28. It has been estimated that individuals slept an average of 10 hours per day at the beginning of the twentieth century. Today people average a little over 7 hours per night. Speculate about the various causes for this change. Also, considering the seemingly adaptive nature of sleep and dreaming, consider how this change has influenced our society. What do you think will happen if this reduction in sleep continues?

____

____

____

____

Concept: III Competency: 25
Question Type: *Conceptual*

29. Flipper the Dolphin is playing around his tank at Marineland. Because some new interns like to jump in the tank and swim with Flipper, he keeps an eye on them by watching them with one eye while the other half of his brain sleeps. The peculiar way of sleeping is known as:
    a. split brain sleep
    b. unihemispherical sleep
    c. paradoxical sleep
    d. circadian sleep

Concept: III. C. 1. a Competency: 26
Question Type: *Applied*

30. Based on the restorative theory of sleep, what would happen if we never slept?

____

____

____

____

Concept: III. C. 1. b Competency: 27
Question Type: *Conceptual*

31. Which of the following statements about the effects of sleep deprivation on physical and cognitive performance is FALSE?
    a. Chronic sleep deprivation leads to lapses in attention.
    b. Chronic sleep deprivation leads to reduced short-term memory.
    c. Two or three days of deprivation greatly reduces performance on complex tasks.
    d. Two or three days of deprivation has little effect on strength or athletic ability.

Concept: III. C. 1. b. 1 Competency: 28
Question Type: *Applied*

32. Nancy has been depressed throughout the winter. She tries something new and cuts her sleep in half for a week. Amazingly, this helps lift her spirits. This effect likely works because sleep deprivation leads to increased activation of __________ receptors.
    a. acetylcholine
    b. dopamine
    c. serotonin
    d. GABA

Concept: III. C. 1. b. 1 Competency: 28
Question Type: *Applied*

33. Ryan has been up late for several days watching sports on television. At the end of a boring business meeting, he realizes that he missed various parts of the discussion. Which of the following is the most likely explanation for this?
    a. REM rebound
    b. REM behaviour disorder
    c. unihemispherical sleep
    d. microsleeps

Concept: III. C. 1. b. 2 Competency: 29
Question Type: *Applied*

34. The finding that many small animals sleep a great deal while vulnerable large animals such as cows and deer sleep little provides support for which sleep theory?
    a. restorative
    b. Freudian
    c. circadian rhythm
    d. facilitation of learning

Concept: III. C. 2 Competency: 30
Question Type: *Applied*

35. The finding that university students have more REM sleep during final exams, and that infants spend more time sleeping and in REM sleep, provides support for which sleep theory?
    a. restorative
    b. Freudian
    c. circadian rhythm
    d. facilitation of learning

Concept: III. C. 3 Competency: 31
Question Type: *Applied*

36. The ____
in the brain stem is responsible for regulating arousal. If fibres in this are cut, an animal will
____.

Concept: III. D   Competency: 32
Question Type: *Factual*

37. After coming home from a late night of studying at the library, you find your roommate asleep at his computer. He is obviously dreaming, and is moving around as if he is running. Which stage of sleep is he most likely in?
a. Stage 1
b. Stage 2
c. Stage 3/4
d. REM

Concept: III. E. 1   Competency: 33
Question Type: *Applied*

38. During breakfast, your friend tells you about a dream she had last night in which she was driving in her car, and then was stuck in traffic. This is most likely a ________________________________
dream. If her car had transformed itself into a magical sleigh pulled by a fleet of unicorns, then it would most likely have been a ______________________
dream.

Concept: III. E. 2   Competency: 34
Question Type: *Applied*

39. Kendall describes a dream during her first year of university in which her teeth fell out. Jaime tells her that this dream symbolizes the anxiety that is associated with the transition to university. According to Freud, Jaime is describing the ________________
content of Kendall's dream.
a. unconscious
b. latent
c. manifest
d. Oedipal

Concept: III. E. 3. a   Competency: 35
Question Type: *Applied*

40. Barry describes a dream in which he is climbing a ladder. Alan tells him that his dream reflects the fact that his eyes were going up and down during REM sleep and that dreams are epiphenomenal. Alan obviously supports which theory of dreaming?
a. activation–synthesis hypothesis
b. Freudian
c. manifest content
d. evolved threat rehearsal

Concept: III. E. 3. b   Competency: 36
Question Type: *Applied*

41. Tim reports having a dream in which he is awakened from sleep by an intense tornado that broke his window, and that he then had to determine a way to escape to safety. This type of dream is best explained by which theory of dreaming?
a. activation–synthesis hypothesis
b. Freudian
c. manifest content
d. evolved threat rehearsal

Concept: III. E. 3. b   Competency: 37
Question Type: *Applied*

42. Concept: IV   Competency: 38
Question Type: *Factual*

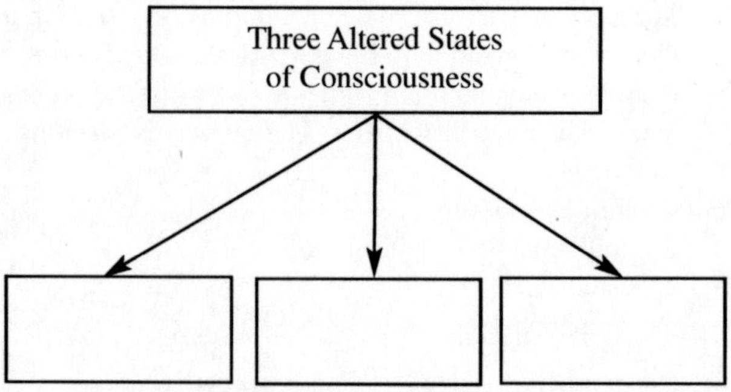

43. During a hypnotist show on campus, several students are hypnotized on stage through a series of suggestions. Once clearly hypnotized, the hypnotist instructs them that they will see everyone in the audience as chickens, and that they won't remember the hypnotist giving them these directions. This is known as:
a. a posthypnotic suggestion
b. a prehypnotic suggestion
c. a hypnotic trance
d. dissociative hypnosis

Concept: IV. A. 1   Competency: 39
Question Type: *Applied*

44. Stacey is not very susceptible to hypnosis. Which of the following characteristics does she most likely possess?
    a. high suggestibility
    b. gets easily distracted
    c. has a rich imagination
    d. gets easily absorbed in activities

    Concept: IV. A. 1 Competency: 40
    Question Type: *Applied*

45. Which theory of hypnosis would Freud most likely endorse? Why?

    ____

    ____

    ____

    ____

    Concept: IV. A. 3 Competency: 41
    Question Type: *Conceptual*

46. Research on hypnosis in the context of pain management shows that hypnosis is highly ______________. This is due to the fact that hypnosis focuses on ______________.
    a. effective; people's interpretations of pain
    b. effective; diminishing pain itself
    c. ineffective; people's interpretations of pain
    d. ineffective; diminishing pain itself

    Concept: IV. A. 4 Competency: 42
    Question Type: *Factual*

47. Harry is meditating before giving a speech in his public speaking course. He meditates by paying attention to his free-flowing thoughts, but tries not to react to them. What type of meditation is this?
    a. transcendental
    b. concentrative
    c. premeditated
    d. mindfulness

    Concept: IV. B Competency: 43
    Question Type: *Applied*

48. All of the following are benefits of transcendental meditation EXCEPT:
    a. improved blood pressure, blood lipids, and insulin
    b. decreased reports of stress
    c. increased grey matter
    d. increased intelligence

    Concept: IV. B. 3 Competency: 44
    Question Type: *Factual*

49. Concept: IV. C Competency: 45
    Question Type: *Factual*

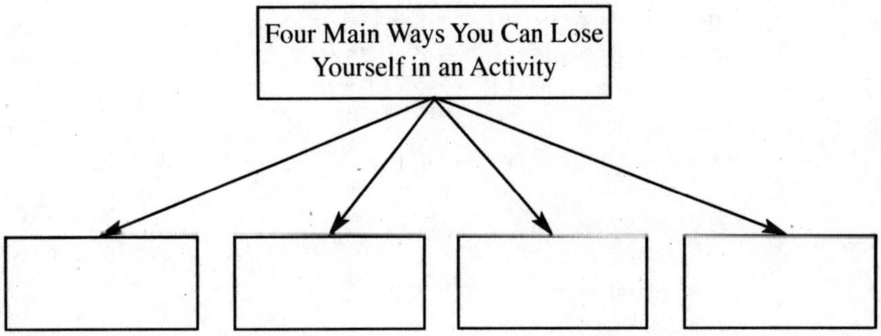

50. Chuck and Larry are both runners. Chuck runs as a way of distracting himself from stress at home and work, while Larry runs for the sake of running. Both find that they become engrossed in the experience. Chuck most likely is experiencing ____________; Larry is most likely experiencing ____________.
    a. escaping the self; escaping the self
    b. flow; escaping the self
    c. escaping the self; flow
    d. flow; flow

    Concept: IV. C   Competency: 46
    Question Type: *Applied*

51. Concept: V. A   Competency: 47
    Question Type: *Factual*

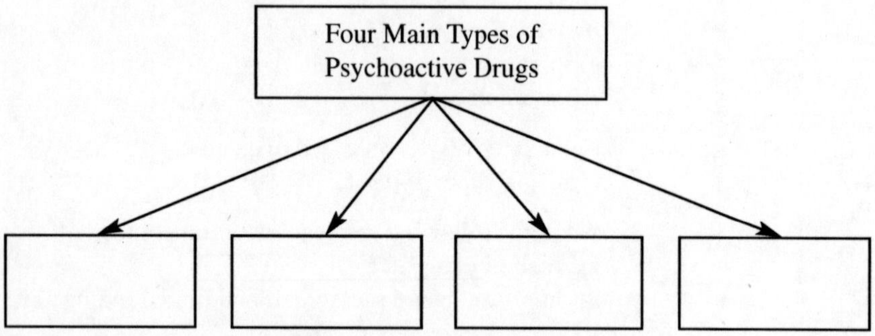

52. For each of the following, please match the description with the most appropriate psychoactive drug.

    a) Marijuana
    b) Stimulants
    c) Ecstasy (MDMA)
    d) Opiates

    ____ Produces feelings of relaxation, analgesia, and euphoria
    ____ Depletes serotonin—users often feel depressed when the rewarding properties of the drug wear off
    ____ Activates the sympathetic nervous system, improves mood, causes people to become restless, and disrupts sleep
    ____ Works by interfering with the normal reuptake of dopamine by the releasing neuron
    ____ Produces an energizing effect but also causes slight hallucinations
    ____ Relaxed mental state, uplifted or contented mood, and some perceptual and cognitive distortions
    ____ Involves receptors in the hippocampus
    ____ Enormous reward value by increasing dopamine activation in the nucleus accumbens

    Concept: V. A   Competency: 48
    Question Type: *Factual*

53. Concept: V. B. 1 Competency: 49
    Question Type: *Factual*

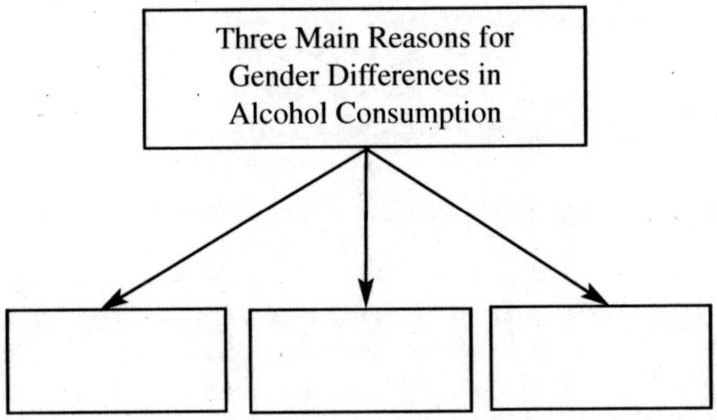

54. Concept: V. B. 1. c Competency: 50
    Question Type: *Factual*

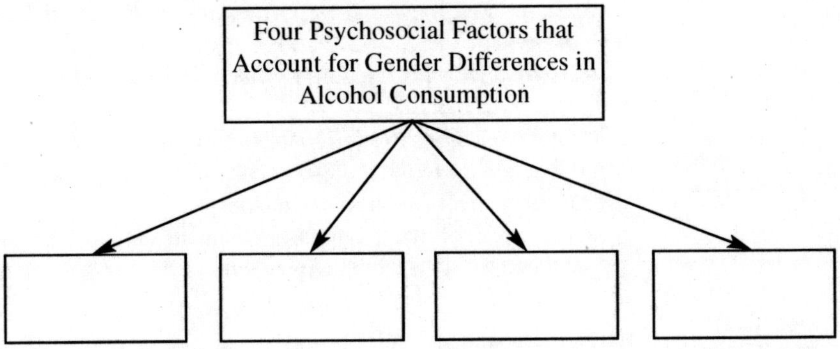

55. Will is doing his senior thesis on expectations related to alcohol and how they influence sociability. He randomly assigns participants to two groups, one that thinks they are drinking beer with alcohol, one that thinks they are drinking non-alcoholic beer. (In reality they are both drinking non-alcoholic beer.) After drinking for an hour, participants have a chance to chat with a group of confederates, and are measured for how outgoing they are. Based on past research in this area, what is he likely to find?
    a. Both groups will be very outgoing and social.
    b. Both groups will be reserved and not very outgoing.
    c. The non-alcoholic beverage group will be more outgoing and social.
    d. The alcoholic beverage group will be more outgoing and social.

    Concept: V. B. 2 Competency: 51
    Question Type: *Applied*

56. Which of the following is NOT a physical effect of alcohol consumption?
    a. It involves activation of acetylcholine receptors.
    b. It interferes with the neurochemical processes involved in memory.
    c. It involves activation of dopamine receptors.
    d. It causes intellectual deterioration.

    Concept: V. B. 3 Competency: 52
    Question Type: *Factual*

57. Physical dependence is synonymous with ________________________, a physiological state in which failing to ingest a substance leads to symptoms of ________________________, a state characterized by anxiety, tension, and cravings. Physical dependence is associated with ________________________, so that a person needs to consume more of the drug to achieve the same subjective effect. The region of the brain called the ________________________ is important for craving and addiction

Concept: V. C. 1 Competency: 53
Question Type: *Factual*

58. Using the social level of analysis, provide your own example of a factor that can facilitate addiction.

____

____

____

____

Concept: V. C. 2. a Competency: 54
Question Type: *Applied*

59. Which of the following statements about individuals and addiction are true?
    a. About 85 to 90 percent of those who use drugs become addicted.
    b. Most people who have used drugs have used them only occasionally or tried them for a while and then gave them up completely.
    c. Those who didn't use any drugs during adolescence were more well-adjusted than those who had.
    d. Only adolescents who were heavy drug users had adjustment problems.

Concept: V. C. 2. b Competency: 55
Question Type: *Factual*

60. Research on drug use among U.S. soldiers after they returned home from Vietnam found that:
    a. only a handful of those who were addicts in Vietnam remained addicts
    b. more than half of those who were addicts in Vietnam remained addicts
    c. those with addictive personalities tended to go to Vietnam in the first place
    d. approximately 10 percent of the addicts no longer used drugs within months of their return

Concept: V. C. 3 Competency: 56
Question Type: *Factual*

SUMMING UP AND MEASURING UP

How Is the Conscious Mind Experienced?

Although the relationship between the physical brain and consciousness has been debated at least since Descartes' time, psychological scientists have developed methods of assessing both the contents and the variations of consciousness. Consciousness refers to a person's experience of the world, including thoughts and feelings. The brain gives rise to consciousness by bringing multiple systems' activities together in a global workspace. Most brain activities do not rise to the level of consciousness, but these unconscious processes influence behaviour.

In a person with an intact brain, what might the interpreter do?

a. Guide reactions to subliminal stimuli.
b. Give a voice to the mute hemisphere.
c. Help connect the brain's hemispheres.
d. Direct the left hand's motor movements, which are connected by the right hemisphere.

What Is Sleep?

Almost all animals experience sleep, an altered state of consciousness in which the sleeper loses most contact with the external world. Sleep's several stages can be identified through different patterns on EEG recordings. REM sleep and non-REM sleep differ, and different neural mechanisms produce each type, although the brain stem figures prominently in the regulation of sleep/wake cycles. Dreams occur in REM sleep and non-REM sleep, but the dreams' contents differ between the types. This variation may be due to differential activation of brain structures associated with both emotion and cognition. Theories have been proposed to explain why sleeping and dreaming happen, but the biological functions of both sleeping and dreaming are unknown.

Match the sleep stage to its dominant type of brain wave.

____	Stage 1	a. theta waves
____	Stage 2	b. sleep spindles and k-complexes
____	Stage 3	c. beta waves
____	Stage 4	d. delta waves (slow waves)
____	REM stage	

ANSWER KEY

Item **Answer**

1. Consciousness
2. a
3. b
4. b
5. This idea suggests that we can only devote our consciousness fully to one thing at a time. By trying to pay attention to more than one thing at a time, aspects of the experience will be missed. So if you pay too much attention to your cellphone, you will miss parts of the lecture, and if you pay too much attention to the lecture you will miss calls on your cellphone. Both activities can't be done simultaneously with 100 percent effectiveness.
6. b
7. b
8. d
9. a
10. d
11. You should bet on red every time. However, the speculative interpreter leads our left hemisphere to want to discern patterns. This generally leads us to try and guess what colour will occur next. (Of course, on a real roulette wheel the odds are relatively even, with no one colour having an advantage).
12. subliminal perception; Freudian slips; priming
13. b
14. There are an infinite number of possibilities here but any example should show that you said something that was on your mind, but didn't really intend to say.
15. b
16. blindsight
17. demonstrates that there appears to be no single area in the brain responsible for general "awareness."
18. c
19. d
20. c, b, d, a, e
21. A person has been sleeping for a very long time, but the brain shows activity that is very similar to when a person is awake. Although the brain is very active, the body is unable to move.
22. b
23. a
24. One of the major causes of insomnia is worrying so it would be good to have your roommate address their worries in some fashion (perhaps write them down). You might also suggest they try cognitive-behavioural therapy, but that they avoid sleeping pills.
25. c
26. d
27. Wake them up. The idea that waking them up might be harmful is a myth.
28. Answers will vary. Ideas for reasons that we sleep less may include the invention of the electric lightbulb and that there are more activities available at night, including television and the Internet. The effect of less sleep on society is unclear, but one might address how this undermines the adaptive function of sleeping (restoration, facilitation of learning) that took thousands of years to evolve. Other possible influences may be increased stress, loss of coping mechanisms (e.g., road rage), sleep-related errors (e.g., work and vehicle accidents), and bodily breakdown (e.g., immune problems, cancer, coronary heart disease). Either we will need to concede the need for more sleep or other bodily systems will have to pick up these functions.
29. b
30. Our body and brain would systematically break down because they wouldn't be able to repair themselves. Damaged tissue would remain due to lack of growth hormone. Our immune system would also be compromised.
31. c
32. c
33. d
34. c
35. d
36. reticular formation; fall asleep and not wake up
37. c
38. non-REM; REM
39. b
40. a
41. d
42. hypnosis; meditation; losing yourself in an activity
43. a
44. b
45. Freud would most likely endorse the dissociation theory because of its emphasis on the idea of separate consciousness in which we are aware of some aspects, but unaware of others.
46. a
47. d
48. d
49. exercise; religious ecstasy; flow; escaping the self
50. c
51. marijuana; stimulants; ecstasy (MDMA); opiates
52. d, c, b, b, c, a, a, d
53. body volume; underreporting; psychosocial
54. power; sex; risks; responsibilities
55. d
56. a
57. addiction; withdrawal; tolerance; insula

58. There are an infinite number of possibilities here but any example that emphasizes the role of parents, peers, and mass media would be acceptable.
59. b
60. a

Summing Up and Measuring Up

How Is the Conscious Mind Experienced?

a. Guide reactions to subliminal stimuli.

What Is Sleep?

stage 1-a; stage 2-b; stages 3–4-d; REM stage-c

KEY TERM EXERCISES

activation-synthesis hypothesis

Textbook Definition:
Your Own Definition:
Your Own Example:

consciousness

Textbook Definition:
Your Own Definition:
Your Own Example:

blindsight

Textbook Definition:
Your Own Definition:
Your Own Example:

dreams

Textbook Definition:
Your Own Definition:
Your Own Example:

circadian rhythms

Textbook Definition:
Your Own Definition:
Your Own Example:

hypnosis

Textbook Definition:
Your Own Definition:
Your Own Example:

insomnia

Textbook Definition:
Your Own Definition:
Your Own Example:

interpreter

Textbook Definition:
Your Own Definition:
Your Own Example:

latent content

Textbook Definition:
Your Own Definition:
Your Own Example:

manifest content

Textbook Definition:
Your Own Definition:
Your Own Example:

meditation

Textbook Definition:
Your Own Definition:
Your Own Example:

microsleeps

Textbook Definition:
Your Own Definition:
Your Own Example:

narcolepsy

Textbook Definition:
Your Own Definition:
Your Own Example:

REM sleep

Textbook Definition:
Your Own Definition:
Your Own Example:

sleep apnea

Textbook Definition:
Your Own Definition:
Your Own Example:

subliminal perception

Textbook Definition:
Your Own Definition:
Your Own Example:

split brain

Textbook Definition:
Your Own Definition:
Your Own Example:

CHAPTER 5 Sensation and Perception

CONCEPT MAP

I. How Do We Sense Our Worlds?
    A. Sensation vs. Perception
        1. Sensation
        2. Perception
    B. Coding Stimuli
        1. Sensory Coding
            a. Transduction
            b. Receptors
                1. Types of Information
                    A. Qualitative
                    B. Quantitative
                2. Coarse Coding
    C. Psychophysics
    D. Sensory Thresholds
        1. Absolute Threshold
        2. Difference Threshold
            a. Weber's Law
    E. Signal-Detection Theory
        1. Hit
        2. Miss
        3. False Alarm
        4. Correct Rejection
        5. Response Bias
    F. Sensory Adaptation

II. Basic Sensory Processes
    A. Taste (Gustation)
        1. Taste Buds
            a. Positioning
            b. Five Basic Qualities
        2. Other Influences on Taste
            a. Food Characteristics
            b. Individual Differences
                1. Supertasters
            c. Cultural Differences
    B. Smell (Olfaction)
        1. Olfactory Epithelium
            a. Nature of Receptors
        2. Olfactory Bulb
        3. Smell and the Amygdala
        4. Sex Differences in Smell
    C. Touch (Haptic Sense)
        1. Tactile Stimulation
            a. Temperature
            b. Pressure
            c. Pain
            d. Location in Space
        2. Two Types of Pain
            a. Fast Fibres
            b. Slow Fibres
        3. Gate-Control Theory of Pain
            a. The Role of Mental Processes
            b. Sex Differences in Pain Sensitivity
            c. Pain Treatment
                1. Brain-Based Treatment of Pain
                2. Traditional Pain Treatment
    D. Hearing (Auditory Sense)
        1. Sound Wave
            a. Amplitude
            b. Frequency
        2. The Ear
            a. Outer Ear
            b. Eardrum
                1. Ossicles

c. Cochlea
1. Basilar Membrane
2. Ethics: Cochlear Implant
d. Hair Cells
3. Locating Sounds
E. Vision
1. The Eye
a. Cornea
b. Lens
1. Pupil
2. Iris
A. Accommodation
c. Retina
2. Receptor Cells
a. Rods
b. Cones
1. Fovea
c. Photopigments
d. Transmission from the Eye to the Brain
1. Ganglion Cells
2. Optic Nerve
A. Blind Spots
3. Optic Chiasm
4. Primary Visual Cortex
3. Detection of Visual Information
a. Receptive Field
4. Lateral Inhibition
5. Colour Vision
a. Characteristics of Colour
1. Hue
2. Brightness
3. Lightness
4. Saturation
b. Colour Mixing
1. Subtractive
2. Additive
c. Explaining Colour Vision
1. Three Different Types of Cones
2. Opposite Processes
A. Afterimages
3. McCollough Effect
6. Simultaneous Contrast
F. Beyond the Five Primary Senses
1. Kinesthetic Sense
2. Vestibular Senses
3. Senses in Animals
G. Extrasensory Perception (ESP)

III. Basic Perceptual Processes
A. Perception Occurs in the Brain
1. Primary Sensory Areas
a. Hearing
1. Primary Auditory Cortex
b. Touch
1. Primary Somatosensory Cortex
c. Vision
1. Primary Visual Cortex
2. What vs. Where
A. Ventral Stream
B. Dorsal Stream
3. Object Agnosia
B. Object Perception Requires Construction
1. Gestalt Principles
a. Proximity
b. Similarity
c. Good Continuation
2. Figure and Ground
a. Reversible Figure Illusion
3. Types of Processing
a. Bottom-Up
b. Top-Down
4. Face Perception
a. Fusiform Gyrus
b. Prosopagnosia
c. Recognizing Emotion
d. Sex Differences
e. Influence of Race/Ethnicity
C. Regaining Vision by Fixing the Eyes
D. Depth Perception
1. Binocular Depth Perception
a. Binocular Disparity
2. Monocular Depth Perception
a. Occlusion
b. Relative Size
c. Familiar Size
d. Linear Perspective
e. Texture Gradient
f. Position Relative to Horizon
3. Culture Influences Perception
a. Mueller-Lyer Illusion
4. Motion Cues to Depth
a. Motion Parallax
5. Size Perception Depends on Distance Perception
a. Ames Boxes
b. Ponzo Illusion
E. Motion Perception
1. Motion After-effects
a. Waterfall Effect
2. Compensatory Factors
3. Stroboscopic Movement
F. Perceptual Constancies
1. Size Constancy
2. Shape Constancy
3. Colour Constancy
4. Light Constancy

CHAPTER SUMMARY

How Do We Sense Our Worlds?

• Stimuli Must Be Coded to Be Understood by the Brain: Stimuli reaching the receptors are converted to neural impulses through the process of transduction.

• Psychophysics Relates Stimulus to Response: By studying how people respond to different sensory levels, scientists can determine thresholds and perceived change (based on signal detection theory). Our sensory systems are tuned to both adapt to constant levels of stimulation and detect changes in our environment.

What Are the Basic Sensory Processes?

• In Taste, Taste Buds Detect Chemicals: The gustatory sense uses taste buds to respond to the chemical substances that produce at least five basic sensations: sweet, sour, salty, bitter, and umami (savoury). The number and distribution of taste buds vary among individuals.

• In Smell, the Nasal Cavity Gathers Odorants: Receptors in the olfactory epithelium respond to chemicals and send signals to the olfactory bulb in the brain. Females are generally more accurate than males at detecting and identifying odours.

• In Touch, Sensors in the Skin Detect Pressure, Temperature, and Pain: The haptic sense relies on tactile stimulation to activate receptors for temperature, for sharp and dull pain, and for other sensations. Neural "gates" in the spinal cord also control pain. We can reduce pain perception by distraction, visualizing pain as more pleasant, being rested and relaxed, learning how to change brain activity that underlies pain perception, and taking drugs that interfere with the neural transmission of pain or render us unconscious.

• In Hearing, the Ear Detects Sound Waves: The size and shape of sound waves activate different hair cells in the inner ear. The receptors' responses depend on the sound waves' frequency and timing and on the activated receptors' location along the basilar membrane. Having two ears allows us to locate the source of a sound.

• In Vision, the Eye Detects Light Waves: Receptors (rods and cones) in the retina detect different forms of light waves. The lens helps the eye focus the stimulation on the retina for near versus far objects. Colour is determined by wavelengths of light, which activate certain types of cones; by the absorption of wavelengths by objects; or by the mixing of wavelengths of light.

• Humans and Animals Have Other Sensory Systems: In addition to the five "basic" senses, humans and other animals have a kinesthetic sense (ability to judge where one's limbs are in space) and a vestibular sense (ability to compare one's bodily position to the upright position). Some animals can use sound waves or disruptions in an electrical field to navigate.

• The Evidence for Extrasensory Perception (ESP) Is Weak or Nonexistent: Little or no good evidence supports the intriguing idea that some people have additional sensory systems that allow them to know what other people are thinking, for example, or to see through objects.

What Are the Basic Perceptual Processes?

• Perception Occurs in the Brain: Neural activity in the primary auditory cortex gives rise to hearing. Touch is mediated by neural activity in the primary somatosensory cortex. Vision results from a complex series of events in various areas of the brain but primarily in the occipital lobe.

• Object Perception Requires Construction: The Gestalt principles of stimulus organization account for some of the brain's perceptions of the world. Those perceptions involve cues about similarity, proximity, form, figure and background properties, and shading. Perception involves dual processes: bottom-up (sensory information) and top-down (expectations about what we will perceive).

• Depth Perception Is Important for Locating Objects: An object's pattern of stimulation on each of the two retinas (binocular) informs the brain about depth. The brain uses pictorial (monocular) cues—information about the object's appearance relative to the surroundings—to perceive depth and relative motion.

• Culture Influences Perception: People raised in a carpentered world—who have interacted with carpentered structures—are more prone to illusions based on cues such as linear perspective than are people raised in a noncarpentered world.

• Size Perception Depends on Distance Perception: Illusions of size can be created when the retinal size conflicts with the known size of objects in the visual field, as in the Ames and Ponzo illusions.

• Motion Perception Has Internal and External Cues: Motion detectors in the cortex respond to stimulation. The perceptual system establishes a stable frame of reference and relates object movement to it. Intervals of stimulation of repeated objects give the impression of continuous movement. Motion after-effects, which are opposite in motion from things that have been observed, tell us about the fatigue of neural receptors that fire in response to motion in certain directions.

• Perceptual Constancies Are Based on Ratio Relationships: We create expectancies about the world that allow us to use information about the shape, size, colour, and lightness of objects in their surroundings to achieve constancy.

COMPETENCY MODEL

How Do We Sense Our Worlds?

Sensation vs. Perception

1. Distinguish between sensation and perception.

Coding Stimuli

2. Explain the general process of how we encode physical information from the outside world.
3. Distinguish between qualitative and quantitative types of information.
4. What does coarse coding allow us to do?

Psychophysics

5. Explain psychophysics.

Sensory Thresholds

6. Distinguish between absolute and difference thresholds.
7. Explain Weber's Law.

Signal Detection Theory

8. Describe Signal Detection Theory and its components.
9. Identify how response bias can influence sensation.

Sensory Adaptation

10. Explain how sensory adaptation is good for general adaptation/survival.

Basic Sensory Processes

Taste (Gustation)

11. Identify the basic qualities of taste buds and their positioning on the tongue.
12. Describe the factors that influence taste.
13. Identify characteristics of supertasters.

Smell (Olfaction)

14. Be able to describe how a person is able to smell (including the structures involved).
15. What is the role of the amygdala in smell?
16. Describe the sex differences associated with smell.

Touch (Haptic Sense)

17. Identify the four types of tactile stimulation.
18. Distinguish between the two types of pain.
19. Explain the gate-control theory of pain.
20. Describe the sex differences associated with pain sensitivity.
21. Identify how the brain is being used to treat pain.
22. Identify pain treatments that focus on the emotional response.

Hearing (Auditory Sense)

23. Describe the characteristics of a sound wave that influence hearing.
24. Be able to describe how a person is able to hear sound (including the structures involved).
25. Identify the primary auditory receptors.
26. Describe how humans are able to locate sound. What animal helps us understand this?

Vision

27. Identify the importance of vision to human adaptation.
28. Be able to describe how a person is able to see (including the structures involved).
29. Explain accommodation.
30. Distinguish between rods and cones.
31. Describe the transmission of information from the eye to the brain.
32. Explain why everyone has "blind spots" based on the structure of the eye.
33. What does lateral inhibition help us see?
34. Describe the four main characteristics of colour.
35. Distinguish between subtractive and additive colour mixing.
36. Be able to explain how three different types of cones help our colour vision.
37. Be able to explain how opposite processes allow us to see afterimages.

Beyond the Five Primary Senses

38. Identify two internal sensory systems that humans possess that are not part of the five primary senses.

Extrasensory Perception (ESP)

39. Is extrasensory perception a real phenomenon?

Basic Perceptual Processes

Perception Occurs in the Brain

40. What is the role of the brain in perception?
41. Match the primary cortex area with its corresponding sense.
42. Distinguish between the ventral and dorsal stream.
43. How would you know if someone was suffering from object agnosia?

Object Perception Requires Construction

44. What is the underlying idea behind Gestalt principles?
45. How do the ideas of proximity, similarity, and good continuation influence perception?
46. Distinguish between figure and ground. How does this operate in reversible figures?
47. Distinguish between bottom-up and top-down processing.
48. What does, "faulty expectations can lead to faulty perceptions" mean?
49. How would you know if someone was suffering from prosopagnosia?
50. Identify which emotions humans recognize easier in others.
51. What sex differences have been identified in face recognition?
52. How does race or ethnicity influence face recognition?

Depth Perception

53. Distinguish between binocular and monocular depth perception.
54. Identify the characteristics that contribute to binocular depth perception.
55. Identify the characteristics that contribute to monocular depth perception.
56. How does culture influence the perception of the Mueller-Lyer illusion?
57. How does motion parallax help us see depth?
58. Describe how the Ames boxes (also called Ames rooms) and the Ponzo illusion rely on depth cues to fool us into seeing depth when it is not really there.

Motion Perception

59. Describe the factors that influence our perception of motion.

Perceptual Constancies

60. Identify the four main perceptual constancies.

KNOWLEDGE CHECK

1. After going home for the weekend, you return to your dorm room and notice a strange odour. This process is known as ________________. Upon thinking about it for a moment you conclude that it smells like rotten pizza. This process is known as ________________.
   a. sensation; sensation
   b. perception; sensation
   c. sensation; perception
   d. perception; perception

   Concept: I. A   Competency: 1
   Question Type: *Applied*

2. When Mary hears her alarm ring, the sensory receptors in her ears respond to the sound waves producing neural impulses. This process is called:
   a. transduction
   b. place coding
   c. psychophysics
   d. sound localization

   Concept: I. B. 1   Competency: 2
   Question Type: *Applied*

3. When Pete sees a bright light, his neurons fire more rapidly than when he sees a dim light. This is an example of:
   a. quantitative sensory coding
   b. qualitative sensory coding
   c. psychophysics
   d. just noticeable differences

   Concept: I. B. 1. b. 1   Competency: 3
   Question Type: *Applied*

4. Karen and Esteban are picking out paint colours for their apartment. They know they want to paint the wall red, but can't decide between brick red, deep merlot, rusty red, and Georgia clay. Their ability to recognize different shades is due to which process?
   a. place coding
   b. coarse coding
   c. psychophysics
   d. just noticeable differences

   Concept: I. B. 1. b. 2   Competency: 4
   Question Type: *Applied*

5. ____ assesses how much physical energy is required for our sense organs to detect a stimulus and how much change is required before we notice that change. This was developed by Gustav Fechner.

Concept: I. C Competency: 5
Question Type: *Factual*

6. When they went into the mall, Mickey complained that she could hear a high-pitched whine. Her friend Donna could not hear it. When they asked a mall employee about it, he told them that it was the security system and most people could not hear it. Mickey and Donna have different ______________ for sound.
   a. signal detectors
   b. tolerances
   c. transduction mechanisms
   d. absolute thresholds

Concept: I. D Competency: 6
Question Type: *Applied*

7. ____ explains why the difference between a 5-pound weight and 10-pound weight is more noticeable than the difference between a 100-pound and 105-pound weight.

Concept: I. D. 2. a Competency: 7
Question Type: *Applied*

8. Mehdi was in an experiment where he had to say whether a very faint light was shown. Sometimes the lights were presented and sometimes they were not. He often had to guess. Which perspective takes into account the factors that influence his judgments about the lights?
   a. absolute threshold theory
   b. difference threshold theory
   c. Weber's law
   d. signal detection theory

Concept: I. D Competency: 8
Question Type: *Applied*

		Signal	
		Presented	*Absent*
Observer	Detected	a	b
	Not-Detected	c	d

9. Using the table above, match the letter from the appropriate combination with the event described below.
   ____ miss
   ____ hit
   ____ false alarm
   ____ correct rejection

Concept: I. E Competency: 8
Question Type: *Conceptual*

10. Which of the following outcomes of signal detection is response bias most like?
   a. miss
   b. hit
   c. false alarm
   d. correct rejection

Concept: I. E. 5 Competency: 9
Question Type: *Conceptual*

11. When Kumar sat down to study biology, he noticed that his lamp made a buzzing noise. After a while, he no longer heard it. This demonstrates:
   a. response bias
   b. threshold detection
   c. sensory adaptation
   d. just noticeable difference

Concept: I. F Competency: 10
Question Type: *Applied*

12. Which of the following statements about taste buds is FALSE?
   a. Taste buds are found on the tongue, as well as in other parts of the mouth.
   b. Different regions of the tongue are more sensitive to certain tastes.
   c. People can have between 500 and 10,000 taste buds.
   d. There are specialized taste buds that respond most strongly to each of the primary taste sensations.

Concept: II. A. 1 Competency: 11
Question Type: *Factual*

13. Taste is affected by all of the following EXCEPT:
   a. texture of the food
   b. temperature of the food
   c. how your brain combines the signals
   d. your sense of smell

Concept: II. A. 2 Competency: 12
Question Type: *Factual*

14. When Lili eats very spicy food, her mouth hurts; she hates bitter foods, and she has many more taste buds than most people do. Lili may be a(n):
    a. olfactory respondent
    b. supertaster
    c. gustatorian
    d. somnambulist

Concept: II. A. 2. b Competency: 13
Question Type: *Applied*

15. Which sense has the most direct route to the brain?
    a. gustation
    b. haptic
    c. olfactory
    d. vision

Concept: II. B Competency: 14
Question Type: *Factual*

16. Every time Susie smells onions and peppers or fried food, she immediately has pleasant memories of going to the carnival as a child. This connection is due to smell being processed in which two brain regions?
    a. prefrontal cortex and thalamus
    b. prefrontal cortex and amygdala
    c. amygdala and thalamus
    d. prefrontal cortex and hypothalamus

Concept: II. B. 3 Competency: 15
Question Type: *Applied*

17. There is a sex difference for smell such that

    ____

    are better able to perceive and identify odour and have better memory for smell. This difference lasts over the life span.

Concept: II. B. 3 Competency: 16
Question Type: *Factual*

18. Concept: II. C. 1 Competency: 17
Question Type: *Factual*

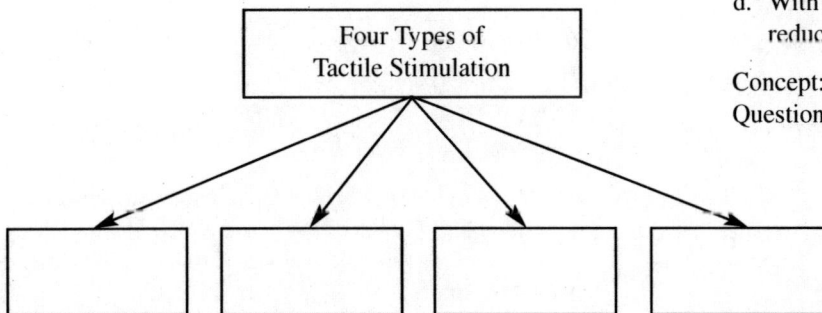

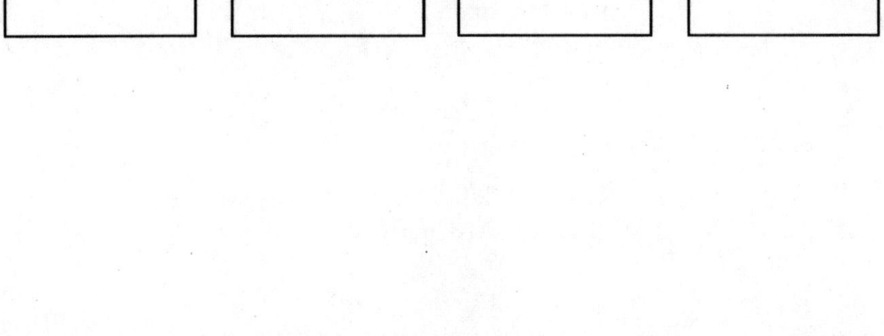

19. Paco has a constant and dull pain in his neck. He senses this due to ________________ fibres. He also has a chronic back ache. He senses this due to ________________ fibres.
    a. fast; fast
    b. fast; slow
    c. slow; fast
    d. slow; slow

Concept: II. C. 2 Competency: 18
Question Type: *Applied*

20. When Emma goes to the pediatrician for her shots, the nurse distracts her with a stuffed animal, gives her the shot, and then rubs the area. The rubbing minimizes pain because it stimulates other haptic receptors, which overwhelms the signals from pain receptors. This is best explained by the:
    a. fast fibres
    b. slow fibres
    c. gate-control theory of pain
    d. pressure reception theory of pain

Concept: II. C. 3 Competency: 19
Question Type: *Applied*

21. There is a sex difference for pain such that

    ____

    have a higher pain threshold. This is seen in automatic processes such as pupil dilation.

Concept: II. C. 3. b Competency: 20
Question Type: *Factual*

22. Which of the following statements about how brain imaging can help pain treatment is TRUE?
    a. Patients engage in mental activities that reduce the activity in the areas that underlie pain perception.
    b. TMS is used to desensitize the pain areas of the brain.
    c. An fMRI distinguishes those people who experience more pain from those who experience less.
    d. With EEG, we can alter the brain's response, thus reducing pain.

Concept: II. C. 3. c. 1 Competency: 21
Question Type: *Factual*

23. Your friend has been rushed to the hospital to have an emergency appendectomy. You want to use what you've learned to help manage his pain. Which of the following would NOT be helpful?
   a. Suggest he use pain medication.
   b. Distract him from thinking about the procedure.
   c. Don't tell your friend what to expect about the procedure.
   d. Have him listen to music.

   Concept: II. C. 3. c. 1 Competency: 22
   Question Type: *Applied*

24. Kambon was in an experiment where he was presented with sounds varying in amplitude. He will hear these sounds as varying in:
   a. timbre
   b. pitch
   c. loudness
   d. frequency

   Concept: II. D. 1 Competency: 23
   Question Type: *Applied*

25. Judy had an accident that damaged her hammer, anvil, and stirrup. She damaged her:
   a. cochleas
   b. ossicles
   c. ear drums
   d. basilar membranes

   Concept: II. D. 2. a Competency: 24
   Question Type: *Factual*

26. The primary auditory receptors are the:
   a. hair cells
   b. ossicles
   c. cochleas
   d. basilar membranes

   Concept: II. D. 2. d Competency: 25
   Question Type: *Factual*

27. Due to a childhood accident, Johan has hearing in only one ear. As a result, he will most likely have trouble with:
   a. place coding in his good ear
   b. temporal coding in his good ear
   c. basilar processing
   d. auditory localization

   Concept: II. D. 3 Competency: 26
   Question Type: *Applied*

28. If humans did not have a sense of vision, how would that have changed our adaptations to our environment?

   ____

   ____

   ____

   ____

   Concept: II. E Competency: 27
   Question Type: *Conceptual*

29. Light first passes through the__________________, a thick, transparent outer layer of the eye that focuses incoming light in a process called refraction. Light rays then enter and are bent farther inward by the

   ____,

   which focuses the light to form an image on the

   ____,

   the inner surface of the back of the eyeball.

   Concept: II. E Competency: 28
   Question Type: *Factual*

30. As he got older, Brett had increased difficulties visually focusing on objects close to his eyes. He was having problems with:
   a. place vision
   b. accommodation
   c. photopigments
   d. his optic nerve

   Concept: II. E. 1. b. 2. A Competency: 29
   Question Type: *Applied*

31. When walking through town on a moonless night, Harry noticed that everything looked grey. He was relying on which receptors for vision that night?
   a. rods
   b. cones
   c. pupils
   d. ganglion cells

   Concept: II. E. 2 Competency: 30
   Question Type: *Applied*

32. During her photography class, Nina is looking at several colour photos of the beach and is noticing the small details in the sand and water. She is relying on which receptors?
   a. rods
   b. cones
   c. pupils
   d. ganglion cells

   Concept: II. E. 2 Competency: 30
   Question Type: *Applied*

33. Light is transduced into neural impulses by the ____ and ____.
Afterward, other cells perform a series of sophisticated computations on those impulses that help the visual system process incoming information. The outputs from these cells converge on about 1 million retinal ____ cells.
Axons from these cells are gathered into a bundle called the ____
that exits the eye at the back of each retina.

Concept: II. E. 2. d Competency: 31
Question Type: *Factual*

34. Everyone has a "blind spot" in their visual field. This is due to:
    a. an insufficient number of rods in the centre of the visual field
    b. an insufficient number of cones in the periphery of the visual field
    c. where the optic nerve leaves the eye
    d. where the fovea meets up with the ganglion cells

Concept: II. E. 2. d. 2. A Competency: 32
Question Type: *Factual*

35. When baby Zachary looks around his room, he is able to distinguish the edges of his crib and his bureau, and he can easily identify where objects begin and end. His ability to do this is best described as due to:
    a. lateral inhibition
    b. his optic chiasm
    c. additive colour mixing
    d. simultaneous contrast

Concept: II. E. 4 Competency: 33
Question Type: *Applied*

36. Cheryl and Tomas are both wearing blue shirts, but all their friends can see that the shirts are not the same colour even though both are blue. The shirts are seen as different colours because:
    a. perception of colour is influenced by saturation, hue, brightness, and lightness
    b. the shirts differ in saturation, the only important variable for seeing colour
    c. the shirts differ in hue, the most important variable for seeing colour
    d. perception of colour relies on differences in brightness and context

Concept: II. E. 5. a Competency: 34
Question Type: *Applied*

37. Samantha wants to paint a ceramic frog green. To get that colour she mixes yellow and blue paint. This demonstrates:
    a. substitute colour mixing
    b. additive colour mixing
    c. subtractive colour mixing
    d. secondary colour mixing

Concept: II. E. 5. b Competency: 35
Question Type: *Applied*

38. Jessica is working for the stage crew for her school's play. To get the white lighting on the stage, she uses several different colours of light. This demonstrates:
    a. substitute colour mixing
    b. additive colour mixing
    c. subtractive colour mixing
    d. secondary colour mixing

Concept: II. E. 5. b Competency: 35
Question Type: *Applied*

39. There are three types of cones that respond to short, medium, and long wavelengths. These three cones correspond with which three colours?
    a. blue; orange; yellow
    b. red; yellow; green
    c. red; blue; yellow
    d. red; blue; green

Concept: II. E. 5. c. 1 Competency: 36
Question Type: *Applied*

40. If you stare at a yellow square and then look at a white wall, you will see a blue afterimage. This is explained by the functioning of the:
    a. retinal ganglion cells
    b. cones in the retina
    c. rods in the retina
    d. bipolar cells

Concept: II. E. 5. c. 2 Competency: 37
Question Type: *Factual*

41. Humans have several internal sensory systems in addition to the five primary ones. The
____
sense refers to sensations we gather from receptors in muscles, tendons, and joints that pinpoint the position and movements of our limbs and body in space. The
____
senses are linked to the experience of being seasick or carsick.

Concept: II. F Competency: 38
Question Type: *Factual*

42. According to the text, most of the research on ESP indicates that:
    a. we should consider ESP a sixth sense
    b. it is largely an individual phenomenon where a select few have the ability, while most people do not
    c. several studies have proven it exists
    d. it probably does not exist

Concept: II. G Competency: 39
Question Type: *Factual*

43. If we were able to do a brain transplant operation where we exchanged your brain with your friend's, how would that influence sensation and perception?

____

____

____

____

Concept: III. A Competency: 40
Question Type: *Conceptual*

44. The ____________________________ cortex is responsible for hearing, the ____________________________ cortex is responsible for touch, and the ____________________________ cortex is responsible for vision.

Concept: III. A. 1 Competency: 41
Question Type: *Factual*

45. Max is watching some friends play intramural softball. His ability to recognize objects is due to the ________________, while his ability to track the flight of the ball in space is due to the ________________.
    a. dorsal stream; ventral stream
    b. ventral stream; dorsal stream
    c. the "where" pathway; the "what" pathway
    d. primary visual pathway; secondary visual pathway

Concept: III. A. 1. c. 2 Competency: 42
Question Type: *Applied*

46. Lucy has experienced brain damage from a car accident. As a result, if you show her a picture of a dog, she does not know what it is. But if you ask her to draw a dog from memory she is able to do it. Lucy most likely suffers from:
    a. somatosensory failure
    b. visual blindness
    c. object agnosia
    d. prosopagnosia

Concept: III. A. 1. c. 3 Competency: 43
Question Type: *Applied*

47. The Gestalt psychologists believed that ____________________________________.

Concept: III. B Competency: 44
Question Type: *Factual*

48. When looking at the following 00 0000 00 000 00 you are likely to see five distinct groups of zeros. This is due to which Gestalt principle?
    a. similarity
    b. proximity
    c. good continuation
    d. closure

Concept: III. B. 1 Competency: 45
Question Type: *Applied*

49. Mariela notices that the FedEx symbol contains the letters for FedEx, but also an arrow between the letter *E* and *x*. When she looks at the FedEx symbol and sees the word *FedEx,* the word is the ________________. When she looks at the FedEx symbol and sees the arrow, the arrow is the ________________.
    a. figure; figure
    b. figure; ground
    c. ground; figure
    d. ground; ground

Concept: III. B. 1. c. 3 Competency: 46
Question Type: *Applied*

50. After Maria photocopied an article she noticed that one letter was chopped off the end of each line. She was happy to find she had no trouble reading the article even though the letters were missing. Her ability to read the article reflects:
    a. parallel processing
    b. continuation processing
    c. bottom-up processing
    d. top-down processing

Concept: III. B. 3 Competency: 47
Question Type: *Applied*

51. How might the idea that "faulty expectations can lead to faulty perceptions" influence how you perceive an instructor on the first day of class? Which type of processing is this most like?

____

____

____

____

Concept: III. B. 3 Competency: 48
Question Type: *Applied*

52. A person suffering from ________________ would be unable to recognize faces. This is also known as face blindness.

Concept: III. B. 4. b Competency: 49
Question Type: *Factual*

53. Mark is given a test to determine his ability to recognize emotions in facial expressions. If he is typical of research in this area, which emotion will he have the easiest time recognizing?
    a. anger
    b. happiness
    c. sadness
    d. fear

Concept: III. B. 4. c Competency: 50
Question Type: *Applied*

54. There is a sex difference for facial recognition such that ______________________________ are more accurate at face recognition tasks, and are able to recognize female faces better than male faces.

Concept: III. B. 4. d Competency: 51
Question Type: *Factual*

55. Which of the following statements about face recognition is true at the social level of analysis?
    a. Faces would be hard to recognize if the person has damage to the fusiform gyrus.
    b. Faces are harder to recognize if they are upside down.
    c. Faces are more easily recognized if they are from one's same race.
    d. Faces are more easily recognized if they are from a different race.

Concept: III. B. 4. e Competency: 52
Question Type: *Factual*

56. Brian is playing a video game that involves driving around a city. His roommate Mike is impressed with how real things look, particularly as he drives into a tunnel. What type of cues did the video game makers use to make things look so real?
    a. monocular depth cues
    b. binocular depth cues
    c. three-dimensional depth cues
    d. stereographic depth cues

Concept: III. D Competency: 53
Question Type: *Applied*

57. When bored in class, Denise stares at her index finger first with only her left eye, then with only her right eye, to watch her finger seem to dance back and forth. Denise's dancing finger demonstrates:
    a. the effects of relative size
    b. monocular cues for depth
    c. motion parallax
    d. binocular disparity

Concept: III. D. 1. a Competency: 54
Question Type: *Applied*

58. When Dave and Chuck walk past Anne, Anne knows that Dave is closer to her because he blocks part of Chuck from view. Anne is using which monocular cue to make her judgment about who is closer?
    a. occlusion
    b. relative size
    c. familiar size
    d. linear perspective

Concept: III. D. 2 Competency: 55
Question Type: *Applied*

59. If you grew up and only lived in an igloo, would you succumb to the Mueller-Lyer illusion? Why?

____

____

____

____

Concept: III. D. 3 Competency: 56
Question Type: *Applied*

60. When staring out the passenger window in his dad's car while riding down the highway, Steve noticed that the fence close to the road seemed to flash past him while trees at the far end of a field seemed to move by more slowly. This demonstrates:
    a. the effects of relative size
    b. a pictorial cue for depth
    c. motion parallax
    d. binocular disparity

Concept: III. D. 4 Competency: 57
Question Type: *Applied*

61. For each of the following, please match the explanation with the most appropriate illusion.

____	Monocular depth cues make the two-dimensional figure seem three-dimensional. Your brain defaults to using depth cues even when there is no depth present.	a) Ames box
____	Normally, a nearby object projects a larger retinal image than a far object. If the depth cues are wrong, the disproportionate size of the image on your retina makes an object look huge.	b) Ponzo illusion

Concept: III. D. 5 Competency: 58
Question Type: *Factual*

62. Nick and Chris are hanging up lights on the outside of their house for the holidays. The type of lights they are using have the appearance of movement when they are on and look like they move continuously. This is due to which cue to motion perception?
   a. waterfall effect
   b. compensatory factors
   c. stroboscopic motion
   d. the induced movement illusion

Concept: III. E Competency: 59
Question Type: *Applied*

63. Concept: III. F Competency: 60
Question Type: *Factual*

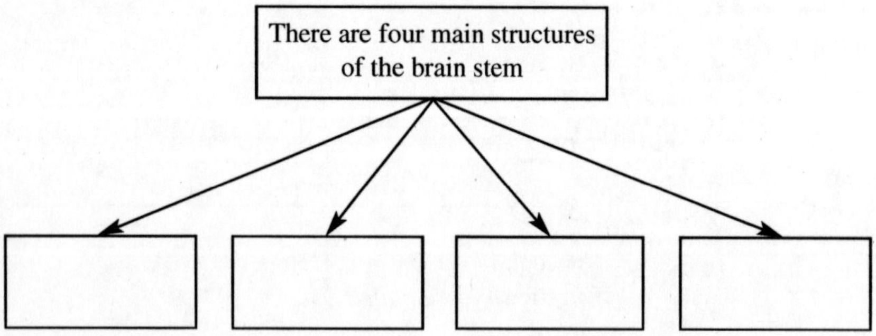
There are four main structures of the brain stem

SUMMING UP AND MEASURING UP

What Are the Basic Sensory Processes?

All the senses share similar processes. Each has receptors that respond to different physical or chemical stimuli by transducing them into some pattern of brain activity. Typically, different receptors respond to different types of stimuli, and most sensory systems integrate signals from these different receptors into an overall sensation. This system allows a relatively small number of receptors to code a wide variety of stimuli. For example, the visual system can interpret the entire range of colours with only three cone types, and all the taste sensations are made up of five primary taste receptors. These various sensory receptors help the perceptual system receive important information that assists in solving adaptive problems. Sensory information, although obtained from the outside world, is processed entirely in the brain to produce sensory experience through perception.

Neurons in the visual system and other sensory systems have receptive fields. For vision, they are:

a. areas, on the retina, in which light must fall for the neurons to increase or decrease their firing rate
b. areas, in the brain, where information from all areas of the retina are combined so we can make sense of the sensory input

ANSWER KEY

Item **Answer**

1. c
2. a
3. a
4. b
5. Psychophysics
6. d
7. Weber's law
8. d
9. c, a, b, d
10. c
11. c
12. b
13. c
14. b
15. c
16. b
17. females
18. Temperature; Pain; Pressure; Location in Space
19. d
20. c
21. males
22. a
23. c
24. c
25. b
26. a
27. d
28. Possibilities for this are numerous, but the most likely change would be that we would no longer act as predators. This would mean we would hunt less (if at all) and instead rely on gathering or grazing for sustenance. As a result, we would likely develop a better sense of smell to find food, and hearing to sense predators. We might also become more reliant on others, and would not be able to be solitary/independent.
29. cornea; lens; retina
30. b
31. a
32. b
33. rods; cones; ganglion, optic nerve
34. c
35. a
36. a
37. c
38. b
39. d
40. a
41. kinesthetic; vestibular
42. d
43. Sensation would not be affected because transduction of external stimuli takes place outside of the brain in the receptors. However, perception occurs in the brain. You would still be able to perceive the stimuli you sense because you would still have the primary sensory areas of the brain (just from your friend's instead of your own). However, because perception is often influenced by past experiences and expectations, things that are unique to different individuals, your perception of things might be different. For example, if you perceived roller coasters as scary, and your friend did not, with your friend's brain you would no longer perceive roller coasters as scary.
44. primary auditory; primary somatosensory; primary visual
45. b
46. c
47. our perceptions are different from the sum of their constituent sensations.
48. b
49. a
50. d
51. Everyone has expectations for what a class is like depending on the topic. We expect a yoga class to be different from a biochemistry class. Similarly we might expect different instructors for those two classes. Our expectations might also come from what friends or classmates tell us. If we hear the instructor is really nice and funny, we would be more likely to perceive it that way. In any case, these expectations could be without any merit. Because this involves a higher level of processing influencing lower levels, it is most like top-down.
52. prosopagnosia
53. a
54. females
55. c
56. a
57. d
58. a
59. Most likely you would not make the mistake of perceiving one line longer than the other. Culturally, those who grow up in a linear world, particularly living in buildings based on square rooms, are more susceptible to the illusion.
60. c
61. b, c, a, d
62. c
63. Size; Shape; Colour; Light

Summing Up and Measuring Up

Answer: a. areas, on the retina, in which light must fall for the neurons to increase or decrease their firing rate

KEY TERM EXERCISES

additive colour mixing

Textbook Definition:
Your Own Definition:
Your Own Example:

audition

Textbook Definition:
Your Own Definition:
Your Own Example:

binocular depth cues

Textbook Definition:
Your Own Definition:
Your Own Example:

binocular disparity

Textbook Definition:
Your Own Definition:
Your Own Example:

bottom-up processing

Textbook Definition:
Your Own Definition:
Your Own Example:

cones

Textbook Definition:
Your Own Definition:
Your Own Example:

cornea

Textbook Definition:
Your Own Definition:
Your Own Example:

eardrum (tympanic membrane)

Textbook Definition:
Your Own Definition:
Your Own Example:

fovea

Textbook Definition:
Your Own Definition:
Your Own Example:

gustation

Textbook Definition:
Your Own Definition:
Your Own Example:

haptic sense

Textbook Definition:
Your Own Definition:
Your Own Example:

iris

Textbook Definition:
Your Own Definition:
Your Own Example:

kinesthetic sense

Textbook Definition:
Your Own Definition:
Your Own Example:

lateral inhibition

Textbook Definition:
Your Own Definition:
Your Own Example:

monocular depth cues

Textbook Definition:
Your Own Definition:
Your Own Example:

olfaction

Textbook Definition:
Your Own Definition:
Your Own Example:

olfactory bulb

Textbook Definition:
Your Own Definition:
Your Own Example:

olfactory epithelium

Textbook Definition:
Your Own Definition:
Your Own Example:

perception

Textbook Definition:
Your Own Definition:
Your Own Example:

perceptual constancy

Textbook Definition:
Your Own Definition:
Your Own Example:

pupil

Textbook Definition:
Your Own Definition:
Your Own Example:

receptive field

Textbook Definition:
Your Own Definition:
Your Own Example:

retina

Textbook Definition:
Your Own Definition:
Your Own Example:

rods

Textbook Definition:
Your Own Definition:
Your Own Example:

sensation

Textbook Definition:
Your Own Definition:
Your Own Example:

sensory adaptation

Textbook Definition:
Your Own Definition:
Your Own Example:

signal detection theory (SDT)

Textbook Definition:
Your Own Definition:
Your Own Example:

sound wave

Textbook Definition:
Your Own Definition:
Your Own Example:

subtractive colour mixing

Textbook Definition:
Your Own Definition:
Your Own Example:

transduction

Textbook Definition:
Your Own Definition:
Your Own Example:

taste buds

Textbook Definition:
Your Own Definition:
Your Own Example:

vestibular sense

Textbook Definition:
Your Own Definition:
Your Own Example:

top-down processing

Textbook Definition:
Your Own Definition:
Your Own Example:

CHAPTER 6 Learning

CONCEPT MAP

I. How Did the Behavioural Study of Learning Develop?
  A. General Information
    1. Learning
    2. Rise of Learning Theory
    3. Classical Conditioning
    4. Operant Conditioning
    5. Behaviourism

II. Classical Conditioning
  A. Behavioural Responses are Conditioned
    1. Pavlov
    2. Pavlov's Experiments
      a. Neutral Stimulus
      b. Conditioning Trial
      c. Critical Trials
      d. Classical (Pavlovian) Conditioning
        1. Unconditioned Response (UR)
        2. Unconditioned Stimulus (US)
        3. Conditioned Stimulus (CS)
        4. Conditioned Response (CR)
  B. Key Classical Conditioning Concepts
    1. Acquisition
      a. Contiguity
    2. Extinction
    3. Spontaneous Recovery
    4. Stimulus Generalization vs. Stimulus Discrimination
    5. Second-Order Conditioning
  C. Application of Classical Conditioning: Treatments
    1. Phobia
      a. Fear Conditioning
      b. Watson and Little Albert
      c. Counterconditioning
        1. Systematic Desensitization
    2. Drug Addiction
  D. Classical Conditioning Involves More Than Events Occurring at the Same Time
    1. Evolutionary Significance
      a. Conditioned Food Aversion
      b. Biological Preparedness
    2. Sex Differences in Learning
    3. Cognitive Perspective
      a. Rescorla-Wagner Model
      b. Blocking Effect

III. Operant Conditioning
  A. General Information
    1. Passive vs. Active
      a. Operant (Instrumental) Conditioning
    2. Thorndike
      a. Law of Effect
  B. Reinforcement Increases Behaviour
    1. Reinforcer
    2. Skinner Box (Operant Chamber)
    3. Shaping
      a. Successive Approximations
    4. Reinforcers Can Be Conditioned
      a. Primary Reinforcers
      b. Secondary Reinforcers
    5. Reinforcer Potency
      a. Premack Principle
  C. Reinforcement and Punishment Can Be Positive or Negative
    1. Reinforcement
      a. Positive Reinforcement
      b. Negative Reinforcement

2. Punishment
   a. Positive Punishment
   b. Negative Punishment
   c. Parental Punishment
      1. Effective
      2. Ineffective
      3. Outcomes

D. Schedules of Reinforcement
   1. Continuous Reinforcement
   2. Partial Reinforcement
      a. Ratio Schedule
      b. Interval Schedule
      c. Fixed Schedule
      d. Variable Schedule
      e. Behavioural Persistence
         1. Partial-Reinforcement Extinction Effect

E. Application of Operant Conditioning
   1. Behaviour Modification
      a. Token Economy

F. Biology and Cognition Influence Operant Conditioning
   1. Biological Constraints
   2. Acquisition-Performance Distinction
      a. Cognitive Maps
      b. Latent Learning
      c. Insight Learning
   3. The Value of Reinforcement Follows Economic Principles
      a. Present vs. Future Rewards
      b. Optimal Foraging Theory

IV. Observational Learning
   A. Cultural Transmission
      1. Memes
      2. Cultural Beliefs about Learning
   B. Learning Can Occur through Observation
      1. Observational Learning
      2. Bandura's Observational Studies
      3. Social Learning of Fear
      4. Teaching through Demonstration
      5. Animals and Humans Imitate Others
         a. Modelling
      6. Vicarious Reinforcement
      7. Media and Violence
         a. Support for the Link
         b. Issues with the Link
         c. How Does Media Violence Promote Aggression?
         d. Ethics
      8. Mirror Neurons

V. Biological Basis of Learning
   A. Dopamine Activity Underlies Reinforcement
      1. Pleasure Centres
         a. Intracranial Self-Stimulation (ICSS)
      2. Nucleus Accumbens Activation
      3. Secondary Reinforcers
   B. Habituation and Sensitization Are Simple Models of Learning
      1. Engram
      2. Habituation
         a. Orienting Response
      3. Sensitization
   C. Long-Term Potentiation Is a Candidate for the Neural Basis of Learning
      1. LTP and the NMDA Receptor
      2. Fear Conditioning

CHAPTER SUMMARY

How Did the Behavioural Study of Learning Develop?

• Behavioural Responses Are Conditioned: Pavlov established the principles of classical conditioning, a process that occurs when associations are made between two stimuli, such as the clinking of a metronome and a piece of meat. This type of learning is based on reflexes, such as the salivation that occurs in response to the meat. Acquisition, discrimination, generalization, and extinction are measured in classical conditioning. Some emotional responses are learned through conditioning.

• Phobias and Addictions Have Learned Components: Phobias are learned fear associations. Similarly, addiction involves a conditioned response, which can result in withdrawal symptoms at the mere sight of drug paraphernalia, and tolerance: the need for more of the particular drug, when that drug is administered in a familiar context, to get a high comparable to the one obtained earlier.

• Classical Conditioning Involves More Than Events Occurring at the Same Time: Not all stimuli are equally potent in producing conditioning. Animals are biologically prepared to make connections between stimuli that are potentially dangerous, such as learning to freeze when shock is administered. Animals are also predisposed to form predictions that enhance survival, such as judging the likelihood that food will continue to be available at one location.

How Does Operant Conditioning Differ from Classical Conditioning?

• Reinforcement Increases Behaviour: A behaviour's positive consequences will likely strengthen it or make it more likely to occur. Shaping is a procedure in which successive approximations of a behaviour are reinforced, leading to the desired behaviour. Reinforcers may be primary (those that satisfy biological needs) or secondary (those that do not directly satisfy biological needs).

• Both Reinforcement and Punishment Can Be Positive or Negative: In either positive reinforcement or positive punishment, a stimulus is delivered after the animal responds. In negative reinforcement or negative punishment, a stimulus is removed after the animal responds. Positive and negative reinforcements increase a behaviour's likelihood; positive and negative punishments decrease a behaviour's likelihood.

• Operant Conditioning Is Influenced by Schedules of Reinforcement: Reinforcement can be delivered at either a fixed rate or a variable rate that depends on the number (ratio) or time (interval) of responses. A variable rate of reinforcement leads to resistance to extinction.

• Biology and Cognition Influence Operant Conditioning: An organism's biological makeup restricts the types of behaviours the organism can learn. Latent learning takes place without reinforcement. Such learning often is not performed until a reinforcer is introduced.

• The Value of Reinforcement Follows Economic Principles: In choosing between reinforcers, human and nonhuman animals consider the likelihood of obtaining each reward and the amount of time it might take to receive each one.

How Does Watching Others Affect Learning?

• Learning Can Be Passed On through Cultural Transmission: Memes (knowledge transferred within a culture) are analogous to genes, in that behaviours are selectively passed on from generation to generation.

• Learning Can Occur through Observation: Observational learning is a powerful adaptive tool. Humans and other animals learn by watching others' behaviours and the consequences of those behaviours.

• Animals and Humans Imitate Others: Modelling occurs when one individual reproduces another individual's behaviour. Vicarious learning occurs as the result of one individual seeing another individual's behaviour reinforced or punished. Mirror neurons are activated when we watch a behaviour, just as when we actually perform the behaviour.

What Is the Biological Basis of Learning?

• Dopamine Activity Underlies Reinforcement: The brain has specialized centres that produce pleasure when stimulated. Behaviours that activate these centres are reinforced. The nucleus accumbens (a part of the limbic system) has dopamine receptors, which are activated by pleasurable behaviours. Through conditioning, secondary reinforcers can also activate dopamine receptors. Drugs also increase activation, which can lead to addiction.

• Habituation and Sensitization Are Simple Models of Learning: Repeated exposure to a stimulus results in habituation, a decrease in behavioural response. Sensitization is an increase in behavioural response to a new threatening stimulus.

• Long-Term Potentiation Is a Candidate for the Neural Basis of Learning: Synaptic connections are strengthened when neurons fire together. This occurs in the hippocampus and, in fear responses, in the amygdala. The receptor NMDA is required for long-term potentiation. Genetically altered mice that had more efficient NMDA receptors were superlearners. LTP is also important for fear conditioning.

COMPETENCY MODEL

How Did the Behavioural Study of Learning Develop?

1. Define learning.
2. What helps explain the rise of learning theory?
3. Distinguish between classical and operant conditioning.
4. Describe the basic idea behind behaviourism. Upon what philosophical idea is this based?

Classical Conditioning

Behavioural Responses Are Conditioned

5. Describe Pavlov's early work that later applied to learning.
6. Explain how a neutral stimulus, conditioning trial, and critical trial relate to one another.
7. Identify unconditioned stimulus/response and conditioned stimulus/response.

Key Classical Conditioning Concepts

8. What is critical for acquisition?
9. How does extinction occur?
10. How does spontaneous recovery occur?
11. Distinguish stimulus generalization from stimulus discrimination.
12. Explain second-order conditioning.

Application of Classical Conditioning: Treatments

13. What is a phobia?
14. What is fear conditioning?
15. Describe the Little Albert experiment.
16. Explain how systematic desensitization can be used in treatment.
17. Understand the role of classical conditioning in drug addiction.

Classical Conditioning Involves More Than Events Occurring at the Same Time

18. What is the evolutionary significance of food aversions?
19. What is biological preparedness?
20. Identify sex differences in learning.
21. What does the Rescorla-Wagner model add to classical conditioning?

Operant Conditioning

22. Distinguish passive learning from active learning.
23. Identify the law of effect.

Reinforcement Increases Behaviour

24. Provide examples of reinforcers.
25. What is a Skinner Box?
26. Describe the process of shaping.
27. Distinguish between primary and secondary reinforcers.
28. What is the Premack principle?

Reinforcement and Punishment Can Be Positive or Negative

29. Distinguish between positive and negative reinforcement.
30. Distinguish between positive and negative punishment.
31. Provide evidence for the effectiveness of parental punishment.
32. Describe the general effectiveness of punishment vs. reinforcement.

Schedules of Reinforcement

33. Extrapolate the concepts of continuous and partial reinforcement to punishment.
34. Distinguish between continuous and partial reinforcement.
35. Identify the different schedules of reinforcement.
36. Explain the partial-reinforcement extinction effect.

Application of Operant Conditioning

37. Explain how token economies can be used in treatment.

Biology and Cognition Influence Operant Conditioning

38. How do animals' adaptations influence learning?
39. What are cognitive maps?
40. Distinguish latent learning from operant conditioning.
41. Which are better reinforcers, present or future rewards?

Observational Learning

Cultural Transmission

42. Explain memes and how they relate to genetics.

Learning Can Occur through Observation

43. Explain the concept of observational learning.
44. Describe Bandura's classic study.
45. Describe modelling.
46. How do we learn fear vicariously?
47. Provide evidence that supports and undermines the link between media and violence.
48. Describe the function of mirror neurons.

Biological Basis of Learning

49. Identify the neurotransmitter most closely associated with reinforcement.

Dopamine Activity Underlies Reinforcement

50. What does ICSS involve?

Habituation and Sensitization Are Simple Models of Learning

51. How does habituation occur?
52. What does sensitization involve?

Long-Term Potentiation Is a Candidate for the Neural Basis of Learning

53. What does long-term potentiation involve?

KNOWLEDGE CHECK

1. ______________________ is a relatively enduring change in behaviour that results from experience.

   Concept: I. A. 1   Competency: 1
   Question Type: *Factual*

2. Learning theory was largely a reaction to all of the following EXCEPT:
   a. a dissatisfaction with introspection
   b. Freudian ideas that were at the heart of psychological theorizing
   c. the belief that Freudian ideas were unscientific
   d. an overemphasis on observable behaviour

   Concept: I. A. 2 Competency: 2
   Question Type: *Factual*

3. In high school, students often begin packing up their materials to go to another class when they hear a bell. This is an example of which type of conditioning?
   a. operant conditioning
   b. classical conditioning
   c. response conditioning
   d. vicarious conditioning

   Concept: I. A. 3 Competency: 3
   Question Type: *Applied*

4. On sports teams, players will earn symbols on their helmet for each positive contribution they made to the team during a game. This is an example of which type of conditioning?
   a. operant conditioning
   b. classical conditioning
   c. response conditioning
   d. vicarious conditioning

   Concept: I. A. 3 Competency: 3
   Question Type: *Applied*

5. Watson believed that any baby could be made into any kind of person based on the environment in which the baby was brought up. This idea indicates he thought of the baby as a:
   a. positive reinforcer
   b. vicarious learner
   c. tabula rasa
   d. conditioned stimulus

   Concept: I. A. 5 Competency: 4
   Question Type: *Factual*

6. Which of the following statements about Pavlov's early work is true?
   a. He was a psychologist interested in the learning behaviour of dogs.
   b. He was a physiologist interested in the digestive system.
   c. He was a student of John Watson.
   d. He was a psychologist interested in dogs' reflexes.

   Concept: II. A. 1 Competency: 5
   Question Type: *Factual*

7. In a typical Pavlovian experiment, a ______________________________ stimulus is presented along with a stimulus that reliably produces the desired reflex. This pairing, known as a ______________________________, is repeated a number of times; then, on ______________________________, the desired response is measured.

   Concept: II. A. 2 Competency: 6
   Question Type: *Factual*

8. Every time Jon feeds his dog he first opens the can with an electric can opener. He then gives the dog its food. Initially the dog would salivate while eating. Now the dog salivates when it hears the can opener. What is the conditioned stimulus in this example? What is the unconditioned response?
   a. the sound of the can opener; the food
   b. the food; salivation
   c. the sound of the can opener; salivation
   d. salivation; the sound of the can opener

   Concept: II. A. 2. d Competency: 7
   Question Type: *Applied*

9. Denise was recently in a car accident, which made her very afraid. Following the accident, she also became afraid of cars. What is the conditioned stimulus in this example?
   a. the accident
   b. the car
   c. the fear
   d. an increase in her heart rate

   Concept: II. A. 2. d Competency: 7
   Question Type: *Applied*

10. Todd wants to teach his sister to laugh every time he says the word *bananas*. To do this, he needs to pair up the conditioned and unconditioned stimuli in order to achieve acquisition. With whatever stimuli he chooses, what is the key element for acquisition?
    a. spontaneous recovery
    b. contiguity
    c. stimulus generalization
    d. the critical trial

    Concept: II. B. 1 Competency: 8
    Question Type: *Applied*

11. Vivian is afraid of dogs. However, she has decided to force herself to interact with dogs and has noticed she is no longer afraid. This exemplifies which process?
    a. stimulus discrimination
    b. stimulus generalization
    c. extinction
    d. contiguity

    Concept: II. B. 2 Competency: 9
    Question Type: *Applied*

12. Rafael has successfully extinguished his fear of balloons. At a recent birthday party he saw balloons and became afraid again. However, after a small amount of time near the balloons he was no longer afraid. The return of his fear is known as:
    a. stimulus discrimination
    b. stimulus generalization
    c. extinction
    d. spontaneous recovery

    Concept: II. B. 3 Competency: 10
    Question Type: *Applied*

13. When Chris went to the dentist he had to have his teeth drilled. Following the visit, Chris was very afraid of the dentist. Soon after, Chris had to go to the doctor. Which of the following would indicate Chris generalized from the situation with the dentist to the situation with the doctor?
    a. He would be comfortable with the doctor.
    b. He would have no feelings about the doctor.
    c. He would also be afraid of the doctor.
    d. He would choose going to the doctor over going to the dentist.

    Concept: II. B. 4 Competency: 11
    Question Type: *Applied*

14. After a bad fall from her bicycle, Jenny was afraid to ride any bicycle. She was not afraid to ride on a motorcycle. The difference in her reaction to bicycles and motorcycles reflects:
    a. extinction
    b. spontaneous recovery
    c. stimulus generalization
    d. stimulus discrimination

    Concept: II. B. 4 Competency: 11
    Question Type: *Applied*

15. Pavlov trained dogs to salivate by presenting a tone followed by food. After this, he repeatedly presented the dogs with a black square concurrent with the tone. He did not present the food. After many trials he found the dogs salivated when presented with the black square alone. This is a demonstration of:
    a. second-order conditioning
    b. spontaneous recovery
    c. stimulus generalization
    d. stimulus discrimination

    Concept: II. B. 5 Competency: 12
    Question Type: *Applied*

16. A ________________________________ is an acquired fear that is out of proportion to the real threat.

    Concept: II. C. 1 Competency: 13
    Question Type: *Factual*

17. In fear conditioning, fear is always the:
    a. conditioned stimulus
    b. unconditioned stimulus
    c. conditioned response
    d. punishment

    Concept: II. C. 1. a Competency: 14
    Question Type: *Conceptual*

18. For each of the following, please match the aspect of the Little Albert experiment with the proper term:

____	Smashing sound	a) Unconditioned stimulus
____	Fear from smashing sound	b) Unconditioned response
____	Fear	c) Conditioned stimulus
____	Rat	d) Conditioned response

    Concept: II. C. 1. b Competency: 15
    Question Type: *Factual*

19. Patty wants to overcome her fear of clowns so she engages in a series of relaxation exercises first while thinking of a clown, then while looking at a picture of a clown, then with a clown in the room, then finally while hugging a clown. This process is known as:
    a. systematic desensitization
    b. systematic deconditioning
    c. extinction
    d. deacquisition

    Concept: II. C. 1. c Competency: 16
    Question Type: *Applied*

20. From the perspective of classical conditioning, why are those in drug treatment told to avoid people, places, and things that relate to their drug use?

____

____

____

____

Concept: II. C. 2 Competency: 17
Question Type: *Conceptual*

21. From an evolutionary standpoint, why is it important to develop conditioned food aversions? What other types of aversion should be easily conditioned?

____

____

____

____

Concept: II. D. 1 Competency: 18
Question Type: *Conceptual*

22. People are more likely to have irrational fears of snakes or dogs than of flowers or butterflies. This reflects:
   a. fear conditioning
   b. biological preparedness
   c. counterconditioning
   d. the contiguity principle

Concept: II. D. 1. b Competency: 19
Question Type: *Applied*

23. For each of the following, please match the characteristic used to solve mazes and navigate through space with the sex who is more likely to use it:

____	More likely to use a learning strategy that consisted of a series of turns (e.g., right, right, left, right)	a) Females b) Males
____	Rely on landmarks to find their way	
____	When the conditions were such that participants could use either strategy, they learned the task more quickly.	
____	More likely to attend to and keep track of the compass direction in which they are traveling	

Concept: II. D. 2 Competency: 20
Question Type: *Factual*

24. Teresa wants to classically condition her dog to salivate. According to the Rescorla-Wagner model, which of the following would be the most effective conditioned stimulus to pair with food?
   a. the smell of almonds
   b. the smell of dog biscuits
   c. the smell of the dog food
   d. the sight of the can of dog food

Concept: II. D. 3. a Competency: 21
Question Type: *Applied*

25. ____ conditioning is considered active, while ____ is considered passive.

Concept: III. A. 1 Competency: 22
Question Type: *Factual*

26. When a hungry dog searches in a trash can and finds food, he is more likely to search the trash can in the future. According to Thorndike, this demonstrates:
   a. the Law of Effect
   b. classical conditioning
   c. secondary reinforcement
   d. use of an unconditioned stimulus

Concept: III. A. 2. a Competency: 23
Question Type: *Applied*

27. By studying and using this study guide you are engaging in learned behaviour. Identify several things that serve as reinforcers for your behaviour.

____

____

____

____

Concept: II. D. 1 Competency: 24
Question Type: *Conceptual*

28. A _______________________________ is a simple device for assessing operant conditioning that consists of a small chamber or cage in which a lever (or response key) is connected to a food or water supply. An animal, usually a rat or a pigeon, is placed inside; when it presses the lever, food or water becomes available.

Concept: III. B. 2 Competency: 25
Question Type: *Factual*

29. When Ichiro wanted to teach his puppy to roll over, he first rewarded the puppy for lying down, then he rewarded the puppy for moving to its side, then for moving to its back, and finally for totally rolling over. The process through which Ichiro trained his puppy is called:
    a. observational learning
    b. classical conditioning
    c. shaping
    d. secondary reinforcement

Concept: III. B. 3. a Competency: 26
Question Type: *Applied*

30. Food, sex, and water are examples of _______________________________ reinforcers, while money, gold stars, and trophies are examples of _______________________________ reinforcers.
    a. primary; secondary
    b. secondary; primary
    c. motivational; Skinnerian
    d. stimulus; response

Concept: III. B. 4 Competency: 27
Question Type: *Applied*

31. When not in class, studying, or working, Petra spends a lot of time at the gym while her roommate Jeanine never goes to the gym. The Premack principle suggests that:
    a. going to the gym is not a reinforcer
    b. going to the gym is a primary reinforcer for Petra, but a secondary reinforcer for Jeanine
    c. going to the gym is a secondary reinforcer for Petra, but a primary reinforcer for Jeanine
    d. going to the gym is a potent reinforcer for Petra, but not for Jeanine

Concept: III. B. 5. a Competency: 28
Question Type: *Applied*

32. After trying a number of different products, Meagan finds that her headaches will go away if she takes ibuprofen. Now she takes ibuprofen every time she has a headache. Her taking of ibuprofen has increased because of:
    a. positive reinforcement
    b. negative reinforcement
    c. positive punishment
    d. negative punishment

Concept: III. C. 1 Competency: 29
Question Type: *Applied*

33. Selma's mother saw Selma speeding on the highway. Following this, to try to make Selma less likely to speed, Selma's mother took the car keys away for a week. Selma's mother is using ____________________ to decrease Selma's speeding.
    a. positive reinforcement
    b. negative reinforcement
    c. positive punishment
    d. negative punishment

Concept: III. C. 2 Competency: 30
Question Type: *Applied*

34. Based on the available research evidence, what advice would you give parents about punishing their children?

____

____

____

____

Concept: III. C. 2. c Competency: 31
Question Type: *Applied*

35. Madison is throwing a temper tantrum in the store because her mom won't buy her a chocolate bar. Based on what you know about the effectiveness of punishment vs. reinforcement, which of the following should Madison's mom do?
    a. Punish her by putting her in time out when they get home from the store.
    b. Give her the candy if she stops crying.
    c. Ignore the tantrum, and reinforce her behaviour with praise when she is acting appropriately.
    d. Punish her right on the spot by giving her a slap on her wrist.

Concept: III. C. 2. c. 3 Competency: 32
Question Type: *Applied*

36. We know that partial reinforcement is more effective than continuous reinforcement. Would the same be true for punishment? Why? Provide an example to support your point.

____

____

____

____

Concept: III. D Competency: 33
Question Type: *Conceptual*

37. Bruce is training his pet horse to raise its front legs on command. He decides to take an approach where he gives the horse oats every six times the horse raises its legs, rather than every time. Is this a smart thing to do?
    a. Yes, the horse will respond more to partial reinforcement.
    b. No, the horse will respond more to continuous reinforcement.
    c. No, it is more natural to get reinforced every time.
    d. Yes, only reinforcing sometimes helps to punish the unwanted behaviour while simultaneously reinforcing the desired behaviour.

Concept: III. D Competency: 34
Question Type: *Applied*

38. Caitlin receives a paychecque from her job every two weeks. This is an example of what schedule of reinforcement?
    a. fixed-ratio
    b. fixed-interval
    c. variable-ratio
    d. variable-interval

Concept: III. D. 2 Competency: 35
Question Type: *Applied*

39. As a child, Albert's parents gave him a dollar for every A he received on a test. After a while, they didn't give him a dollar every time, but did every once in a while. To this day Albert still wants to get A's because his parents might give him a dollar. This demonstrates:
    a. the partial-reinforcement extinction effect
    b. a fixed-interval schedule of reinforcement
    c. a fixed-ratio schedule of reinforcement
    d. continuous reinforcement

Concept: III. D. 2. e. 1 Competency: 36
Question Type: *Applied*

40. Reynold is having trouble with doing his homework for school. How could you help him using a token economy?

____

____

____

____

Concept: III. E. 1. a Competency: 37
Question Type: *Applied*

41. John Watson once remarked that he could teach children to be whatever type of profession he wanted. Does the same idea apply to animals? Why or why not?

____

____

____

____

Concept: III. F Competency: 38
Question Type: *Conceptual*

42. Rebecca has a mental representation of the locations of the dorms, the library, and the commons on her campus. This is called:
    a. three-dimensional representation
    b. latent learning
    c. a cognitive map
    d. observational learning

Concept: III. F. 2. a Competency: 39
Question Type: *Applied*

43. Tolman's latent learning differs from operant conditioning because it:

____

Concept: III. F. 2. b Competency: 40
Question Type: *Factual*

44. How can the distinction between present vs. future rewards help us understand why dieting is so difficult? To what other experience can this apply?

____

____

____

____

Concept: III. F. 3. a Competency: 41
Question Type: *Conceptual*

45. ____
involve the transmission of cultural knowledge and are analogous to genes, in that they are selectively passed on from one generation to the next.

Concept: IV. A. 1 Competency: 42
Question Type: *Factual*

46. The key difference between observational learning and classical or operant learning is

____

Concept: IV. B. 1 Competency: 43
Question Type: *Factual*

47. Bandura's classic "Bobo Study" showed which of the following?
    a. Children who saw other children act aggressively on film acted aggressively themselves.
    b. Children who saw other children act aggressively acted aggressively themselves, but only if they saw the actor do so in person.
    c. The presence of a "Bobo" doll led to aggressive reactions from children.
    d. Children who saw an adult act aggressively on film acted aggressively themselves.

Concept: IV. B. 2 Competency: 44
Question Type: *Factual*

48. Alex wears baggy pants because he noticed that Dr. Sloan does so. This illustrates the importance of:
    a. shaping
    b. modelling
    c. vicarious reinforcement
    d. immediate reinforcement

Concept: IV. B. 5. a Competency: 45
Question Type: *Applied*

49. Debbie was playing outside and saw her sister poke a bee hive with a stick. Debbie then saw her sister get stung. Debbie could describe what her sister did—but she would not do the behaviour herself. Her reaction reflects:
    a. latent learning
    b. vicarious learning
    c. the transmission of a meme
    d. modelling

Concept: IV. B. 6 Competency: 46
Question Type: *Applied*

50. Based on the available evidence, should parents let children be exposed to violent media content? Support your claim.

____

____

____

____

Concept: IV. B. 7 Competency: 47
Question Type: *Applied*

51. ____
fire in the brain when you watch someone engage in behaviour. They are the same neurons that would fire if you were engaging in the behaviour yourself.

Concept: IV. B. 8 Competency: 48
Question Type: *Factual*

52. Ben wants to develop a new energy drink that contains ingredients that will produce neurotransmitters that create the greatest sense of reinforcement. He should try to produce which neurotransmitter?
    a. dopamine
    b. serotonin
    c. epinephrine
    d. GABA

Concept: V. A Competency: 49
Question Type: *Applied*

53. A study of hungry rats on a near-starvation diet for 10 days showed that when the rats were given a choice between food and the opportunity to administer intracranial self-stimulation to their pleasure centres the rats chose:
    a. eating 100 percent of the time
    b. eating more than 80 percent of the time
    c. electrical stimulation more than 80 percent of the time
    d. eating and electrical stimulation, each about 50 percent of the time

    Concept: V. A. 1. a Competency: 50
    Question Type: *Factual*

54. Tim was teasing his friend Rita by tapping her on the back. At first Rita jumped when Tim tapped her, but after a while she stopped responding to the taps entirely. Her decrease in responding reflects:
    a. an orienting response
    b. habituation
    c. sensitization
    d. secondary reinforcement

    Concept: V. B. 2 Competency: 51
    Question Type: *Applied*

55. Sensitization is associated with:
    a. a reduction of neurotransmitters
    b. a complete cessation in the production of neurotransmitters
    c. an increase in the release of neurotransmitters
    d. extinction of neurotransmitter production

    Concept: V. B. 3 Competency: 52
    Question Type: *Factual*

56. The strengthening of synaptic connections so that postsynaptic neurons are more easily activated is called:
    a. an orienting response
    b. long-term potentiation
    c. intracranial self-stimulation
    d. latent learning

    Concept: V. B. 3 Competency: 53
    Question Type: *Factual*

PSYCHOLOGY AND SOCIETY

Using the principles of sound experimental design (see Chapter 2, "Research Methodology," of your textbook), design a study to test the hypothesis that exposure to media violence causes adolescents to become more aggressive. How will you select your participants, and how will you assign them to experimental conditions? What are your independent variable(s) and your dependent variable(s)? How will you measure the dependent variable?

SUMMING UP AND MEASURING UP

How Does Operant Conditioning Differ from Classical Conditioning?

Whereas classical conditioning involves the learned association between two events, operant conditioning involves the learned association between a behaviour and its consequences. B. F. Skinner developed the concept of operant conditioning to explain why some behaviours are repeated and others are not. Reinforcement increases a behaviour's likelihood of being repeated, whereas punishment reduces that likelihood. If a reinforcer increases a behaviour when presented, it is a positive reinforcer; if it increases the behaviour when removed, it is a negative reinforcer. Although Skinner was confident that operant conditioning could ultimately explain all behaviour, his theories have faced a number of challenges. Chief among these are that it is difficult to change instinctive behaviours and that learning can take place without reinforcement. Modern learning theorists recognize cognitive processes' influence on behaviour and biology's constraints on it. Models based on economic theory have become increasingly useful for understanding how animals choose among reinforcers.

1. When arriving at their preschool class each day, most of the children drop their belongings by the door; a few throw their belongings near the coat rack and cubby area. The teacher asks all of them to always hang up their coats and place their lunch boxes in the cubbies. Which strategy would increase the likelihood that the children will engage in the desired behaviours?
    a. At nap time, the teacher should give stickers to children who put away their belongings upon entering the classroom.
    b. As the children enter the classroom, the teacher should give stickers to those who put away their belongings.
    c. Initially, the teacher should give stickers to children who leave their belongings near the coat rack and cubby area. Later, the teacher should give stickers only to children who put away a coat or a lunch box. Later, the teacher should give stickers only to children who put away both coat and lunch box.

2. In the above preschool example, which of the following strategies likely would harness the power of social learning? Choose as many as apply.
    a. The teacher could put on a short skit, playing a child entering the classroom and being rewarded

for putting coat and lunch box in the correct places.

b. The teacher could send the children's parents a weekly newsletter announcing which child received the "Most Responsible Student" award.

c. As soon as the teacher saw a child put his or her belongings away, the teacher could say something like, "Wow, you really know how to take care of your things. You are so grown up and responsible!"

ANSWER KEY

Item **Answer**

1. Learning
2. d
3. b
4. a
5. c
6. b
7. neutral; conditioning trial; critical trials
8. c
9. b
10. b
11. c
12. d
13. c
14. d
15. a
16. phobia
17. c
18. c, d, b, a
19. c
20. Classical conditioning focuses on the associations between stimuli. When someone uses drugs, the experiences (people, places, things) that coincide with that experience become linked. Often these associations are hard to break. During drug recovery, anything associated with drug use runs the risk of increasing cravings.
21. By quickly and easily associating the food that makes us sick we can avoid becoming poisoned. This makes us more likely to survive and pass on our genes. We should also quickly learn aversions to dangerous animals (e.g., lion vs. mouse), situations (e.g., heights, fire, submersion in water), and the dark (because we have very poor night vision it is easier for predators to successfully attack us under this condition).
22. b
23. a, a, b, b
24. a
25. Operant/Instrumental/Skinnerian; classical/respondent/Pavlovian
26. a
27. Examples will vary, but anything that increases the likelihood that the response (studying) will be repeated. Some possibilities include: learning new information, good grades, praise from parent(s), praise from your instructor, and a feeling of satisfaction. You might also reinforce yourself by saying, "if I finish 10 questions with correct answers I will let myself watch TV."
28. Skinner Box (Operant Chamber)
29. c
30. a
31. d
32. b
33. d
34. Punishment is most effective when it is reasonable, immediate, and unpleasant. However, punishment leads to a desire to avoid the punishment and not necessarily to act appropriately. Punishment may also lead to negative feelings such as fear and anxiety. Physical forms of punishment are particularly ineffective.
35. c
36. No. In fact, it would most likely work in an opposite fashion where punishment is more effective when it is continuous and less effective when it is partial. For example, if a speeding ticket is the punishment for speeding, punishing speeding every single time with a ticket would reduce speeding much more than if you got a ticket only some of the times you speed.
37. a
38. b
39. a
40. Institute a system where every time Reynold does his homework, he gets a check mark. Then identify a reinforcer that Reynold really wants so that he has to accumulate enough check marks to get the reinforcer. For example, if he gets 10 check marks he can play video games for an extra hour.
41. The idea of animals being a tabula rasa is a bit of a stretch. Animals can be taught to do a wide range of behaviours, but only within their biological constraints. A dolphin can be taught to jump through hoops, but it may be much more difficult, if not impossible, to have it lie on its back or toss a ball.
42. c
43. shows that learning can occur without reinforcement.
44. Dieting involves foregoing positive experiences (i.e., rewards) in the present for rewards in the future, while skipping one's diet involves reaping rewards in the present and foregoing rewards in the future. People much prefer present rewards. The same concept can be applied to putting purchases on one's credit card.
45. Memes
46. observational experience does not involve direct experience (classical and operant do)

47. d
48. b
49. b
50. Most of the evidence points to negative consequences of media violence. Studies routinely show that children who are exposed to aggression subsequently act more aggressive. The statistical effect size for the link is nearly the same as the link between smoking and lung cancer. In contrast, some point out that the studies consider some behaviour aggressive that others would consider playful. It is also impossible to establish cause and effect in a real life context because there are so many other intervening variables.
51. Mirror neurons
52. a
53. c
54. b
55. c
56. b

Psychology and Society

Your answer should mention the need for random assignment to conditions, the need for a control condition, and the use of outcome measures that can be measured objectively. You may also mention the need to define the population (e.g., all adolescents or just 10–12-year-olds? boys and girls, or just one or the other?), the need to define the IV (e.g., what specific kind or kinds of violence?), the need to define the DV (e.g., what exactly constitutes an aggressive behaviour? only one specific aggressive behaviour?), the need to test for alternative explanations, and so forth.

Summing Up and Measuring Up

1. c. Initially, the teacher should give stickers to children who leave their belongings near the coat rack and cubby area. Later, the teacher should give stickers only to children who put away a coat or a lunch box. Later, the teacher should give stickers only to children who put away both coat and lunch box.

2. a. The teacher could put on a short skit, playing a child entering the classroom and being rewarded for putting coat and lunch box in the correct places.; c. As soon as the teacher saw a child put her or his belongings away, the teacher could say something like, "Wow, you really know how to take care of your things. You are so grown up and responsible!"

KEY TERM EXERCISES

acquisition

Textbook Definition:
Your Own Definition:
Your Own Example:

behaviour modification

Textbook Definition:
Your Own Definition:
Your Own Example:

classical conditioning, or Pavlovian conditioning

Textbook Definition:
Your Own Definition:
Your Own Example:

cognitive map

Textbook Definition:
Your Own Definition:
Your Own Example:

conditioned response (CR)

Textbook Definition:
Your Own Definition:
Your Own Example:

conditioned stimulus (CS)

Textbook Definition:
Your Own Definition:
Your Own Example:

continuous reinforcement

Textbook Definition:
Your Own Definition:
Your Own Example:

extinction

Textbook Definition:
Your Own Definition:
Your Own Example:

fixed schedule

Textbook Definition:
Your Own Definition:
Your Own Example:

habituation

Textbook Definition:
Your Own Definition:
Your Own Example:

interval schedule

Textbook Definition:
Your Own Definition:
Your Own Example:

latent learning

Textbook Definition:
Your Own Definition:
Your Own Example:

law of effect

Textbook Definition:
Your Own Definition:
Your Own Example:

learning

Textbook Definition:
Your Own Definition:
Your Own Example:

long-term potentiation (LTP)

Textbook Definition:
Your Own Definition:
Your Own Example:

meme

Textbook Definition:
Your Own Definition:
Your Own Example:

mirror neurons

Textbook Definition:
Your Own Definition:
Your Own Example:

modelling

Textbook Definition:
Your Own Definition:
Your Own Example:

negative punishment

Textbook Definition:
Your Own Definition:
Your Own Example:

negative reinforcement

Textbook Definition:
Your Own Definition:
Your Own Example:

observational learning

Textbook Definition:
Your Own Definition:
Your Own Example:

operant conditioning, or instrumental conditioning

Textbook Definition:
Your Own Definition:
Your Own Example:

partial reinforcement

Textbook Definition:
Your Own Definition:
Your Own Example:

partial-reinforcement extinction effect

Textbook Definition:
Your Own Definition:
Your Own Example:

phobia

Textbook Definition:
Your Own Definition:
Your Own Example:

positive punishment

Textbook Definition:
Your Own Definition:
Your Own Example:

positive reinforcement

Textbook Definition:
Your Own Definition:
Your Own Example:

ratio schedule

Textbook Definition:
Your Own Definition:
Your Own Example:

reinforcer

Textbook Definition:
Your Own Definition:
Your Own Example:

Rescorla-Wagner model

Textbook Definition:
Your Own Definition:
Your Own Example:

sensitization

Textbook Definition:
Your Own Definition:
Your Own Example:

shaping

Textbook Definition:
Your Own Definition:
Your Own Example:

spontaneous recovery

Textbook Definition:
Your Own Definition:
Your Own Example:

stimulus discrimination

Textbook Definition:
Your Own Definition:
Your Own Example:

stimulus generalization

Textbook Definition:
Your Own Definition:
Your Own Example:

unconditioned response (UR)

Textbook Definition:
Your Own Definition:
Your Own Example:

unconditioned stimulus (US)

Textbook Definition:
Your Own Definition:
Your Own Example:

variable schedule

Textbook Definition:
Your Own Definition:
Your Own Example:

vicarious learning

Textbook Definition:
Your Own Definition:
Your Own Example:

CHAPTER 7 Attention and Memory

CONCEPT MAP

I. How Does Attention Determine What Is Remembered?
   A. Attention
      1. Multi-tasking
   B. Visual Attention Is Selective and Serial
      1. Parallel Processing
   C. Auditory Attention Allows Selective Listening
      1. Cocktail Party Phenomenon
      2. Shadowing
   D. Selective Attention Can Operate at Multiple Stages of Processing
      1. Filter Theory
      2. Change Blindness

II. What Are the Basic Stages of Memory?
   A. Definition of Memory
   B. Three Phases of Information Processing
      1. Acquisition/Encoding Phase
      2. Storage
      3. Retrieval
   C. Three Parts of the Modal Memory Model
      1. Sensory Memory
      2. Short-Term Memory
         a. Memory Span and Chunking
         b. Working Memory
            1. Central Executive
            2. Phonological Loop
            3. Visuospatial Sketchpad
            4. Episodic Buffer
      3. Long-Term Memory
         a. Long-Term vs. Working Memory
            1. Serial Position Effect
               A. Primacy Effect
               B. Recency Effect
         b. Encoding into Long-Term Memory
            1. Overlearning
            2. Distributed vs. Massed Practice
         c. Memory for Familiar Objects
         d. Evolutionary Theory and Long-Term Memory

III. What Are the Different Long-Term Memory Systems?
   A. Old View vs. New View
   B. Explicit Memory
      1. Explicit vs. Declarative Memory
      2. Types of Explicit Memory
         a. Episodic Memory
         b. Semantic Memory
   C. Implicit Memory
      1. False Fame Effect
      2. Repetition Priming
      3. Procedural (Motor) Memory
   D. Prospective Memory

IV. How Is Information Organized in Long-Term Memory?
   A. Long-Term Storage
      1. Explicit and Implicit Processes
      2. Levels of Processing
         a. Maintenance Rehearsal
         b. Elaborative Rehearsal
   B. Schemas
      1. Organizational Framework
      2. Biased Encoding
   C. Networks of Association
      1. Spreading Activation Model
   D. Retrieval Cues
      1. Recognition vs. Recall

2. Encoding Specificity
    a. Context-Dependent Memory
    b. State-Dependent Memory

V. What Brain Processes Are Involved in Memory?
  A. Physical Location of Memory
    1. Equipotentiality
  B. Medial Temporal Lobes and the Consolidation of Declarative Memories
    1. Anterograde Amnesia
    2. Consolidation
      a. Reconsolidation
  C. The Hippocampus and Spatial Memory
    1. Morris Water Maze Test
  D. The Frontal Lobes
    1. Types of Memory Involved
    2. Role in Encoding
    3. Role in Working Memory
  E. Neurochemistry Influences Memory
    1. Meaningfulness of Stimuli
      a. Ephinephrine
    2. The Amygdala and the Neurochemistry of Emotion
      a. Norepinephrine
      b. Sex Differences
      c. Trauma and Stress
        1. Posttraumatic Stress Disorder (PTSD)
          A. Ethics of Altering Memory

VI. When Do People Forget?
  A. Forgetting
    1. Methods of Savings
  B. Sins of Memory Related to Forgetting
    1. Transience
      a. Interference
        1. Proactive
        2. Retroactive
    2. Blocking
      a. Tip-of-the-Tongue Phenomenon
    3. Absentmindedness
      a. Shallow Encoding
      b. Cultural Differences in Change Blindness
  C. Amnesia
    1. Retrograde Amnesia
    2. Anterograde Amnesia

VII. How Are Memories Distorted?
  A. Flashbulb Memories
    1. Inaccuracy of Flashbulb Memories
    2. Stress and Memory
      a. von Restorff Effect
  B. Source Misattributions
    1. Cryptomnesia
  C. Accuracy of Eyewitnesses
    1. Cross-Ethnic Identification
    2. Suggestibility and Misinformation
    3. Eyewitness Confidence
  D. People Have False Memories
    1. Source Amnesia
    2. Childhood Amnesia
    3. Creating False Memories
    4. Confabulation
      a. Capgras Syndrome
  E. Repressed Memories
  F. Memory Bias
  G. Neuroscience May Make It Possible to Distinguish "True" and False Memories
    1. Imaging as Lie Detector

VIII. How Can We Improve Learning and Memory?
  A. Mnemonic Strategies
    1. Practice
    2. Elaborate the Material
    3. Overlearn
    4. Get Adequate Sleep
    5. Use Verbal Mnemonics
      a. Acronyms
    6. Use Visual Imagery
      a. Method of Loci

CHAPTER SUMMARY

How Does Attention Determine What Is Remembered?

• Visual Attention Is Selective and Serial: Simple searches for stimuli that differ in only one primary factor (e.g., size, colour, orientation) occur automatically and rapidly, but searches for objects that are the conjunction of two or more properties (e.g., red and large) occur slowly and serially.

• Auditory Attention Allows Selective Listening: We can attend to more than one message at a time but not well. Evidence indicates that we weakly process some unattended information.

• Selective Attention Can Operate at Multiple Stages of Processing: We often miss large objects in our visual field when we are attending to something else, a phenomenon known as change blindness.

What Are the Basic Stages of Memory?

• Sensory Memory Is Brief: Visual and auditory memories are maintained long enough to ensure a continuous sensory experience.

• Working Memory Is Active: Immediate active memory is limited. Chunking reduces information into units that are easier to remember. The four components of working memory are the central executive, the phonological loop, the visuospatial sketchpad, and the episodic buffer.

• Long-Term Memory Is Relatively Permanent: Long-term memory (LTM) is the potentially indefinite storage of all memories. Meaningful memories are stored in LTM in networklike structures.

What Are the Different Long-Term Memory Systems?

• Explicit Memory Involves Conscious Effort: Explicit, declarative memories that we consciously remember include personal events (episodic memory) and general knowledge (semantic memory).

• Implicit Memory Occurs without Deliberate Effort: Procedural (motor) memories of how to do things automatically are implicit.

• Prospective Memory Is Remembering to Do Something: Prospective memory has "costs" in terms of reducing attention and reducing working memory capacity.

How Is Information Organized in Long-Term Memory?

• Long-Term Memory Is Based on Meaning: Memory processes include encoding, storage, and retrieval. Elaborative rehearsal involves encoding information in more meaningful ways and results in better memory than maintenance (repetition) rehearsal.

• Schemas Provide an Organizational Framework: Schemas, cognitive structures of meaning, aid the organization of memories. Cultural variations in schemas produce differences in what and how information is remembered.

• Information Is Stored in Association Networks: Networks of associations are formed by nodes of information, which are linked together and are activated by spreading activation.

• Retrieval Cues Provide Access to Long-Term Storage: According to the encoding specificity principle, any stimulus encoded along with an experience can later trigger the memory of the experience. The memory's context is also activated.

What Brain Processes Are Involved in Memory?

• There Has Been Intensive Effort to Identify Memory's Physical Location: Research has revealed that a number of specific brain regions contribute to learning and memory.

• The Medial Temporal Lobes Are Important for Consolidation of Declarative Memories: The process of consolidation of new memories involves changes in neural connections. The hippocampus, a structure in the medial temporal lobe, is important for declarative memories. Place cells in the hippocampus aid spatial memory.

• The Frontal Lobes Are Involved in Many Aspects of Memory: Extensive neural networks connect the frontal lobes with other memory regions of the brain. Activation of neurons in the frontal lobe is associated with deeper meaning.

• Neurochemistry Underlies Memory: Neurochemicals modulate the storage of memories. Epinephrine enhances memory. The amygdala is probably responsible for memory modulation through activity in its norepinephrine receptors.

When Do People Forget?

• Transience Is Caused by Interference: Forgetting over time occurs because of interference from both old and new information.

• Blocking Is Temporary: The tip-of-the-tongue phenomenon is a person's temporary trouble retrieving the right word, usually due to interference from a similar word.

• Absentmindedness Results from Shallow Encoding: Inattentive or shallow processing causes memory failure.

• Amnesia Is a Deficit in Long-Term Memory: Both injury and disease can result in amnesia, either the inability to recall past memories (retrograde) or the inability to form new memories (anterograde).

How Are Memories Distorted?

• Flashbulb Memories Can Be Wrong: The strong emotional response that attends a flashbulb memory may affect the memory's strength and accuracy.

• People Make Source Misattributions: A person can misremember the source of a memory (source misattribution). In cryptomnesia, a person thinks he or she has come up with a new idea, but has only retrieved a memory.

• People Are Bad Eyewitnesses: Poor eyewitness recall occurs, particularly when people try to identify those of other ethnicities. Suggestibility leads to misinformation.

• People Have False Memories: Immature frontal lobes cause childhood amnesia. False memories can be implanted. Confabulation can occur because of brain damage.

• Repressed Memories Are Controversial: Some therapeutic techniques can result in false repressed memories.

• People Reconstruct Events to Be Consistent: People tend to maintain consistency between their past memories, their current knowledge, and their current attitudes.

• Neuroscience May Make It Possible to Distinguish between "True" and "False" Memories: By examining brain activity at encoding and retrieval, researchers hope to distinguish true from false memories. The current research has many flaws, but the techniques may be improved.

How Can We Improve Learning and Memory?

• Mnemonics Are Useful Strategies for Learning: Mnemonics include practicing at retrieval through frequent testing, overlearning, getting enough sleep, spacing study sessions, and using imagery.

COMPETENCY MODEL

How Does Attention Determine What Is Remembered?

Attention

1. Describe the effects of multi-tasking.
2. Which features are processed quickly, automatically, and effortlessly in a visual search?

Auditory Attention Allows Selective Listening

3. What is the cocktail party phenomenon?
4. How does the technique of shadowing tell us about auditory attention?

Selective Attention Can Operate at Multiple Stages of Processing

5. Explain filter theory.
6. What is change blindness? What does it tell us about memory?

What Are the Basic Stages of Memory?

Definition of Memory

7. Define memory.

Three Phases of Information Processing

8. Identify the three phases of information processing.

Three Parts of the Modal Memory Model

9. Identify the three parts of the modal memory model.
10. Distinguish between sensory, short-term, and long-term memory.
11. How does chunking aid short-term memory?
12. Identify the three main components of working memory.
13. Explain the serial position effect.
14. Distinguish between primacy and recency effects.
15. What does it mean to overlearn something?
16. Distinguish between distributed and massed practice.
17. How good is our memory for familiar objects?
18. What does evolutionary theory suggest about the contents of long-term memory?

What Are the Different Long-Term Memory Systems?

Old View vs. New View

19. Distinguish between the old and new view of memory.

Explicit Memory

20. Distinguish between explicit and declarative memory.
21. Distinguish between episodic and semantic memory.

Implicit Memory

22. Understand how the false fame effect works.
23. How is procedural memory different from most other types of memory?

Prospective Memory

24. What is prospective memory?

How Is Information Organized in Long-Term Memory?

Long-Term Storage

25. Know how are memories are stored.
26. Distinguish between maintenance and elaborative rehearsal.
27. Explain how to make use of elaborative rehearsal.

Schemas

28. Identify the utility of using schemas.
29. Be aware of the potential problems of using schemas.

Networks of Association

30. Explain the spreading activation model.

Retrieval Cues

31. Distinguish between recognition and recall.

32. Understand the distinction between context-dependent and state-dependent memory.

What Brain Processes Are Involved in Memory?

Physical Location of Memory

33. Explain the idea of equipotentiality. Is it correct?

Medial Temporal Lobes and the Consolidation of Declarative Memories

34. How does anterograde amnesia influence memories?
35. What is consolidation? How is it different from reconsolidation?
36. Identify the brain structure involved in consolidation.

The Hippocampus and Spatial Memory

37. What is the role of the hippocampus in spatial memory?

The Frontal Lobes

38. What is the role of the frontal lobes in memory?

Neurochemistry Influences Memory

39. Identify the neurotransmitter that indicates an experience is meaningful.
40. Identify the role of the amygdala in memory.
41. Describe the findings on sex differences related to memory for emotional events.

When Do People Forget?

Forgetting

42. Understand the process of forgetting.
43. Explain how Ebbinghaus studied the method of savings.

Sins of Memory Related to Forgetting

44. What is transience?
45. Distinguish between proactive and retroactive interference.
46. What occurs during blocking?
47. Explain what leads to absentmindedness.

Amnesia

48. Distinguish between retrograde and anterograde amnesia.

How Are Memories Distorted?

Flashbulb Memories

49. What characterizes a flashbulb memory?
50. What is the von Restorff effect?

Source Misattributions

51. What is source misattribution?
52. What is cryptomnesia?

Accuracy of Eyewitnesses

53. Describe factors that influence the accuracy of eyewitness testimony.
54. Explain suggestibility and the misinformation effect.
55. Identify ways in which laboratory studies may not be ideal for eyewitness accuracy.
56. How does confidence relate to eyewitness accuracy?

People Have False Memories

57. What does source amnesia involve? What is childhood amnesia?
58. What does confabulation involve?
59. How is Capgras syndrome an example of confabulation?

Memory Bias

60. Understand how memory bias influences memory.

Neuroscience May Make It Possible to Distinguish between "True" and "False" Memories

61. Explain how neuroscience techniques could be used as a lie detector.

How Can We Improve Learning and Memory?

Mnemonic Strategies

62. Identify six mnemonic strategies that can help improve memory.

KNOWLEDGE CHECK

1. Olivia is a busy university student and seemingly always has more to do than there are hours in the day. As a result she tends to multi-task by doing several things at once such as checking email, text-messaging, doing homework, and watching television. Research on multi-tasking suggests that:
   a. her performance on all tasks will be diminished
   b. her performance on her homework will be diminished, but the other activities will not
   c. her performance on the social tasks (email and texting) will be diminished, but the other activities will not
   d. her performance will not be diminished for any of the tasks

   Concept: I. A. 1 Competency: 1
   Question Type: *Applied*

2. At a party, Frank was listening to his friend Eddy. Suddenly, Frank told Eddy to be quiet because he heard a pretty girl across the room mention his name, and he wanted to listen in on her conversation. Frank's hearing his name from across the room reflects:
   a. screened processing
   b. unconscious inference
   c. visual search
   d. the cocktail party phenomenon

   Concept: I. C. 1 Competency: 3
   Question Type: *Applied*

3. Pete is in an experiment where he has different information presented in each of his ears, but his task is to repeat back information from only one ear. Research on auditory attention suggests that:
   a. he will hear sound and understand meaning from the unattended ear
   b. he will hear sound from the unattended ear but not discern meaning
   c. he won't be able to detect any sound from the unattended ear
   d. he won't be able to detect any sound from the unattended ear and will have a very hard time repeating information from the ear he is listening to

   Concept: I. C. 2 Competency: 4
   Question Type: *Factual*

4. ________________________________
   suggests that people have a limited capacity for sensory information and thus screen incoming information, letting in only the most important.

   Concept: I. D. 1 Competency: 5
   Question Type: *Factual*

5. Siena and Steve were out having dinner at a local restaurant. Their waiter came over to introduce himself. At that moment a loud crash came from the kitchen that distracted Siena and Steve, during which time their waiter went to see what happened. The original waiter was replaced by another waiter. Siena and Steve never realized it was a different waiter. This is known as:
   a. filtered memory
   b. change blindness
   c. face blindness
   d. selective blindness

   Concept: I. D. 2 Competency: 6
   Question Type: *Factual*

6. ________________________________
   is the capacity of the nervous system to acquire and retain usable skills and knowledge, allowing organisms to benefit from experience.

   Concept: II. A Competency: 7
   Question Type: *Factual*

7. Concept: II. B Competency: 8
   Question Type: *Factual*

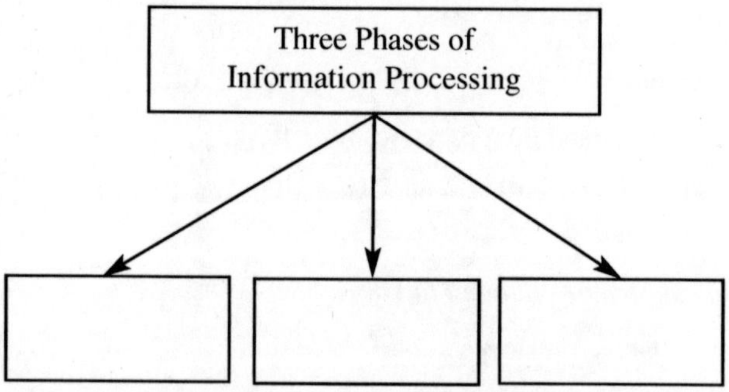

8. Concept: II. C Competency: 9
   Question Type: *Factual*

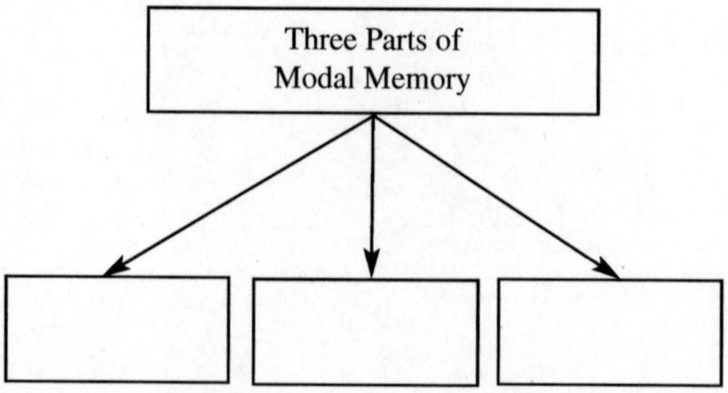

9. Joe looked up his friend Jack's phone number. He was repeating the number to himself as he looked for the phone. He repeated the number to keep it in which memory system?
   a. sensory memory
   b. short-term memory
   c. echoic memory
   d. long-term memory

   Concept: II. C Competency: 10
   Question Type: *Applied*

10. For each of the following, please match the aspect of the modal memory model with the proper term:

____	Consists of our fleeting thoughts, feelings, and impressions of the world	a) Sensory memory
____	Consists of iconic and echoic memory	b) Short-term memory
____	Holds information indefinitely	c) Long-term memory
____	Holds information for less than one second	
____	Also called working or immediate memory	
____	The "hard drive" in the computer analogy	

   Concept: II. C Competency: 10
   Question Type: *Factual*

11. Which of the following lists would probably be most difficult to keep in STM (short-term memory)?
   a. UNHYTFE
   b. NBC BMW IPOD TXT MTV
   c. PSYCHOLOGICAL ASSESSMENT
   d. 17762008911

   Concept: II. C. 2. a Competency: 11
   Question Type: *Applied*

12. Concept: II. C. 2. b Competency: 12
   Question Type: *Factual*

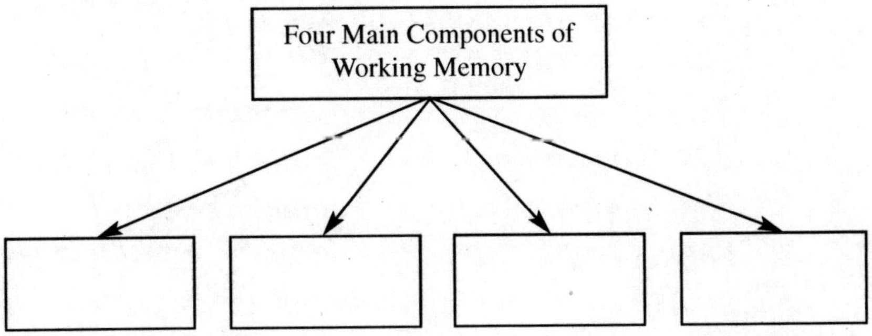

13. Avi wrote a grocery list of 12 items. Unfortunately he forgot the list at home and could only remember the first few items on the list and the last few. His recall demonstrates:
   a. anterograde amnesia
   b. the serial position effect
   c. the encoding specificity principle
   d. the phonological loop effect

   Concept: II. C. 3. a. 1 Competency: 13
   Question Type: *Applied*

14. Based on your knowledge of the primacy and recency effects, when you are studying for a big test that has lots of information that covers multiple chapters (e.g., 1–6), what is the worst thing you could do? What is the solution?

   ____

   ____

   ____

   ____

   Concept: II. C. 3. a. 1 Competency: 14
   Question Type: *Conceptual*

15. Sara is with a group of her friends when they are introduced to a guy she would really like to get to know. According to the research on primacy effects, when among her friends should she be introduced if she wants the guy to remember her?
   a. first
   b. last
   c. in the middle
   d. either first or last

   Concept: II. C. 3. a. 1 Competency: 14
   Question Type: *Applied*

16. Madeline is studying the periodic table for her chemistry class. She is confident she knows all the information but keeps studying because she learned in her psychology class that it was helpful for her memory. What concept does this demonstrate?
    a. the long-term memory effect
    b. distributed practice
    c. massed practice
    d. overlearning

    Concept: II. C. 3. b. 1 Competency: 15
    Question Type: *Applied*

17. Liam has a history test tomorrow and has decided to pull an all-nighter. This is known as ________________. Unfortunately it does not promote long-term memory.
    a. the long-term memory effect
    b. distributed practice
    c. massed practice
    d. overlearning

    Concept: II. C. 3. b. 2 Competency: 16
    Question Type: *Applied*

18. Think of a friend who is frequently on his cellphone. The next time you see him, ask him to describe the screen on his cellphone without looking at it. Chances are, your friend will have a hard time doing so accurately. Why?
    a. People have a hard time describing the details of anything.
    b. A cellphone screen is very familiar and we often don't encode details for familiar things.
    c. People have a hard time describing things, and an easier time describing animals.
    d. Your friend likely has experienced insufficient repetition to commit it to long-term memory.

    Concept: II. C. 3. c Competency: 17
    Question Type: *Applied*

19. According to evolutionary theory our memory is best for information that assists ________________ and________________________________.

    Concept: II. C. 3. d Competency: 18
    Question Type: *Factual*

20. The old view of memory stated: ________________________________.
    However the new view states: ________________________________.

    Concept: III. A Competency: 19
    Question Type: *Factual*

21. Antonia is taking a test in her health class. She is most likely using which type of memory?
    a. procedural
    b. explicit
    c. episodic
    d. declarative

    Concept: III. B. 1 Competency: 20
    Question Type: *Applied*

22. When Cybil asked Marcia what the word *mnemonics* means, Marcia had no difficulty providing the definition. Marcia's knowledge of the word exemplifies her:
    a. semantic memory
    b. explicit memory
    c. episodic memory
    d. declarative memory

    Concept: III. B. 2 Competency: 21
    Question Type: *Applied*

23. If someone asked you whether Todd Heatherton was famous you might say the name sounds familiar but you might not know where you heard it, leading you to conclude he must be famous. This is an example of:
    a. declarative memory
    b. the false fame effect
    c. episodic memory
    d. the false consensus effect

    Concept: III. C. 1 Competency: 22
    Question Type: *Applied*

24. Which of the following is an example of procedural memory?
    a. knowing how to hold a pencil and sign your name in cursive writing
    b. remembering the type of bike you first learned to ride
    c. knowing the definition of the word *perspicacious*
    d. recalling you had a really terrible meal at a specific restaurant

    Concept: III. C. 3 Competency: 23
    Question Type: *Applied*

25. After class Morrison has to remember to pay a parking ticket at the campus police station. He is relying on which type of memory?
    a. procedural
    b. prospective
    c. episodic
    d. declarative

    Concept: III. D Competency: 24
    Question Type: *Applied*

26. Memories are stored based on ________________________________.

    Concept: IV. A. 2 Competency: 25
    Question Type: *Factual*

27. When studying for a biology test Juan repeated the definitions of the words over and over to himself. Which of the following is true of this method of study?
    a. It is maintenance rehearsal.
    b. It is elaborative rehearsal.
    c. It results in deep processing.
    d. It is the most effective way to study for an exam.

    Concept: IV. A. 2 Competency: 26
    Question Type: *Applied*

28. We know from levels of processing that elaborative rehearsal promotes greater long-term memory. How could you use this to study?

    ____

    ____

    ____

    ____

    Concept: IV. A. 2 Competency: 27
    Question Type: *Applied*

29. Stan walks into a fast food restaurant chain that he has never been to before. Although he has never been to this chain, he has a good idea of how to order his food, and what he has to pay for (food and drink) and what is complementary (he doesn't have to pay for napkins, salt, pepper, etc.). What is Stan using?
    a. maintenance rehearsal
    b. elaborative rehearsal
    c. encoding specificity
    d. a schema

    Concept: IV. B. 1 Competency: 28
    Question Type: *Applied*

30. Schemas help us process information and focus our attention on the key information. In the context of stereotypes, how could this be a bad thing?

    ____

    ____

    ____

    ____

    Concept: IV. B. 2 Competency: 29
    Question Type: *Conceptual*

31. Every time Stacy has mint chocolate chip ice cream she always remembers getting ice cream from the ice cream truck the very first time when she was a kid. This then conjures up memories of the summer, spending time at the lake, and fireworks. This demonstrates which concept?
    a. networking
    b. elaborative rehearsal
    c. spreading activation
    d. equipotentiality

    Concept: IV. C. 1 Competency: 30
    Question Type: *Applied*

32. When you take exams, multiple-choice questions involve ________________ while fill-in-the-blank and short-answer involve ________________. The former is easier, while the latter is more challenging.
    a. recognition; recall
    b. recall; recognition
    c. encoding; recognition
    d. recall; reconsolidation

    Concept: IV. D. 1 Competency: 31
    Question Type: *Applied*

33. Terri studied for her psychology test in the room where the test was given. Jenn studied for the exam in her dorm. If everything else about Jenn and Terri was the same, but Terri did better on the exam, what could account for this?
    a. context-dependent memory
    b. procedural memory
    c. state-dependent memory
    d. recognition

    Concept: IV. D. 2 Competency: 32
    Question Type: *Applied*

34. According to the research on state-dependent memory, if you drink a lot of coffee when studying, what should you do when taking the exam?
    a. You should avoid coffee to highlight the differences between studying and testing.
    b. You should avoid all fluids.
    c. You should drink alcohol.
    d. You should drink coffee.

    Concept: IV. D. 2 Competency: 32
    Question Type: *Applied*

35. The idea that memory is distributed throughout the brain is known as ________________. This idea has been shown to be ________________.
    a. reconsolidation; incorrect
    b. equipotentiality; incorrect
    c. equipotentiality; partially correct
    d. reconsolidation; partially correct

    Concept: V. A Competency: 33
    Question Type: *Factual*

36. Suki watched a TV show in which the main character had an accident and could not remember her name, her husband, or her profession. This character is suffering from:
a. retrograde amnesia
b. anterograde amnesia
c. blocking
d. the von Restorff effect

Concept: V. B. 1 Competency: 34
Question Type: *Applied*

37. Chloe read a book about European history. Now her brain is different than it was before due to ____________________. Later when recalling the information, she'll store information in memory through ____________________.
a. reconsolidation; consolidation
b. consolidation; reconsolidation
c. reconsolidation; blocking
d. procedural memory; blocking

Concept: V. B. 2. a Competency: 35
Question Type: *Applied*

38. When he recovered from his accident, Bruno discovered he could remember things like his name, his elementary school, and his mother's birthday. However, he could not put any new information into his long-term memory. Bruno is probably suffering from:
a. damage to the hypothalamus
b. damage to the cerebellum
c. damage to the medial parietal lobe
d. damage to the medial temporal lobe

Concept: V. B. 2 Competency: 36
Question Type: *Applied*

39. On the first day of classes Jordon located all of his classes on campus. Later that night he dreamed about how to get from class to class. This is because dreams help with ____________________, thanks in part to the ____________________.
a. reconsolidation; hippocampus
b. consolidation; hippocampus
c. reconsolidation; amygdala
d. consolidation; amygdala

Concept: V. C Competency: 37
Question Type: *Applied*

40. Activity in the ____________________ lobe is indicative of deeper encoding. Activity in the ____________________ lobe is indicative of which information will be remembered compared to what will be forgotten.
a. frontal; temporal
b. temporal; frontal
c. frontal; frontal
d. temporal; temporal

Concept: V. D Competency: 38
Question Type: *Applied*

41. The neurotransmitter that indicates an experience is meaningful is ____________________.

Concept: II. E. 1. a Competency: 39
Question Type: *Factual*

42. Which brain structure seems to be most important for influencing the effects of neurotransmitters on memory?
a. the amygdala
b. the corpus callosum
c. the cerebellum
d. the hypothalamus

Concept: VI. B 1 Competency: 40
Question Type: *Applied*

43. There is a sex difference for memory of emotional events such that ____________________ not only reported greater emotional reactions to negative pictures but also showed much better memory for those pictures.

Concept: VI. B. 1. b Competency: 41
Question Type: *Factual*

44. Is it possible to purposefully forget something?

____

____

____

____

Concept: VI. A Competency: 42
Question Type: *Conceptual*

45. Ebbinghaus had people memorize nonsense syllables (nuh, jad, rep) to see how long it took them to memorize them all. At a later time he tested them to see how long it took them to relearn the lists. He found that people were quicker the second time. This best demonstrates the concept of:
a. consolidation
b. reconsolidation
c. transcience
d. savings

Concept: VI. B. 1 Competency: 43
Question Type: *Applied*

46. It is easier for high school sophomores to remember the names of their teachers from freshman year, but much more difficult for a senior to remember his or her freshman teachers. This example best demonstrates which concept?
    a. blocking
    b. reconsolidation
    c. transience
    d. savings

    Concept: VI. B. 1 Competency: 44
    Question Type: *Applied*

47. Sanjay just got a new combination lock. He is upset because he keeps trying to open it with his old combination. His problem demonstrates:
    a. blocking
    b. proactive interference
    c. transience
    d. retroactive interference

    Concept: VI. B. 1. a Competency: 45
    Question Type: *Applied*

48. Ginny knows that she knows the name of the guy who sat next to her in biology, but she just can't think of it. Her memory lapse exemplifies:
    a. blocking
    b. proactive interference
    c. transience
    d. retroactive interference

    Concept: VI. B. 2 Competency: 46
    Question Type: *Applied*

49. When Brett was introduced to a friend's cousin, he was not paying attention. Later, when asked the cousin's name, Brett had no idea what it was. Brett's memory problem exemplifies:
    a. transience
    b. absentmindedness
    c. amnesia
    d. retroactive interference

    Concept: VI. B. 3 Competency: 47
    Question Type: *Applied*

50. La'roi had perfect memory for everything up until his 21st birthday. Since that time he hasn't been able to form new memories. He most likely suffers from:
    a. proactive interference
    b. anterograde amnesia
    c. retrograde amnesia
    d. retroactive interference

    Concept: VI. C Competency: 48
    Question Type: *Applied*

51. All of the following are likely to be flashbulb memories EXCEPT:
    a. what you did yesterday
    b. your first kiss
    c. the time you broke your leg
    d. the day your child is born

    Concept: VII. A Competency: 49
    Question Type: *Applied*

52. The von Restorff effect refers to the finding that:
    a. distinctive information is recalled more easily than less distinctive information
    b. familiar information is recalled more easily than less familiar information
    c. emotional memories are less accurate than other kinds of episodic recall
    d. alcohol abuse can cause anterograde amnesia

    Concept: VII. A. 2. a Competency: 50
    Question Type: *Factual*

53. Noah believes he first learned about the facts of life from his older brother. In reality, his parents were the first to discuss this subject with him. Noah's mistaken recall reflects:
    a. absentmindedness
    b. source misattribution
    c. cryptomnesia
    d. the von Restorff effect

    Concept: VII. B Competency: 51
    Question Type: *Applied*

54. When writing a paper, Jenn thought she defined a term in a new way; in fact she had directly quoted one of the articles she had read. This exemplifies:
    a. absentmindedness
    b. source misattribution
    c. cryptomnesia
    d. the von Restorff effect

    Concept: VII. B. 1 Competency: 52
    Question Type: *Applied*

55. Liz, a Caucasian, was an eyewitness to a crime. She will be most likely to correctly identify the perpetrator if the perpetrator:
    a. is a university student
    b. is Caucasian
    c. is black
    d. carried a gun

    Concept: VII. C. 1 Competency: 53
    Question Type: *Applied*

56. Donna's older sisters kept telling her that she had been lost as a little kid and they could not find her for two hours. In fact, this never happened. But Donna believes that she can remember it. Donna is demonstrating:
    a. cryptomnesia
    b. source misattribution
    c. absentmindedness
    d. suggestibility

    Concept: VII. C. 2 Competency: 54
    Question Type: *Applied*

57. Why might memory be better for real life events than it is in laboratory experiments in the context of eyewitness accuracy?

    ____

    ____

    ____

    ____

    Concept: VII. C. 2 Competency: 55
    Question Type: *Conceptual*

58. Erin, Allison, and Fortune all witnessed a robbery while they were out at a local coffee shop. When police interview them afterward and they independently give their description of the robber, Fortune is extremely confident about what she saw, Allison is not confident at all, and Erin is moderately confident. Which of the following is true about their accuracy?
    a. Allison is likely to be the least accurate.
    b. Erin is likely to be the least accurate.
    c. Fortune is likely to be the most accurate.
    d. Allison and Erin will have similar accuracies, but Fortune will be the least accurate.

    Concept: VII. C. 3 Competency: 56
    Question Type: *Applied*

59. Jodi surprised all her friends when she could supply the definition of *narcolepsy* in class. When asked where she had learned it, Jodi had no idea. She just knew it. Jodi is demonstrating:
    a. false recognition
    b. childhood amnesia
    c. the sleeper effect
    d. source amnesia

    Concept: VII. D. 1 Competency: 57
    Question Type: *Applied*

60. After his stroke, Mr. Smith had problems with his memory. When asked about his family he will report what he knows and then will seem to just make things up—even though he has no intent to deceive anyone. Mr. Smith demonstrates:
    a. confabulation
    b. childhood amnesia
    c. the sleeper effect
    d. source amnesia

    Concept: VII. D. 4 Competency: 58
    Question Type: *Applied*

61. Mr. Wendel believes his family has been replaced by imposters. He is probably suffering from:
    a. Korsakoff's syndrome
    b. childhood amnesia
    c. Capgras syndrome
    d. source amnesia

    Concept: VII. D. 4 Competency: 59
    Question Type: *Factual*

62. Edyta is a professor in the English Department. When recalling her early school performance she recalls herself excelling in school. However, her parents recall her being an average student. Edyta's memory best exemplifies:
    a. confabulation
    b. childhood amnesia
    c. memory bias
    d. source amnesia

    Concept: VII. F Competency: 60
    Question Type: *Applied*

63. In terms of lie detection, brain imaging may be helpful in making the key distinction between a lie, which occurs when the person reports something he or she knows is not true, and ______________________.

    Concept: VII. G Competency: 61
    Question Type: *Factual*

64. Concept: VIII Competency: 62
    Question Type: *Factual*

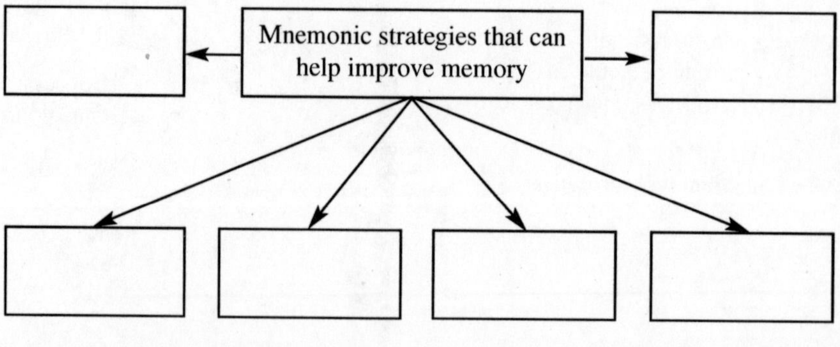

PSYCHOLOGY AND SOCIETY

Search the Internet and newspapers for a story about a person who has suffered a traumatic brain injury (e.g., a soldier, a motorcyclist, or a skateboarder). Many such individuals experience significant memory impairment. Prepare a short lecture discussing the nature of the brain injury, its relevance to memory impairment, and an explanation of how your understanding of material from this chapter contributes to your understanding of the news story.

SUMMING UP AND MEASURING UP

How Does Attention Determine What Is Remembered?

Attention is the ability to focus on certain stimuli, which are passed along to be encoded into a neural code that can be retrieved later. It is an adaptation that enables a person to handle the huge amounts of information in an environment without becoming overloaded. Still, a person can fail to notice major changes in an environment because his or her attention is focused on something else. Visual search tasks indicate that we process visual information about basic features (e.g., colour, motion, orientation, and size) quickly, automatically, and effortlessly. Searching for stimuli that are the conjunction of two basic features (e.g., trying to find large, red numbers) is slow, serial, and effortful. A key aspect of attention is that it is selective; we can choose the stimuli to which we attend, as when we ignore a nearby conversation in favour of a more interesting one farther away. However, to an extent we can process some information contained in sensory stimuli to which we are not consciously attending. Attention can operate in multiple stages of perceptual processing, and unattended stimuli are reduced rather than eliminated from further processing. Because of change blindness, people have difficulty remembering events to which they did not attend.

When can we successfully multi-task?

a. when we are young and have the capacity to handle large amounts of information
b. when we can effectively focus attention on events important for our survival
c. when the tasks meet the requirements for preattentive processing and thus happen automatically
d. when the tasks are easy

What Brain Processes Are Involved in Memory?

Research during the past 30 years has demonstrated that memories are encoded in distributed networks of neurons in relatively specific brain regions. We now know that damage to the medial temporal lobes, especially to the hippocampus, causes significant memory disturbances. These medial temporal regions are important for the consolidation of declarative memories into storage. The sites of memory storage are the brain structures involved in perception. Fear causes activation of the amygdala, which is associated with the strengthening of memories. There are sex differences in which of the brain regions underlie emotional memories and perhaps in the processing of emotional memories. Memories for highly traumatic events can result in posttraumatic stress disorder, a clinical disorder diagnosed when the traumatic memories intrude into everyday life.

Which of the following statements are accurate about glucose's role in learning and in memory? Indicate as many as apply.

a. Glucose is detrimental to learning and memory.
b. Glucose is necessary for learning and memory.
c. The amygdala has glucose receptors that help strengthen neural connections.
d. Epinephrine and norepinephrine cause more glucose to be released so the brain can use it during learning and remembering.
e. Sugary drinks have a positive effect on memory in older adults.

ANSWER KEY

Item Answer

1. a
2. d
3. a
4. Filter theory
5. b
6. Memory
7. acquisition/encoding phase; storage; retrieval
8. sensory; short-term; long-term
9. b
10. b, a, c, a, b, c
11. a
12. central executive; the phonological loop; the visuospatial sketchpad; the episodic buffer
13. b
14. Primacy suggests we remember the things we look at first, recency suggests we remember the things we looked at last. For a test we want to remember everything so the worst thing we could do is to study the chapters/information in the same order. By doing that we are likely to remember chapter 1 and 6 very well, and not the others. To solve this, you should study things in different orders so that all information can benefit from primacy and recency. Keeping study times short will also decrease the amount that falls in the middle (i.e., between primacy and recency).

15. a
16. d
17. c
18. b
19. reproduction; survival
20. memories differed in terms of their strength and accessibility; memory is not just one entity; rather, it is a process that involves several interacting systems
21. d
22. a
23. b
24. a
25. b
26. meaning
27. a
28. The basic idea behind elaborative rehearsal is giving yourself more cues to help remember things. This is accomplished by linking new information to other information. If you learn a concept in class, you should think of how it could be used in other contexts, how it relates to other information you have learned, or how it relates to you. All of these are means of elaboration.
29. d
30. Answers will vary, but generally if we have a negative view of a group of people our schema would help us maintain that belief. For example, if we distrust lawyers and meet someone new who happens to be a lawyer, our schema could make us pay extra attention to signs of dishonesty. This may lead us to not notice all of the positive qualities our new lawyer acquaintance may have.
31. c
32. b
33. a
34. d
35. c
36. a
37. b
38. d
39. b
40. c
41. epinephrine
42. a
43. females
44. This would be extremely difficult, and probably impossible. For example, do everything in your power to forget the letters ARL. It may seem easy to say, "don't try to remember it in the first place." But for something to be forgotten it has to be encoded initially. Otherwise it wasn't forgotten; it was never put into memory. You may try to forget something by not rehearsing or repeating it, but how will you know what to avoid repeating (ARL) without remembering what it is you are trying not to repeat (ARL).
45. d
46. c
47. d
48. a
49. b
50. b
51. a
52. a
53. b
54. c
55. b
56. d
57. In a real life accident or crime, there are many more cues in the environment to help our memory. Additionally, a real life event may be more surprising, emotional, and consequently memorable, whereas participants in a lab expect that they will be safe and that things aren't real. Eyewitnesses also have the ability in real life to retell their story numerous times, making it more consistent.
58. d
59. d
60. a
61. c
62. c
63. a false or faulty memory, which occurs when the person remembering the event honestly believes it is true.
64. practice; elaborate the material; overlearn; get adequate sleep; use verbal mnemonics; use visual imagery

Psychology and Society

A complete and accurate answer will reflect authentic understanding of brain anatomy, of brain function, and of the related processes and impairments of memory. The "lecture" should connect ideas from the chapter to the individual news story (e.g., naming the kind of amnesia a person is suffering).

Summing Up and Measuring Up

How Does Attention Determine What Is Remembered?

d. when the tasks are easy

What Brain Processes Are Involved in Memory?

b. Glucose is necessary for learning and memory.
d. Epinephrine and norepinephrine cause more glucose to be released so the brain can use it during learning and remembering.
e. Sugary drinks have a positive effect on memory in older adults.

KEY TERM EXERCISES

absentmindedness

Textbook Definition:
Your Own Definition:
Your Own Example:

amnesia

Textbook Definition:
Your Own Definition:
Your Own Example:

anterograde amnesia

Textbook Definition:
Your Own Definition:
Your Own Example:

blocking

Textbook Definition:
Your Own Definition:
Your Own Example:

change blindness

Textbook Definition:
Your Own Definition:
Your Own Example:

chunking

Textbook Definition:
Your Own Definition:
Your Own Example:

confabulation

Textbook Definition:
Your Own Definition:
Your Own Example:

consolidation

Textbook Definition:
Your Own Definition:
Your Own Example:

cryptomnesia

Textbook Definition:
Your Own Definition:
Your Own Example:

declarative memory

Textbook Definition:
Your Own Definition:
Your Own Example:

encoding

Textbook Definition:
Your Own Definition:
Your Own Example:

encoding specificity principle

Textbook Definition:
Your Own Definition:
Your Own Example:

episodic memory

Textbook Definition:
Your Own Definition:
Your Own Example:

explicit memory

Textbook Definition:
Your Own Definition:
Your Own Example:

flashbulb memories

Textbook Definition:
Your Own Definition:
Your Own Example:

forgetting

Textbook Definition:
Your Own Definition:
Your Own Example:

implicit memory

Textbook Definition:
Your Own Definition:
Your Own Example:

long-term memory (LTM)

Textbook Definition:
Your Own Definition:
Your Own Example:

memory

Textbook Definition:

Your Own Definition:

Your Own Example:

memory bias

Textbook Definition:

Your Own Definition:

Your Own Example:

mnemonics

Textbook Definition:

Your Own Definition:

Your Own Example:

modal memory model

Textbook Definition:

Your Own Definition:

Your Own Example:

parallel processing

Textbook Definition:

Your Own Definition:

Your Own Example:

post-traumatic stress disorder (PTSD)

Textbook Definition:

Your Own Definition:

Your Own Example:

proactive interference

Textbook Definition:

Your Own Definition:

Your Own Example:

procedural memory

Textbook Definition:

Your Own Definition:

Your Own Example:

prospective memory

Textbook Definition:

Your Own Definition:

Your Own Example:

reconsolidation

Textbook Definition:

Your Own Definition:

Your Own Example:

retrieval

Textbook Definition:
Your Own Definition:
Your Own Example:

retrieval cue

Textbook Definition:
Your Own Definition:
Your Own Example:

retroactive interference

Textbook Definition:
Your Own Definition:
Your Own Example:

retrograde amnesia

Textbook Definition:
Your Own Definition:
Your Own Example:

schema

Textbook Definition:
Your Own Definition:
Your Own Example:

semantic memory

Textbook Definition:
Your Own Definition:
Your Own Example:

sensory memory

Textbook Definition:
Your Own Definition:
Your Own Example:

serial position effect

Textbook Definition:
Your Own Definition:
Your Own Example:

short-term memory (STM)

Textbook Definition:
Your Own Definition:
Your Own Example:

source amnesia

Textbook Definition:
Your Own Definition:
Your Own Example:

source misattribution

Textbook Definition:
Your Own Definition:
Your Own Example:

suggestibility

Textbook Definition:
Your Own Definition:
Your Own Example:

spatial memory

Textbook Definition:
Your Own Definition:
Your Own Example:

transience

Textbook Definition:
Your Own Definition:
Your Own Example:

storage

Textbook Definition:
Your Own Definition:
Your Own Example:

working memory (WM)

Textbook Definition:
Your Own Definition:
Your Own Example:

CHAPTER 8 Thinking and Intelligence

CONCEPT MAP

- I. How Does the Mind Represent Information?
  - A. Cognition
    - 1. Analogical Representation
    - 2. Symbolic Representation
  - B. Mental Images are Analogical Representations
    - 1. Rotated Images
    - 2. Mind's Eye vs. Actual Sight
    - 3. Limits of Analogical Representations
  - C. Concepts Are Symbolic Representations
    - 1. Categorization
    - 2. Concept
      - a. Defining Attribute Model
        - 1. Problems with the Model
      - b. Prototype Model
      - c. Exemplar Model
  - D. Schemas Organize Useful Information about Environments
    - 1. Schema
      - a. Scripts
      - b. Gender Roles
        - 1. Gender Traits are Not Mutually Exclusive
      - c. Essential Elements of Schemas
      - d. Utility of Schemas
- II. Cognition
  - A. Reasoning
    - 1. Deductive
      - a. Conditional Syllogism
      - b. Categorical Syllogism
    - 2. Inductive
  - B. Decision Making
    - 1. Normative Models
      - a. Expected Utility Theory
    - 2. Descriptive Models
      - a. Algorithms
      - b. Heuristics
        - 1. Availability
        - 2. Representativeness
          - A. Base Rate
      - c. Framing
        - 1. Prospect Theory
          - A. Loss Aversion
      - d. Affective Forecasting
    - 3. Good Decision Makers
  - C. Problem-Solving
    - 1. Organization of Subgoals
    - 2. Sudden Insight
    - 3. Changing Representations
      - a. Restructuring
      - b. Mental Sets
        - 1. Functional Fixedness
    - 4. Conscious Strategies
      - a. Working Backward
      - b. Finding an Appropriate Analogy
    - 5. Paradox of Choice
      - a. Satisficer vs. Maximizer
      - b. Jobs and Marriage
  - D. Ethics: Cognition-Enhancing Drugs
- III. Intelligence
  - A. Intelligence Is Assessed with Psychometric Tests
    - 1. Achievement
    - 2. Aptitude
    - 3. Intelligence Scales
    - 4. Intelligence Quotient
      - a. Mental Age vs. Chronological Age
      - b. Normal Distribution

    5. Validity
    6. Cultural Bias
B. General Intelligence Involves Multiple Components
    1. Fluid vs. Crystallized Intelligence
    2. Multiple Intelligences
    3. Sternberg's Intelligences
        a. Analytical
        b. Creative
        c. Practical
    4. Emotional Intelligence
    5. Importance of g
C. Intelligence Is Associated with Cognitive Performance
    1. Speed of Mental Processing
        a. Simple vs. Choice Reaction Time
        b. Inspection Time
    2. Working Memory
    3. Brain Structure and Function
        a. Overall Size
        b. Brain Regions
    4. Savants
D. Genes and Environment Influence Intelligence
    1. Behavioural Genetics
        a. Social Multiplier
    2. Environmental Factors
        a. Nutrition
        b. Adoption
        c. Enriched Environments
        d. Schooling
        e. Flynn Effect
    3. Group Differences
        a. Sex
        b. Race
            1. Biologically Meaningful?
            2. Different Life Circumstances
            3. Stereotype Threat

CHAPTER SUMMARY

How Does the Mind Represent Information?

• Mental Images Are Analogical Representations: Thoughts can take the form of visual images. The primary visual cortex is activated proportionately to the size of an image in the mind's eye; therefore, mental visual imagery involves the same underlying brain processes involved in seeing the external world. Symbolic knowledge affects the ways we use visual imagery.

• Concepts Are Symbolic Representations: Concepts are mental representations of subtypes of broad knowledge categories; the concept of *cat,* for example, is a subcategory of *animals.* Concepts may be formed by defining attributes, prototypes, or exemplars. Many categories have fuzzy boundaries; we have no simple way of telling a cat from a dog or a rat, for example, since conceptually they are similar (*four-legged, hairy animals*).

• Schemas Organize Useful Information about Environments: We develop schemas based on our real-life experiences. Scripts are schemas that allow us to form expectations about the sequence of events in a given context.

How Do We Make Decisions and Solve Problems?

• People Use Deductive and Inductive Reasoning: Deductive reasoning proceeds from a general statement to specific applications. Syllogisms are formal structures of deduction. For example: If all psychology textbooks are fun to read and this is a psychology textbook, then this textbook will be fun to read. Inductive reasoning proceeds from specific instances to general conclusions. For example: If you read many psychology textbooks and find them interesting, you can infer that psychology books generally are interesting.

• Decision Making Often Involves Heuristics: Expected utility models assume people behave according to logical processes, such as always selecting the outcome that will yield the greatest reward. Descriptive models highlight reasoning shortcomings, specifically the use of mental shortcuts (i.e., heuristics) that sometimes lead to faulty decisions. We select information to confirm our conclusions, to avoid loss or regret or both, and to be consistent with a problem's framing.

• Problem Solving Achieves Goals: Problem solving involves reaching a goal, which usually is broken down into subgoals. Insights come suddenly, when we see elements of a problem in new ways. Restructuring aids solutions; mental sets and functional fixedness inhibit solutions.

How Do We Understand Intelligence?

• Intelligence Is Assessed with Psychometric Tests: The Binet-Simon Intelligence Test was the first modern test of mental ability and led to the concept of IQ as a ratio of mental age and chronological age. This test was later normed to a distribution with a mean of 100 and standard deviation of 15; therefore, average ability is between 85 and 115. The question of the validity of intelligence tests persists, and one significant criticism is cultural bias. Other ways of assessing intelligence also have the potential for bias, as when interview questions are ambiguous.

• General Intelligence Involves Multiple Components: Charles Spearman concluded that a general intelligence component exists, known as g. Fluid intelligence is involved when people solve novel problems, whereas crystallized intelligence is accumulated knowledge retrieved from memory.

Howard Gardner has proposed a theory of multiple intelligences that includes linguistic, mathematical/logical, spatial, bodily-kinesthetic, intrapersonal, and interpersonal abilities. Robert Sternberg has proposed that there are three types of intelligence: analytical, creative, and practical. Emotional intelligence is the ability to understand emotions and use them appropriately.

• Intelligence Is Associated with Cognitive Performance: Speed of mental processing (e.g., reaction time, inspection time) is part of intelligence. The relationship of working memory to intelligence seems to involve attention. The size and activity of the brain's frontal lobes are related to qualities of intelligence, but since brain size is altered by experience, we cannot infer cause from this correlation.

• Genes and Environment Influence Intelligence: Behavioural genetics has revealed genes' substantial influence in setting the limits of the expression of intelligence. Environmental factors, including nutrition, parenting, schooling, and intellectual opportunities generally seem to establish where IQ falls within the genetic limits.

• Group Differences in Intelligence Have Multiple Determinants: One of the most contentious areas in psychology concerns group differences in intelligence. Females and males score differently, on average, on different measures of intelligence, with some measures favouring males and others favouring females. Thus there is no overall sex difference in intelligence. Race differences in intelligence are confounded with a multitude of environmental differences, including income, discrimination, and health care. Additionally, many scientists question the idea of race as referring to anything more than a small number of human differences, such as skin colour.

COMPETENCY MAP

How Does the Mind Represent Information?

Cognition

1. Define cognition.
2. Distinguish between analogical and symbolic representations.

Mental Images Are Analogical Representations

3. Explain mind's eye.
4. Describe the limits of analogical representations.

Concepts Are Symbolic Representations

5. What is the benefit of categorization?
6. Explain the defining attribute model and identify problems with it.
7. Explain the prototype model.

Schemas Organize Useful Information about Environments

8. What is a schema?
9. What is useful about scripts?
10. Understand how gender roles can be problematic.
11. What does it mean to say that gender traits are not mutually exclusive?

How Do We Make Decisions and Solve Problems?

Cognition

12. Distinguish among reasoning, decision making, and problem solving.

Reasoning

13. How are deductive and inductive reasoning different?
14. Distinguish between conditional and categorical syllogisms.
15. What concepts are deductive and inductive reasoning similar to?

Decision Making

16. How do normative and descriptive models view human decision making?
17. How are algorithms different from heuristics?
18. Distinguish between an algorithm and a heuristic approach.
19. Describe the availability and representativeness heuristics.
20. Describe how framing influences decision making.
21. What does prospect theory suggest about decision making?
22. What is affect forecasting?
23. What are some benefits of being a good decision maker?

Problem Solving

24. How can organizing subgoals facilitate problem solving?
25. What does it mean to have insight?
26. What does it mean to restructure one's thinking?
27. Provide an example of functional fixedness.
28. What two conscious strategies can we employ to help problem solving?

29. Describe the paradox of choice. How does this apply to jobs and marriage?

How Do We Understand Intelligence?

Ethics: Cognition-Enhancing Drugs

30. Identify the ethical issues related to cognition-enhancing drugs.

Intelligence Is Assessed with Psychometric Tests

31. Define intelligence.
32. Distinguish between achievement and aptitude.
33. Provide examples of prominent intelligence scales, what they measure, and who developed them.
34. Explain how IQ is calculated.
35. What is considered "normal" for intelligence? How do we know?
36. Address the validity of intelligence tests.
37. Explain the issue of cultural bias in intelligence tests.

General Intelligence Involves Multiple Components

38. Distinguish between fluid and crystallized intelligence.
39. Explain the theory behind Gardner's multiple intelligences.
40. Identify Sternberg's three main types of intelligence.
41. What are the four components of emotional intelligence?
42. What is the importance of g?

Intelligence Is Associated with Cognitive Performance

43. Distinguish simple and choice reaction time.
44. Understand how brain structure relates to intelligence.
45. Describe what it means to be a savant.

Genes and Environment Influence Intelligence

46. What is the role of a social multiplier?
47. What are the four main environmental factors that are known to influence intelligence?
48. Explain the Flynn effect.
49. Identify intelligence differences based on sex.
50. Identify the problems associated with making claims of intelligence differences based on race.
51. Explain how stereotype threat influences performance.

KNOWLEDGE CHECK

1. ________________________________ is directly associated with manipulating how the brain represents information and the act of thinking.

   Concept: I. A Competency: 1
   Question Type: *Factual*

2. Your mental image of a bicycle shares some physical characteristics with an actual bicycle and so is a(n) ____________ representation.
   a. symbolic
   b. physical
   c. deficient
   d. analogical

   Concept: I. A Competency: 2
   Question Type: *Applied*

3. Your mental image of love is a(n) ____________________ representation.
   a. symbolic
   b. physical
   c. deficient
   d. analogical

   Concept: I. A Competency: 2
   Question Type: *Applied*

4. While in her art history class, the professor asked everyone to think of the Mona Lisa. As Chelsea complied, it was as if she was seeing a picture in her brain that was identical to the first time she saw a picture of the Mona Lisa. This is known as:
   a. a physical representation
   b. categorization
   c. the mind's eye
   d. an analogical representation

   Concept: I. B. 2 Competency: 3
   Question Type: *Applied*

5. On a geography quiz, Marc mistakenly indicated that Toronto was further north than Minneapolis, and that Los Angeles was further west than Spokane, Washington. His analogical representation was most likely undermined by:
   a. his physical representation
   b. his symbolic representation
   c. his mind's eye
   d. his incomplete prototype

   Concept: I. B. 3 Competency: 4
   Question Type: *Applied*

6. In an experiment, Janice was given a rose, a toy car, a toy truck, a tulip, a daisy, and a toy ambulance. When told to put these in groups, she put the rose, tulip, and daisy together because they had petals, leaves, and stems. This kind of grouping is called ______________ and is useful because ______________.
   a. symbolic representation; improves the strength of our conceptual thought
   b. symbolic representation; it reduces the amount of knowledge we must hold in memory
   c. categorization; it reduces the amount of knowledge we must hold in memory
   d. prototyping; improves the strength of our conceptual thought

   Concept: I. C. 1 Competency: 5
   Question Type: *Applied*

7. According to the defining attribute model, each concept is characterized by a list of features that are necessary to determine if an object is a member of a category. All of the following are problems with the model EXCEPT:
   a. the model suggests that membership within a category is on an all-or-none basis
   b. all attributes of a category are equally salient in terms of defining the given category
   c. the concepts are organized hierarchically, such that they can be superordinate or subordinate to each other
   d. all members of a category are equal in category membership—no one item is a better fit than any other

   Concept: I. C. 2. a Competency: 6
   Question Type: *Factual*

8. According to which model is an apple more repre - sentative of the category of fruits than a kiwi is?
   a. prototype model
   b. representativeness model
   c. defining attribute model
   d. hierarchical model

   Concept: I. C. 2. a Competency: 7
   Question Type: *Factual*

9. Chase believes that classrooms contain seats, desks, blackboards, students, and professors, so this is what he expects to see. This may be a description of Chase's ______________ for classrooms.
   a. script
   b. validity
   c. schema
   d. analog

   Concept: I. D. 1 Competency: 8
   Question Type: *Applied*

10. Shyla is going on a job interview. She knows ahead of time about the company with which she is interviewing, what questions to expect, to dress professionally and to bring a resume. This is due to her ______________ for job interviews.
    a. analog
    b. prototype
    c. exemplar
    d. script

    Concept: I. D. 1. a Competency: 9
    Question Type: *Applied*

11. Shane is in the process of hiring a general manager for his sporting goods store. Although several women appear qualified based on their previous experience, Shane is reluctant to hire a woman. He believes women are generally unsuited for positions of leadership because they lack assertiveness. This demonstrates Shane's use of:
    a. scripts
    b. gender roles
    c. sex-typed behaviours
    d. prototypes

    Concept: I. D. 1. b Competency: 10
    Question Type: *Applied*

12. A common "male" trait is assertiveness, while a common "female" trait is caring. What do we know about these traits?
    a. Nearly all men tend to be assertive.
    b. Nearly all women tend to be caring.
    c. If a person is assertive they are unlikely to be caring.
    d. The traits are not mutually exclusive.

    Concept: I. D. 1. b. 1 Competency: 11
    Question Type: *Applied*

13. In ______________________________, we determine if a conclusion is valid using information we believe is true.

    ______________________________ usually involves selecting among alternatives.

    ______________________________ involves moving from a present state to a goal state.

    Concept: II Competency: 12
    Question Type: *Factual*

14. Mary is a philosophy professor. Sue believes that all philosophy professors are fascinating. She is therefore sure that Mary will be fascinating. Sue is using which kind of reasoning to make this judgment?
    a. analysis reasoning
    b. deductive reasoning
    c. inductive reasoning
    d. meta-reasoning

    Concept: II. A Competency: 13
    Question Type: *Applied*

15. After meeting four intelligent people on the swim team, Albert concludes that swimmers must be a bright group. Albert drew this conclusion based on what kind of reasoning?
    a. analysis reasoning
    b. deductive reasoning
    c. inductive reasoning
    d. meta-reasoning

    Concept: II. A Competency: 13
    Question Type: *Applied*

16. Cooper is a dog. All dogs are friendly. Therefore Cooper is friendly. This is an example of:
    a. a categorical syllogism
    b. a conditional syllogism
    c. a premise
    d. inductive reasoning

    Concept: II. A. 1 Competency: 14
    Question Type: *Applied*

17. Deductive reasoning is to ______________, as inductive reasoning is to ______________.
    a. top-down processing; top-down processing
    b. top-down processing; bottom-up processing
    c. bottom-up processing; top-down processing
    d. bottom-up processing; bottom-up processing

    Concept: II. A Competency: 15
    Question Type: *Conceptual*

18. ______________________________ models of decision making have viewed humans as optimal decision makers, while ______________________________ models have tried to account for the tendencies humans have to misinterpret and misrepresent the probabilities underlying many decision-making scenarios.

    Concept: II. B Competency: 16
    Question Type: *Factual*

19. Why does it make sense for computers to use algorithms instead of heuristics?

    ____

    ____

    ____

    ____

    Concept: II. B. 2 Competency: 17
    Question Type: *Conceptual*

20. Imagine that your professor gave you a set of keys and asked you to go to her car to get her textbook. Once in the parking you realize she never told you which type of car she had. You decide to try every key in every car. This is an example of a ______________ approach.
    a. representativeness heuristic
    b. availability heuristic
    c. algorithm
    d. prototype

    Concept: II. B. 2 Competency: 18
    Question Type: *Applied*

21. When asked whether more words begin with the letter "k" or whether more have "k" in the third position, Monique said that more started with "k" because she could think of them more easily. She is using:
    a. representativeness heuristic
    b. availability heuristic
    c. confirmation bias
    d. the gambler's fallacy

    Concept: II. B. 2. b Competency: 19
    Question Type: *Applied*

22. When Marion first met Khoung she figured he must be an engineer because he liked math puzzles, woodworking, and computers. Her guess about his profession can be explained by the:
    a. representativeness heuristic
    b. availability heuristic
    c. confirmation bias
    d. the gambler's fallacy

    Concept: II. B. 2. b Competency: 19
    Question Type: *Applied*

23. Tristan needs to buy a new shirt. At the store, he finds two shirts that he likes. Shirt A is priced at 39.99, marked down from 49.99; Shirt B is priced at 39.99 with no markdown. Tristan gets Shirt A because it is a better value. This demonstrates the effect of _______________ on decision making.
    a. the representativeness heuristic
    b. the availability heuristic
    c. confirmation bias
    d. framing

    Concept: II. B. 2. c Competency: 20
    Question Type: *Applied*

24. MacKenzie is an investor who wants to buy stocks. At company A, making a trade costs 19.99, but there is a surcharge of 5 dollars if the trade is done over the phone. At company B, making a trade costs 24.99, but there is a discount of 5 dollars if the trade is done online. According to prospect theory and the concept of loss aversion MacKenzie will choose:
    a. company A
    b. company B
    c. company A or B because both cost essentially the same for online trading
    d. neither company because they both involve risk

    Concept: II. B. 2. c. 1 Competency: 21
    Question Type: *Applied*

25. Boyd and Stefan are talking about their futures. According to affective forecasting, what will Stefan predict about how he would feel if he got a divorce?
    a. Stefan will accurately predict his ability to cope, but underestimate how negatively he will feel.
    b. Stefan will overestimate how negatively he will feel about divorce, and underestimate his ability to cope with it.
    c. Stefan will overestimate how negatively he will feel about divorce, and overestimate his ability to cope with it.
    d. Stefan will accurately predict his emotional feeling, but underestimate his ability to cope.

    Concept: II. B. 2. d Competency: 22
    Question Type: *Applied*

26. Good decision makers have been shown to have better life outcomes. Why might this be?

    ____

    ____

    ____

    ____

    Concept: II. B. 3 Competency: 23
    Question Type: *Conceptual*

27. Isabelle has to write a senior thesis in order to graduate with honours. What is the best approach for her to take?
    a. Think of the end product and work backward.
    b. Focus on the overall thesis and work on everything simultaneously.
    c. Break up the larger task of doing a thesis into several smaller issues. Then work on everything simultaneously.
    d. Break up the larger task of doing a thesis into several smaller issues. Then work on each smaller problem individually.

    Concept: II. C. 1 Competency: 24
    Question Type: *Applied*

28. Little Tony's room is a mess: Books are on the floor, clothing is all over, the bed is unmade, and so on. His mother helps him out by telling him to first put the books back on the shelf. When that is done she tells him to hang up the clothing. Finally she tells him to make his bed. Tony's mom has helped him solve his problem by using:
    a. subgoals
    b. functional fixedness
    c. framing
    d. a mental set

    Concept: II. C. 1 Competency: 24
    Question Type: *Applied*

29. Sheryl was trying to solve a statistics problem and getting nowhere until she suddenly saw how to get to the answer. Once she saw this, the problem was easy. Sheryl's experience demonstrates:
    a. functional fixedness
    b. sudden insight
    c. affective problem solving
    d. counterfactual reasoning

    Concept: II. C. 2 Competency: 25
    Question Type: *Applied*

30. The common phrase "thinking outside of the box" is most like which concept?
    a. restructuring
    b. finding an appropriate analogy
    c. working backward
    d. a mental set

    Concept: II. C. 3 Competency: 26
    Question Type: *Conceptual*

31. When she got to class, Mona noticed that the seam of her shirt was opened. She was embarrassed by this and wanted some way to close the seam until she could get home and mend it. Although she knew she had tape with her, it did not occur to her that she could tape the seam closed. Mona is suffering from:
    a. the availability heuristic
    b. the framing effect
    c. functional fixedness
    d. counterfactual thinking

    Concept: II. C. 1 Competency: 27
    Question Type: *Applied*

32. Conscious strategies to problem solve can include working backward, which involves

    ______________________________________.

    Another strategy, finding an appropriate analogy, involves ______________________________.

    Concept: II. C. 3 Competency: 28
    Question Type: *Factual*

33. Rihanna has it all. She is very popular, wealthy, and accomplished. She can pretty much have any job she wants, and could marry any person she wants. As a result, she is frustrated and finds her predicament unsatisfying. She often wishes there were fewer options. This demonstrates:
    a. the paradox of choice
    b. failure to think outside of the box
    c. the influence of mental sets
    d. counterfactual thinking

    Concept: II. C. 4 Competency: 29
    Question Type: *Applied*

34. What concerns are associated with the use of cognition-enhancing drugs? Does a good memory guarantee success?

    ____

    ____

    ____

    ____

    Concept: II. D Competency: 30
    Question Type: *Conceptual*

35. The human ability to use knowledge to solve problems, understand complex ideas, learn quickly, and adapt to environmental changes is known as:
    a. framing
    b. intelligence
    c. cognition
    d. insight

    Concept: III Competency: 31
    Question Type: *Factual*

36. The test a person takes to get their driver's permit is an example of an ______________ test, while the driving (i.e., road) portion of the test is an example of an ______________ test.
    a. achievement; application
    b. achievement; aptitude
    c. aptitude; application
    d. aptitude; achievement

    Concept: III. A Competency: 32
    Question Type: *Applied*

37. For each of the following, please match the description of the intelligence test with the creator:

    ____ Developed a test that has a verbal part that measures such aspects as comprehension, vocabulary, and general knowledge
    ____ Developed the first intelligence test
    ____ Measured children's vocabulary, memory, skill with numbers, and other mental abilities
    ____ Modified an existing test for use in the United States
    ____ Developed a test that has a performance part that involves arranging pictures in proper order, assembling parts to make a whole object, and identifying missing features from a picture

    a) Alfred Binet and Théodore Simon
    b) Lewis Terman
    c) David Wechsler

    Concept: III. A. 3 Competency: 33
    Question Type: *Factual*

38. What would be the IQ, as defined by Stern, of a child with a mental age of 12 and a chronological age of 12?
a. 100
b. 90
c. 120
d. 200

Concept: III. A. 4 Competency: 34
Question Type: *Applied*

39. A ______________ shows that most people are average. In the case of intelligence, most people have an IQ around ______________.
a. average distribution; 120
b. average distribution; 200
c. normal distribution; 100
d. normal distribution; 10

Concept: III. A. 4. b Competency: 35
Question Type: *Applied*

40. What may be concluded from the finding that children with higher IQs tend to do better in school than children with lower IQs?
a. IQ is the only important variable that influences school performance.
b. Children with high IQs are more valuable students than children with lower IQs.
c. People with higher IQs will grow up to have more satisfying lives than people with lower IQs.
d. IQ tests have some validity.

Concept: III. A. 5 Competency: 36
Question Type: *Factual*

41. Delilah is from Saskatchewan and has never left her home province. She just took an intelligence test that had a logic question dealing with how subways operate and their schedule. What is a potential issue?
a. The test is not reliable.
b. The test has a gender bias.
c. The test is culturally biased.
d. The test is a measure of achievement.

Concept: III. A. 6 Competency: 37
Question Type: *Applied*

42. Abe is 70 years old. He knows a lot more words than does his 20-year-old granddaughter, Monika, but he does not think as quickly as she does. According to Cattell, Abe may score better than Monika on tests of which type of intelligence?
a. intrapersonal intelligence
b. crystallized intelligence
c. fluid intelligence
d. kinesthetic intelligence

Concept: III. B Competency: 38
Question Type: *Applied*

43. Sun has an extensive vocabulary, is good in math, deals well with other people, and is excellent at solving logic puzzles. Patrick knows a lot about nature, is a good tennis player, and plays the harp in the orchestra. According to Gardner's theory of multiple intelligences, who is more intelligent?
a. Sun, because she has high verbal and math ability.
b. Sun, because Patrick's abilities don't demonstrate intelligence.
c. Sun, because she has more abilities than Patrick.
d. Neither, they are just differently talented.

Concept: III. B. 2 Competency: 39
Question Type: *Applied*

44. Concept: III. B. 3 Competency: 40
Question Type: *Factual*

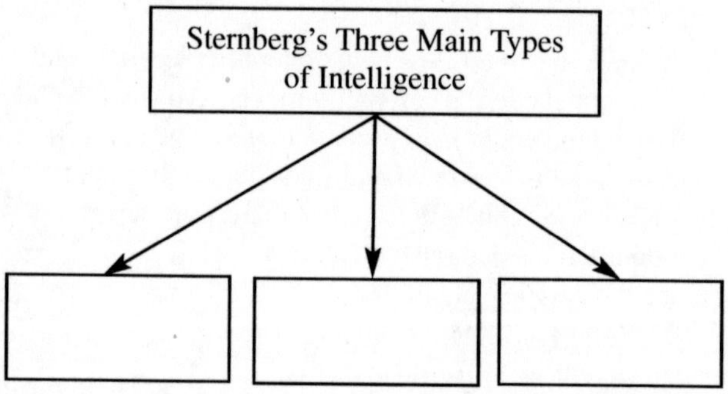

45. Concept: III. B. 4 Competency: 41
Question Type: *Factual*

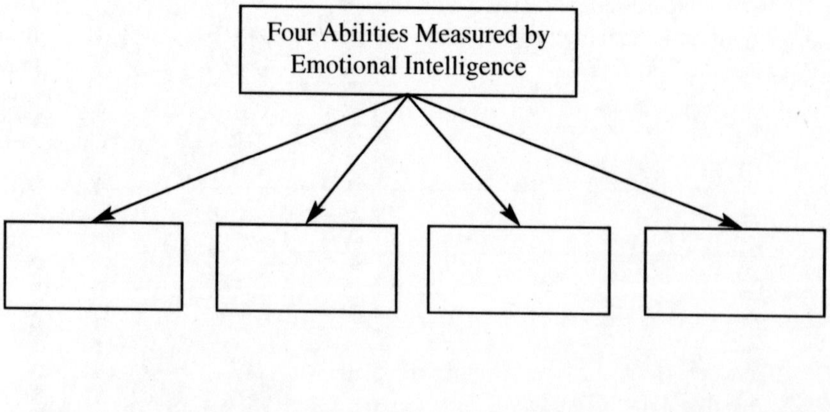

46. Peter is not only in touch with his own feelings but understands the feelings of others and gets along well with almost everyone he meets. He may be high in which kind of intelligence?
    a. linguistic
    b. emotional
    c. intimate
    d. fluid

    Concept: III. B. 4 Competency: 41
    Question Type: *Applied*

47. Possessing a high g is associated with positive outcomes in each of the following EXCEPT:
    a. parenting
    b. work performance
    c. health
    d. school performance

    Concept: III. B. 5 Competency: 42
    Question Type: *Factual*

48. Roberta is an air traffic controller who often has to divert planes to one of several different areas of air space in a short period of time. Thankfully, she has high g and does a fantastic job. Her job represents a type of:
    a. factor analysis
    b. inspection time
    c. simple reaction time
    d. choice reaction time

    Concept: III. C. 1. a Competency: 43
    Question Type: *Applied*

49. Which of the following has been found regarding brain structure and intelligence?
    a. All parts of the brain seem to be equally important for intelligence.
    b. Brain size is in no way related to intelligence.
    c. As of yet, no relationship between brain functioning and intelligence has been found.
    d. The frontal brain regions seem to be particularly associated with intelligence.

    Concept: III. B. 3 Competency: 44
    Question Type: *Applied*

50. Peter is 5 years old and experiences great difficulty in school. He has no ability to read, or do arithmetic, but is an exceptional artist. He most likely:
    a. is academically gifted
    b. is a savant
    c. has a high g
    d. is low in Gardner's intelligences

    Concept: III. C. 4 Competency: 45
    Question Type: *Applied*

51. Research on the behavioural genetics of intelligence show that:
    a. genetics are responsible for a vast majority of intelligence differences
    b. the environment is responsible for a vast majority of intelligence differences
    c. the environment acts as a social multiplier, making small genetic advantages even greater
    d. genetics can be altered to create lifelong superlearners

    Concept: III. D. 1. a Competency: 46
    Question Type: *Factual*

52. Concept: III. D. 2 Competency: 47
    Question Type: *Factual*

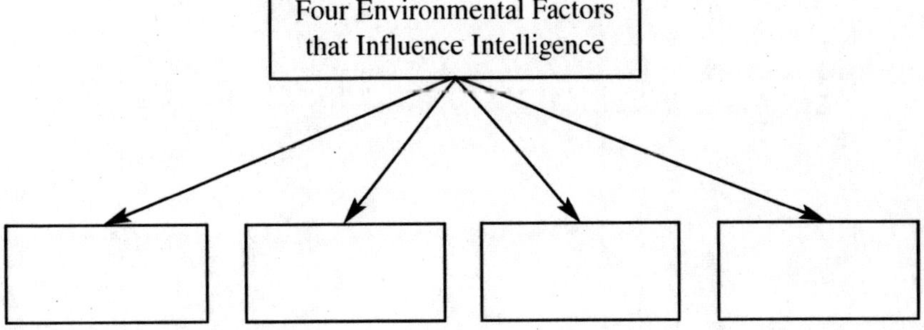

53. If the Flynn effect continues, in 100 years which of the following is most likely to be true?
    a. By today's standard, everyone will have below average intelligence.
    b. By today's standard, the average intelligence will be 70.
    c. By today's standard, the average intelligence will be 100.
    d. By today's standard, the average intelligence will be 160.

    Concept: III. D. 2. e Competency: 48
    Question Type: *Factual*

54. There is a sex difference for intelligence such that ______________________ get better grades in school and tend to have the advantage on measures of writing and language usage. ______________________ tend to get higher scores on some standardized tests of math aptitude and visuospatial processing. Therefore the smarter sex is ______________________.

    Concept: III. D. 3. a Competency: 49
    Question Type: *Factual*

55. What is the problem with concluding that one race is smarter than another? What can the qualities of good experimentation tell us about this?

    ____

    ____

    ____

    ____

    Concept: III. D. 3. b Competency: 50
    Question Type: *Conceptual*

56. Right before a math test, Anita's teacher told the class that he did not expect the girls to do well because girls are not good in math. Sure enough Anita, an excellent math student, did worse on the test than she should have. Anita's performance reflects ______________________.

    Concept: III. D. 3. b. 3 Competency: 51
    Question Type: *Applied*

SUMMING UP AND MEASURING UP

How Do We Understand Intelligence?

Intelligence is the ability of humans to reason, solve problems, think quickly and efficiently, and adapt to environmental challenges. The psychometric approach reveals multiple components to intelligence but also a central dimension that has been called general intelligence, or g. Fluid intelligence is the type of intelligence we use when faced with novel problems that do not have solutions we can simply pull from memory; it is related to cognitive measures, such as working memory and speed of mental processing. By contrast, crystallized intelligence reflects knowledge we have already acquired, as in finding the area of a triangle after having been taught the formula. Multiple forms of intelligence have been identified, including emotional, although debate continues as to whether they reflect the same kind of intelligence captured in traditional definitions. Intelligence is measured through standardized psychometric tests, reaction times, inspection times, and responses to situations. Both genes and environment influence intelligence, and researchers seek to understand how environmental factors lead to differential gene expression in regard to intelligence. Data from twin and adoption studies are often used to garner evidence for the contributions of nature and nurture to intelligence. Group differences in intelligence cannot be attributed to genetic differences when those groups have experienced environmental differences. Group differences in intelligence, specifically by sex and race, can be altered somewhat by inducing or removing the threat posed by societal stereotypes about particular groups' intelligence. Members of groups stereotyped as being less intelligent may improve their scores when the stereotype is not activated or is removed. Considerable controversy exists over whether stereotype threat changes scores on intelligence and aptitude tests, but the possibility that it does creates concerns about test scores' validity.

ANSWER KEY

Item **Answer**

1. Cognition
2. d
3. a
4. c
5. b
6. c
7. c
8. a
9. c
10. d
11. b
12. d
13. reasoning; Decision making; Problem solving
14. b
15. c
16. a
17. b
18. Normative; descriptive
19. Algorithms try every possible solution and are guaranteed to get the correct solution. Often the number of possible solutions is very high, making this approach time consuming (particularly for humans). However, because a computer can try the solutions very quickly, the algorithm approach is better than heuristics (which can be flawed).
20. c
21. b
22. a
23. d
24. b
25. b
26. Good decision making involves good critical thinking. As a result, a good decision maker may more accurately weigh the pros and cons of any number of decisions from which job to take, whom to marry, and what financial decisions to make. They might also be more skeptical of others' attempts to take advantage of them.
27. d
28. a
29. b
30. a
31. c
32. starting at the solution or conclusion and determining the steps it would have taken to get there; finding an approach that works in another context that could work for the problem you are currently trying to solve.
33. a
34. If hard work is not involved in learning there will be decreased admiration for achievement and perseverance, and a decreased sense of accomplishment. It may also be a case where everyone must take the drugs or run the risk of being surpassed by everyone else for jobs. While this is possible, a good memory does not guarantee success. There are successful people with poor memories, and unsuccessful people with perfect memory. Ultimately, a person must properly apply his or her ability.
35. b
36. b
37. c, a, a, b, c
38. a
39. c
40. d
41. c
42. b
43. d
44. analytical; creative; practical
45. recognize other's emotions; use one's own emotions to facilitate activities; understand emotional language; manage one's own emotions
46. b
47. a
48. d
49. d
50. b
51. c
52. nutrition, adoption, enriched environment, schooling
53. d
54. females; Males; neither is "smarter"
55. Race may not be a biologically meaningful concept due to the fact that the vast majority of genes are identical among people (perhaps as many as 99.9 percent). It is also often hard to classify race due to the blended nature of our society. Good experimentation requires equivalent groups with a high degree of control. Comparing race involves comparing non-equivalent/non-randomized groups that may not have similar environments. Due to the lack of similar environments, there is a lack of control such that we can't ever be sure what factors cause what levels of intellignece. For example, is it race that influences intelligence, or lower socio-economic status?
56. stereotype threat

Summing Up and Measuring Up

Answer: b. evidence for nature because later-born children show the same effect when older siblings die, a situation that changes their environment, not their heredity

KEY TERM EXERCISES

analogical representations

Textbook Definition:
Your Own Definition:
Your Own Example:

availability heuristic

Textbook Definition:
Your Own Definition:
Your Own Example:

cognition

Textbook Definition:
Your Own Definition:
Your Own Example:

concept

Textbook Definition:
Your Own Definition:
Your Own Example:

crystallized intelligence

Textbook Definition:
Your Own Definition:
Your Own Example:

decision making

Textbook Definition:
Your Own Definition:
Your Own Example:

deductive reasoning

Textbook Definition:
Your Own Definition:
Your Own Example:

defining attribute model

Textbook Definition:
Your Own Definition:
Your Own Example:

emotional intelligence (EQ)

Textbook Definition:
Your Own Definition:
Your Own Example:

exemplar model

Textbook Definition:
Your Own Definition:
Your Own Example:

fluid intelligence

Textbook Definition:
Your Own Definition:
Your Own Example:

framing

Textbook Definition:
Your Own Definition:
Your Own Example:

general intelligence (g)

Textbook Definition:
Your Own Definition:
Your Own Example:

heuristics

Textbook Definition:
Your Own Definition:
Your Own Example:

inductive reasoning

Textbook Definition:
Your Own Definition:
Your Own Example:

insight

Textbook Definition:
Your Own Definition:
Your Own Example:

intelligence

Textbook Definition:
Your Own Definition:
Your Own Example:

intelligence quotient (IQ)

Textbook Definition:
Your Own Definition:
Your Own Example:

mental age

Textbook Definition:
Your Own Definition:
Your Own Example:

mental set

Textbook Definition:
Your Own Definition:
Your Own Example:

multiple intelligences

Textbook Definition:
Your Own Definition:
Your Own Example:

problem solving

Textbook Definition:
Your Own Definition:
Your Own Example:

prototype model

Textbook Definition:
Your Own Definition:
Your Own Example:

reasoning

Textbook Definition:
Your Own Definition:
Your Own Example:

representativeness heuristic

Textbook Definition:
Your Own Definition:
Your Own Example:

restructuring

Textbook Definition:
Your Own Definition:
Your Own Example:

stereotype threat

Textbook Definition:
Your Own Definition:
Your Own Example:

symbolic representations

Textbook Definition:
Your Own Definition:
Your Own Example:

CHAPTER 9 Motivation and Emotion

CONCEPT MAP

I. How Does Motivation Activate, Direct, and Sustain Behaviour?
  A. Motivation
    1. Energizing
    2. Directive
    3. Persist
    4. Strength
  B. Multiple Factors Motivate Behaviour
    1. Need
      a. Need Hierarchy
        1. Self-actualization
    2. Drives
      a. Arousal
      b. Homeostasis
      c. Habits
    3. Incentives
    4. Arousal and Performance
      a. Yerkes-Dodson Law
      b. Optimal Level of Arousal
    5. Pleasure
      a. Hedonism
  C. Some Behaviours Are Motivated for Their Own Sake
    1. Extrinsic Motivation
    2. Intrinsic Motivation
      a. Creativity
    3. Rewarding Intrinsic Motives
      a. Self-determination theory
      b. Self-perception Theory
  D. People Set Goals to Achieve
    1. Goals
      a. Self-regulation
      b. Qualities of a Good Goal
        1. Challenging
        2. Not Overly Difficult
        3. Specific
    2. Self-efficacy
    3. Achievement Motivation
    4. Delayed Gratification
  E. People Have a Need to Belong
    1. Making and Keeping Friends
    2. Anxiety and Affiliation

II. What Determines How We Eat?
  A. Time and Taste
    1. Time of Day
    2. Flavour
      a. Sensory-specific Satiety
  B. Culture Determines What We Eat
    1. Neophobia
    2. Cuisine
  C. Multiple Neural Processes Control Eating
    1. Hypothalamus
      a. Hyperphagia vs. Aphagia
    2. Other Brain Structures
    3. Internal Sensations
      a. Stomach
      b. Bloodstream
        1. Glucostatic Theory
        2. Lipostatic Theory
        3. Leptin
        4. Ghrelin

III. What Factors Motivate Sexual Behaviour?
  A. Biological Factors Influence Sexual Behaviour
    1. Sexual Response Cycle
      a. Excitement Phase

b. Plateau Phase
c. Orgasm Phase
d. Resolution Phase
2. Hormones
a. Development of Brain and Body
1. Puberty
2. Secondary Sexual Characteristics
b. Motivation
1. Testosterone
3. Neurotransmitters
a. Nitric Oxide
4. Variations across the Menstrual Cycle
5. Neural Correlates of Viewing Erotica
B. Cultural Scripts and Cultural Rules Shape Sexual Interactions
1. Double Standards
2. Sex Differences in Sexual Motives
a. Erotic Plasticity
b. Sexual Strategies Theory
C. Mating Strategies Differ between the Sexes
1. Traits Desired by Both Men and Women
2. Sex Differences
a. Evolutionary Theory
D. There Are Differences in Sexual Orientation
1. Parents' Role
2. Biological Contribution
a. Prenatal Hormones
b. Behavioural Genetics
c. Hypothalamus
1. Correlational Nature of Findings
d. Biology and Environment

IV. How Are Emotions Adaptive?
A. Emotion
1. Mood
B. Facial Expressions Communicate Emotion
1. Infants
2. Part of the Face
3. Facial Expressions across Cultures
4. Display Rules and Gender
a. Display Rules
C. Emotions Serve Cognitive Functions
1. Influence of Mood
2. Decision Making
a. Affect as Information
3. Somatic Marker Theory
D. Emotions Strengthen Interpersonal Relations
1. Guilt Strengthens Social Bonds
a. Three Mechanisms
2. Embarrassment and Blushing

V. How Do People Experience Emotions?
A. Three Parts of Emotions
1. Subjective Experience
2. Physical Changes
3. Cognitive Appraisal
B. Emotions Have a Phenomenological (Subjective) Component
1. Alexithymia
2. Distinguishing among Types of Emotions
a. Primary Emotions
b. Secondary Emotions
c. Circumplex Model
1. Valence
2. Activation
C. Emotions Have a Physiological Component
1. James-Lange Theory of Emotion
a. Facial Feedback Hypothesis
2. Cannon-Bard Theory of Emotion
3. The Amygdala
a. Functions
b. Two Pathways
c. Influence on Memory
d. Perception of Social Stimuli
4. Prefrontal Cortex
a. Cerebral Asymmetry
D. Emotions Have a Cognitive Component
1. Two-Factor Theory of Emotion
a. Schachter and Singer Experiment
2. Misattribution of Arousal
a. Excitation Transfer
E. People Regulate Their Moods
1. Humour
2. Thought Suppression
a. Rebound Effect
3. Rumination

CHAPTER SUMMARY

How Does Motivation Activate, Direct, and Sustain Behaviour?

• Multiple Factors Motivate Behaviour: Motives activate, direct, and sustain behaviours that will satisfy a need. Needs create arousal, and the response to being aroused is a drive to satisfy the need. *Homeostasis* refers to the body's attempts to maintain a state of equilibrium. The Yerkes-Dodson law states that a person performs best when his or her level of arousal is neither too low nor too high.

• Some Behaviours Are Motivated for Their Own Sake: Behaviours such as playing games are unrelated to needs. People are intrinsically motivated by the joy of engaging in these behaviours.

• People Set Goals to Achieve: People with a high need to achieve set reasonably high goals and believe that with hard work, they can achieve their goals. These people are high in self-efficacy. They are able to delay gratification as they work toward difficult goals.

• People Have a Need to Belong: For most people, social motivation is very strong. Evolutionary theorists point out the survival advantage of having others to share dangerous tasks and care for one another. When people were made anxious in an experimental setting, they preferred to be with other people in a similar situation, most likely because they could interpret their own situation by comparing themselves to similar others.

What Determines How We Eat?

• Time and Taste Play Roles: Customs and local norms strongly determine the foods we find appetizing and the times of day when we have our meals. Sensory-specific satiety is people's tendency to eat less when there is little variety in their food choices.

• Culture Determines What We Eat: Culture determines what a person considers edible. Neophobia is the reluctance to eat unfamiliar foods. Researchers have found that infants are more likely to try a new food when a family member offers it.

• Multiple Neural Processes Control Eating: The hypothalamus is the brain structure most closely identified with eating. Rats whose ventromedial hypothalamus was damaged experienced hyperphagia—they consumed huge quantities of food. By contrast, rats whose lateral hypothalamus was damaged exhibited aphagia—they stopped eating to the point of death. The limbic system, which is involved in reward, shows more activity when overweight people look at food than when people of normal weight do. Set-point sensors for body fat, blood glucose monitors, and hormones also play important roles in how much we eat.

What Factors Motivate Sexual Behaviour?

• Biological Factors Influence Sexual Behaviour: The four stages of the human sexual response cycle are excitement, plateau, orgasm, and resolution. Men have a refractory period following orgasm, during which time they cannot become sexually aroused; women do not have a refractory period. Both men's and women's sexual responsiveness depends on their having a minimal amount of testosterone available. Some data show that heterosexual women's preferences for masculine-looking men vary over the menstrual cycle.

• Cultural Scripts and Cultural Rules Shape Sexual Interactions: Our beliefs about how we should behave sexually are influenced by cultural scripts defining sexual behaviour for men and women. The double standard allows men greater sexual latitude than it allows women.

• Mating Strategies Differ between the Sexes: According to the evolutionary view, women want men to be faithful and be good providers for their children because women's investments in pregnancy and child care are intensive. By contrast, men want—at least subconsciously—to impregnate many women as a strategy to promote the survival of as many of the men's offspring as possible.

• People Differ in Sexual Orientation: Evolutionary theorists have difficulty explaining homosexuality because same-sex relations do not result in offspring. A portion of the hypothalamus was found to be smaller in gay men than in heterosexual men, but as with any correlational data, the causal relation is unclear. Research suggests that prenatal hormones may be important in determining sexual orientation.

How Are Emotions Adaptive?

• Facial Expressions Communicate Emotion: People from multiple cultures interpret a particular facial expression as representing the same emotion. Men appear to be less emotional than women, possibly because of societal display rules.

• Emotions Serve Cognitive Functions: We use our emotions as a guide when making decisions. One theory is that we use emotions as somatic markers informing our behaviours—meaning we interpret our body's responses and use that information to help make decisions.

• Emotions Strengthen Interpersonal Relations: Social bonds are strengthened when we can read other people's emotions accurately.

How Do People Experience Emotions?

• Emotions Have a Subjective Component: Primary emotions are adaptive across cultures. They include anger, fear, sadness, disgust, happiness, surprise, and content. Secondary emotions are blends of the primary emotions.

• Emotions Have a Physiological Component: Emotions are associated with changes in bodily states. Research points to important roles of the amygdala and the prefrontal cortex in the production and experience of emotion.

• Emotions Have a Cognitive Component: According to the two-factor theory, emotions have an arousal component and a cognitive or interpretive component. The interpretation determines which emotion is felt.

• People Regulate Their Moods: When experiencing intense moods, we can use strategies such as distraction to manage them. Thought suppression and ruminating are not effective strategies.

COMPETENCY MAP

How Does Motivation Activate, Direct, and Sustain Behaviour?

Motivation

1. Define motivation.
2. Identify the four essential qualities of motivational states.
3. Differentiate the four essential qualities of motivational states.

Multiple Factors Motivate Behaviour

4. Distinguish needs from drives.
5. Explain Maslow's need hierarchy.
6. Explain how homeostasis relates to motivation.
7. Identify the unique nature of incentives.
8. What does the Yerkes-Dodson law suggest about arousal and performance?
9. Explain optimal level of arousal.
10. Describe hedonism.

Some Behaviours Are Motivated for Their Own Sake

11. Distinguish between extrinsic and intrinsic motivation.
12. What happens if you reward intrinsic motives?
13. Describe self-perception theory.

People Set Goals to Achieve

14. Identify the qualities of good goals.
15. Understand how self-efficacy influences motivation.
16. How can you identify achievement motivation?
17. What is delayed gratification?

People Have a Need to Belong

18. What is meant by a need to belong?
19. What is the role of anxiety in affiliation?

What Determines How We Eat?

Time and Taste

20. Identify how taste influences how we eat.

Culture Determines What We Eat

21. Identify ways that culture influences how we eat.

Multiple Neural Processes Control Eating

22. Differentiate between hyperphagia and aphagia.
23. Differentiate between glucostatic and lipostatic theory.
24. Identify the role of leptin and ghrelin in eating.

What Factors Motivate Sexual Behaviour?

Biological Factors Influence Sexual Behaviour

25. Identify the four phases of the sexual response cycle.
26. Understand the ways that hormones influence sexual behaviour.
27. Describe the role of testosterone in sexual behaviour.
28. Identify how neurotransmitters influence sexual behaviour.
29. How does the menstrual cycle influence sexual behaviour?

Cultural Scripts and Rules Shape Sexual Interactions

30. Explain what is meant by a double standard.
31. What factors influence erotic plasticity?
32. What is the sexual strategies theory?

Mating Strategies Differ between the Sexes

33. Understand the similarities and differences between men and women in mating.
34. Evaluate how evolutionary theory applies to mating behaviour.

There Are Differences in Sexual Orientation

35. Describe the biological contribution to sexual orientation.

How Are Emotions Adaptive?

Emotion

36. Differentiate emotions from moods.

Facial Expressions Communicate Emotion

37. Describe evidence for facial expressions communicating emotion.

38. Identify how display rules differ by gender and culture.

Emotions Serve Cognitive Functions

39. Explain how emotions influence decision making.
40. Describe how somatic markers influence emotions.

Emotions Strengthen Interpersonal Relations

41. Identify three ways that guilt strengthens social bonds.

How Do People Experience Emotions?

Three Parts of Emotions

42. Identify the three components of emotions.

Emotions Have a Phenomenological (Subjective) Component

43. Identify characteristics of alexithymia.
44. Distinguish between primary and secondary emotions.
45. Explain the circumplex model of emotions.

Emotions Have a Physiological Component

46. Understand the distinction between the James-Lange and Cannon-Bard theories of emotion.
47. How does facial feedback influence emotion?
48. Describe the role of the amygdala in emotion.
49. Describe the role of the prefrontal cortex in emotion.

Emotions Have a Cognitive Component

50. Describe the two-factor theory of emotions.
51. How does misattribution of arousal take place?
52. Describe strategies people use to regulate their moods.

KNOWLEDGE CHECK

1. ______________________________ is the area of psychological science that studies the factors that energize, or stimulate, behaviour.

   Concept: I. A   Competency: 1
   Question Type: *Factual*

2. Concept: I. A   Competency: 2
   Question Type: *Factual*

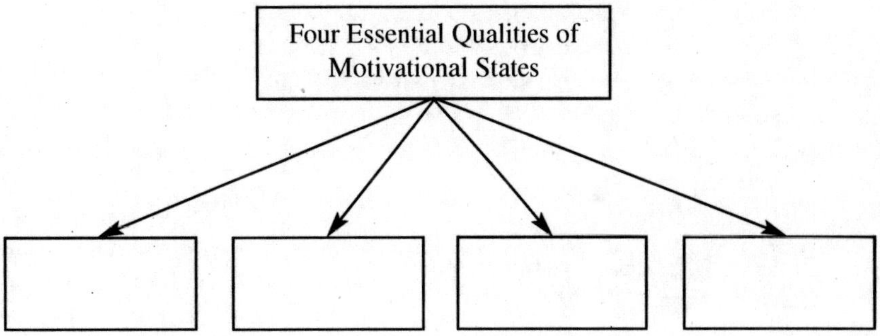

3. Corgan's goal is to graduate from university in 3 years. For this reason, he takes overloads each semester, as well as several classes each summer. This is an example of which essential quality of motivational states?
   a. energizing
   b. directive
   c. persistence
   d. strength

   Concept: I. A Competency: 3
   Question Type: *Applied*

4. Dion is training for a marathon. During a long run she becomes dehydrated. Her dehydration is a ______________. As a result she starts thinking of ways to get something to drink. This represents a ______________.
   a. need; need
   b. drive, need
   c. need; drive
   d. drive; drive

   Concept: I. B. 1 Competency: 4
   Question Type: *Applied*

5. Chet is a contestant on a TV show where he and several others have to survive on an island. According to Maslow's hierarchy of needs, which of the following should Chet do first?
   a. Be sure he has shelter for safety.
   b. Focus on getting others in the group to like and accept him.
   c. Demonstrate his hunting skills to others so they will respect him.
   d. Find food and clean water.

   Concept: I. B. 1. a Competency: 5
   Question Type: *Applied*

6. Carmela needs 8 hours of sleep a night to function at her optimal level. Last night, she only slept 4 hours, leading her to want to nap a lot today. The goal of napping is best described as an attempt to:
   a. refocus her drive
   b. fix her set-point
   c. obtain optimal arousal
   d. re-establish homeostasis

   Concept: I. B. 2. b Competency: 6
   Question Type: *Applied*

7. Leo works at two jobs because he wants to earn enough money to buy a new car. In this situation, what is the incentive motivating Leo?
   a. money to buy the car
   b. feelings of satisfaction for a job well done
   c. basic hedonism
   d. anxiety about not having enough money

   Concept: I. B. 3 Competency: 7
   Question Type: *Applied*

8. According to the Yerkes-Dodson law, who of the following should perform best on an exam?
   a. Anita, who is so anxious she can't eat or sleep
   b. Marco, who is so anxious he spelled his name wrong
   c. Maria, who is a little nervous
   d. Joe, who is not nervous at all

   Concept: I. B. 4. a Competency: 8
   Question Type: *Applied*

9. Penelope and Ben couldn't be more different. She likes loud music, rollercoaster rides, and driving fast. Ben prefers quiet, reading a book, and driving slow. This demonstrates a difference in their:
   a. Yerkes-Dodson law
   b. optimal level of arousal
   c. homeostasis
   d. hedonism

   Concept: I. B. 4. b Competency: 9
   Question Type: *Applied*

10. Charlotte believes in eating good foods, having good sex, and staying happy. She avoids all activities that make her uncomfortable. Her behaviour exemplifies:
    a. homeostasis
    b. an optimal level of arousal
    c. incentive theory
    d. hedonism

    Concept: I. B. 5. a Competency: 10
    Question Type: *Applied*

11. Jackie is currently in university and is constantly studying for her classes. Her roommates think she is boring and only studying to keep her parents happy. However, Jackie explains that she is doing it for herself, because she really likes to learn, enjoys the challenge, and likes the sense of fulfillment it gives her. This example best describes which type of motivation?
    a. extrinsic
    b. intrinsic
    c. achievement
    d. delay of gratification

    Concept: I. C Competency: 11
    Question Type: *Applied*

12. Jose, a 10-year-old, loves playing the piano and will play for hours just for his own enjoyment. Based on the research presented in the textbook, what would happen if Jose's mother starts to give him $5 for every hour that he plays?
    a. His playing will increase because the money is a reward.
    b. His playing will increase because the money is an incentive.
    c. His playing will be unaffected because he plays so much already.
    d. His playing will decrease because it was intrinsically motivated initially.

    Concept: I. C. 3 Competency: 12
    Question Type: *Applied*

13. Sara is an undecided major. She has recently noticed that whenever she has free time she tends to read a lot about history. As a result, she realized that she likes history and has decided to make it her major. Which theory best accounts for this?
    a. self-perception theory
    b. self-determination theory
    c. drive reduction theory
    d. self-regulation

    Concept: I. C. 3. b Competency: 13
    Question Type: *Applied*

14. Goals motivate behaviour. Good goals have been shown to be ______________________________,
    ______________________________,
    and ______________________________.

    Concept: I. D. 1. b Competency: 14
    Question Type: *Factual*

15. Monica believes that if she studies for her exam, she will do well on it. According to Bandura, Monica is displaying a strong sense of:
    a. self-perception
    b. self-actualization
    c. self efficacy
    d. self-regulation

    Concept: I. C. 2. Competency: 15
    Question Type: *Applied*

16. Angela is starting a new company and wants to hire employees with a high level of achievement motivation. To test achievement motivation, she has potential employees engage in a task where they throw ping pong balls into cups, and can choose to complete the task from three distances (short, medium, and far). The task is to get as many in as possible. Who should she hire?
    a. those that go from a short distance
    b. those that go from a medium distance
    c. those that go from a far distance
    d. those that go from a short or far distance because it is the best combination of accomplishment and risk-taking

    Concept: I. D. 3 Competency: 16
    Question Type: *Applied*

17. Steve would really like to go to a party on Thursday night, but he studies for an exam instead. He knows that if he studies he will do well and then will have a better chance of getting a good job. Steve is displaying:
    a. hedonism
    b. the pleasure principle
    c. delay of gratification
    d. deindividuation

    Concept: I. D. 4 Competency: 17
    Question Type: *Applied*

18. When Noreen was ill, she spent a lot of time alone in her room. She found that she became starved for company and was delighted when people visited her. Her reaction reflects:
    a. delay of gratification
    b. a need to belong
    c. deindividuation
    d. social exclusion theory

    Concept: I. E Competency: 18
    Question Type: *Applied*

19. Troy was called down to the principal's office. He has some idea what it is about, and is really anxious because he could be in a lot of trouble. When he gets to the office he has to wait in the waiting room. Based on the research in the book he should most prefer to wait with:
    a. no one
    b. other students who are not anxious at all
    c. other students who are as anxious as he is
    d. others, but those who are not students

    Concept: I. E. 2 Competency: 19
    Question Type: *Applied*

20. When JR eats dinner at his mom's house, he doesn't eat too much of the burger, salad, and potatoes that she serves. However, when he goes to his grandma's he eats a lot of the chicken, burgers, salad, fruit, chips, candy, cake, and pie that she loves to make. JR's increased eating at his grandma's house may reflect:
    a. the effects of time on eating
    b. sensory-specific satiety
    c. neophobia
    d. gourmand syndrome

    Concept: II. A. 2. a Competency: 20
    Question Type: *Applied*

21. Local norms of not only what to eat but also how to prepare it, known as ______________________, influence food preference.

    Concept: II. B. 2 Competency: 21
    Question Type: *Factual*

22. Debra's dog Chunky is morbidly obese. The problem is that Chunky never stops eating. He most likely suffers from ______________ due to a problem in his ______________.
    a. aphagia; thalamus
    b. aphagia; hypothalamus
    c. hyperphagia; thalamus
    d. hyperphagia; hypothalamus

    Concept: II. C. 1. a Competency: 22
    Question Type: *Applied*

23. Research suggests that the bloodstream's nutrient levels produce hunger. One theory, ______________________________________, proposes that glucose is the key nutrient. Another theory, the ______________________________, proposes a set-point for body fat in which deviations from the set-point initiate compensatory behaviours to return to homeostasis.

    Concept: II. C. 3. b Competency: 23
    Question Type: *Factual*

24. There are two key hormones that regulate eating. ______________ helps regulate fat, and ______________ surges before meals and then decreases after people eat, suggesting that it plays an important role in triggering eating.
    a. Leptin; ghrelin
    b. Ghrelin; leptin
    c. Ghrelin; pectin
    d. Pectin; leptin

    Concept: II. C. 3. b Competency: 24
    Question Type: *Factual*

25. Concept: III. A. 1 Competency: 25
    Question Type: *Factual*

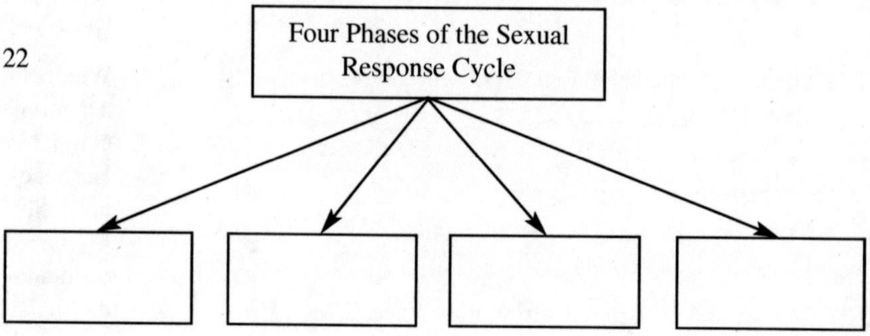

26. All of the following about how hormones influence sexual behaviour are true, EXCEPT:
    a. Estrogens play a major role in human female sexuality.
    b. Hormones aid the development of secondary sexual characteristics.
    c. Hormones activate reproductive behaviour.
    d. Hormones aid brain development during puberty.

    Concept: III. A. 2 Competency: 26
    Question Type: *Factual*

27. Imagine a situation where you had to determine the amount of sexual thoughts an unknown person had on a daily basis. Would you rather know the person's gender or the person's testosterone level? Why?

    ____

    ____

    ____

    ____

    Concept: III. A. 2. b Competency: 27
    Question Type: *Conceptual*

28. Which neurotransmitter is enhanced by Viagra?
    a. dopamine
    b. nitric oxide
    c. MDMA
    d. Oxytocin

    Concept: III. A. 3. a Competency: 28
    Question Type: *Factual*

29. Trishelle is out at a dance club with several of her friends who are pointing out guys they think are most attractive. Trishelle seems to prefer guys who appear very masculine, athletic, and hyper-confident. It is most likely that Trishelle:
    a. has high levels of oxytocin
    b. has high levels of estrogen
    c. is in the least fertile stage of her menstrual cycle
    d. is in the most fertile stage of her menstrual cycle

    Concept: III. A. 4 Competency: 29
    Question Type: *Applied*

30. Cherise comes from a family where girls are expected to be virgins when they marry but boys are expected to get as much experience as they can. Her family's values:
    a. reflect a double standard
    b. are unknown in any culture
    c. are pheromone based
    d. reflect erotic plasticity

    Concept: III. B. 1 Competency: 30
    Question Type: *Applied*

31. The idea of erotic plasticity emphasizes the role of each of the following, EXCEPT:
    a. religion
    b. family upbringing
    c. the influence of testosterone
    d. the influence of peers

    Concept: III. B. 2 Competency: 31
    Question Type: *Factual*

32. In one study of 96 university students, an attractive stranger approached people of the opposite sex and said, "I have been noticing you around campus. I find you attractive. Would you go to bed with me tonight?" Although not one woman said yes, three-quarters of the men agreed to the request. Which theory best accounts for these findings?
    a. double standard theory
    b. erotic plasticity theory
    c. sexual strategies theory
    d. sexual motivation theory

    Concept: III. B. 2. b Competency: 32
    Question Type: *Factual*

33. Jen and Tim are both looking for a romantic partner. According to research, both will equally desire a partner who is ______________. Tim, however, will put more emphasis on ______________.
    a. kind, honest, and good-natured; physical appearance
    b. highly physically attractive; personality characteristics
    c. capable of earning a good salary; physical appearance
    d. kind, honest, and good-natured; capability of earning a good salary

    Concept: III. C. 1 Competency: 33
    Question Type: *Applied*

34. Is it valid to use evolutionary theory to mating behaviour? Give reasons why it would and would not be valid.

    ____

    ____

    ____

    ____

    Concept: III. C. 2. a Competency: 34
    Question Type: *Conceptual*

35. The best available evidence suggests that the biggest influence on sexual orientation is:
a. a specific gene
b. exposure to hormones, especially androgens, in the prenatal environment
c. parenting style
d. which parent the child is closer to

Concept: III. D. 2 Competency: 35
Question Type: *Factual*

36. ______________________________ refers to feelings that involve subjective evaluation, physiological processes, and cognitive beliefs. ______________________________ are diffuse and long-lasting states that influence rather than interrupt thought and behaviour.

Concept: IV. A. 1 Competency: 36
Question Type: *Factual*

37. Jon is on his first date with a woman he really likes. She is being polite, but he wonders how she actually feels about him. Based on research on nonverbal displays of emotion, Jon should look at her ______________ for clues about her inner states, moods, and needs.
a. eyebrows
b. eyes
c. cheek muscles
d. mouth

Concept: IV. B. 2 Competency: 37
Question Type: *Applied*

38. Jean-Claude is at the movies with his girlfriend. Because he lost a bet, they are watching a love story. When the heroine dies at the end of the movie, Jean-Claude feels tears rush to the corners of his eyes. He tries to look away and subtly wipe his eyes because crying would violate the ______________ in his culture for how emotions are exhibited by tough guys.
a. affective standards
b. mood heuristics
c. display rules
d. feelings norms

Concept: IV. B. 4. a Competency: 38
Question Type: *Applied*

39. Portia is at the mall when she is asked to evaluate a new soft drink, a combination of vanilla, cherry, and cola. Portia is fairly neutral about the beverage, but she gives it a positive evaluation because she is in a good mood and it is nice to be out of the house. This behaviour, in which individuals use their current emotional state to make judgments and appraisals, is predicted by the:
a. affect-as-information theory
b. somatic marker hypothesis
c. emotional heuristic theory
d. affective information guide

Concept: IV. C. 2. a Competency: 39
Question Type: *Applied*

40. Lacey is eating lunch with several friends when a really attractive guy comes over to their table and starts making conversation. He is very friendly, and after a few minutes asks Lacey for her phone number. She turns him down and later explains to her friends that "it just didn't feel right" and that he didn't give her "butterflies." What theory best explains Lacey's explanation?
a. affect-as-information theory
b. somatic marker hypothesis
c. emotional heuristic theory
d. affective information guide

Concept: IV. C. 3 Competency: 40
Question Type: *Applied*

41. Guilt strengthens social bonds in all of the following ways EXCEPT:
a. Guilt keeps people from doing things that would harm their relationships.
b. Guilt is often experienced in isolation and serves to makes you less remorseful.
c. Displays of guilt demonstrate that people care about their relationship partners.
d. Guilt is an influence tactic that can be used to manipulate the behaviour of others.

Concept: IV. D. 1. a Competency: 41
Question Type: *Factual*

42. Concept: V. A Competency: 42
Question Type: *Factual*

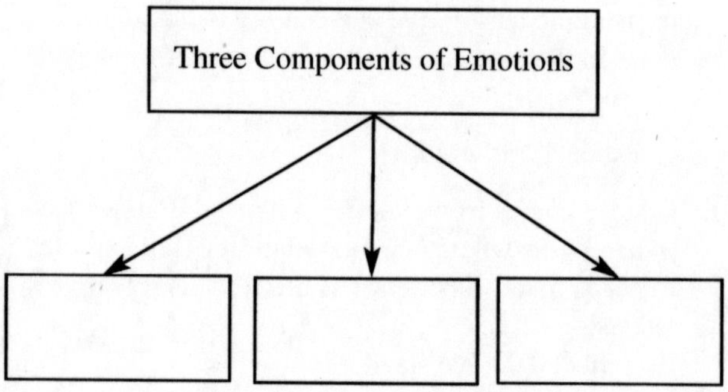

43. Leonard was in a car accident and suffered damage to his prefrontal cortex. Suddenly he seemed detached from his problems, and his relationships and job have fallen apart because he does not experience the subjective component of emotions. Leonard most likely suffers from:
    a. anti-social personality disorder
    b. affective constriction
    c. alexithymia
    d. major depressive disorder

    Concept: V. B. 1 Competency: 43
    Question Type: *Applied*

44. For each of the following, please match the emotion with the most appropriate type.

____	Anger	a) Primary emotion
____	Anticipation	b) Secondary emotion
____	Fear	
____	Guilt	
____	Happiness	
____	Remorse	
____	Sadness	

    Concept: V. B. 2 Competency: 44
    Question Type: *Applied*

45. Excitement is an affective state that can be described by its valence (high pleasantness) as well as its activation (high arousal). This description in which two basic factors of emotion are arranged in a circle around intersections of the core dimensions of affect is an example of a(n):
    a. alexithymic report
    b. phenomenological taxonomy
    c. primary emotion categorization
    d. circumplex model

    Concept: V. B. 1 Competency: 45
    Question Type: *Applied*

46. While Sara was on safari in Africa, the Land Rover in which she was riding was charged by a lion. Before she could even think that she was safe in the car, her heart began pounding and her brain received specific physiological feedback from her body, so she automatically knew she was experiencing fear! This experience supports the ______________ theory of emotion.
    a. James-Lange
    b. Cannon-Bard
    c. two-factor
    d. circumplex model

    Concept: V. C. 1 Competency: 46
    Question Type: *Applied*

47. Your friend Jesse has a theory that if a person is sad, all they need to do is bounce their foot up and down and that this will make the person happy. Which established idea is this most similar to?
    a. facial feedback hypothesis
    b. Cannon-Bard theory
    c. two-factor theory
    d. circumplex model

    Concept: V. C. 1 Competency: 47
    Question Type: *Conceptual*

48. Wes was in a really bad mood because he got fired from his job, and he had been frowning all day. That evening his friends were attempting to cheer him up. Finally one friend suggested that if he smiled, the change in his facial expression would produce a corresponding change in his mood. This process the friend suggested is based on which of the following?
    a. two-factor theory
    b. Cannon-Bard theory
    c. facial feedback hypothesis
    d. circumplex model

    Concept: V. C. 1 Competency: 47
    Question Type: *Applied*

49. The ________________________________ processes the emotional significance of stimuli and generates immediate emotional and behavioural reactions. If this structure is damaged a person will not be able to engage in what type of learning?

    Concept: V. C. 3 Competency: 48
    Question Type: *Factual*

50. Niles, a local psychologist, is diagnosed as having brain damage, but he still is performing psychotherapy. However, he can no longer recognize when his clients are experiencing fear or highly intense emotions. Which of the following brain structures is most likely damaged?
    a. amygdala
    b. hippocampus
    c. hypothalamus
    d. medulla

    Concept: V. C. 3 Competency: 48
    Question Type: *Applied*

51. Unequal activation of the left and right hemispheres of the prefrontal cortex is associated with specific emotional states, a pattern known as

_________________________________.

In a series of studies, Davidson and his colleagues found that greater activation of the right prefrontal cortex is associated with ____________________ affect, whereas greater activation of the left hemisphere is associated with ____________________ affect.

Concept: V. C. 3. a Competency: 49
Question Type: *Factual*

52. Kathi is watching a television special about puppies and kittens. She thinks they are adorable and feels happy when she watches them. Based on studies of cerebral asymmetry, we would expect an increase in activation in which of the following cortical brain areas?
   a. right prefrontal
   b. left hemisphere
   c. anterior parietal
   d. amygdala

Concept: V. C. 3. a Competency: 49
Question Type: *Applied*

53. Lenny is at a local comedy club. The comedian is making some cruel jokes about people in a recent tragedy. Lenny is unsure how he feels about this, but everyone around him is laughing hysterically. Because of this environmental influence, he finds the comedian uproariously funny also. Lenny's reaction is best predicted by which theory of emotion?
   a. James-Lange
   b. Cannon-Bard
   c. two-factor
   d. circumplex model

Concept: V. D. 1 Competency: 50
Question Type: *Applied*

54. Corey is pumping iron at the gym and really gets her heart rate up. Afterward she is cooling down and doesn't even realize that she is still aroused. Just then she bumps into a guy and notices that she is attracted to him. Which of the following explains why she is highly attracted to this guy she does not even know?
   a. emotion regulation through suppression
   b. misattribution of arousal
   c. two-factor theory of emotion
   d. circumplex model of emotion

Concept: V. D. 2 Competency: 51
Question Type: *Applied*

55. Courtney's roommates are worried about her. She was crushed by the revelation that her boyfriend was cheating on her. She has been miserable and unable to eat or attend classes. Courtney's roommates should recommend which of the following techniques to help her regulate her mood?
   a. thought suppression
   b. distraction
   c. rumination
   d. rebound effect

Concept: V. D. 3 Competency: 52
Question Type: *Applied*

56. Klaus is a juror in a high-profile murder case. At one point the defense lawyer stated that the victim was a prostitute who was once convicted for spousal abuse. In response to the prosecutor's objections, the judge had this comment stricken from the record and ordered the jurors to ignore it. Despite his best efforts, this is all Klaus can think about for the rest of the day. This common failure of thought suppression is known as:
   a. thought suppression
   b. distraction
   c. rumination
   d. the rebound effect

Concept: V. D. 3. b. 1 Competency: 52
Question Type: *Applied*

SUMMING UP AND MEASURING UP

How Are Emotions Adaptive?

Emotions are adaptive because they bring about states of behavioural readiness. The evolutionary basis for emotions is supported by research on the crosscultural recognition of emotional displays. Facial expressions communicate meaning to others and enhance emotional states. Emotions aid in memory processes by garnering increased attention and deeper encoding of emotionally relevant events. Positive and negative emotions serve as guides for action. Emotions also repair and maintain close interpersonal relationships.

Research has shown that women smile more than men do. What is the most likely explanation for this?
   a. Women tend to be happier than men are.
   b. Men's facial muscles are not as pliant as women's.
   c. Smiling shows agreement, and men are more likely to be independent thinkers.
   d. It is more socially acceptable for women to smile—as both girls and boys learn in a cultural context.

How Do People Experience Emotions?

Emotions are often classified as primary emotions, which are similar across cultures and have an evolutionarily adaptive purpose, or secondary emotions, which are blends of primary emotions. Emotions have a valence (positive or negative) and a level of activation (level of arousal). The three main theories of emotion differ in their relative emphases on subjective experience, physiological changes, and cognitive interpretation. The James-Lange theory states that specific patterns of physical changes give rise to the perception of associated emotions. The Cannon-Bard theory proposes that two separate pathways, physical changes and subjective experience, occur at the same time. Schachter's two-factor theory emphasizes the combination of generalized physiological arousal and cognitive appraisals in determining specific emotions. We often misattribute the causes of our emotions, seeking environmental explanations for our feelings. People also use various strategies to alter their moods. The best methods for regulating negative affect include humor and distraction.

1. Primary emotions are:
   a. the emotions we feel as soon as we are in a new situation
   b. the same across cultures
   c. more common in men than in women
   d. the first emotions we feel as infants

2. Secondary emotions are:
   a. blends of primary emotions
   b. learned from intense experiences
   c. not as activated as primary emotions
   d. more subjective and phenomenological than primary emotions

ANSWER KEY

Item **Answer**

1. Motivation
2. Energizing; Directive; Persistence; Strength
3. b
4. c
5. d
6. d
7. a
8. c
9. b
10. d
11. b
12. d
13. a
14. challenging; not overly difficult; specific
15. c
16. b
17. c
18. b
19. c
20. b
21. cuisine
22. d
23. glucostatic theory; lipostatic theory
24. a
25. Excitement Phase; Plateau Phase; Orgasm Phase; Resolution Phase
26. a
27. Testosterone level. While males generally have higher testosterone levels than females, it is not a perfect relationship. There are men with low testosterone, and women with high testosterone. Testosterone has a direct relationship with number of sexual thoughts so it is more informative.
28. b
29. d
30. a
31. c
32. c
33. c
34. Thinking about things in an evolutionary context may be valid because our modern experience is quite brief relative to human history. Thus, it stands to reason that some of the ways our brain worked hundreds of years ago still influence our behaviour today. That said, we have very few behavioural indications of those prehistoric tendencies. For example, our eating behaviour is dictated by our schedules, our aggression tempered by perceived consequences, our desire for food and other goods does not result in stealing because of societal norms. Similarly, even though our evolutionary tendency may push us toward certain sexual behaviour, it does not dictate it. We have to adapt to our current society and doing so necessitates appropriate behaviour.
35. a
36. Emotion; Moods
37. d
38. c
39. a
40. b
41. b
42. Subjective Experience; Physical Changes; Cognitive Appraisal
43. c
44. a, b, a, b, a, b, a
45. d
46. a
47. a

48. c
49. amygdala; fear conditioning
50. a
51. cerebral asymmetry; negative; positive
52. b
53. c
54. b
55. b
56. d

Summing Up and Measuring Up

How Are Emotions Adaptive?

d. It is more socially acceptable for women to smile—as both girls and boys learn in a cultural context.

How Do People Experience Emotions?

1. b. the same across cultures
2. a. blends of primary emotions

KEY TERM EXERCISES

arousal

Textbook Definition:
Your Own Definition:
Your Own Example:

display rules

Textbook Definition:
Your Own Definition:
Your Own Example:

drive

Textbook Definition:
Your Own Definition:
Your Own Example:

emotion

Textbook Definition:
Your Own Definition:
Your Own Example:

extrinsic motivation

Textbook Definition:
Your Own Definition:
Your Own Example:

homeostasis

Textbook Definition:
Your Own Definition:
Your Own Example:

incentives

Textbook Definition:
Your Own Definition:
Your Own Example:

intrinsic motivation

Textbook Definition:
Your Own Definition:
Your Own Example:

motivation

Textbook Definition:
Your Own Definition:
Your Own Example:

need

Textbook Definition:
Your Own Definition:
Your Own Example:

need hierarchy

Textbook Definition:
Your Own Definition:
Your Own Example:

need to belong theory

Textbook Definition:
Your Own Definition:
Your Own Example:

primary emotions

Textbook Definition:
Your Own Definition:
Your Own Example:

secondary emotions

Textbook Definition:
Your Own Definition:
Your Own Example:

self-actualization

Textbook Definition:
Your Own Definition:
Your Own Example:

sexual response cycle

Textbook Definition:
Your Own Definition:
Your Own Example:

sexual strategies theory

Textbook Definition:
Your Own Definition:
Your Own Example:

Yerkes-Dodson law

Textbook Definition:
Your Own Definition:
Your Own Example:

somatic markers

Textbook Definition:
Your Own Definition:
Your Own Example:

CHAPTER 10 Health and Well-Being

Concept Map

- I. Can Psychosocial Factors Affect Health?
  - A. Background
    - 1. Health Psychology
    - 2. Well-Being
  - B. Biopsychosocial Model
    - 1. Biological Characteristics
    - 2. Behavioural Factors
    - 3. Social Conditions
    - 4. Circular Nature
  - C. Leading Causes of Death Are Behavioural
    - 1. Physical Health
    - 2. Accidents
  - D. Placebos Can Be Powerful Medicine
    - 1. Placebo Effect
      - a. Belief it Will Work
      - b. Decreased Anxiety
- II. How Do People Cope with Stress?
  - A. Stress
    - 1. Stressor
    - 2. Coping Response
    - 3. Two Types
      - a. Eustress
      - b. Distress
    - 4. Environmental Influences
      - a. Catastrophic Events
      - b. Positive and Negative Life Events
      - c. Daily Hassles
  - B. Stress Has Physiological Components
    - 1. Hypothalamic-Pituitary-Adrenal Axis
      - a. Influence on Memory
  - C. Sex Differences in Response to Stressors
    - 1. Fight-or-Flight Response
    - 2. Tend-and-Befriend Response
      - a. Oxytocin
  - D. General Adaptation Syndrome
    - 1. Alarm Stage
    - 2. Resistance Stage
    - 3. Exhaustion Stage
  - E. Stress Affects Health
    - 1. Immune System
      - a. Psychoneuroimmunology
      - b. Lymphocytes
    - 2. Heart Disease
      - a. Personality
        - 1. Type A Behaviour Pattern
          - A. Hostility
        - 2. Type B Behaviour Pattern
      - b. How Personality Influences Health
        - 1. Poor Behavioural Coping
        - 2. Direct Physiological Changes
      - c. Allostatic Load Theory of Illness
  - F. Coping Is a Process
    - 1. Appraisals
      - a. Primary Appraisal
      - b. Secondary Appraisal
    - 2. Types of Coping
      - a. Anticipatory Coping
      - b. Emotion-Focused Coping
        - 1. Positive Reappraisal
        - 2. Downward Comparisons
        - 3. Creation of Positive Events
      - c. Problem-Focused Coping
      - d. Emotion vs. Problem-Focused Coping
    - 3. Individual Differences in Coping
      - a. Hardiness
        - 1. Commitment
        - 2. Challenge

3. Control
4. Family-Focused Interventions

III. What Behaviours Affect Mental and Physical Health?
   A. Obesity
      1. Body Mass Index (BMI)
      2. Genetic Influence
         a. Interaction with Environment
      3. Stigma of Obesity
         a. Medical Effects
         b. Psychological Effects
         c. Cultural Differences
      4. Restrictive Dieting Does Not Work
         a. Weight is Socially Contagious
      5. Restrained Eating
      6. Disordered Eating
         a. Anorexia Nervosa
         b. Bulimia Nervosa
   B. Smoking
      1. Starting Smoking
         a. False-Consensus Effect
      2. Quitting Smoking
   C. Exercise
      1. Physical Health
      2. Mental Health
   D. Ethnic Differences
      1. Acculturation

IV. Can a Positive Attitude Keep Us Healthy?
   A. Being Positive Has Health Benefits
      1. Positive Psychology
      2. Learning to Be Happier
      3. Health Effects of Positive Emotions
   B. Social Integration and Social Support
      1. Buffering Hypothesis
      2. Emotional Disclosure
      3. Marriage
         a. Good vs. Bad Marriages
   C. Trust and Health
      1. Oxytocin and Trust
      2. Testosterone and Distrust
   D. Spirituality and Well-Being

CHAPTER SUMMARY

Can Psychosocial Factors Affect Health?

• The Biopsychosocial Model of Health Incorporates Multiple Perspectives for Understanding and Improving Health: The biopsychosocial model describes the reciprocal and multiple influences of biological predispositions, individual thoughts and actions, and societal variables on health. According to this model, people are active participants in shaping health outcomes.

• Behaviour Contributes to the Leading Causes of Death: The leading causes of death are all behavioural, especially among teenagers and young adults, who are most likely to die from accidents, homicide, and suicide. Many lifestyle variables, such as eating unhealthy foods, being obese, and leading a sedentary life, contribute to heart disease, cancer, respiratory disease, and other disease states that reduce the quality and length of life. People with certain personality types, such as those with hostile personalities, are at an increased risk for heart disease and earlier death.

• Placebos Can Be Powerful Medicine: Placebos can have powerful effects on health and well-being, but a placebo works only if the person taking it believes in its ability to reduce pain or disease. The same brain processes involved in responses to chemically active (nonplacebo) drugs are involved when patients respond to placebos.

How Do People Cope with Stress?

• Stress Has Physiological Components: Stressful events cause a cascade of physiological events, most importantly the release of hormones from the hypothalamus, the pituitary gland, and the adrenal glands. Stress-related hormones circulate through the bloodstream, affecting organs throughout the body.

• There Are Sex Differences in Responses to Stressors: Women and men respond somewhat differently to stress. Women will more likely tend and befriend, whereas men will more likely have a fight-or-flight response. Consistent with an evolutionary perspective on psychology, these different styles may be related to sex-differentiated roles in hunter-gatherer societies and to higher estrogen concentrations in women during childbearing years.

• The General Adaptation Syndrome Is a Bodily Response to Stress: Selye outlined the general adaptation syndrome, the steps by which the body responds to stress. The initial response, alarm, is followed by resistance; if the stressor continues, the final response is exhaustion.

• Stress Affects Health: A small amount of stress may be healthy, but excessive stress negatively affects health by placing a heavy allostatic load on the physical system, impairing memory and cognition. When we are constantly stressed, our bodies do not have enough time to return to homeostasis, the resting state, to recover from stress reactions.

• Coping Is a Process: Coping means adjusting to stress. We have emotion-focused and problem-focused coping strategies. The latter are usually more constructive in the long run because they allow us to find ways to change a stressful situation.

What Behaviours Affect Mental and Physical Health?

• Obesity Results from a Genetic Predisposition and Overeating: In industrialized countries around the world, an increasing number of people are obese. Obesity results from a combination of a genetic predisposition and overeating. Restrictive diets rarely help obese people lose weight.

• Smoking Is a Leading Cause of Death: Smoking contributes to all the major diseases that kill people, including heart disease and many cancers. People usually start smoking as children or adolescents and continue because of the attractive traits sometimes associated with people who smoke, such as defying authority.

• Exercise Has Physical, Emotional, and Cognitive Benefits: Exercise has been shown to reduce depression, improve memory, and speed healing, in addition to its positive effects on muscles and the respiratory system. Exercise can reduce cognitive decline in older adults. Despite these positive effects, too many people fail to exercise.

• There Are Ethnic Differences in Health Behaviours: Ethnic and racial differences in health behaviours can explain some of the disparities in health outcomes. As groups become more acculturated to the mainstream culture, they tend to adopt the health behaviours of that culture, positive and negative. Health interventions intended to bring about changes need to consider the behaviours of different groups.

Can a Positive Attitude Keep Us Healthy?

• Being Positive Has Health Benefits: A range of evidence shows that there are health benefits to having a positive, optimistic outlook.

• Social Support and Social Integration Are Associated with Good Health: Social support is critical to good health because when others care about us, they provide material and psychological support. They can help us reinterpret events more positively. Socially integrated individuals have meaningful relations with others.

• Trust and Health Are Related across Cultures: Oxytocin, sometimes called the trust hormone, is secreted during trusting encounters; it is involved in infant/parent attachment and love relationships.

• Spirituality Contributes to Well-Being: Being spiritual can give meaning to people's lives; members of religious communities also provide physical assistance to one another and support healthy behaviours.

COMPETENCY MAP

Can Psychosocial Factors Affect Health?

Background

1. What does health psychology involve?
2. How does well-being differ from health?

Biopsychosocial Model

3. Identify the main components of the biopsychosocial model.
4. Describe how the main components of the biopsychosocial model interact.

Leading Causes of Death Are Behavioural

5. How do our own behaviours relate to our chances of death?

Placebos Can Be Powerful Medicine

6. Explain the placebo effect.

How Do People Cope with Stress?

Stress

7. Understand what leads to stress.
8. What is the purpose of the coping response relative to a stressor?
9. Distinguish between eustress and distress.
10. Identify misconceptions concerning stress.
11. Describe how the environment can influence stress.

Stress Has Physiological Components

12. Explain the hypothalamic-pituitary-adrenal axis and its influences.

Sex Differences in Response to Stressors

13. What is the fight-or-flight response?
14. What is the tend-and-befriend response?

General Adaptation Syndrome

15. Identify the three stages of the general adaptation syndrome.
16. Distinguish between the three stages of the general adaptation syndrome.

Stress Affects Health

17. Explain how stress influences the immune system.
18. What is the role of personality in heart disease?

19. Give the key characteristic of personality that relates to heart disease.
20. In what two ways can personality influence the heart or health more generally?
21. Explain the allostatic load theory of illness. What theory is this similar to?

Coping Is a Process

22. Distinguish between primary and secondary appraisals.
23. How is anticipatory coping different from other types of coping?
24. Describe positive techniques of emotion-focused coping.
25. Distinguish between emotion-focused and problem-focused coping.
26. Identify the characteristics of hardiness.
27. Describe family-focused interventions.

What Behaviours Affect Mental and Physical Health?

Obesity

28. What is body mass index?
29. How do genes directly and indirectly influence obesity?
30. Identify medical and psychological effects of obesity.
31. What are the cultural differences regarding the stigma of obesity?
32. Identify problems with restrictive dieting.
33. What does it mean to say that weight is socially contagious?
34. How does restrained eating differ from restricted eating?
35. Distinguish between anorexia nervosa and bulimia nervosa.

Smoking

36. Identify how the false-consensus effect promotes smoking.

Exercise

37. How does exercise influence physical and mental health?

Ethnic Differences

38. Explain acculturation.

Can a Positive Attitude Keep Us Healthy?

Being Positive Has Health Benefits

39. Describe the basic idea behind positive psychology.
40. Identify techniques people can use to become happier.
41. How do positive emotions influence health?

Social Integration and Social Support

42. Explain the buffering hypothesis.
43. What are the key elements of emotional disclosure that help it work best?
44. How does marriage positively and negatively influence health for husbands and wives?

Trust and Health

45. Differentiate the influence of oxytocin from testosterone as it applies to trust and health.

Spirituality and Well-Being

46. How does spirituality influence well-being?

KNOWLEDGE CHECK

1. ______________________________ is the area of psychological science that applies psychological principles to promote well-being.

   Concept: I. A   Competency: 1
   Question Type: *Factual*

2. ______________ involves the absence of disease. In contrast, ______________ focuses on a positive state in which we feel our best.
   a. Wellness; health
   b. Wellness; well-being
   c. Health; well-being
   d. Well-being; health

   Concept: I. A   Competency: 2
   Question Type: *Factual*

3. Concept: I. B   Competency: 3
   Question Type: *Factual*

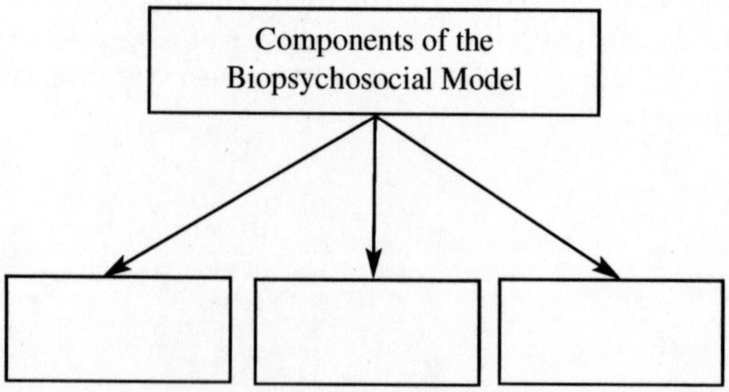

4. Thalia is constantly sick with either the cold, the flu, or a stomach virus. Her doctor suggests that her problem may be related to a combination of factors including the fact that Thalia's mother is frequently sick, that Thalia works in a high stress environment, and that it is part of her culture to work long hours resulting in less sleep. Thalia's doctor is applying the:
   a. health and wellness model
   b. biopsychosocial model
   c. global factors theory
   d. general adaptation syndrome

   Concept: I. B Competency: 4
   Question Type: *Applied*

5. According to statistics, we are most likely to die from which of the following?
   a. flying
   b. shark attacks
   c. terrorist attacks
   d. heart disease

   Concept: I. C Competency: 5
   Question Type: *Factual*

6. Two roommates, Mona and Steph, go to the health centre on campus with the same stomach illness. Because the health centre has run out of medicine, Mona and Steph are both given sugar water, but are told it is medicine. Mona believes it will work while Steph does not. In three days Mona is better, and Steph is better in four days. Mona most likely got better due to ______________. Steph most likely got better due to ______________.
   a. the sugar water actually helping; the placebo effect
   b. the placebo effect; the placebo effect
   c. the sugar water actually helping; her body getting better on its own
   d. the placebo effect; her body getting better on its own

   Concept: I. D Competency: 6
   Question Type: *Conceptual*

7. Imagine that you walk into your history class and find out you have a surprise 50-page paper due. Is this inherently stressful? Based on what leads to stress, under what circumstances would this assignment not be stressful?

   ____

   ____

   ____

   ____

   Concept: II. A Competency: 7
   Question Type: *Conceptual*

8. A ____________________________ is an environmental event or stimulus that threatens an organism; it elicits a ____________________________, which is any response an organism makes to avoid, escape from, or minimize an aversive stimulus.

   Concept: II. A Competency: 8
   Question Type: *Factual*

9. Natalia was engaged and her fiancé called off the marriage at the last minute. As a result Natalia experiences strain on her body resulting from the experience of:
   a. microstressors
   b. distress
   c. eustress
   d. macrostressor

   Concept: II. A. 3 Competency: 9
   Question Type: *Applied*

10. All of the following statements about stress are true EXCEPT:
    a. stress arises from negative experiences; positive events are not stressful
    b. some stress, in low doses, is beneficial
    c. the greater the number of changes a person experiences, the greater the stress
    d. different levels of stress are optimal for different people

    Concept: II. A. 3 Competency: 10
    Question Type: *Applied*

11. Monica is on her way to class when traffic is slowed by an accident. She is already late for class when she finds there are no parking spaces near her building. When she finally arrives at class and gets an annoyed stare from her professor, she finds she has no pen to write with. These stressors that are known as:
    a. major life stressors
    b. daily hassles
    c. eustress
    d. macrostressor

    Concept: II. A. 4 Competency: 11
    Question Type: *Applied*

12. Out of nowhere, a bird crashes into your windshield while you are driving your car on the highway. According to the hypothalamic-pituitary-adrenal axis how does your body react?

    ____

    ____

    ____

    ____

    Concept: II. B   Competency: 12
    Question Type: *Applied*

13. While walking home from a party, Ken believes someone is following him and thinks he hears the click of a gun. As a result, Ken's body experiences a physiological reaction known as the:
    a. general adaptation syndrome
    b. eustress reaction
    c. fight-or-flight response
    d. tend-and-befriend response

    Concept: II. C. 1   Competency: 13
    Question Type: *Applied*

14. While in a business meeting about new marketing ideas, Sam has her ideas directly challenged. She responds by pointing out that several coworkers at the meeting share her view, and looks to them for support. This reaction is most consistent with the:
    a. general adaptation syndrome
    b. eustress reaction
    c. fight-or-flight response
    d. tend-and-befriend response

    Concept: II. C. 2   Competency: 14
    Question Type: *Applied*

15. Concept: II. D   Competency: 15
    Question Type: *Factual*

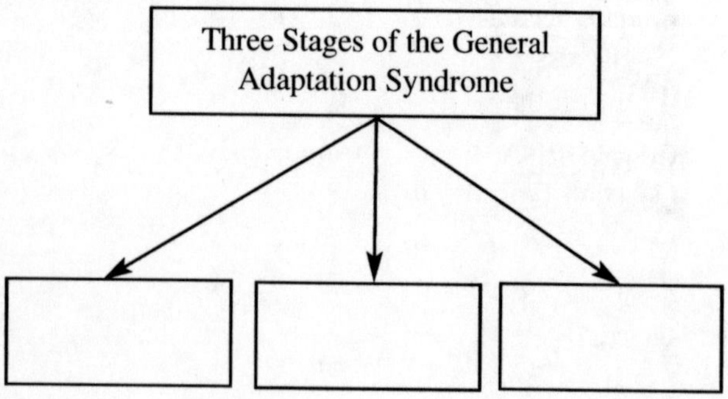

16. Mike is driving along the highway when a huge 18-wheeler truck drifts into his lane right in front of him. His heart begins to pound and his blood pressure escalates as he swerves to avoid the truck. At this point Mike is in which stage of the general adaptation syndrome?
    a. alarm
    b. reactive
    c. resistance
    d. exhaustion

    Concept: II. D   Competency: 16
    Question Type: *Applied*

17. Kyle is under a great deal of stress from work, school, and problems at home. As a result, all of the following are true about how stress negatively affects his health EXCEPT:
    a. stress leads to a lower lymphocyte (i.e., white blood cell) count in the blood
    b. stress increases the number of toxins and germs in your system that cause you to get sick
    c. stress increases the chances of engaging in unhealthy behaviours (i.e., poor diet)
    d. stress decreases the chances of engaging in healthy behaviours (i.e., exercise)

    Concept: II. E   Competency: 17
    Question Type: *Applied*

18. Lori is a busy person, and she always speed-walks through campus, never stopping to talk to people. When she does stop to talk, she speaks rapidly and interrupts the other person constantly. She also is frustrated and hostile, especially when waiting in line or competing with other students. Lori can best be described as having which type of personality?
    a. type A
    b. type B
    c. type C
    d. hardiness

    Concept: II. E. 2   Competency: 18
    Question Type: *Applied*

19. Research has identified ______________________ as the key characteristic of personality that relates to heart disease.

    Concept: II. E. 2. a. 1. A Competency: 19
    Question Type: *Factual*

20. Hostility may lead to greater heart disease in all of the following ways EXCEPT:
    a. increased activation of the parasympathetic nervous system
    b. increase in overeating, drinking too much, or smoking
    c. activating the fight-or-flight response
    d. elevating levels of cortisol and blood pressure

    Concept: II. E. 2. b Competency: 20
    Question Type: *Factual*

21. According to the ____________________, the body regulates the response to excessive stress and tries to return to a steady state. If stress is too excessive, returning to a steady state is more difficult and makes the body prone to illness. The idea of a steady state is similar to the idea of ____________________.

    Concept: II. E. 2. c Competency: 21
    Question Type: *Factual*

22. Xavier has four exams and a paper due in the next week. He also has an athletic event and a party that he should attend. He constructs a schedule that will allow him to get his work done as well as meet his social obligations. This evaluation of response options and potential coping behaviours is an example of:
    a. primary appraisals
    b. secondary appraisals
    c. emotion-focused behaviours
    d. positive reappraisals

    Concept: II. F. 1 Competency: 22
    Question Type: *Applied*

23. Zeke has looked ahead in his day planner and knows that the upcoming month is going to present a lot of stressors. As a result of this, he decides that he should make a point to exercise more frequently, get a full night's sleep, and eat better. What type of coping best describes his behaviour?
    a. anticipatory coping
    b. problem-focused coping
    c. emotion-focused coping
    d. positive reappraisal coping

    Concept: II. F. 2 Competency: 23
    Question Type: *Applied*

24. Melinda was upset about the grade she received in her psychology course. The combination of exams and papers resulted in an 89.6 percent average. However, her professor refused to round this number up and gave her a B rather than an A. She was whining about the unfairness of it all when a student came by crying because she had flunked out of school. Oh well, she thought, at least I am not in that situation! This is an example of the positive reappraisal process of:
    a. creation of positive events
    b. secondary appraisals
    c. delusional thinking
    d. downward comparisons

    Concept: II. F. 2. b. 2 Competency: 24
    Question Type: *Applied*

25. Raoul is trying to get a class he needs to graduate next December, and he just found out that it won't be offered until next spring. Although he is upset, he realizes that there is nothing he can do about it and that the situation is out of his control. So he just gripes about it to his friends, who comfort him and tell him they will all have a good time next year anyhow. What course of action is Raoul taking to deal with his stress?
    a. anticipatory coping
    b. thought suppression
    c. emotion-focused coping
    d. problem-focused coping

    Concept: II. F. 2. d Competency: 25
    Question Type: *Applied*

26. Meg, a hard-working CEO, is committed to her work and family. She enjoys the challenges she experiences in her job and in her personal life. She has a sense of being in control of her life and of her destiny. Overall, she doesn't experience much stress despite her busy life. Meg is high in the personality characteristic of:
    a. hardiness
    b. extraversion
    c. realistic pessimism
    d. Type A personality

    Concept: II. F. 3 Competency: 26
    Question Type: *Applied*

27. Evidence for the effectiveness of family-focused interventions is ____________. The key determinant may be which aspect of hardiness?
    a. not strong; commitment
    b. not strong; control
    c. strong; commitment
    d. strong; control

    Concept: II. F. 4 Competency: 27
    Question Type: *Factual*

28. Albert's physician is concerned about Albert's weight. To determine whether Albert would qualify as obese, she computes a ratio of his body weight to his height in a measure known as the:
    a. actuarial cutoff technique
    b. body mass index
    c. weight-density indicator
    d. scale of morbid obesity

    Concept: III. A Competency: 28
    Question Type: *Applied*

29. If genes primarily determine body weight, why has the percentage of Americans who are obese doubled over the past few decades?

    ____

    ____

    ____

    ____

    Concept: II. A. 2 Competency: 29
    Question Type: *Conceptual*

30. All of the following statements about obesity are true, EXCEPT:
    a. Obesity is associated with a significant number of medical problems, including heart disease, high blood pressure, and gastric ailments.
    b. Perceiving oneself as overweight is linked to depression, anxiety, and low self-esteem.
    c. Obesity causes low self-esteem.
    d. Obese individuals are viewed as less attractive, less socially adept, less intelligent, and less productive than their normal-weight peers.

    Concept: III. A. 3 Competency: 30
    Question Type: *Factual*

31. Why would being obese be desirable in some cultures?

    ____

    ____

    ____

    ____

    Concept: III. A. 3. c Competency: 31
    Question Type: *Conceptual*

32. Restrictive dieting tends to be ineffective for all of the following reasons EXCEPT:
    a. the body slows its metabolism to compensate for the lack of food
    b. a person's ability to gain or lose weight is determined in part by genetics
    c. weight gain occurs much faster in previously starved animals than would be expected by caloric intake alone
    d. people on diets rarely lose weight in the first place

    Concept: III. A. 4 Competency: 32
    Question Type: *Factual*

33. The idea that weight is socially contagious suggests that if you want to lose weight, which of the following would be most effective?
    a. Cook the same meals as people who are the weight you want to be.
    b. Spend lots of time with a group of people who are the weight you want to be.
    c. Spend lots of time with a group of people who are heavier than you want to be.
    d. Spend lots of time with close same-sex friends who are the weight you want to be.

    Concept: III. A. 4 Competency: 33
    Question Type: *Applied*

34. Nishit is trying to lose weight. He does a good job all week keeping his calories down but tends to binge on the weekend because he feels he has blown his diet anyway. What type of eating pattern does he display?
    a. restrained eating
    b. restricted eating
    c. obesity-prone eating
    d. socially contagious eating

    Concept: III. A. 5 Competency: 34
    Question Type: *Applied*

35. Alexia is average to slightly overweight and routinely diets with periods of binge eating that are often followed by forced vomiting. She worries excessively about her weight and exercises excessively to compensate. She most likely suffers from what type of disordered eating?
    a. binge-eating disorder
    b. anorexia nervosa
    c. bulimia nervosa
    d. None, her behaviour is not disordered.

    Concept: III. A. 6 Competency: 35
    Question Type: *Applied*

36. Larry is an adolescent who desperately wants to fit in with the crowd. He takes up smoking because he incorrectly believes that this behaviour is common among his peer group. This overestimation of the number of adolescent and adult smokers is known as the:
    a. partial reinforcement extinction effect
    b. social referencing effect
    c. associative reward effect
    d. false-consensus effect

    Concept: III. B. 1. a Competency: 36
    Question Type: *Applied*

37. Morrison spends at least 40 minutes a day doing aerobic exercise. Based on the research, exercise will likely benefit him in all of the following ways EXCEPT:
    a. promotes neurogenesis, the growth of new neurons and neural connections
    b. decreases the amount of time he needs to sleep each night
    c. enhances memory and cognition
    d. reduces depression, stress, and improves mood

    Concept: III. C Competency: 37
    Question Type: *Applied*

38. ______________________ is the extent to which individuals assimilate the customs, values, beliefs, and behaviours of the mainstream culture—it is an important variable in understanding why different groups have disparate health outcomes and behaviours.

    Concept: III. D Competency: 38
    Question Type: *Factual*

39. Positive psychology emphasizes ______________________.

    Concept: IV. A. 1 Competency: 39
    Question Type: *Factual*

40. Onc of your friends has been really unhappy lately and has asked you for suggestions to help get them feeling happy again. All of the following are good suggestions EXCEPT:
    a. Write a letter of gratitude and deliver it in person to someone who has been kind to you but whom you have never thanked.
    b. Keep a journal that focuses on the positive aspects of your life, health, freedom, friends, etc.
    c. Suggest that they spend a little time being selfish and focusing on their own needs and wants.
    d. Act like a happy person by just going through the motions of being a happy person will create a happy emotion.

    Concept: IV. A. 2 Competency: 40
    Question Type: *Applied*

41. Research shows that all of the following are associated with positive emotions EXCEPT:
    a. enhanced immune system functioning
    b. greater longevity
    c. higher levels of hope were associated with reduced risk of all medical diseases
    d. less exposure to germs

    Concept: IV. A. 3 Competency: 41
    Question Type: *Applied*

42. Alex is having a tough time at home with his wife and children. He comes into work every day and shares many of these interactions with his colleagues, who offer sympathy, advice, and support. The fact that this social support actually lessens the negative effects of stress is an example of the:
    a. resilience phenomenon
    b. buffering hypothesis
    c. familial intervention theory
    d. dampening phenomenon

    Concept: IV. B. 1 Competency: 42
    Question Type: *Applied*

43. Assume your roommate has just experienced an emotional break-up. You know emotional disclosure could help, and to make it the most beneficial what key features should you suggest?

    ____

    ____

    ____

    ____

    Concept: IV. B. 2 Competency: 43
    Question Type: *Applied*

44. Marital conflict has more negative health outcomes for ______________. The positive effects of marriage are stronger for ______________. Unmarried people are ______________ than those in bad marriages.
   a. wives; wives; less happy
   b. wives; husbands; happier
   c. husbands; wives; less happy
   d. husbands; husbands; happier

   Concept: IV. B. 3 Competency: 44
   Question Type: *Factual*

45. Jonesy is a fantastic used car salesman. He has a way about him that leads customers to trust him. Research suggests that Jonesy may secrete which hormone? However, some male customers don't trust him and likely secrete which hormone?
   a. oxytocin; testosterone
   b. testosterone; oxytocin
   c. oxytocin; estrogen
   d. estrogen; oxytocin

   Concept: IV. C Competency: 45
   Question Type: *Applied*

46. Harry has experienced several bad events in the past year. His parents died, his wife left him, and he found out he has cancer. According to research, which of the following will be most likely to help Harry deal with his problems?
   a. making a lot of money
   b. not talking about his problems
   c. maintaining his independence and not relying too much on others' help
   d. having a strong religious faith

   Concept: IV. D Competency: 46
   Question Type: *Applied*

PSYCHOLOGY AND SOCIETY

Write a brief description of your current level of happiness. Place your description in an envelope and seal it. Then, for one week, engage in one of the happiness interventions described in the chapter. At the end of one week, write another brief description of your level of happiness. Then, open your sealed envelope and reread your initial description. Write an essay commenting on your subjective experience of the happiness intervention (e.g., what did it feel like to complete the intervention?) and describing how your preintervention and postintervention happiness descriptions are similar or different. If they are different, to what do you attribute these differences? To what extent is it appropriate to attribute these differences to the intervention?

SUMMING UP AND MEASURING UP

Can Psychosocial Factors Affect Health?

The biopsychosocial model of health and illness posits the interaction of biological variables (such as genetic predispositions), psychological variables (such as personality types and health behaviours), and social variables (such as social support and cultural beliefs about diseases). The leading causes of serious illness and death are, at least in part, behavioural. Behaviours such as overeating, lack of exercise, and smoking contribute in large measure to the development of coronary heart disease and other illnesses. For teens and young adults, accidents, homicides, and suicides are the leading causes of death; almost half of all deaths in this age range are due to accidents, many of them preventable. Placebos can powerfully affect health, so it is not surprising that they activate the same areas of the brain and respond to other drugs in ways that are similar to validated treatments.

A doctor claims to have developed a new treatment for Alzheimer's disease, a serious disease that progresses to severe cognitive impairments. The treatment consists of transplanting the lining of a cow's stomach into the patient's brain. The doctor has tried this method with two patients, and his preliminary testing indicated that both patients had improved abilities to remember. Why might the doctor have achieved these results?

a. The patients could not have improved, so he must be lying.
b. It is possible that immediately after the surgery, the two patients believed their memory was somewhat improved even when it was not and may have tried harder when performing simple tests of memory.
c. The surgery was done in a major hospital, so the technique must be valid.
d. The stomach and the brain have many similarities, so the patients likely did improve.

How Do People Cope with Stress?

Stress occurs when people feel overwhelmed by the challenges they face, as when major change happens in their lives. Hans Selye's general adaptation theory conceptualizes the stages of physiological coping. Stresses include major life changes as well as daily hassles. Females' responses to stress include the tendency to affiliate with a group in which members care for each other, whereas males tend to have a fight-or-flight response in which their bodies prepare them for combat or fast escape. Cognitive appraisals, such as determining the relevance of the stressor and adopting a problem-focused versus emotion-focused approach, can alleviate stress or minimize its harmful effects. Hardy people handle stress well because they believe they can control events in their lives, are committed to and actively engaged in what they do, and see obstacles as challenges to be overcome. A positive appraisal of events is also a good way to regulate emotions. When providing care for an ill person, it is important to allow the patient to maintain control over his or her life. Maintaining such control is a trait of hardy people.

You enter the classroom a bit late and find everyone seated, with a pencil and test form on each desk. You forgot there is an exam today! After settling in your seat, you calm down, gather your thoughts, and do your best to answer the questions. Your response is consistent with which type of coping?

a. emotion-focused coping
b. alarmed coping
c. problem-focused coping
d. termination coping

What Behaviours Affect Mental and Physical Health?

How people behave in their daily lives profoundly affects their physical and mental health. People engage in many unhealthy behaviours when they are stressed, such as eating fatty foods and smoking. Other behaviours that directly affect health include suicides, homicides, and accidents. People who eat too much may become obese, especially if they have a genetic predisposition to put on weight, and obesity poses some serious health risks. Smoking is especially bad for health and is a leading cause of death. Unfortunately, smoking typically starts in adolescence, when people give little thought to long-term consequences. Exercise is one of the best things people can do for their health. Regular physical activity enhances emotional experiences, improves memory and cognition, and builds a strong, healthy body. Racial and ethnic groups exhibit health disparities, some of which can be attributed to differences in their health behaviours. Interventions may work best if they are grounded in an understanding of the health behaviours of different ethnicities.

Which of the following strategies would likely be most effective in persuading junior high school kids not to smoke?

a. Tell kids how expensive it is to smoke.
b. Deliver a message that smokers are not cool because they smell bad and develop stained teeth.
c. Explain the health consequences of smoking and the physiological aspects of addiction.

Can a Positive Attitude Keep Us Healthy?

A variety of evidence shows that optimistic people are healthier and live longer than their more negative counterparts. These findings show the flip side of the negative health consequences associated with hostile personalities. Social support and being socially integrated in a group are also protective health factors, because concerned others provide material and psychological support. Marriages low in conflict have a positive association with health, though these effects are greater for men than for women. Women are more likely than men to feel the stress of conflictual marriages and initiate divorce when marriages are troubled. Similarly, trust is associated with attachment, love, and better health across Canada. Spirituality is also associated with better health due to the sense of meaning that can be derived from religious beliefs and the support people receive from communities of faith.

What is the relationship between marriage and health?

a. Married people are always healthier than never-married, divorced, or widowed adults.
b. Married people tend to be healthier, but only when there is not too much conflict in their marriages.
c. Divorced adults are the healthiest group because they are happy to be out of bad marriages.
d. Single adults are the healthiest because they usually have more money to take care of their health.

ANSWER KEY

Item **Answer**

1. Health psychology
2. c
3. biological characteristics; behavioural factors; social conditions
4. b
5. d
6. d
7. Things in life are not inherently stressful. Instead, we dictate what is stressful by how we think about and react to situations. Because stress results from a mismatch between the demands of a situation and our perceived ability to deal with them, anything that helps us better deal with the situation makes it less stressful. That might be our own perspective: "The paper has been assigned so I have no choice but to do it and do my best"; or could result from an increase in resources (e.g., having 3 days to write the paper vs. 3 months or 3 years). Having 3 years to write 50 pages is MUCH less stressful because your resources are much more able to meet the demand of the situation.
8. stressor; coping response
9. b
10. a
11. b
12. When the bird hits, the hypothalamus sends a chemical message to the pituitary gland, which then secretes hormones that travel through the bloodstream until they reach the adrenal glands, which in turn secrete cortisol, or glucocorticoids. Cortisol is responsible for many of

the feelings that we have when we are stressed, including a rush of energy. The influence of hormones is somewhat delayed so you will likely feel the rush of energy long after the shock of the bird-windshield encounter has passed.

13. c
14. d
15. alarm; resistance; exhaustion
16. a
17. b
18. a
19. hostility
20. a
21. allostatic load theory of illness; homeostasis
22. b
23. a
24. d
25. c
26. a
27. b
28. b
29. As with almost any outcome, there is more than one cause. While genes may be the primary influence, they are not the only influence. Genes may influence our predisposition toward becoming obese, but environmental factors influence whether we will actually become obese. For example, a person with a strong genetic disposition for obesity will likely not become obese if they are in an environment where food is scarce.
30. c
31. In cultures where food is more scarce, being obese may be a sign of wealth or status. It also makes a person less susceptible to some infectious diseases, reduces the chance of starvation, and increases successful pregnancies in women.
32. d
33. d
34. a
35. c
36. d
37. b
38. Acculturation
39. the strengths and virtues that help people thrive, as well as what makes people happy.
40. c
41. d
42. b
43. Try to discern meaning from the event as you write to help gain a better understanding. Write for 15 minutes straight. Express what is troubling you and how you feel about it.
44. b
45. a
46. d

Psychology and Society

Answer: There really is no one correct answer to this question. Responses should reflect openness to trying the interventions. If you come to either of the following conclusions, remember the problems with using individual data points to test predictions: "I don't feel happier. Therefore, the intervention doesn't work." and "I feel happier. Therefore, this intervention is an amazing panacea."

Summing Up and Measuring Up

Can Psychosocial Factors Affect Health?

b. It is possible that immediately after the surgery, the two patients believed their memory was somewhat improved even when it was not and may have tried harder when performing simple tests of memory.

How Do People Cope with Stress?

c. problem-focused coping

What Behaviours Affect Mental and Physical Health?

b. Deliver a message that smokers are not cool because they smell bad and develop stained teeth.

Can a Positive Attitude Keep Us Healthy?

b. Married people tend to be healthier, but only when there is not too much conflict in their marriages.

KEY TERM EXERCISES

allostatic load theory of illness

Textbook Definition:
Your Own Definition:
Your Own Example:

anorexia nervosa

Textbook Definition:
Your Own Definition:
Your Own Example:

biopsychosocial model

Textbook Definition:
Your Own Definition:
Your Own Example:

body mass index (BMI)

Textbook Definition:
Your Own Definition:
Your Own Example:

buffering hypothesis

Textbook Definition:
Your Own Definition:
Your Own Example:

bulimia nervosa

Textbook Definition:
Your Own Definition:
Your Own Example:

coping response

Textbook Definition:
Your Own Definition:
Your Own Example:

emotion-focused coping

Textbook Definition:
Your Own Definition:
Your Own Example:

fight-or-flight response

Textbook Definition:
Your Own Definition:
Your Own Example:

general adaptation syndrome

Textbook Definition:
Your Own Definition:
Your Own Example:

health psychology

Textbook Definition:
Your Own Definition:
Your Own Example:

hypothalamic-pituitary-adrenal (HPA) axis

Textbook Definition:
Your Own Definition:
Your Own Example:

immune system

Textbook Definition:
Your Own Definition:
Your Own Example:

lymphocytes

Textbook Definition:
Your Own Definition:
Your Own Example:

oxytocin

Textbook Definition:
Your Own Definition:
Your Own Example:

placebo effect

Textbook Definition:
Your Own Definition:
Your Own Example:

primary appraisal

Textbook Definition:
Your Own Definition:
Your Own Example:

problem-focused coping

Textbook Definition:
Your Own Definition:
Your Own Example:

secondary appraisal

Textbook Definition:
Your Own Definition:
Your Own Example:

social integration

Textbook Definition:
Your Own Definition:
Your Own Example:

stress

Textbook Definition:
Your Own Definition:
Your Own Example:

stressor

Textbook Definition:
Your Own Definition:
Your Own Example:

tend-and-befriend response

Textbook Definition:
Your Own Definition:
Your Own Example:

Type A behaviour pattern

Textbook Definition:
Your Own Definition:
Your Own Example:

Type B behaviour pattern

Textbook Definition:
Your Own Definition:
Your Own Example:

well-being

Textbook Definition:
Your Own Definition:
Your Own Example:

CHAPTER 11 Human Development

CONCEPT MAP

I. What Shapes a Child?
   A. Developmental Psychology
      1. Predictable
      2. Environmental Influences
   B. Development Starts in the Womb
      1. Physical Development
         a. Zygote, Embryo, Fetus
         b. Brain Development
         c. Hormones
      2. Teratogens
         a. Fetal Alcohol Syndrome (FAS)
      3. Ethics: Alcohol and Drug Use During Pregnancy
   C. Brain Development Promotes Learning
      1. Processing Sensory Stimuli
      2. Reflexes
         a. Grasping
         b. Rooting
      3. Myelination and Neuronal Connections
         a. Synaptic Pruning
         b. Plasticity
      4. Sensitive Learning Periods
   D. Attachment Promotes Survival
      1. Attachment
      2. Attachment in Other Species
         a. Imprinting
         b. Harlow's Monkeys
      3. Attachment Style
         a. Strange Situation
         b. Secure Attachment
         c. Avoidant Attachment
         d. Anxious-ambivalent Attachment
      4. Chemistry of Attachment

II. How Do Children Learn about Their Worlds?
   A. Perception Introduces the World
      1. Research Techniques with Infants
         a. Preferential Looking Technique
         b. Orienting Reflex
      2. Vision
         a. Preference
         b. Acuity
         c. Depth Perception
      3. Auditory Perception
   B. Memory Improves over Childhood
      1. Infantile Amnesia
      2. Inaccurate Memory
         a. Source Amnesia
         b. Confabulation
   C. Piaget's Stages of Development
      1. General Concepts
         a. Schemas
         b. Assimilation
         c. Accommodation
      2. Stages
         a. Sensorimotor Stage
            1. Object Permanence
         b. Preoperational Stage
            1. Conservation
         c. Concrete Operational Stage
         d. Formal Operational Stage
      3. Challenges to Piaget
   D. Infants Have Early Knowledge about the World
      1. Understanding the Laws of Nature
         a. Physics
         b. Mathematics
   E. Humans Learn from Interacting with Others
      1. Theory of Mind
         a. False Belief Test

b. Culturally Universal
2. Kohlberg Stages of Moral Reasoning
a. Preconventional
b. Conventional
c. Postconventional
3. Moral Emotions
a. Empathy
b. Sympathy
4. Physiological Basis of Morality
a. Somatic Marker Hypothesis
F. Language Develops in an Orderly Fashion
1. From Zero to 60,000
a. First Words
1. Phonemes
b. Telegraphic Speech
2. Acquiring Language with the Hands
3. Universal Grammar
a. Language Acquisition Device
b. Vygotsky
c. Interaction Across Culture
4. Learning to Read
a. Phonics
b. Whole-Language
5. Animal Communication

III. How Do Children and Adolescents Develop Their Identities?
A. Social Development
B. Social Systems Influence Development
1. Biocultural Systems Theory
a. Microsystem
b. Exosystem
c. Macrosystem
d. Chronosystem
C. Friends Influence Identity and Behaviour
1. Parents versus Peers
a. Group Socialization Theory
D. Parental Style Can Affect Children's Well-Being
1. Role of Temperament
2. Parents' Behaviour
3. Parents' Attitudes
E. Divorce Is Difficult for Children
1. Divorce vs. Single Parent Homes
2. Staying Together vs. Divorce
F. Gender Identity Is Determined by Biology and Cultural Norms
1. Gender vs. Sex Differences
a. Gender Identity
b. Gender Roles
c. Gender Schemas
2. Cultural and Situational Factors
3. Biological Bases of Sexual Identity
G. People Define Themselves in Terms of Race and Ethnicity

IV. What Brings Meaning to Adulthood?
A. Life-Span Perspective
1. Erikson Stages of Adult Development
a. Intimacy vs. Isolation
b. Generativity vs. Stagnation
c. Integrity vs. Despair
B. Adults Are Affected by Life Transitions
1. Career
2. Marriage
3. Having Children
C. Aging Can Be Successful
1. Contribution to Society
2. Physical Changes
3. Mental Ability
4. Socioemotional Selectivity Theory
D. Cognition Changes during Aging
1. Memory
a. Recognition vs. Recall
b. Younger vs. Older Adults
2. Intelligence

CHAPTER SUMMARY

What Shapes a Child?

• Development Starts in the Womb: Many factors in the prenatal environment, such as nutrition and hormones, can affect development. Exposure to teratogens (e.g., drugs, alcohol, viruses) can result in death, deformity, or mental disorders.

• Brain Development Promotes Learning: Brain development involves both maturation and experience. The brain's plasticity allows changes in the development of connections and in the synaptic pruning of unused neural connections. The timing of experiences necessary for brain development is particularly important in the early years.

• Attachment Promotes Survival: The emotional bond that develops between a child and a caregiver increases the child's chances of survival. Attachment styles are generally categorized as secure, avoidant, anxious/ambivalent, and disorganized. At the biological level, the hormone oxytocin facilitates attachment.

How Do Children Learn about Their Worlds?

• Perception Introduces the World: Experiments using habituation and the preferential-looking technique have revealed infants' considerable perceptual ability. Vision and hearing develop rapidly as neural circuitry develops.

• Memory Improves over Childhood: Infantile memory is limited by a lack of both language ability and autobiographical reference. Source amnesia is common in children. Confabulation, common in young children, may result from underdevelopment of the frontal lobes.

• Piaget Emphasized Stages of Development: Jean Piaget proposed that through interaction with the environment, children develop mental schemas and proceed through stages of cognitive development. In the sensorimotor stage, children experience the world through their senses and develop object permanence. In the preoperational stage, children's thinking is dominated by the appearance of objects rather than by logic. In the concrete operational stage, children learn the logic of concrete objects. In the formal operational stage, children become capable of abstract, complex thinking.

• Infants Have Early Knowledge about the World: Experiments using the habituation paradigm have revealed that infants innately understand some basic laws of physics and of mathematics.

• Humans Learn from Interacting with Others: Being able to infer another's mental state is known as theory of mind. Through socialization, children move from egocentric thinking to being able to take another's perspective.

• Language Develops in an Orderly Fashion: Infants can discriminate phonemes. Language proceeds from sounds to words to telegraphic speech to sentences. According to Noam Chomsky, all human languages are governed by universal grammar, an innate set of relations between linguistic elements. According to Lev Vygotsky, social interaction is the force that develops language. For language to develop, a child must be exposed to it during the sensitive period.

How Do Children and Adolescents Develop Their Identities?

• Social Systems Influence Development: Urie Bronfenbrenner's biocultural theory of development recognizes four levels of context that affect development: The microsystem includes family and classroom; the exosystem includes less direct forces, such as parents' workplace norms; the macrosystem broadens to cultural aspects such as ethnicity; and the chronosystem consists of sociohistorical context.

• Friends Influence Identity and Behaviour: Social comparisons help shape children's development.

• Parental Style Can Affect Children's Well-Being: Although some psychologists believe that parents play a minimal role in their children's development, data show that parents influence many areas of their children's lives, including religiosity and how children experience emotions.

• Divorce Is Difficult for Children: Many children suffer adverse consequences when their parents divorce, but some children manage this life-changing event well. The reduced income following divorce likely contributes to the negative outcomes.

• Gender Identity Is Determined by Biology and Cultural Norms: Shaped by biology and culture, gender identity develops in children and shapes their behaviours (i.e., gender roles). Gender schemas are the cognitive constructs of gender.

• People Define Themselves in Terms of Race and Ethnicity: By 3 months of age, infants show a preference for faces of their own race, except for infants reared around large majorities of people from different races. By age 4, children begin to categorize themselves and others with regard to race and ethnicity. Ethnic identity is complicated by social prejudice.

What Brings Meaning to Adulthood?

• Adults Are Affected by Life Transitions: Erikson believed that people develop throughout the life span and theorized that each stage of life presents important social issues to be resolved. For adults, development focuses on generativity with regard to career and family. Marriage is a central issue, though in Western societies about half of contemporary marriages fail.

• Aging Can Be Successful: As the population in many Western societies ages, more research is being done on aging, which inevitably brings physical and mental changes. Dementia has various causes, including Alzheimer's disease. Most older adults are healthy, remain productive, and become selective about their relationships and activities.

• Cognition Changes during Aging: Short-term memory, including complex memory and divided attention, is affected by aging. Crystallized intelligence increases; fluid intelligence declines in old age as processing speed declines. Being mentally active and socially engaged preserves cognitive functioning.

COMPETENCY MAP

What Shapes a Child?

1. What does developmental psychology involve?

Development Starts in the Womb

2. Describe the physical development in the womb.
3. Distinguish between a zygote, embryo, and fetus.
4. How does the brain develop in the womb?
5. What is the role of teratogens in development?
6. Explain ethical issues associated with alcohol and drug use during pregnancy.

Brain Development Promotes Learning

7. Describe how a baby processes sensory stimuli.
8. Identify the reflexes that babies possess.
9. Explain how synaptic pruning and plasticity influence neuronal connections.
10. What is a sensitive learning period? Contrast this with a critical period.

Attachment Promotes Survival

11. What is the role of attachment in social development?
12. Identify attachment in other species.
13. Identify the important contribution of Harlow's research.
14. Distinguish between the three main attachment styles.
15. Describe the strange situation paradigm.
16. Explain how the cognitive and social abilities of older and younger children differ.

How Do Children Learn about Their Worlds?

Perception Introduces the World

17. Explain how researchers use preferential looking and the orienting reflex.
18. Understand the qualities of infants' vision.
19. Understand the qualities of infants' hearing.

Memory Improves over Childhood

20. What is infantile amnesia?
21. Distinguish between source amnesia and confabulation.

Piaget's Stages of Development

22. Distinguish between assimilation and accommodation.
23. Identify Piaget's stages of cognitive development.
24. Distinguish between Piaget's stages of cognitive development.
25. Explain object permanence.
26. Explain conservation.
27. Identify challenges to Piaget's stages of cognitive development.

Infants Have Early Knowledge about the World

28. Describe infants' understanding of physics.
29. Describe infants' understanding of mathematics.

Humans Learn from Interacting with Others

30. Explain the theory of mind.
31. Identify Kohlberg's stages of moral development.
32. Distinguish characteristics associated with Kohlberg's stages of moral development.
33. Distinguish between the moral emotions.
34. Describe the somatic marker hypothesis.

Language Develops in an Orderly Fashion

35. What characteristics do first words have?
36. What is telegraphic speech?
37. Describe how deaf children acquire language.
38. Distinguish the contributions of Chomsky and Vygotsky.
39. Differentiate the phonics and whole language approaches.
40. Identify which method of learning to read has more support.

How Do Children and Adolescents Develop Their Identities?

Social Development

41. What does social development involve?

Social Systems Influence Development

42. Identify the systems in biocultural systems theory.

Friends Influence Identity and Behaviour

43. What is the relative role of parents and peers on identity and behaviour?
44. How can parental style affect children's well-being?
45. Describe temperament.

Parental Style and Divorce Affect a Child's Well-Being

46. How do children of divorce compare to those in single-parent homes?
47. How do children of divorce compare to those whose parents stay together for the good of the child?

Gender Identity Is Determined by Cultural Norms and Biology

48. Distinguish between gender and sex differences.

49. Distinguish between gender identity, gender roles, and gender schemas.

50. How do cultural and situational factors influence gender?

People Define Themselves in Terms of Race and Ethnicity

51. How do people define themselves in terms of race and ethnicity?

What Brings Meaning to Adulthood?

Life-Span Perspective

52. Identify Erikson's stages of adult development.

53. Describe the crisis associated with each of Erikson's stages of adult development.

Adults Are Affected by Life Transitions

54. Describe how adults are affected by careers.

55. Describe how adults are affected by marriage.

Aging Can Be Successful

56. Describe socioemotional selectivity theory.

Cognition Changes During Aging

57. Identify the cognitive changes that take place during aging.

KNOWLEDGE CHECK

1. Developmental psychology is concerned with changes in ______________________________,
______________________________,
and ______________________________
over the life span.

Concept: I. A Competency: 1
Question Type: *Factual*

2. Harold's mother was very stressed while she was pregnant with him. This stress resulted in his having lower birth weight than he would have had otherwise. The influence Harold's mother's stress had on his development exemplifies the effects of:
a. genes
b. the cultural environment
c. the physical environment
d. the FAS environment

Concept: I. B. 1 Competency: 2
Question Type: *Applied*

3. One month after conception is the stage in which the internal organs and the nervous system begin to form. This creates a(n):
a. fetus
b. embryo
c. critical period
d. scheme

Concept: I. B. 1. a Competency: 3
Question Type: *Factual*

4. Which of the following is NOT true about brain development in the womb?
a. The cells that will form the cortex are visible by week 7.
b. The left and right hemispheres are visible by week 12.
c. By birth, the brain has cortical layers, connections among its neurons, and myelination.
d. All brain development takes place in the womb.

Concept: I. B. 1. b Competency: 4
Question Type: *Factual*

5. As a baby, Stefan was exposed to a teratogen during development. In terms of his development:
a. he will develop depending on timing and length of exposure
b. this exposure may result in physical problems
c. this exposure may result in language problems
d. this exposure may interfere with brain development

Concept: I. B. 2 Competency: 5
Question Type: *Applied*

6. In the case of a pregnant woman who consumes alcohol, who has the greater rights: baby or mother? Why?

____

____

____

____

Concept: I. B. 3 Competency: 6
Question Type: *Conceptual*

7. Addie was born 2 hours ago. Research shows that she will prefer _______________ tastes. As a newborn Addie will be able to see approximately _______________.
   a. salty; 24 inches
   b. sweet; 8-12 inches
   c. slightly sour; 8-12 inches
   d. sweet; 3-6 inches

   Concept: I. C. 1 Competency: 7
   Question Type: *Applied*

8. Newborns have a series of reflexes that _______________. One reflex, known as the _______________, involves the automatic turning and sucking that infants engage in when a nipple or similar object is near their mouths.
   a. aid survival while they are newborns; rooting reflex
   b. aid survival while they are newborns; grasping reflex
   c. stay with them throughout their lifetime; sucking reflex
   d. stay with them throughout their lifetime; grasping reflex

   Concept: I. C. 2 Competency: 8
   Question Type: *Factual*

9. During infancy synaptic connections that are not used decay and disappear. This is termed:
   a. myelination
   b. plasticity
   c. teratogenic decay
   d. synaptic pruning

   Concept: I. C. 3 Competency: 9
   Question Type: *Factual*

10. Ruiz is an animal trainer who needs to train two animals to jump through a hoop. Based on previous experience Ruiz knows that Animal A has a critical period for this behaviour, while Animal B has a sensitive period. Since he can only attend to one animal at a time, what should he do?

    ____

    ____

    ____

    ____

    Concept: I. C. 4 Competency: 10
    Question Type: *Conceptual*

11. Describe infant behaviours that promote attachment and aid survival.

    ____

    ____

    ____

    ____

    Concept: I. B. 3 Competency: 11
    Question Type: *Factual*

12. Joey walked through a park shortly after some duck - lings hatched. He was surprised when the ducklings followed him wherever he went. The ducklings were demonstrating:
    a. bonding
    b. anxiety
    c. imprinting
    d. orienting reflex

    Concept: I. D. 2. a Competency: 12
    Question Type: *Applied*

13. In his experiment with infant rhesus monkeys, Harry Harlow found that the infants preferred a surrogate mother who:
    a. made monkeylike noises
    b. provided food
    c. fought off threats
    d. was soft

    Concept: I. D. 2. b Competency: 13
    Question Type: *Applied*

14. Samuel, a 1-year-old, was happy playing in the doctor's office while his mother was nearby. When she had to step out for just a second he started to cry. His mother quickly came back, and he ran to her smiling. Samuel was probably displaying which style of attachment?
    a. avoidant attachment
    b. secure attachment
    c. anxious attachment
    d. ambivalent attachment

    Concept: I. D. 3 Competency: 14
    Question Type: *Applied*

15. The ________________________________ involves observing the child, the caregiver, and a friendly but unfamiliar adult in a standard sequence of separations and reunions between the child and each of the two adults. During the episodes, the child is observed through a one-way mirror, and actions such as crying, playing, level of activity, and attention to the mother and stranger are recorded.

Concept: I. D. 3. a Competency: 15
Question Type: *Factual*

16. Imagine that you are interested in writing children's books. You wish to write one book that will be engaging to children about 3 years old. You want the other book to appeal to 10-year-olds. Given the cognitive and social abilities of these age groups, what will your books be like?

____

____

____

____

Concept: I Competency: 16
Question Type: *Conceptual*

17. Madison works for a children's product manufacturer and wants to design a wall picture that will capture a baby's attention. She has narrowed it down to two choices. Because babies can't say which type of picture they like better, Madison keeps track of which picture babies look at more. Which technique is she using?
   a. preferential looking
   b. orienting reflex
   c. strange situation test
   d. rooting reflex

Concept: II. A. 1 Competency: 17
Question Type: *Applied*

18. Based on the research on babies' vision, if you wanted to buy a toy that a 3-month-old is most likely to look at, you should buy one that has:
   a. a complex design in shades of grey
   b. a bold black-and-white pattern
   c. a picture across the room rather than a pattern that is closer
   d. a picture painted with pale pastel colours

Concept: II. A. 2 Competency: 18
Question Type: *Applied*

19. A researcher read one group of fetuses *The Cat in the Hat*, while another group was read nothing. After birth, the babies were played various recordings of children's books on tape. The babies who had been read *The Cat in the Hat* as fetuses altered their sucking when tapes played *The Cat in the Hat*. This research indicates that:
   a. babies can understand simple books even before they are born
   b. babies' sensory systems are completely developed before birth
   c. babies can hear before birth and have some memory of what they heard
   d. babies are as competent as older children in recognizing stories

Concept: II. A. 3 Competency: 19
Question Type: *Applied*

20. Carl went into the hospital when he was 2 years old for an operation. He has no memory of this, probably reflecting:
   a. preoperational thought
   b. repression
   c. learning amnesia
   d. infantile amnesia

Concept: II. B. 1 Competency: 20
Question Type: *Applied*

21. Three-year-old Stephie was told by her brother that she could watch TV. When Stephie's dad saw her watching TV, and he asked her who said she could watch, Stephie could not remember. Her forgetting is an example of:
   a. confabulation
   b. source amnesia
   c. learning amnesia
   d. infantile amnesia

Concept: II. B. 2 Competency: 21
Question Type: *Applied*

22. Diana has a dog at home and often points at him and says, "Dog!" When her dad takes her to the zoo, she routinely sees the wolves and says, "Dog!" This represents:
   a. assimilation
   b. accommodation
   c. learning amnesia
   d. source amnesia

Concept: II. C. 1 Competency: 22
Question Type: *Applied*

23. Concept: II. C. 2 Competency: 23
Question Type: *Factual*

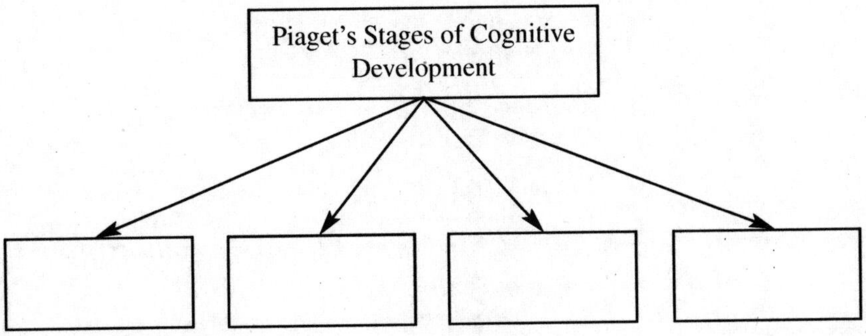

24. Five-year-old Jared is upset when his sister gets a tall thin glass of juice when he gets a short wide one. Jared's mom tries to explain there is the same amount of juice in both cups, but Jared does not believe her. Jared is probably in which of Piaget's stages?
    a. preoperational
    b. concrete operational
    c. formal operational
    d. postformal operational

    Concept: II. C. 2 Competency: 24
    Question Type: *Applied*

25. After Jenny's brother hides her bear under a blanket, Jenny does not seem to know the bear still exists. Jenny has not yet acquired what?
    a. theory of mind
    b. orienting reflex
    c. object permanence
    d. accommodation

    Concept: II. C. 2. a. 1 Competency: 25
    Question Type: *Applied*

26. If a child thinks a tall thin glass has more juice than a short wide glass when both in fact have the same amount, the child is having problems with:
    a. abstract thinking
    b. dialectic thinking
    c. object permanence
    d. conservation

    Concept: II. C. 2. b. 1 Competency: 26
    Question Type: *Applied*

27. Further research into the mental capacities of young children showed that Piaget:
    a. overestimated children's abilities
    b. was correct in his theories
    c. underestimated children's abilities
    d. did not describe conservation

    Concept: II. C. 3 Competency: 27
    Question Type: *Factual*

28. Which of the following does NOT demonstrate an infant's understanding of physics?
    a. Infants believe that objects that move together are connected.
    b. Infants believe that two stationary objects are connected.
    c. Infants prefer to look at a moving stimulus over one that is stationary.
    d. Infants understand what is necessary to support an object in space.

    Concept: II. D. 1. a Competency: 28
    Question Type: *Factual*

29. Pete wants to test his 2-year-old son Max's ability to understand numbers. He puts out two rows of candy as follows:

    Row 1: O O O O O
    Row 2: O O O O

    According to research presented in the book, which row will Max pick?
    a. Row 1 because it is shorter.
    b. Row 1 because it has more.
    c. Row 2 because it is longer.
    d. Max will show no preference.

    Concept: II. D. 1. b Competency: 29
    Question Type: *Applied*

30. When talking on the phone with his grandpa, 3-year-old Ben nodded when asked if his mom was at home. Ben did not realize that his grandpa could not see him. According to Piaget, Ben is reflecting:
    a. egocentrism
    b. a fully developed theory of mind
    c. conservation
    d. formal thought

    Concept: II. E. 1 Competency: 30
    Question Type: *Factual*

31. Concept: II. E. 2 Competency: 31
Question Type: *Factual*

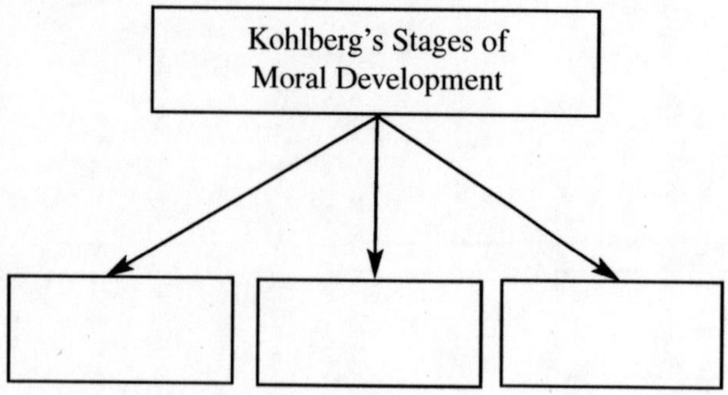

32. If asked whether it was wrong for a man to steal a drug to save his dying wife, a child who responded "He shouldn't steal the drug because it is wrong to steal, so everyone will think he is a bad person" is at which moral level?
a. conventional
b. preconventional
c. postconventional
d. social disapproval

Concept: II. E. 2 Competency: 32
Question Type: *Applied*

33. While listening to her roommate Kim talk about her problems in her math class, Tori finds herself feeling really bad for Kim. This demonstrates:
a. empathy
b. sympathy
c. primary emotions
d. formal operational thinking

Concept: II. E. 3 Competency: 33
Question Type: *Applied*

34. Ben's friends want him to go with them while they sneak into an abandoned house. Ben declines because he "has a bad feeling" about it. This is an example of the ________________________________.

Concept: II. E. 4. a Competency: 34
Question Type: *Applied*

35. The sound of the "R" in the word *rat* is called a:
a. morpheme
b. syntax
c. pragmatic
d. phoneme

Concept: II. F. 1. a. 1 Competency: 35
Question Type: *Applied*

36. "Eat soup. All gone." would be an example of:
a. a morpheme
b. teratogenic speech
c. telegraphic speech
d. a phoneme

Concept: II. F. 1. b Competency: 36
Question Type: *Applied*

37. Robin, a deaf child, was born to deaf parents who used American Sign Language to communicate with each other and with Robin. Based on the research, Robin will acquire language:
a. faster than hearing children of hearing parents
b. slower than hearing children of hearing parents
c. at a rate identical to hearing children of hearing parents
d. in a manner totally different from children who can hear

Concept: II. F. 2 Competency: 37
Question Type: *Applied*

38. ______________ argued that language must be governed by "universal grammar", while ______________ developed the first major theory that emphasized the role of social and cultural context in cognition and language development.
a. Lev Vygotsky; Noam Chomsky
b. Noam Chomsky; Lev Vygotsky
c. Roger Brown; Lev Vygotsky
d. Roger Brown; Noam Chomsky

Concept: II. F. 3 Competency: 38
Question Type: *Factual*

39. Ms. Smith teaches her students to read by focusing on meaning and understanding of how words are connected in sentences. She is using which approach to teaching reading?
a. schema
b. whole language
c. syntax
d. phonics

Concept: II. F. 4 Competency: 39
Question Type: *Applied*

40. Tammy wants to be sure that her three young children become as proficient at reading as possible. Based on existing research which technique should she use?
a. schemas
b. whole language
c. syntax
d. phonics

Concept: II. F. 4 Competency: 40
Question Type: *Applied*

41. Adolescents often question who they are because of three changes. Which of the following is NOT one of them?
    a. heightened pressure to prepare for the future and to make career choices
    b. addressing the conflict of generativity versus stagnation
    c. changing physical appearance
    d. more sophisticated cognitive abilities

    Concept: III. A Competency: 41
    Question Type: *Factual*

42. Concept: III. B. 1 Competency: 42
    Question Type: *Factual*

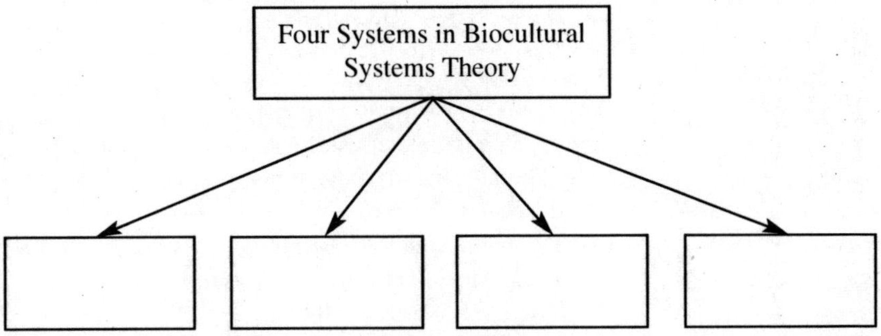

43. As parents of adolescents, Mimi and Fred want to be sure their son and daughter have the most positive experience possible to ensure they have ideal social development. According to research, which of these is the best course of action?
    a. Be good parents and be sure the children come from a good home.
    b. Spend extra time with their children teaching them morals.
    c. Change where they live and what schools the children go to to help make sure the children have good peers.
    d. There really isn't evidence to suggest what influences social development.

    Concept: III. C Competency: 43
    Question Type: *Applied*

44. Otto is a difficult child. According to research, which of these is the best course of action?
    a. His parents should respond in a calm, firm, patient, and consistent style.
    b. His parents should respond in stern fashion and use appropriate discipline.
    c. His parents should respond in very protective fashion to be sure there is little chance that Otto experiences something upsetting.
    d. His parents should punish him for bad behaviour using progressively more severe forms of punishment so that Otto learns consequences.

    Concept: III. C. 2 Competency: 44
    Question Type: *Applied*

45. Baby Abby is generally happy and easygoing. In contrast, baby Diane is often fussy and hard to calm. These babies clearly have different:
    a. temperaments
    b. learning histories
    c. parents
    d. attachment objects

    Concept: III. C. 2. a Competency: 45
    Question Type: *Applied*

46. According to the text, what may be concluded about whether divorce harms children?
    a. Children always do better if their parents stay together.
    b. There are no negative effects associated with divorce.
    c. Parental conflict may produce more negative outcomes than divorce.
    d. There is nothing more harmful to a child's emotional well-being than divorce.

    Concept: III. C. 3. a Competency: 46
    Question Type: *Factual*

47. Bob and Patricia are having a tough time in their marriage and are considering a divorce. However, they want to do what is best for their child and so have decided to stay together. What does research suggest about this?
   a. They should get divorced. The impact on children is minimal.
   b. Parents who stay together unhappily are worse for children than divorced parents.
   c. Staying together is the most important thing for children.
   d. Staying together is good provided the parents don't talk to each other in order to avoid conflict.

   Concept: III. C. 3. b Competency: 47
   Question Type: *Applied*

48. Laura wants to research how masculinity influences preference for video games between boys and girls. Her research will focus most closely on:
   a. gender differences
   b. sex differences
   c. gender schemas
   d. cultural influences

   Concept: III. D Competency: 48
   Question Type: *Factual*

49. Whether people think of themselves as male or female reflects their:
   a. gender
   b. gender role
   c. gender schema
   d. gender identity

   Concept: III. D Competency: 49
   Question Type: *Factual*

50. What are the cognitive structures that influence how people perceive the behaviours of females and males?
   a. gender
   b. gender role
   c. gender schema
   d. gender identity

   Concept: III. D Competency: 49
   Question Type: *Factual*

51. While shopping for clothes for his daughter in a suburb of Ottawa, Mike noticed a shirt that read "Future Prime Minister." However, the shirt only came in dark blue, and was only in the boys section of the store. How does this demonstrate the role of cultural factors on gender?

   Concept: III. D Competency: 50
   Question Type: *Conceptual*

52. When asked to sort pictures of people, 5-year-old Sally puts all the pictures of Asian people in one pile and all the pictures of Caucasian people in another pile. Three-year-old Matt cannot do this: He does not see the difference between Asians and Caucasians. What may we conclude from this?
   a. Matt is unable to form ethnic categories.
   b. Matt is concrete operational.
   c. Sally has stereotypes based on race.
   d. Sally has a clear ethnic identity.

   Concept: III. E Competency: 51
   Question Type: *Applied*

53. Concept: IV. A. 1 Competency: 52
   Question Type: *Factual*

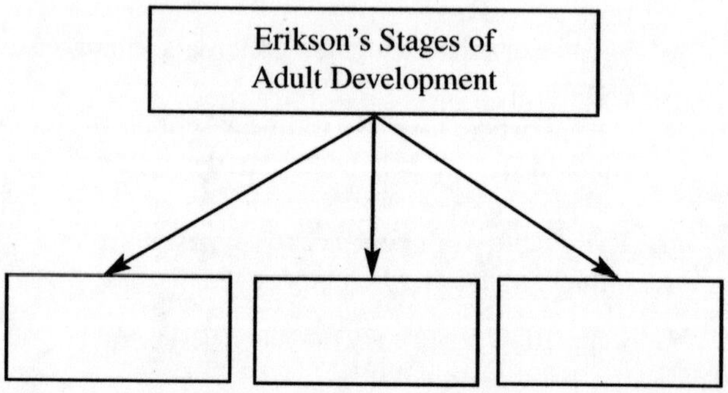

54. Who proposed a theory of development that emphasizes age-related psychological processing and their effects on social functioning across the life span?
   a. Sigmund Freud
   b. Erik Erikson
   c. Lev Vygotsky
   d. Lawrence Kohlberg

   Concept: IV. A. 1 Competency: 52
   Question Type: *Factual*

55. According to Erikson, middle-aged adults, such as the parents of most typically aged university students, are in the stage of generativity versus stagnation. Describe the characteristics of an individual who is successfully dealing with this stage. Give specific examples of what this adult may be doing.

____

____

____

____

Concept: IV. A. 1 Competency: 53
Question Type: *Conceptual*

56. When making her choice of careers, Haley should find a career that:
   a. pays very well
   b. her parents have approved of
   c. involves something she is passionate about
   d. is very prestigious

Concept: IV. B. 1 Competency: 54
Question Type: *Applied*

57. Marriages that are most satisfying are those that have what three characteristics?

____,
____,
and ____

Concept: IV. B. 1 Competency: 55
Question Type: *Factual*

58. Yolanda, aged 84, spends most of her time taking care of her flowers and talking with her two best friends. She avoids going places or seeing people she does not like. Yolanda's behaviour supports Carstensen's ideas on:
   a. socioemotional selectivity theory
   b. identity versus role confusion
   c. postformal thought
   d. dementia

Concept: IV. C. 4 Competency: 56
Question Type: *Applied*

59. Milo is 75 years old and in good physical and mental health. Which of the following tasks will he most likely have the most difficulty with?
   a. remembering a list of groceries he needs, while remembering where to find them in the store
   b. recalling important events from his childhood
   c. learning the name of someone he just met
   d. being able to efficiently use new information he has learned

Concept: IV. D Competency: 57
Question Type: *Applied*

PSYCHOLOGY AND SOCIETY

Imagine you are a pediatrician. The father of one of your patients becomes worried when he reads a parenting magazine article that indicates that babies should be able to sit up on their own by 5 or 6 months of age. He emails you, concerned because his daughter is already 8 months old and has not yet managed to sit up on her own. Respond to the father's email. Explain why he should or should not worry about his daughter's development.

SUMMING UP AND MEASURING UP

What Shapes a Child?

The human genome consists of instructions for building a functioning human being, but from the earliest moment of human development, environmental factors influence how each individual is formed. Throughout the prenatal period, various environmental agents, from the mother's hormones to substances she consumes, can alter the formation of the fetus and its cognitive capacities. Once the child is born, learning is constrained by the development of both brain and body. Except in cases of abuse or some serious illnesses, children crawl and walk when their bodies develop the appropriate musculature and when their brains mature sufficiently to coordinate motor actions. Almost from the moment of birth, humans are social creatures, forming bonds of attachment with caregivers. The quality of these attachments, as well as the children's attitudes, values, and beliefs, are shaped by interactions with their caregivers. Parents and other caregivers influence many aspects of children's lives.

When is a teratogen, such as a drug taken by a pregnant woman, most likely to affect the developing fetus's brain?
   a. Approximately 4 months after conception, when the brain is developing.
   b. Approximately 1 year after birth, when synaptic pruning is reducing the number of synapses.
   c. Immediately after conception, when the zygote is developing rapidly.
   d. All times are critical because the brain develops throughout gestation.

How Do Children Learn about Their Worlds?

Children acquire information through perception. Research, drawing on the fact that young infants look longer at novel stimuli than at familiar stimuli, indicates that infants are capable of learning at very young ages. Piaget emphasized that most young children's cognitive development occurs in consistent stages, each of which builds on previous stages. Though his theory was influential, recent evidence suggests that infants understand much more about objects' physical properties than Piaget believed and that he underestimated infants' innate and early knowledge. For instance, infants can use laws of physics and even demonstrate a basic understanding of addition and subtraction. An important part of learning occurs through social interaction, as young children develop the ability for theory of mind, a capacity that allows people to live in human society. A developing memory system helps children build a store of useful knowledge. The human capacity for language is innate, as there appear to be built-in methods of acquiring words and forming them into sentences. Although language development occurs in an orderly fashion, the specific language a child develops is influenced by environmental and cultural factors. These processes develop together to enable young children to learn and survive as they become members of society.

Which of the following research techniques tell us what infants know? Check as many as apply.

____ a. We can measure how long infants look at two objects presented simultaneously, to determine if infants can tell between them.

____ b. Infants can learn simple motor skills such as kicking a leg to make a mobile move. By altering the time between trials, we can determine how long an infant remembers this trick.

____ c. We can use an infant's theory of mind to determine which of Kohlberg's levels of moral development applies.

____ d. Infants understand speech at birth, so their throat movements enable us to determine what infants can understand.

How Do Children and Adolescents Develop Their Identities?

How people define themselves is influenced by cultural beliefs about factors such as race, sex, and age. Even young children classify themselves on the basis of biological sex, but how they come to understand the meaning of being a boy or a girl is largely determined through their socialization into gender roles, in which children adopt behaviours viewed as appropriate for their sex. Adolescents struggle for identity by questioning social values and personal goals, as they try to figure out who they are and what they want to become. Moral development helps people define what they value and what is important to them. Race and ethnicity shape our beliefs and attitudes regarding how we fit into the cultures in which we are raised.

The pervasiveness of gender roles can be seen in multiple contexts. Indicate whether each of the following statements exemplifies a gender role. Either mark the statement "GR" or leave it blank.

____ a. Most firefighters shown on television are male.

____ b. Most firefighters are male.

____ c. Sally's mother is trying to raise Sally to be anything she wants to be.

____ d. In many societies around the world, women and men wear pants at work.

____ e. Most single parents are women.

____ f. Very few boys are allowed to play with tea sets or doll carriages.

ANSWER KEY

Item **Answer**

1. physiology, cognition, and social behaviour
2. c
3. b
4. d
5. a
6. The major argument for the baby's rights would be that alcohol has documented negative effects on newborns, including mental retardation and fetal alcohol syndrome. The argument for the mother's rights is that it is her body and her baby. The mother has personal rights and autonomy, including the right to not have treatment forced upon her.
7. b
8. a
9. d
10. Ruiz should focus his attention on Animal A. Because that animal has a critical period for the behaviour, if Ruiz misses that time, the animal will never learn the behaviour. In contrast, Animal B has a sensitive period which means it is easiest to learn the behaviour during a certain time, but it could be learned at another time.
11. Infants engage in many behaviours that promote contact and give them a sense of safety and security that is important because they are not able to survive on their own. For instance, an infant will put out their arms to be lifted, smile when they see their caregivers, and cry when they feel abandoned.
12. c
13. d
14. b

15. strange situation test
16. Three-year-olds have very different cognitive skills, language skills, and social skills than do 10-year-olds. To write engaging books for these age groups consider Piaget's stages, language development, and social development. For example, 3-year-olds are probably preoperational, whereas 10-year-olds are concrete operational. The language skills of 3-year-olds are not as developed as those of 10-year-olds. Three-year-olds are still very attached to their parents; 10-year-olds, though still attached to their parents, are spending increasing time with peers.
17. a
18. b
19. c
20. d
21. b
22. a
23. Sensorimotor; Preoperational; Concrete Operational; Formal Operational
24. a
25. c
26. d
27. c
28. b
29. b
30. a
31. Preconventional; Conventional; Postconventional
32. a
33. b
34. somatic marker hypothesis
35. d
36. c
37. c
38. b
39. b
40. d
41. b
42. Microsystem; Exosystem; Macrosystem; Chronosystem
43. c
44. a
45. a
46. c
47. b
48. a
49. d
50. c
51. Up to this point in Canada, the elected Prime Minister has always been a man. Thus, in the Canadian culture a "Future Prime Minister" shirt for boys may seem appropriate. However, in other cultures and countries (e.g., England, New Zealand) this is not the case. There is the possibility that this reflects the culture, but also that it influences the culture by making girls less likely to see their potential to be Prime Minister.
52. a
53. Intimacy vs. Isolation; Generativity vs. Stagnation; Integrity vs. Despair
54. b
55. According to Erikson, people successfully address this stage when they are generative. This means that they feel they produce something of value or give back something to society. People accomplish this in many different ways: jobs, families, scientific contributions, and art are just some forms of generativity.
56. c
57. Partners have sufficient economic resources; Partners share decision making; Partners both hold the view that marriage should be a lifelong commitment.
58. a
59. a

Psychology and Society

Your response should encourage the father not to worry about his daughter. Although predictable ages exist for developmental milestones, some babies reach the milestones earlier than the target ages and others reach them later. Also, remember environment. It is possible, for example, that family members carry this baby a lot or that she spends most of her time in a carrier of some sort; environmental factors of this sort might influence the baby's muscle development and thus the timing of her sitting up.

Summing Up and Measuring Up

What Shapes a Child?

a. Approximately 4 months after conception, when the brain is developing.

How Do Children Learn about Their Worlds?

a. We can measure how long infants look at two objects presented simultaneously, to determine if infants can tell between them.; b. Infants can learn simple motor skills such as kicking a leg to make a mobile move. By altering the time between trials, we can determine how long an infant remembers this trick.

How Do Children and Adolescents Develop Their Identities?

a, b, e, f

KEY TERM EXERCISES

accommodation

Textbook Definition:
Your Own Definition:
Your Own Example:

anxious-ambivalent attachment

Textbook Definition:
Your Own Definition:
Your Own Example:

assimilation

Textbook Definition:
Your Own Definition:
Your Own Example:

attachment

Textbook Definition:
Your Own Definition:
Your Own Example:

avoidant attachment

Textbook Definition:
Your Own Definition:
Your Own Example:

concrete operational stage

Textbook Definition:
Your Own Definition:
Your Own Example:

conventional

Textbook Definition:
Your Own Definition:
Your Own Example:

critical periods

Textbook Definition:
Your Own Definition:
Your Own Example:

developmental psychology

Textbook Definition:
Your Own Definition:
Your Own Example:

disorganized attachment

Textbook Definition:
Your Own Definition:
Your Own Example:

formal operational stage

Textbook Definition:
Your Own Definition:
Your Own Example:

gender identity

Textbook Definition:
Your Own Definition:
Your Own Example:

gender roles

Textbook Definition:
Your Own Definition:
Your Own Example:

gender schemas

Textbook Definition:
Your Own Definition:
Your Own Example:

infantile amnesia

Textbook Definition:
Your Own Definition:
Your Own Example:

object permanence

Textbook Definition:
Your Own Definition:
Your Own Example:

postconventional

Textbook Definition:
Your Own Definition:
Your Own Example:

preconventional

Textbook Definition:
Your Own Definition:
Your Own Example:

preoperational stage

Textbook Definition:
Your Own Definition:
Your Own Example:

secure attachment

Textbook Definition:
Your Own Definition:
Your Own Example:

sensitive periods

Textbook Definition:
Your Own Definition:
Your Own Example:

sensorimotor stage

Textbook Definition:
Your Own Definition:
Your Own Example:

social development

Textbook Definition:
Your Own Definition:
Your Own Example:

synaptic pruning

Textbook Definition:
Your Own Definition:
Your Own Example:

telegraphic speech

Textbook Definition:
Your Own Definition:
Your Own Example:

teratogens

Textbook Definition:
Your Own Definition:
Your Own Example:

theory of mind

Textbook Definition:
Your Own Definition:
Your Own Example:

CHAPTER 12 Social Psychology

CONCEPT MAP

I. How Do Attitudes Guide Behaviour?
  A. Social Psychology
  B. Attitude Formation
    1. Attitudes
    2. Mere Exposure
    3. Classical Conditioning
    4. Socialization
  C. Attitude Behaviour Consistency
    1. Attitude Strength
    2. Attitude Accessibility
    3. Explicit vs. Implicit Attitudes
      a. Implicit Associations Test
  D. Discrepancies Lead to Dissonance
    1. Cognitive Dissonance
      a. Postdecisional Dissonance
      b. Attitude Change
      c. Justifying Effort
  E. Attitudes Can Be Changed through Persuasion
    1. Persuasion
      a. Elaboration Likelihood Model
      b. Central vs. Peripheral Route
        1. Cues that Influence a Message's Persuasiveness
          A. Source
          B. Content
          C. Receiver
      c. The Message
        1. Supportive vs. Skeptical Audiences

II. How Do We Form Our Impressions of Others?
  A. Nonverbal Actions and Expressions
    1. Nonverbal Behaviour
    2. Facial Expressions
    3. Body Language
      a. Thin Slices of Behaviour
  B. We Make Attributions about Others
    1. Attributions
    2. Just World Hypothesis
    3. Attributional Dimensions
      a. Personal Attributions
      b. Situational Attributions
    4. Attributional Bias
      a. Fundamental Attribution Error
      b. Correspondence Bias
      c. Actor-Observer Discrepancy
  C. Stereotypes
    1. Purpose
    2. Maintaining Stereotypes
    3. Ethics: Testing for Prejudice
    4. Self-fulfilling Prophecy
      a. Stereotype Threat
  D. Prejudice
    1. Prejudice and Discrimination
    2. Ingroup-Outgroup Bias
      a. Outgroup Homogeneity Effect
      b. Ingroup Favouritism
    3. Stereotypes and Perception
    4. Inhibiting Stereotypes
  E. Cooperation Can Reduce Prejudice
    1. Sherif's Camp Study
      a. Superordinate Goals
    2. Jigsaw Classroom

III. How Do Others Influence Us?
  A. Groups Influence Individual Behaviour
    1. Social Facilitation
      a. Three Steps
        1. Others Create Arousal

        2. Arousal Leads to Dominant Response
        3. Improved Performance for Simple Tasks
    2. Social Loafing
    3. Deindividuation
    4. Group Decision Making
        a. Risky-Shift Effect
        b. Group Polarization
        c. Groupthink
  B. We Conform to Social Norms
    1. Social Norms
    2. Conformity
        a. Autokinetic Effect
        b. Asch Studies
            1. Factors that Decrease Conformity
  C. We Are Compliant
    1. Compliance
        a. Foot-in-the-Door Effect
        b. Door in the Face
        c. Low-Balling Strategy
  D. We Are Obedient to Authority
    1. Obedience
    2. Milgram Experiment
        a. Details
        b. Rate of Obedience
        c. Reducing Obedience

IV. When Do We Harm or Help Others?
  A. Aggression Can Be Adaptive
    1. Biological Factors
        a. Brain Regions
        b. Neurotransmitters
    2. Individual Factors
        a. Frustration-Aggression Hypothesis
        b. Cognitive-neoassociationistic Model
  B. Aggression Has Social and Cultural Aspects
    1. Culture of Honor
  C. Many Factors May Influence Helping Behaviour
    1. Prosocial Behaviour
    2. Altruism
        a. Inclusive Fitness
        b. Kin Selection
        c. Reciprocal Helping
    3. Bystander Intervention Effect
        a. Diffusion of Responsibility

V. What Determines the Quality of Relationships?
  A. Situational and Personal Factors Influence Friendships
    1. Proximity
    2. Familiarity
        a. Neophobia
        b. Mere Exposure Effect
    3. Similarity
    4. Personal Characteristics
    5. Physical Attractiveness
        a. Face Attractiveness
        b. What Is Beautiful Is Good Stereotype
            1. Actual Correlates of Attractiveness
  B. Love
    1. Passionate and Companionate Love
    2. Attachment Style
  C. Making Love Last Is Difficult
    1. Jealousy and Possessiveness
    2. Dealing with Conflict
        a. "Four Horsemen"
            1. Being Overly Critical
            2. Holding the Partner in Contempt
            3. Being Defensive
            4. Mentally Withdrawing from the Relationship
    3. Attributional Style and Accommodation
    4. Myths of Marriage
    5. Creating Positive Feelings in the Relationship
        a. Show Interest in Your Partner
        b. Be Affectionate
        c. Show You Care
        d. Spend Quality Time Together
        e. Maintain Loyalty and Fidelity
        f. Handle Conflict

CHAPTER SUMMARY

How Do Attitudes Guide Behaviour?

• We Form Attitudes through Experience and Socialization: Attitudes are influenced by familiarity (the mere exposure effect) and can be shaped by conditioning and through socialization.

• Behaviours Are Consistent with Strong Attitudes: Implicit attitudes (those that are automatic and easily activated from memory) can influence behaviour and may differ from explicit attitudes (those we profess).

• Discrepancies Lead to Dissonance: A mismatch between attitudes or between an attitude and a behaviour causes cognitive dissonance, which is usually resolved by a change in attitude. A behavioural change is possible but more difficult to accomplish. To justify behaviour that does not reflect attitudes, people often inflate positive aspects of the experience.

• Attitudes Can Be Changed through Persuasion: Persuasion often works by focusing on either the message (the central route) or the feelings the message generates (the peripheral route).

How Do We Form Our Impressions of Others?

• Nonverbal Actions and Expressions Affect Our Impressions: Nonverbal behaviour (body language) is interpreted quickly and provides valuable information.

• We Make Attributions about Others: We use personal dispositions and situational factors to explain others' behaviour. Fundamental attribution error occurs when personal attributions are favoured over situational attributions in explaining others' behaviour.

• Stereotypes Are Based on Automatic Categorization: Stereotypes are cognitive schemas that allow for fast, easy processing of social information; they can lead to bias and illusory correlations. Self-fulfilling prophecies occur when people behave in ways that confirm the biases of stereotypes.

• Stereotypes Can Lead to Prejudice: Prejudice occurs when the attitude associated with a stereotype is negative. Having a negative bias can lead to discriminatory action. We show a preference for members of our ingroup versus those in outgroups.

• Cooperation Can Reduce Prejudice: Sharing superordinate goals that require cooperation leads to reduced prejudice and discrimination.

How Do Others Influence Us?

• Groups Influence Individual Behaviour: The presence of others can improve performance (social facilitation) or create laziness (social loafing). Loss of personal identity and of self-awareness (deindividuation) can occur in groups. Group decisions can be extreme.

• We Conform to Social Norms: Socially determined influences on behaviour occur through awareness of social norms. Lack of unanimity diminishes conformity.

• We Are Compliant: Various factors influence the likelihood of compliance, among them what mood we are in and whether we have previously agreed to a lesser request (foot-in-the-door effect).

• We Are Obedient to Authority: People readily behave in ways directed by authorities, even to the extent of harming others.

When Do We Harm or Help Others?

• Aggression Can Be Adaptive: Brain structures, neurochemistry, and hormones influence aggression. Biologically based responses can be adaptive. Frustration can lead to aggression.

• Aggression Has Social and Cultural Aspects: Aggression is not entirely adaptive and is influenced by our social and cultural experiences.

• Many Factors May Influence Helping Behaviour: Prosocial behaviours maintain social relations. Altruism toward kin may favour inclusive fitness. Reciprocal helping is more likely in social groups in which survival depends on cooperation.

• Some Situations Lead to Bystander Apathy: The presence of others in an emergency may diffuse responsibility and lead to individual inaction.

What Determines the Quality of Relationships?

• Situational and Personal Factors Influence Friendships: People affiliate with others who are similar to themselves and who possess valued characteristics, such as attractiveness.

• Love Is an Important Component of Romantic Relationships: In successful romantic relationships, passionate love tends to evolve into companionate love.

• Making Love Last Is Difficult: As passion fades, couples must develop other areas of satisfaction. Jealousy arises out of fears of infidelity. How a couple deals with conflict influences the stability of the relationship. Generally, in a happy couple the partners have positive views of each other and their relationship.

COMPETENCY MAP

How Do Attitudes Guide Behaviour?

Social Psychology

1. What does social psychology involve?

Attitude Formation

2. Define attitudes.
3. What is the mere exposure effect?
4. How are attitudes influenced by classical conditioning and socialization?

Attitude Behaviour Consistency

5. What factors of attitudes make them more likely to influence behaviour?
6. Distinguish between explicit and implicit attitudes.
7. Why is the implicit associations test useful?

Discrepancies Lead to Dissonance

8. Explain cognitive dissonance.
9. How does dissonance relate to decisions?
10. Understand the Festinger and Carlsmith cognitive dissonance study.

11. How does dissonance relate to justifying effort?

Attitudes Can Be Changed through Persuasion

12. Distinguish the central route from the peripheral route in the elaboration likelihood model.
13. Identify the cues that influence a message's persuasiveness.
14. Know what type of message works best with which type of audience.

How Do We Form Our Impressions of Others?

Nonverbal Actions and Expressions

15. Identify forms of nonverbal behaviour.
16. Can very limited exposure produce accurate impressions?

We Make Attributions about Others

17. What are attributions?
18. Explain the just-world hypothesis.
19. Distinguish between personal and situational attributions.
20. Explain the fundamental attribution error.
21. Explain correspondence bias.
22. Distinguish the actor-observer discrepancy from the fundamental attribution error.

Stereotypes

23. What is the purpose of stereotypes?
24. How do people maintain stereotypes?
25. Identify the ethical issues associated with testing for prejudice.
26. Explain the self-fulfilling prophecy.
27. What is stereotype threat?

Prejudice

28. Distinguish between prejudice and discrimination.
29. Describe the outgroup homogeneity effect.
30. What does ingroup favouritism involve?
31. How do stereotypes influence perception?
32. Can people inhibit stereotypes?

Cooperation Can Reduce Prejudice

33. Explain how superordinate goals and the jigsaw classroom can reduce prejudice.

How Do Others Influence Us?

Groups Influence Individual Behaviour

34. What is social facilitation?
35. What is social loafing?
36. How does deindividuation influence behaviour?
37. Distinguish between how risky-shift, group polarization, and groupthink influence decision making.

We Conform to Social Norms

38. Describe social norms.
39. Explain conformity.
40. Describe Sherif's conformity study and how it used the autokinetic effect.
41. Understand the findings from Asch's conformity study.

We Are Compliant

42. Distinguish between how foot-in-the-door, door in the face, and low-balling lead to compliance.

We Are Obedient to Authority

43. What is obedience? How does it differ from conformity and compliance?
44. Describe Milgram's obedience study.

When Do We Harm or Help Others?

Aggression Can Be Adaptive

45. Identify aggression.
46. Identify biological factors that influence aggression.
47. Describe the frustration-aggression hypothesis.
48. Describe the cognitive-neoassociationistic model.

Aggression Has Social and Cultural Aspects

49. Understand how a "culture of honor" influences aggression.

Many Factors May Influence Helping Behaviour

50. What is altruism?

51. Describe how inclusive fitness and kin selection differ from reciprocal helping.

52. Describe the bystander intervention effect.

53. Explain why the bystander intervention effect occurs.

What Determines the Quality of Relationships?

Situational and Personal Factors Influence Friendships

54. Describe how proximity promotes relationships.

55. Describe how similarity promotes relationships.

56. Identify desirable personal characteristics for relationships.

57. What factors make faces more attractive?

58. Understand the "what is beautiful is good" stereotype.

Love

59. Distinguish between passionate and companionate love.

Making Love Last Is Difficult

60. How could the "Four Horsemen" be used to deal with conflict?

61. How do attributions influence relationships?

62. Identify myths of marriage.

63. Identify ways to create positive feelings in relationships.

KNOWLEDGE CHECK

1. Social psychology is concerned with how ________________________ influence a person's thoughts, feelings, and actions.

   Concept: I. A   Competency: 1
   Question Type: *Factual*

2. ________________________ involve our evaluations of objects, events, or ideas. They are central to social psychology.

   Concept: I. B   Competency: 2
   Question Type: *Factual*

3. We tend to prefer photographs of ourselves with the image reversed, but we prefer photographs of friends as we see them because of:
   a. the mere exposure effect
   b. social exchange theory
   c. need complementarity
   d. elaboration likelihood

   Concept: I. B. 2   Competency: 3
   Question Type: *Applied*

4. Fabio has a tough job. He is in charge of selling cologne using TV commercials where it is impossible for viewers to smell his cologne and form a favourable impression. As a result, he creates commercials that feature rugged men in cool clothes involved in dangerous situations. Fabio is trying to influence attitudes through:
   a. the mere exposure effect
   b. socialization
   c. classical conditioning
   d. elaboration likelihood

   Concept: I. B. 3   Competency: 4
   Question Type: *Applied*

5. A group of friends have all decided to take steps to be more environmentally conscious by recycling, buying "green" products, and reducing energy consumption. Based on the following descriptions, who is LEAST likely to engage in these behaviours?
   a. Sergio who feels he has a personal connection to the Earth.
   b. Julia who easily recalls all the times she engaged in these behaviours in the past.
   c. Chrissy who believes very strongly in being "green."
   d. Bob who saw an informative TV documentary about being environmentally conscious.

   Concept: I. C   Competency: 5
   Question Type: *Applied*

6. Felipe was sitting at home eating dinner when he received a telephone call asking him to talk about his feelings about religion and the upcoming election. The telephone pollster was asking him to talk about his:
   a. explicit attitudes
   b. attitude accessibility
   c. implicit attitudes
   d. implicit associations

   Concept: I. C. 3   Competency: 6
   Question Type: *Applied*

7. Why is the implicit associations test (IAT) useful?

____

____

____

____

Concept: I. B. 3 Competency: 7
Question Type: *Conceptual*

8. Samantha and her boyfriend, Lance, decide to be participants on a couples' reality television show. Before the show Samantha believes she is totally committed to Lance and will not give in to the temptations presented by the show's premise. However, after a few dream dates with a single guy on the show, Samantha gives in to temptation and cheats on Lance. Afterward she feels guilty about it and suddenly realizes that she is not as in love with Lance as she thought she was. What do Samantha's latest realizations illustrate?
   a. social facilitation
   b. implicit attitudes
   c. a consensus effect
   d. cognitive dissonance

Concept: I. D. 1 Competency: 8
Question Type: *Applied*

9. Ozzy has free tickets to a baseball game and a rock concert. He really wants to attend both, but they are at the same time. He finally decides on the baseball game. He immediately focuses on the positive aspect of the baseball game (good weather, good pitching matchup) and the negative aspect of the rock concert (poor parking, hearing loss). Ozzy is motivated by:
   a. social facilitation
   b. postdecisional dissonance
   c. effort justification
   d. elaboration likelihood

Concept: I. D. 1. a Competency: 9
Question Type: *Applied*

10. Leon did an experiment with a group of graduate students who were music teachers. He paid one group of teachers $100 to try to convince an alleged school board member that music education was unimportant and the funding for it should be cut. He paid the other group $1 to accomplish the same task. He found that the group to which he paid $1 actually agreed with the message more because they had ______________ for lying.
    a. insufficient justification
    b. postdecisional dissonance
    c. implicit attitudes
    d. selective exposure

Concept: I. D. 1. b Competency: 10
Question Type: *Applied*

11. Rory is pledging a sorority on a U.S. campus. As part of initiation, she is forced to wear silly clothes, sing silly songs, and disregard her personal hygiene for a couple of weeks. After acceptance, she tells her family it was all worth it because the ridicule brought her pledge class much closer together. Rory is engaging in the dissonance-reducing strategy of:
    a. social facilitation
    b. postdecisional dissonance
    c. effort justification
    d. elaboration likelihood

Concept: I. D. 1. c Competency: 11
Question Type: *Applied*

12. Chris is a first-year student who has not had much luck with studying. After listening to a couple of lectures on memory and studying tips, he tells his psychology professor that he found the lecture and text material influential. He said that because of all these good suggestions, he was beginning to study more effectively. Chris's decision-making process is an example of using:
    a. the central route of persuasion
    b. the peripheral route of persuasion
    c. groupthink
    d. social facilitation

Concept: I. E. 1. b Competency: 12
Question Type: *Applied*

13. Concept: I. E. 1. b. 1 Competency: 13
Question Type: *Factual*

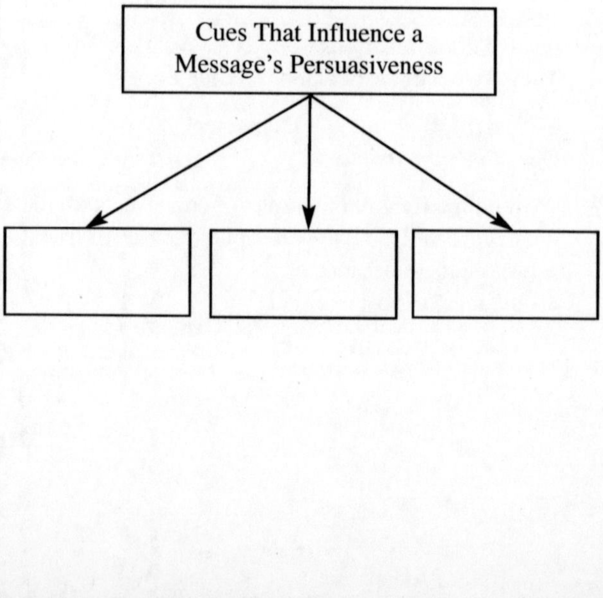

14. Mario is a political candidate who is debating the merits of medical marijuana. He decides to explain both sides of the argument and then focus on his position. This strategy is a better idea if his audience is:
    a. strongly supportive of him
    b. strongly supportive of the idea
    c. skeptical
    d. gullible

    Concept: I. E. 1. c. 1 Competency: 14
    Question Type: *Applied*

15. Please give your own examples of nonverbal behaviour.

    ____

    ____

    ____

    ____

    Concept: II. A Competency: 15
    Question Type: *Conceptual*

16. Shirley is on a campus student committee that has to evaluate each professor teaching. Based on research, what is the least amount of time she can spend that will still produce an accurate rating?
    a. 30 seconds
    b. 30 minutes
    c. 1 class
    d. 3 classes

    Concept: II. A. 3. a Competency: 16
    Question Type: *Applied*

17. Eshkol is on spring break and notices several students from other universities engaging in questionable behaviour. He comes up with several explanations for why they might be doing these things. These causal explanations are known as:
    a. justifications
    b. attributions
    c. just-world hypotheses
    d. attitudes

    Concept: II. B. 1 Competency: 17
    Question Type: *Applied*

18. Tito has the philosophy that if he does good things, good things will happen to him and that if he were to do bad things, bad things would happen. His philosophy is most closely associated with the idea of
    a. justifications
    b. causal attributions
    c. the just-world hypothesis
    d. dispositional attributions

    Concept: II. B. 2 Competency: 18
    Question Type: *Conceptual*

19. A man robbed a convenience store with a gun, escaping with all the money in the register. During the investigation detectives came up with several possible reasons why the man robbed the store. One was that maybe the man was poor and needed money to feed his family. This explanation is an example of:
    a. a personal attribution
    b. a situational attribution
    c. the fundamental attribution error
    d. a dispositional attribution

    Concept: II. B. 3 Competency: 19
    Question Type: *Applied*

20. Kristen scurries into her general psychology professor's office late. Her hair is sticking up and her notebook has papers falling out in every direction. Before she can explain that her electricity went haywire, her professor assumes that she is disorganized and lazy. This is an example of a:
    a. confirmation bias
    b. self-fulfilling prophecy
    c. fundamental attribution error
    d. misattribution

    Concept: II. B. 4. a Competency: 20
    Question Type: *Applied*

21. People often have difficulty accepting that celebrities have substantial drug and alcohol problems because their television characters are so nice and sweet. This expectation that behaviour should correspond with beliefs and personality (even if acting) is known as the:
    a. actor-observer discrepancy
    b. self-fulfilling prophecy
    c. fundamental attribution error
    d. correspondence bias

    Concept: II. B. 4. b Competency: 21
    Question Type: *Applied*

22. Patty falls over a hole in the sidewalk and starts cursing the slowness of the university's maintenance workers. However, she laughed at how clumsy one of her friends was when she tripped over the exact same hole 30 minutes earlier. This tendency to focus on situational factors to explain your behaviour but dispositional factors to explain the behaviour of others is known as the:
    a. actor-observer discrepancy
    b. self-fulfilling prophecy
    c. fundamental attribution error
    d. correspondence bias

    Concept: II. B. 4. b Competency: 22
    Question Type: *Applied*

23. Stereotypes involve ______________, and allow us to ______________.
    a. cognitive schemas that organize information about people; make judgments quickly
    b. cognitive schemas that organize information about people; make accurate judgments
    c. unjustified and inappropriate treatment of people; make judgments quickly
    d. unjustified and inappropriate treatment of people; make accurate judgments

    Concept: II. C. 1 Competency: 23
    Question Type: *Applied*

24. George has a stereotype that guys who play sports are dumb. He maintains this stereotype in all of the following ways EXCEPT:
    a. he will remember all of the times athletes were smart, and then discount those memories
    b. when he meets a smart athlete, he considers that guy the exception to the rule
    c. he pays attention to each instance of a dumb jock
    d. when an athlete is smart, he considers it luck

    Concept: II. C. 2 Competency: 24
    Question Type: *Applied*

25. What is the ethical argument against testing for prejudice? Support your argument with examples.

    ____

    ____

    ____

    ____

    Concept: II. C. 3 Competency: 25
    Question Type: *Conceptual*

26. Vince heard from some older students that his academic advisor was short-tempered and mean. As a result, when they met Vince tended to be defensive, sarcastic, and rude. Subsequently his advisor abruptly suggested he needed an attitude adjustment and asked him to leave. This is an example of a(n):
    a. actor-observer discrepancy
    b. fundamental attribution error
    c. self-fulfilling prophecy
    d. correspondence bias

    Concept: II. C. 4 Competency: 26
    Question Type: *Applied*

27. Chuck is a varsity football player who is trying out for the school play. Prior to his audition someone suggests that "football players don't make good actors because they have no emotions." As a result, Chuck's performance suffered. This was most likely due to:
    a. an actor-observer discrepancy
    b. a fundamental attribution error
    c. a correspondence bias
    d. stereotype threat

    Concept: II. C. 4. a Competency: 27
    Question Type: *Applied*

28. Josh, a Euro-Canadian, has negative feelings about Juo, an Asian-Canadian. Josh has no reason for these feelings and actually has not even talked to Juo. He just dislikes him because he is from a different ethnic background. What are Josh's feelings called?
    a. prejudice
    b. discrimination
    c. a stereotype
    d. a subtype

    Concept: II. D. 1 Competency: 28
    Question Type: *Applied*

29. Since the terrorist attacks on September 11, 2001, some angry Americans have lumped together all people who look even vaguely "Middle Eastern" and believe they all are linked to terrorism in some way. The beliefs of these Americans illustrate:
    a. social categorization
    b. the outgroup homogeneity effect
    c. social role typing
    d. ingroup favouritism

    Concept: II. D. 2. a Competency: 29
    Question Type: *Applied*

30. Sandy, Roxanne, and Carolyn are put into a group in their statistics class. Kristen, Lori, and Melinda are put into a different group. All six of these women were originally friends. However, since being put into opposing groups, they have become bitter toward those not in their group and will share notes and homework only with group members. Their reactions reflect:
    a. social categorization
    b. the outgroup homogeneity effect
    c. social role typing
    d. ingroup favouritism

    Concept: II. D. 2. b Competency: 30
    Question Type: *Applied*

31. When participants in a research study were primed with a _______________ face they identified guns more quickly. In another study when they were primed with weapons, they paid greater attention to _______________ faces.
    a. black; black
    b. black; white
    c. white; black
    d. white; white

    Concept: II. D. 3 Competency: 31
    Question Type: *Applied*

32. Regina meets someone from Mexico and is aware of many negative stereotypes about Mexico people that are automatically activated when she meets this person. Which of the following is most likely to happen?
    a. If she has high levels of prejudice she will be able to inhibit the stereotype.
    b. If she has low levels of prejudice she will be able to inhibit the stereotype.
    c. Stereotypes are automatic and consequently can not be altered consciously.
    d. She will be able to temporarily inhibit the stereotype but it will quickly become activated and influence her behaviour.

    Concept: II. D. 3 Competency: 32
    Question Type: *Applied*

33. You have been brought in as a consultant to a school system that is experiencing considerable racial conflict and gang violence. Consider the research on stereotypes, prejudice, and discrimination and discuss how you might address these problems.

    ____

    ____

    ____

    ____

    Concept: II. E Competency: 33
    Question Type: *Conceptual*

34. Kristen decided to try out for the university's gymnastics team. When she performed her routine in front of team members and the coach, she did well on an easy cartwheel. However, when she tried the difficult double-twisted flip, she fell over and lost her shoe. Kristen's performance was affected by:
    a. social loafing
    b. deindividuation
    c. the bystander effect
    d. social facilitation

    Concept: III. A. 1 Competency: 33
    Question Type: *Applied*

35. Beyonce really likes doing group work in her classes because she can get away with doing less work than she would if she worked alone, basically by letting others do the work. This is known as:
    a. social loafing
    b. deindividuation
    c. the bystander effect
    d. social facilitation

    Concept: III. A. 2 Competency: 35
    Question Type: *Applied*

36. Brandy is at a music concert where she is surrounded by thousands of people. Although she is normally shy and afraid to express her feelings, she soon gets swept up in the madness around her. She joins the mosh pit and begins yelling, laughing, and dancing hysterically. Which of the following best explains her sudden loss of inhibition?
    a. emotional contagion
    b. deindividuation
    c. the bystander effect
    d. social facilitation

    Concept: III. A. 3 Competency: 36
    Question Type: *Applied*

37. The space shuttle *Challenger* was launched despite the fact that it was a cold morning and NASA had been warned about faulty O-rings on the solid-rocket booster. The term that describes this extreme form of group decision-making among NASA engineers is:
    a. risky shift
    b. group polarization
    c. groupthink
    d. social facilitation

    Concept: III. A. 4 Competency: 37
    Question Type: *Applied*

38. Dr. Smith, a Canadian psychologist, went to a professional conference. When she greeted other psychologists, she politely said hello and firmly shook hands with them. What does Dr. Smith's behaviour illustrate?
    a. sanction norms
    b. ingroup rules
    c. social schemas
    d. social norms

    Concept: III. B. 1 Competency: 38
    Question Type: *Applied*

39. When Phoebe stopped by her friend Monica's new apartment, she noticed that the living room walls were covered by hideous orange wallpaper. However, the next day when Monica asked her group of friends if they liked her beautiful wallpaper, all the rest said yes, so Phoebe did too. Phoebe's statement is an example of:
    a. social facilitation
    b. conformity
    c. groupthink
    d. deindividuation

    Concept: III. B. 2 Competency: 39
    Question Type: *Applied*

40. In a famous study, participants looked at a point of light that appeared to move. This is known as _______________. Over time, participants' estimates of how far the light moved _______________.
    a. a risky shift; got bigger and bigger
    b. a risky shift; got smaller and smaller
    c. the autokinetic effect; converged around a common estimate
    d. groupthink; got smaller and smaller

    Concept: III. B. 2. a Competency: 40
    Question Type: *Factual*

41. Stu is always late to class. One day before he got there the teacher told everyone in the class to say that Sir Wilfred Laurier was the first Prime Minister of Canada. When Stu arrived the professor asked five students who the first Prime Minister of Canada was (all said it was Sir Wilfred Laurier), then asked Stu. What would Asch's study suggest about his response if Stu was presented with a similar situation several times?
    a. He would never give the wrong answer to such an obvious question.
    b. He would give the wrong answer about 66 percent of the time.
    c. He would give the wrong answer about 33 percent of the time.
    d. He would always give the wrong answer.

    Concept: III. B. 2. b Competency: 41
    Question Type: *Factual*

42. Ginger is interested in buying a new evening dress. She tells her mother that she will need $300 to purchase it. After her mother goes through an emotional tirade, Ginger asks for $100 to purchase the dress (which is the amount she wanted all along) and her mother agrees. Ginger is engaging in the influence tactic of:
    a. foot-in-the-door
    b. door in the face
    c. low-balling
    d. high rolling

    Concept: III. C. 1. a Competency: 42
    Question Type: *Applied*

43. Pedro is shopping for a car. He finally finds one at a reasonable price with all the options he wants. He agrees to buy it from the salesperson. When he goes to sign the contract, he notices a number of extras have been added at his expense (e.g., pinstripes, floor mats, keys, undercoating). Pedro believes the salesperson is trying the tactic of:
    a. foot-in-the- door
    b. door in the face
    c. low-balling
    d. high rolling

    Concept: III. C. 1. a Competency: 42
    Question Type: *Applied*

44. Bruce is working out at a local gym and doesn't clean up after himself. As he is about to leave, the owner gives him a look and says, "Be sure to clean that stuff up before you leave." Bruce proceeds to clean up. This is best described as:
    a. obedience
    b. conformity
    c. compliance
    d. risky shift

    Concept: III. D. 1 Competency: 43
    Question Type: *Applied*

45. In the famous Milgram obedience study, approximately what proportion of volunteers were willing to deliver the highest level of shock (450 volts) to the innocent volunteer/confederate?
    a. none
    b. one-fifth
    c. one-third
    d. two-thirds

    Concept: III. D. 2 Competency: 44
    Question Type: *Factual*

46. Which of the following is NOT an example of aggression?
    a. Shelton breaks the leg of a pedestrian he does not see by backing over him with a car.
    b. Because of jealousy, Mara starts a vicious, untrue rumor about a girl who talks to her boyfriend.
    c. Mac pushes his professor down the stairs after getting frustrated in a psychology exam.
    d. After Elliot and his girlfriend break up, he goes for a walk and knocks over the little statues on everybody's lawns.

    Concept: IV. A Competency: 45
    Question Type: *Factual*

47. Stimulating the _______________ increases aggression, while damaging the _______________ decreases aggression. The neurotransmitter _______________ has been found to be very low in those who committed suicide.
    a. amygdala; hypothalamus; dopamine
    b. hippocampus; hypothalamus; serotonin
    c. hypothalamus; amygdala; dopamine
    d. amygdala; amygdala; serotonin

    Concept: IV. A. 1 Competency: 46
    Question Type: *Factual*

48. Lori, who was in a hurry to get to school so she could be on time for a big test, became angry because Kristen was driving like a snail in front of her. When then they stopped at a red light, Lori got out of her car and smashed Kristen's windshield. Lori's behaviour can best be explained by:
    a. the projection hypothesis
    b. the frustration-aggression hypothesis
    c. the bystander effect
    d. social facilitation theory

    Concept: IV. A. 2. a Competency: 47
    Question Type: *Applied*

49. Donovan is at a baseball game, where it is extremely hot and his team is losing. As a result he is getting more and more angry. When the person in front of him stands up and obstructs his view, Donovan pours his popcorn on him. Donovan's behaviour can be best explained by:
    a. the cognitive-neoassociationistic model
    b. the frustration-aggression hypothesis
    c. the bystander effect
    d. social facilitation theory

    Concept: IV. A. 2. b Competency: 48
    Question Type: *Applied*

50. While on vacation in the United States, Catherine noticed that the guys with a Southern accent are much more aggressive and tend to get into more altercations. She asked a guy she met from Alabama why that is and he said that he was brought up not to let anyone tarnish his reputation. This best represents which concept?
    a. the cognitive-neoassociationistic model
    b. the culture of honor
    c. the frustration-aggression hypothesis
    d. the just-world hypothesis

    Concept: IV. B. 1 Competency: 49
    Question Type: *Applied*

51. Jerry was involved in a train crash. Although numerous cars were on fire, he rushed back into the train to save as many others as possible. This providing of help without any apparent reward for doing so is known as:
    a. inclusive fitness
    b. reciprocity
    c. hedonism
    d. altruism

    Concept: IV. C. 2 Competency: 50
    Question Type: *Applied*

52. Jake and his son Chase are out in the ocean sailing when a heavy storm throws Chase overboard. Jake dives in to save Chase even though Jake isn't a strong swimmer. This scenario best represents what type of helping?
    a. pro-altruistic
    b. reciprocal helping
    c. kin selection
    d. inclusive fitness

    Concept: IV. C. 2 Competency: 51
    Question Type: *Applied*

53. Jen is leaving a house with friends after a night of partying. In the street, they see several groups and pairs of people staring at and discussing a scene involving a man repeatedly slapping a woman while yelling and cursing at her. Jen experiences the bystander intervention effect, so she:
a. ignores the scene and does not help the woman
b. ignores everyone standing around and runs to help the woman
c. immediately finds a phone and calls the police
d. rallies a bunch of other observers to help the woman

Concept: IV. C. 3 Competency: 52
Question Type: *Applied*

54. Because of diffusion of responsibility, if you need help in a crowded situation you should:
a. ask "can anyone help me?"
b. tell them "I know one of you can help me!"
c. point to one person and tell them to help you
d. shout to everyone that you need help

Concept: IV. C. 3. a Competency: 53
Question Type: *Applied*

55. Norman found that his friends in university were the people in the dorms who lived near him. He saw them a lot and they began hanging out together. His situation illustrates the effects of ______________ on friendship.
a. matching
b. proximity
c. propriety
d. conditioned rewards

Concept: V. A. 1 Competency: 54
Question Type: *Applied*

56. Pam and Tommy have all the same interests. They both like wild parties, tattoos, constant stimulation, and loads of attention. Because of the effects of ______________, they have become close friends.
a. matching
b. proximity
c. similarity
d. familiarity

Concept: V. A. 3 Competency: 55
Question Type: *Applied*

57. Raul wants to have the best online dating profile possible so he should say that he is ______________________________ and is not ______________________________.

Concept: V. A. 4 Competency: 56
Question Type: *Factual*

58. Which of the following characteristics is NOT considered attractive in a face?
a. It has unique and distinct features.
b. It appears as though it is the average of many other attractive faces.
c. It is symmetrical.
d. It is biracial.

Concept: V. A. 5. a Competency: 57
Question Type: *Applied*

59. When Lyle and Erik were facing charges in court, their attorney took great pains to ensure that they had fresh haircuts and were dressed as attractively as possible. Their attorney is using the ______________ stereotype.
a. door in the face
b. what is beautiful is good
c. birds of a feather flock together
d. external similarity

Concept: V. A. 5. b Competency: 58
Question Type: *Applied*

60. Charlie and Lucy have just started dating and are most likely experiencing high levels of ______________ love. Ronald and Nancy have been married for 60 years and are most likely experiencing high levels of ______________ love.
a. companionate; passionate
b. commitment; passionate
c. passionate; companionate
d. companionate; commitment

Concept: V. B. 1 Competency: 59
Question Type: *Applied*

61. You are a psychotherapist at the university counselling centre. The university has instituted a policy that all students who wish to get married can come in for four sessions of free prenuptial advice. Describe how you would assess which couples were at risk for problems and how you might help the couples with future difficulties.

____

____

____

____

Concept: V. C. 2. a Competency: 60
Question Type: *Conceptual*

62. Dennis decides to bring home some flowers to show his girlfriend, Carmen, how much he cares for her. When she sees the flowers, she flies into a rage accusing him of infidelity or doing something else that he is trying to atone for. Carmen is making ______________ attributions.
   a. distress-maintaining
   b. partner-enhancing
   c. external
   d. socially destructive

Concept: V. C. 3 Competency: 61
Question Type: *Applied*

63. Which of the following is true?
   a. Couples who have more sex are happier.
   b. Conflict is symptomatic of a troubled relationship.
   c. Conflict is inevitable in any serious relationship and is one of the healthiest things a couple can do for their relationship when it helps air grievances.
   d. Couples who never fight are the happiest.

Concept: V. C. 4 Competency: 62
Question Type: *Applied*

64. Concept: V. B. 5 Competency: 63
Question Type: *Factual*

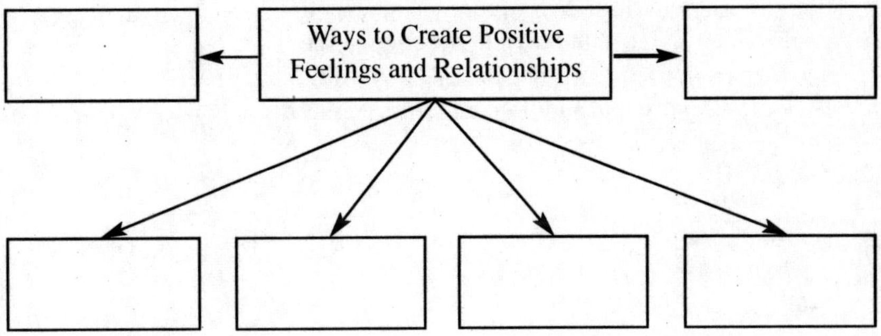

PSYCHOLOGY AND SOCIETY

Imagine that a friend of yours recently moved to another province to attend university. She sends you an email about how lonely she is and asks for advice on how to make new friends. Compose a response to your friend describing at least two situational and/or personal predictors of liking; translate each into a concrete piece of advice for your friend.

ANSWER KEY

Item **Answer**

1. other people
2. Attitudes
3. a
4. c
5. d
6. a
7. Its primary use is that it doesn't rely on self-report (people telling you their attitudes) which can be problematic because people are motivated to make themselves look good. If you want to know how a person feels about a sensitive topic, it may be more accurate to avoid self-report. The IAT gets reaction times to word pairings. People respond quicker to pairings they agree with or find more appropriate. So if a person responded more quickly to CAT=EVIL than DOG=EVIL we could surmise that that person had a stronger dislike for cats.
8. d
9. b
10. a
11. c
12. a
13. source; content; receiver
14. c
15. Many examples are appropriate. Some include posture, if they avoid eye contact, if they have their arms crossed, legs crossed, if they lean toward or away from you, if they play with their hair or something on their clothing, or if they put their hands behind their head.
16. a
17. b
18. c
19. b
20. c
21. d
22. a
23. a
24. a
25. Finding that we make quick and automatic judgments that categorize people is not surprising because we quickly make judgments about everything (e.g., Will that chair hold me? Does that lettuce look spoiled? Did that person give me a look?). What we do with those judgments is a conscious process that can override any unconscious classifications.
26. c
27. d
28. a
29. b
30. d
31. a
32. b
33. Answers will vary but might include a discussion of the contact hypothesis or the idea that simply learning more about outgroups will lessen tension and hostility (it does not). Students might incorporate Sherif's ideas of disparate groups having shared superordinate goals and how this might be incorporated into school activities. In addition, they might propose a variation of Aronson's jigsaw classroom as a way of facilitating more positive attitudes toward other ethnicities. Finally, students might discuss how ingroup and outgroup formation seems to be a natural, and normally adaptive, process of social interaction.
34. d
35. a
36. b
37. c
38. d
39. b
40. c
41. c
42. b
43. c
44. a
45. d
46. a
47. d
48. b
49. a
50. b
51. d
52. d
53. a
54. c
55. b
56. c
57. kind, dependable, trustworthy; dishonest, insincere, or lacking personal warmth
58. a
59. b
60. c

61. Answers will vary. In terms of assessment, students might address the issues of proximity and similarity while taking into account the phenomenon of need complementarity. The couples could also be rated on Sternberg's three components of love: passion, intimacy, and commitment. One also could relate the differences between passionate and companionate love and the toxicity of extramarital affairs. In terms of treatment, the therapist could attempt to alter Gottman's four interpersonal styles that lead to marital discord: being overly critical, holding the partner in contempt, being defensive, and mentally withdrawing from the relationship. One could also try to help the couple make partner-enhancing attributions as opposed to distress-maintaining attributions.
62. a
63. c
64. Show interest in your partner; Be affectionate; Show you care; Spend quality time together; Maintain loyalty and fidelity; Handle conflict

Psychology and Society

Examples of advice you could give that builds on each predictor:

Propinquity/proximity and familiarity
Sit in the same place each day in class to become more familiar to, and thus more liked by, those around you; frequent the same coffee shops.

Similarity
Join clubs based on your interests (e.g., a hiking club); attend protests.

Personal characteristics
People like others who are honest, helpful, and so on. Do not act deceitfully; offer assistance.

Physical attractiveness
Not much we can do about our symmetry or our averageness, but we can hold ourselves with confidence, groom, and wear clean clothes.

KEY TERM EXERCISES

aggression

Textbook Definition:
Your Own Definition:
Your Own Example:

attitudes

Textbook Definition:
Your Own Definition:
Your Own Example:

altruism

Textbook Definition:
Your Own Definition:
Your Own Example:

attributions

Textbook Definition:
Your Own Definition:
Your Own Example:

bystander intervention effect

Textbook Definition:
Your Own Definition:
Your Own Example:

cognitive dissonance

Textbook Definition:
Your Own Definition:
Your Own Example:

compliance

Textbook Definition:
Your Own Definition:
Your Own Example:

conformity

Textbook Definition:
Your Own Definition:
Your Own Example:

deindividuation

Textbook Definition:
Your Own Definition:
Your Own Example:

discrimination

Textbook Definition:
Your Own Definition:
Your Own Example:

elaboration likelihood model

Textbook Definition:
Your Own Definition:
Your Own Example:

explicit attitudes

Textbook Definition:
Your Own Definition:
Your Own Example:

frustration-aggression hypothesis

Textbook Definition:
Your Own Definition:
Your Own Example:

fundamental attribution error

Textbook Definition:
Your Own Definition:
Your Own Example:

implicit attitudes

Textbook Definition:
Your Own Definition:
Your Own Example:

prejudice

Textbook Definition:
Your Own Definition:
Your Own Example:

ingroup favouritism

Textbook Definition:
Your Own Definition:
Your Own Example:

prosocial

Textbook Definition:
Your Own Definition:
Your Own Example:

nonverbal behaviour

Textbook Definition:
Your Own Definition:
Your Own Example:

self-fulfilling prophecy

Textbook Definition:
Your Own Definition:
Your Own Example:

personal attributions

Textbook Definition:
Your Own Definition:
Your Own Example:

situational attributions

Textbook Definition:
Your Own Definition:
Your Own Example:

persuasion

Textbook Definition:
Your Own Definition:
Your Own Example:

social facilitation

Textbook Definition:
Your Own Definition:
Your Own Example:

social loafing

Textbook Definition:
Your Own Definition:
Your Own Example:

stereotypes

Textbook Definition:
Your Own Definition:
Your Own Example:

social norms

Textbook Definition:
Your Own Definition:
Your Own Example:

CHAPTER 13 Personality

CONCEPT MAP

I. How Have Psychologists Studied Personality?
   A. Personality
      1. Organization
      2. Dynamic
      3. Psychophysical Systems
      4. Characteristic
   B. Psychodynamic Theories
      1. Instincts
         a. Pleasure Principle
         b. Libido
      2. Topographical Model of Mind
         a. Conscious
         b. Preconscious
         c. Unconscious
            1. Freudian Slip
      3. Development of Sexual Instincts
         a. Stages
            1. Oral Stage
            2. Anal Stage
            3. Phallic Stage
               A. Oedipus Complex
            4. Latency Stage
            5. Genital Stage
         b. Fixations
      4. Structural Model of Personality
         a. Id
            1. Pleasure Principle
         b. Superego
         c. Ego
            1. Reality Principle
            2. Defense Mechanisms
               A. Rationalize
               B. Reaction Formation
      5. Neo-Freudians: Psychodynamic Theory Since Freud
         a. Neo-Freudians
         b. Object Relations
   C. Humanistic Approaches
      1. Self-Actualization
      2. Phenomenology
      3. Person-Centred Approach
      4. Unconditional Positive Regard
      5. Positive Psychology Movement
         a. Broaden-and-Build Theory
   D. Type and Trait Approaches
      1. Personality Types
         a. Implicit Personality Theory
      2. Trait Approach
         a. Personality Trait
         b. Factor Analysis
      3. Eysenck's Hierarchical Model
         a. Specific Response Level
         b. Habitual Response Level
         c. Superordinate Traits
            1. Introversion-Extroversion
            2. Emotional Stability
            3. Psychoticism (Constraint)
      4. The Big Five
         a. Five-Factor Theory
            1. Openness to Experience
            2. Conscientiousness
            3. Extroversion
            4. Agreeableness
            5. Neuroticism
         b. Empirical Support
   E. Learning and Cognitive Processes
      1. Internal vs. External Locus of Control
      2. Cognitive-Social Theories

- a. Self-Efficacy
- b. Cognitive-Affective Personality System (CAPS)
  1. Defensive Pessimism
  2. Self-Regulatory Capacities

II. How Is Personality Assessed and What Does It Predict?
- A. Personality Refers to Both Unique and Common Characteristics
  1. Idiographic Approach
     - a. Central Traits
     - b. Secondary Traits
     - c. Life Story
  2. Nomothetic Approach
- B. Objective and Projective Methods to Assess Personality
  1. Projective Measures
     - a. Rorschach Inkblot
     - b. Thematic Apperception Test (TAT)
  2. Objective Measures
     - a. NEO Personality Inventory
     - b. California Q-Sort
- C. Observers Show Accuracy in Trait Judgments
  1. Level of Acquaintance
- D. People Are Sometimes Inconsistent
  1. Situationism
     - a. Trait Centrality
     - b. Self-Monitoring
- E. Behaviour Is Influenced by the Interaction of Personality and Situations
  1. Strong vs. Weak Situations
  2. Interactionists
  3. People Influence Their Environment
- F. There Are Cultural and Gender Differences in Personality
  1. Cultural Stereotypes
  2. Gender Stereotypes
- G. On Ethics: Changing Your Personality with Drugs

III. What Are the Biological Bases of Personality?
- A. Animals Have Personality
- B. Personality is Rooted in Genetics
  1. Twin Studies
  2. Adoption Studies
  3. Are There Specific Genes for Personality?
- C. Temperaments Are Evident in Infancy
  1. Temperament
     - a. Activity Level
     - b. Emotionality
     - c. Sociability
  2. Long-Term Implications of Temperaments
  3. Gender and Temperaments
  4. Shyness and Inhibition
- D. Personality Is Linked to Specific Neurophysiological Mechanisms
  1. Arousal and Extroversion/Introversion
     - a. Ascending Reticular Activating System
     - b. Optimal Level of Arousal
     - c. Sensation Seeking
  2. Neurophysiology of Extroversion/Introversion
     - a. Behavioural Approach System
     - b. Behavioural Inhibition System
- E. Personality Is Adaptive
- F. Personality Traits Are Stable over Time
  1. Age Related Change
  2. Characteristic Adaptations

IV. How Do We Know Our Own Personalities?
- A. Our Self-Concept Consists of Self-Knowledge
  1. Self-Concept
  2. Self-Awareness
  3. Self-Discrepancy
  4. Self-Schema
     - a. Memory
  5. Working Self-Concept
- B. Perceived Social Regard Influences Self-Esteem
  1. Self-Esteem
     - a. Reflected Appraisal
  2. Sociometer Theory
  3. Self-Esteem and Death Anxiety
     - a. Terror Management Theory
  4. Self-Esteem and Life Outcomes
     - a. Narcissism
- C. We Use Mental Strategies to Maintain Our Views of Self
  1. Positive Illusions
     - a. Better-Than-Average Effect
     - b. Unrealistic Perception of Control
     - c. Unrealistic Perception of Future
  2. Self-Evaluative Maintenance
  3. Social Comparisons
  4. Self-Serving Biases
- D. Cultural Differences in the Self
  1. Individualistic vs. Collectivistic Cultures
  2. Culture and Self-Serving Bias

CHAPTER SUMMARY

How Have Psychologists Studied Personality?

• Psychodynamic Theories Emphasize Unconscious and Dynamic Processes: Freud believed that personality resulted partly from unconscious conflicts. The personality results from the ego's use of defense mechanisms to reduce the anxiety of the oppositional demands of the id and the superego.

Stages of psychosexual development occur from birth to adolescence. Neo-Freudians have focused on relationships, especially children's emotional attachments to their parents.

• Humanistic Approaches Emphasize Integrated Personal Experience: Humanists view personality as the result of experiences and beliefs. Humans strive to realize their full potential and may be hampered in doing so if they do not receive unconditional positive regard from their parents and/or guardians. The positive psychology movement researches subjective well-being.

• Type and Trait Approaches Describe Behavioural Dispositions: Personality type theories focus more on description than on explanation. Trait theorists assume that personality is a collection of traits that vary and that exist in a hierarchy of importance. In Eysenck's model of personality, lesser traits are organized under larger biologically based traits (extraversion, emotional stability, psychoticism).The Big Five theory considers personality to be composed of openness to new experiences, conscientiousness, extraversion, agreeableness, and neuroticism.

• Personality Reflects Learning and Cognition: Through interaction with their environment, people learn patterns of responding that are guided by both expectancies and values. Self-efficacy, the extent to which people believe they can achieve specific outcomes, is an important determinant of behaviour. The cognitive-affective personality system (CAPS) emphasizes self-regulation.

How Is Personality Assessed, and What Does It Predict?

• Personality Refers to Both Unique and Common Characteristics: Idiographic approaches are person-centred; they evaluate personality by assessing the unique pattern of an individual's characteristics. Nomothetic approaches focus on characteristics common among all people but on which individuals vary (i.e., traits).

• Researchers Use Objective and Projective Methods to Assess Personality: Projective measures subjectively evaluate the unconscious issues a person projects onto ambiguous stimuli. Objective measures are straightforward assessments, usually involving self-report questionnaires or observer ratings.

• Observers Show Accuracy in Trait Judgments: Close acquaintances may better predict a person's behaviour than the person can.

• People Sometimes Are Inconsistent: Mischel proposed that situations are more important than traits in predicting behaviour.

• Behaviour Is Influenced by the Interaction of Personality and Situations: Situations vary in the extent to which they both influence behaviour and interact with personality to determine behaviour.

• There Are Cultural and Gender Differences in Personality: Cross-cultural research presents problems because of translation issues, cultural norms for self-reporting, and individuals' judgments of themselves relative to other people from their own cultures. Some research suggests that the Big Five personality factors are universal for humans.

What Are the Biological Bases of Personality?

• Animals Have Personalities: Research on a wide variety of animal species has shown that animals have distinct personality traits that correspond roughly to the Big Five in humans.

• Personality Is Rooted in Genetics: Twin and adoption studies have found that 40 percent to 60 percent of personality variation is due to genetics. Personality characteristics are influenced by multiple genes, and their expression is the result of interaction with environments.

• Temperaments Are Evident in Infancy: Temperaments, the general tendencies of how people behave, are biologically mediated and observable in infants.

• Personality Is Linked to Specific Neurophysiological Mechanisms: Cortical arousal is regulated by the ascending reticular activating system and results in characteristics of introversion/extroversion. The behavioural approach system and the behavioural inhibition system affect variations in arousal and the behavioural responses.

• Personality Is Adaptive: Variations in individuals' personality and skills benefit a group and provide an advantage for group survival.

• Personality Traits Are Stable over Time: Trait consistency is lowest for young children and highest for those over age 50. Biological and environmental factors are more stable in adulthood. Characteristic adaptations change across time and circumstances.

How Do We Know Our Own Personalities?

• Our Self-Concepts Consist of Self-Knowledge: Self-schemas are the cognitive aspects of self-knowledge, and the working self-concept is the immediate experience of self at any given time.

• Perceived Social Regard Influences Self-Esteem: Self-esteem is influenced by people's beliefs about how other people view them. According to sociometer theory, the need to belong influences social anxiety relative to self-esteem. Self-esteem may also be influenced by death anxiety.

• We Use Mental Strategies to Maintain Our Views of Self: Positive illusions of self are common. Self-esteem is influenced by comparisons to others. A self-serving bias helps maintain positive self-esteem and may be culturally influenced.

• There Are Cultural Differences in the Self: People from collectivist cultures (e.g., regions of Asia and Africa) tend to have interdependent self-concepts; people from individualist cultures (e.g., Canada, the United States, Europe) tend to have independent self-concepts.

COMPETENCY MAP

How Have Psychologists Studied Personality?

Personality

1. Identify the key concepts for defining personality.

Psychodynamic Theories

2. Describe the psychodynamic approach to personality.
3. Explain the relationship between instinct, pleasure principle, and libido.
4. Identify the key components of the topographical model of mind.
5. What do Freudian slips reveal?
6. Identify the stages in the development of sexual instincts.
7. Describe the Oedipus complex.
8. Explain the concept of fixation.
9. Identify the three main aspects of the structural model of personality.
10. Distinguish the three main aspects of the structural model of personality.
11. Distinguish between rationalizing and reaction formation.
12. How do neo-Freudians differ from Freud?

Humanistic Approaches

13. What does it mean to achieve self-actualization?
14. What does a person-centred approach involve?
15. Describe unconditional positive regard.
16. Explain the broaden-and-build theory.

Type and Trait Approaches

17. Describe the type/trait approach to personality.
18. Explain implicit personality theory.
19. What is a personality trait?
20. Describe the process of factor analysis.
21. Distinguish between specific and habitual response levels.
22. Identify the three main types of superordinate traits.
23. Identify the Big Five personality traits.

Learning and Cognitive Processes

24. Distinguish between internal and external locus of control.
25. Describe the cognitive-social approach to personality.
26. Explain self-efficacy.
27. What is defensive pessimism?

How Is Personality Assessed and What Does It Predict?

Personality Refers to Both Unique and Common Characteristics

28. Distinguish between idiographic and nomothetic approaches.

Objective and Projective Methods to Assess Personality

29. Describe key features of projective measures.
30. Identify well-known projective measures.
31. Describe key features of objective measures.
32. Identify well-known objective measures.

Observers Show Accuracy in Trait Judgments

33. Identify determinants of observers' accuracy regarding traits.

People Are Sometimes Inconsistent

34. Explain situationism.
35. Describe what self-monitoring involves.

Behaviour Is Influenced by the Interaction of Personality and Situations

36. Distinguish between strong and weak situations.
37. Describe the interactionists' perspective on behaviour.

There Are Cultural and Gender Differences in Personality

38. Evaluate the cultural stereotypes related to personality.
39. Evaluate the gender stereotypes related to personality.

What Are the Biological Bases of Personality?

Animals Have Personality

40. Describe evidence for animals having personality.

Personality is Rooted in Genetics

41. Provide evidence for personality being rooted in genetics.

Temperaments Are Evident in Infancy

42. Identify the three main components of temperament.
43. Distinguish between the three main components of temperament.
44. What are the long-term implications of temperament?
45. Describe the role of gender in temperament.

Personality Is Linked to Specific Neurophysiological Mechanisms

46. How does optimal level of arousal and sensation-seeking relate to introversion/extroversion?
47. Describe characteristics of those high in sensation seeking.
48. Distinguish between the effects of the behavioural approach and inhibition systems.

Personality Traits Are Stable over Time

49. To what extent are personality traits stable over time?

How Do We Know Our Own Personalities?

Our Self-Concepts Consist of Self-Knowledge

50. What is the self-concept?
51. How does self-awareness influence behaviour?
52. What are implications of self-discrepancy?

Perceived Social Regard Influences Self-Esteem

53. What is the role of reflected appraisal on self-esteem?
54. According to the sociometer theory, where does self-esteem come from?
55. What is narcissism?

We Use Mental Strategies to Maintain Our Views of Self

56. Describe three ways that people carry positive illusions about the self.
57. What is a downward social comparison?
58. What is a self-serving bias?

Cultural Differences in the Self

59. How does culture influence self-construal?

KNOWLEDGE CHECK

1. Concept: I. A Competency: 1
Question Type: *Factual*

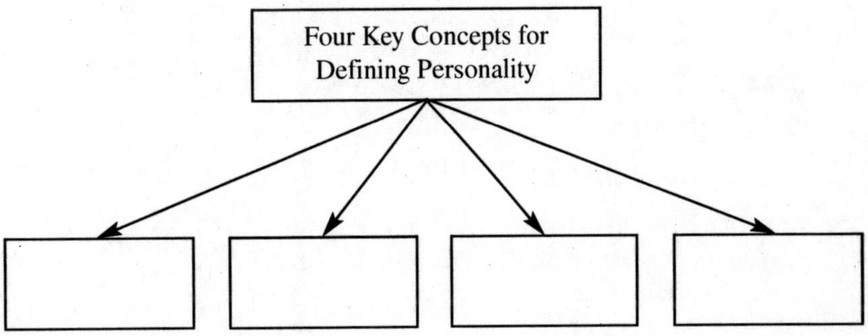

2. Randall has been highly disruptive in university. His poor grades and anti-social behaviour have eventually led him to be expelled. His therapist explains to his parents that Randall is unconsciously acting out because he did not want to attend university. The therapist is taking a ______________ approach to understanding personality.
   a. psychodynamic
   b. trait
   c. cognitive-social
   d. humanistic

   Concept: I. B Competency: 2
   Question Type: *Applied*

3. Freud proposed that people have a life ______________________________ that is satisfied by following the ______________________________, which directs people to seek pleasure and avoid pain. The energy that drives the pleasure principle is called ______________________________.

   Concept: I. B. 1 Competency: 3
   Question Type: *Factual*

4. Concept: I. B. 2 Competency: 4
   Question Type: *Factual*

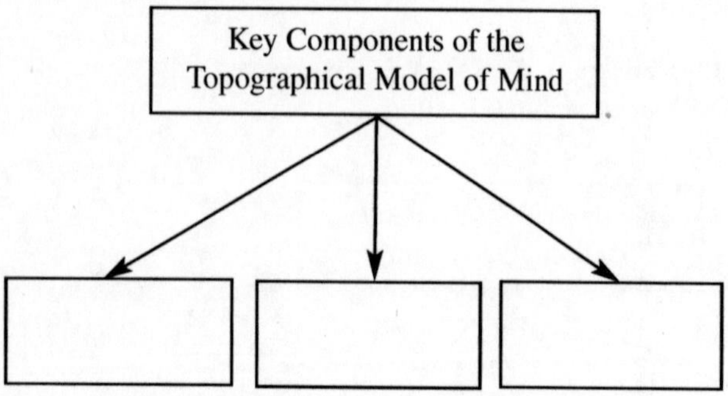

5. Julie is introduced to her biological mother, who abandoned her as an infant. As they shake hands Julie says, "It's nice to beat you." This Freudian slip is an example of information at the ______________ level being accidentally revealed.
   a. conscious
   b. preconscious
   c. subconscious
   d. unconscious

   Concept: I. B. 2. c Competency: 5
   Question Type: *Applied*

6. Which of the following is NOT one of Freud's psychosexual stages of development?
   a. oral
   b. anal
   c. latency
   d. oedipal

   Concept: I. B. 3 Competency: 6
   Question Type: *Factual*

7. TJ is 5 years old and according to Freud would experience an Oedipus complex. This should make TJ want to do which of the following?
   a. Kill his mother.
   b. Kill his father.
   c. Marry his sister.
   d. Experience conscious sexual desires toward his mother.

   Concept: I. B. 3. a. 3. A Competency: 7
   Question Type: *Applied*

8. As a baby, Dave did not receive sufficient gratification from his mother. Now, as an adult, he smokes, drinks excessively, and constantly chews on his fingernails. According to Freud, Dave's behaviour is a result of:
   a. fixation
   b. projection
   c. identification
   d. compression

   Concept: I. B. 3. b Competency: 8
   Question Type: *Applied*

9. Concept: I. B. 4 Competency: 9
   Question Type: *Factual*

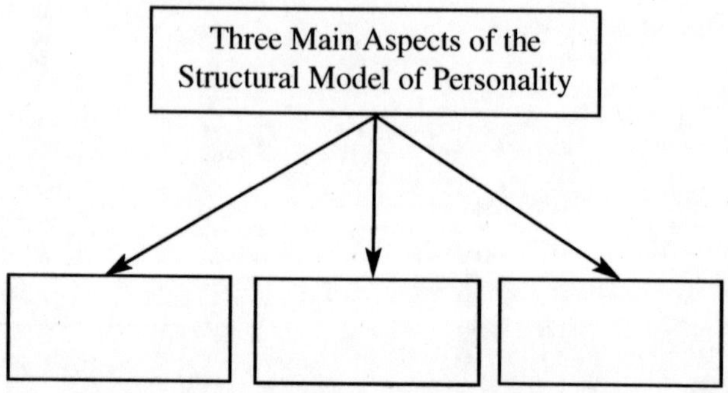

10. Alexander sees a new CD that he really wants. Part of him thinks about just stealing it when the salesperson's head is turned, but part of him feels guilty for thinking in such a selfish, anti-social way. Finally Alexander decides to do a few extra jobs to earn the money for the CD. Which Freudian personality structure is guiding his behaviour?
    a. libido
    b. id
    c. superego
    d. ego

    Concept: I. B. 4. c Competency: 10
    Question Type: *Applied*

11. What would be the ramifications if the structure of personality did not include a superego?

____

____

____

____

Concept: I. B. 4 Competency: 10
Question Type: *Conceptual*

12. Eileen's son is applying for university. He really wants to go to one of the military academies but unfortunately gets rejected. When he gets his rejection letters he states, "I didn't want to go there anyway, those guys are just a bunch of jarheads, and their parents probably paid someone to get them in!" This represents the defense mechanism of:
    a. denial
    b. rationalization
    c. repression
    d. reaction formation

Concept: I. B. 4. c. 2 Competency: 11
Question Type: *Applied*

13. Pete gets turned down for the convenience store employee of the month award because he did not turn in the guy who was stealing breath mints. Rather than beat his employer with a stale danish, Pete tells everyone what a great guy he is and how he only is trying to help him improve. This represents which ego defense mechanism?
    a. projection
    b. rationalization
    c. repression
    d. reaction formation

Concept: I. B. 4. c. 2 Competency: 11
Question Type: *Applied*

14. Which of the following is NOT true about neo-Freudians?
    a. Neo-Freudians included Horney, Jung, and Adler.
    b. Many neo-Freudians considered Freud's views misogynistic and negative toward women.
    c. Neo-Freudians put less emphasis on culture than Freud.
    d. Many neo-Freudians focused less on sexual energy and more on social connections.

Concept: I. B. 5. a Competency: 12
Question Type: *Applied*

15. Omar constantly seeks out opportunities for personal growth. He also spends a great deal of time focused on who he is in an attempt to enhance self-understanding and further promote personal growth. This process is referred to as:
    a. phenomenology
    b. humanitarian motivation
    c. self-actualization
    d. unconditional positive regard

Concept: I. C. 1 Competency: 13
Question Type: *Applied*

16. Leonard is a humanistic therapist who believes it is important to get the client's subjective view of the problem. This approach is considered:
    a. phenomenological
    b. fully functioning
    c. self-actualized
    d. unconditional positive regard

Concept: I. C. 3 Competency: 14
Question Type: *Applied*

17. Holly tries to do her best at everything. Even though she may fail periodically, her boyfriend, Sven, sticks with her in all her endeavours. According to Rogers, Sven is demonstrating ______________ toward Holly.
    a. unconditional love
    b. reciprocal determinism
    c. self-efficacy
    d. unconditional positive regard

Concept: I. C. 4 Competency: 15
Question Type: *Applied*

18. Amelia is working on a tricky problem for her math class and can't seem to figure out the solution. To help her arrive at a new and creative solution she decides to play her favourite song and dance around her room to put herself in a good mood. Sure enough, the solution was quickly apparent. Which of the following best explains this?
    a. self-monitoring
    b. broaden-and-build theory
    c. self-efficacy
    d. unconditional positive regard

Concept: I. C. 5. a Competency: 16
Question Type: *Applied*

19. Ginger's friends are trying to figure out why she would humiliate herself as a stripper at a local cabaret. They finally agree on a type/trait approach to understanding personality. Which of the following explanations best represents that approach?
   a. She is unconsciously trying to get back at her parents who were rather repressed in the area of sexuality.
   b. At her stable core, Ginger is just an exhibitionist.
   c. She has received attention (i.e., reinforcement) for this behaviour.
   d. She is trying to fulfill her potential and sees clothing as an artificial societal constraint.

   Concept: I. D Competency: 17
   Question Type: *Applied*

20. Upon meeting Ashley for the first time, Karen noticed that Ashley was very talkative and immediately predicted that Ashley would like to go to parties and was probably a lot of fun. Karen is basing this on a(n):
   a. implicit personality theory
   b. introversion-extroversion continuum
   c. explicit personality type
   d. phenomenological approach

   Concept: I. D. 1. a Competency: 18
   Question Type: *Applied*

21. A ______________________________ is a dispositional tendency to act in a certain way over time and across circumstances.

   Concept: I. D. 2 Competency: 19
   Question Type: *Factual*

22. Based on a typical factor analysis, which of the following sets of words would MOST likely be a factor?
   a. happy-sad; energetic-lethargic
   b. abysmal; active; adjusted
   c. stressed; anxious; apprehensive
   d. distress-excitement; boring-exciting

   Concept: I. D. 2. b Competency: 20
   Question Type: *Conceptual*

23. Schmitty really wants to figure out his new roommate's personality. On the second day of school Schmitty noticed that when his roommate received a package from home he left the packaging strewn around the room. From this, Schmitty decides his roommate is messy. This represents a:
   a. superordinate response
   b. big five response
   c. specific response level
   d. habitual response level

   Concept: I. D. 3 Competency: 21
   Question Type: *Applied*

24. Concept: I. B. 4 Competency: 22
   Question Type: *Factual*

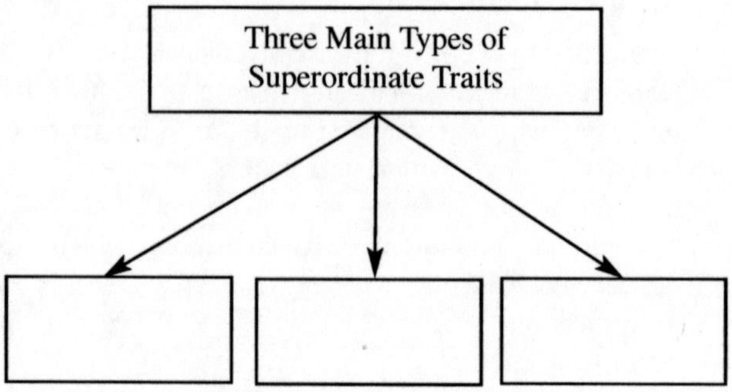

25. Concept: I. B. 4 Competency: 23
   Question Type: *Factual*

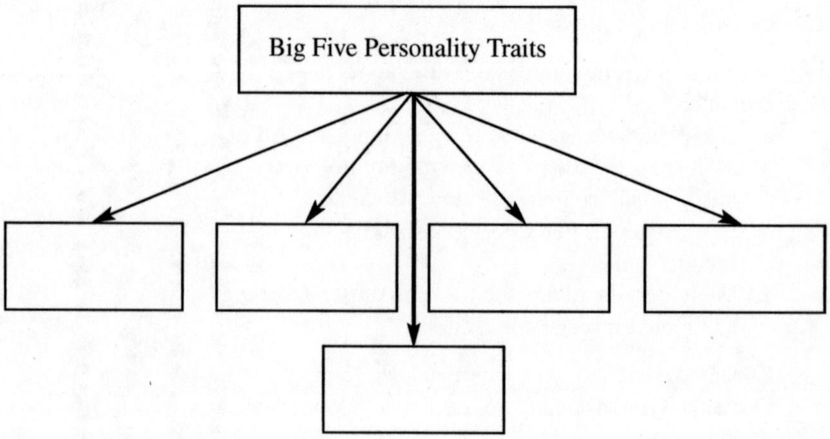

26. Tyshawn gets a 75 on his first psychology exam. He decides that he will have to study harder to receive the A he desires for the class. Tyshawn is exhibiting a(n) ______________ locus of control.
    a. internal
    b. external
    c. efficacious
    d. utilitarian

    Concept: I. E. 1 Competency: 24
    Question Type: *Applied*

27. Professor Perez is trying to figure out why John is consistently disruptive during her lectures. John not only laughs throughout the class but also points and throws unmentionable items up at the stage! Professor Perez finally decides that John has been inadvertently rewarded with attention for his rude behaviour, and he expects to be rewarded for it in the future. Which theory of personality does her approach most closely resemble?
    a. psychodynamic
    b. humanistic
    c. trait
    d. cognitive-social

    Concept: I. E. 2 Competency: 25
    Question Type: *Applied*

28. Addison is taking her first yoga class. Although she has no prior experience, she is fully confident that she can do a downward-facing dog position that her instructor describes. This demonstrates Addison's high level of:
    a. defensive pessimism
    b. external locus of control
    c. self-efficacy
    d. self-monitoring

    Concept: I. E. 2. a Competency: 26
    Question Type: *Applied*

29. Jadja is about to take her driving test to get her license. She is certain she is going to do poorly and that she will fail. This demonstrates her:
    a. defensive pessimism
    b. external locus of control
    c. self-efficacy
    d. self-monitoring

    Concept: I. E. 2. b Competency: 27
    Question Type: *Applied*

30. Latasha is doing a case study about Karen Horney, a famous personality theorist. Latasha is investigating her background and how it contributed to her ideas about human behaviour. Latasha is using a(n) ______________ approach to understanding personality.
    a. idiographic
    b. nomothetic
    c. individual
    d. stratified

    Concept: II. A Competency: 28
    Question Type: *Applied*

31. Tiffany is developing a scale called the Canadian Conscientiousness Chart. She is hoping to describe people on this trait ranging from low to high. Tiffany is using a(n) ______________ approach to understanding personality.
    a. idiographic
    b. nomothetic
    c. individual
    d. stratified

    Concept: II. A Competency: 28
    Question Type: *Applied*

32. Juan was trying his luck as a painter. One day in frustration he just tossed some different paints on the blank canvas in no particular order. When he showed his "masterpiece" to his friends, they began describing the ambiguous splotches according to their personal needs, conflicts, hopes, and fears. Unknowingly, Juan had created a(n) ______________ test.
    a. projective
    b. thematic apperception
    c. Minnesota Multiphasic Personality Inventory
    d. objective

    Concept: II. B. 1 Competency: 29
    Question Type: *Applied*

33. Andrea is in treatment when her therapist decides to do some additional personality assessment. Andrea takes a test in which she is shown an ambiguous picture and asked to tell a story about it. Andrea likely has taken a:
    a. Rorschach inkblot test
    b. Thematic Apperception Test
    c. Minnesota Multiphasic Personality Inventory
    d. NEO personality inventory

    Concept: II. B. 1. a Competency: 30
    Question Type: *Applied*

34. Ramone is administering a self-report questionnaire to his client to learn more about his personality. Ramone is using a(n) _______________ measure of personality.
   a. subjective
   b. projective
   c. multimodal
   d. objective

   Concept: II. B. 2 Competency: 31
   Question Type: *Applied*

35. Paulo is taking a self-report questionnaire designed to assess the Big Five personality traits. Paulo is most likely taking the:
   a. Millon Clinical Multiaxial Inventory
   b. NEO personality inventory
   c. Minnesota Multiphasic Personality Inventory
   d. California Q-Sort

   Concept: II. B. 1. a Competency: 32
   Question Type: *Applied*

36. Frederico considers himself to be a good judge of others and specifically believes he is very accurate when identifying personality traits. According to research, what type of person will Frederico have the most accuracy for?
   a. a complete stranger
   b. an acquaintance
   c. a best friend
   d. a person who tends to be introverted

   Concept: II. C. 1 Competency: 33
   Question Type: *Applied*

37. Wes takes a personality test when he applies for a job at a local prison, and he scores well. However, his answers do not really reflect his behaviour and his personality differs drastically from one situation to the next. His behaviour relative to his measured traits supports Mischel's idea that:
   a. prospective employees must be retested several times to get a true picture of their personality
   b. several personality tests must be used to reliably predict behaviour in a particular situation
   c. only projective personality tests (which cannot be faked) give a true picture of individual's traits
   d. behaviours are determined to a much greater extent by situations than by personality traits

   Concept: II. D. 1 Competency: 34
   Question Type: *Applied*

38. Which of the following statements best describes the relation between the trait of self-monitoring and the consistency of personality?
   a. People who are high in self-monitoring alter their behaviour to match the situation, so they exhibit low levels of consistency.
   b. People who are high in self-monitoring alter their behaviour to match the situation, so they exhibit high levels of consistency.
   c. People who are low in self-monitoring are less able to alter their self-presentation to match situations, so they exhibit low levels of consistency.
   d. People who are low in self-monitoring are less able to alter their self-presentation to match situations, so their personalities are relatively unpredictable.

   Concept: II. D. 1. b Competency: 35
   Question Type: *Applied*

39. Two friends meeting for coffee is an example of a _______________ situation. A classroom is an example of a _______________ situation.
   a. weak; weak
   b. strong; weak
   c. weak; strong
   d. strong; strong

   Concept: II. E. 1 Competency: 36
   Question Type: *Applied*

40. Sasha has been hired by a marketing company to predict customers' buying behaviour. As an interactionist, Sasha will:
   a. focus solely on the interaction between customer and seller
   b. focus solely on the influence of situational and environmental factors on buying
   c. pay equal attention to customers' traits and results of projective measures
   d. pay equal attention to customers' dispositions and the buying situation

   Concept: II. E. 2 Competency: 37
   Question Type: *Applied*

41. Research on cultural stereotypes finds:

   ____

   ____

   ____

   ____

   Concept: II. F. 1 Competency: 38
   Question Type: *Factual*

42. Which of the following has NOT been determined based on research on gender stereotypes?
    a. Women typically report and are rated as being more empathetic and agreeable than men.
    b. Women typically report and are rated as being more neurotic and concerned about feelings than men.
    c. Findings largely contradict stereotypes.
    d. Men tend to report and are rated as being more assertive than women.

    Concept: II. F. 2 Competency: 39
    Question Type: *Factual*

43. Which of the following has NOT been determined by research on personality in animals?
    a. Personality traits for hyenas clustered into five factors that matched those of humans.
    b. Agreement among the raters of hyenas was as high as is typically found in personality studies of humans
    c. Traits similar to extraversion, neuroticism, and agreeableness can be seen in most species.
    d. Only chimpanzees showed any signs of conscientiousness.

    Concept: III. A Competency: 40
    Question Type: *Factual*

44. According to twin studies, genetic influence accounts for approximately what percentage of the variance in personality traits?
    a. 0–10 percent
    b. 10–20 percent
    c. 20–40 percent
    d. 40–60 percent

    Concept: III. B Competency: 41
    Question Type: *Factual*

45. Concept: III. C. 1 Competency: 42
    Question Type: *Factual*

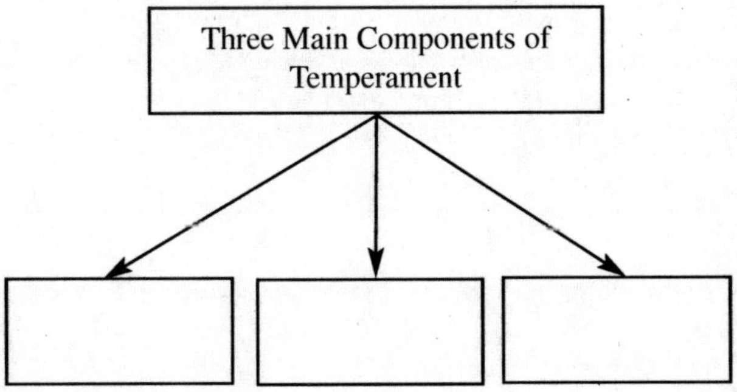

46. Emily is an expressive child. The slightest offense can cause her to cry, and she is easily frightened by new situations. Emily is high in the temperament of:
    a. affectivity
    b. activity level
    c. sociability
    d. emotionality

    Concept: III. C. 1 Competency: 43
    Question Type: *Applied*

47. Three-year-old Luke tends to have a very social temperament. Research on the long-term implications of temperament suggest that:
    a. Luke's current sociability will predict behaviour until age 12 but not beyond
    b. Luke's current sociability will not predict behaviour very well in the future
    c. Luke's current sociability will predict behaviour until early adulthood
    d. Luke's current sociability will reverse itself in adulthood

    Concept: III. C. 2 Competency: 44
    Question Type: *Applied*

48. A meta-analysis of research on gender differences in temperament found that

    ____

    demonstrated a stronger ability to control their attention and to resist their impulses. Also,

    ____

    were physically active and experienced more high-intensity pleasure. However, there were no temperamental differences in negative emotions, such as being angry or neurotic, during childhood.

    Concept: III. C. 3 Competency: 45
    Question Type: *Applied*

49. Cindy is doing a research study on the effects of caffeine on various behaviours. Cindy finds that several of her participants are very arousable or reactive to the caffeine. These individuals likely fit which of the following trait categories?
    a. introverts
    b. extroverts
    c. sensation seekers
    d. sociopaths

    Concept: III. D. 1. b Competency: 46
    Question Type: *Applied*

50. Dan lives an exciting lifestyle. He likes to go bungee jumping and parachuting on a waveboard. Dan seeks arousal through adventures and new experiences. He is easily bored and used to escape this boredom through the use of drugs and alcohol. Dan is high in the arousal-based trait of:
    a. introversion
    b. extraversion
    c. sensation seeking
    d. sociopathy

    Concept: III. D. 1. c Competency: 47
    Question Type: *Applied*

51. Drew the extrovert loves to gamble. He is more influenced by the possibility of winning the big pot than he is by the constant punishment of losing his money. Which of the following neurological systems has the greatest effect on Drew?
    a. behavioural inhibition system
    b. behavioural approach system
    c. ascending reticular activating system
    d. cognitive-affective personality system

    Concept: III. D. 2 Competency: 48
    Question Type: *Applied*

52. Farrah is in a relationship with a man who is demeaning and abusive. In response to her confrontation he tells her, "I can change!" According to a meta-analysis of 150 studies on personality change, personality becomes more stable by:
    a. age 5
    b. adolescence
    c. young adulthood
    d. middle age

    Concept: III. F Competency: 49
    Question Type: *Applied*

53. Stephanie and Said have just met at a party. Stephanie asks him to describe himself. Said states that he is a senior finance major, 22 years old, Moroccan, Muslim, a soccer player, shy, and optimistic. These things Said knows about himself are part of his:
    a. minimal self
    b. self-concept
    c. self-recognition
    d. reflected appraisal

    Concept: IV. A. 1 Competency: 50
    Question Type: *Applied*

54. Seeing yourself can enhance self-awareness which in turn leads people to act in accordance with their personal values and beliefs. Give your own examples of times or contexts when you have seen this used.

    ____

    ____

    ____

    ____

    Concept: IV. A. 2 Competency: 51
    Question Type: *Conceptual*

55. Woody is having a tough time in university. There is a substantial gap between how he sees himself and how he believes he ought to seem to others. According to Higgins's self-discrepancy theory, which of the following emotions is Woody most likely to experience?
    a. disappointment
    b. frustration and helplessness
    c. sadness and depression
    d. anxiety and guilt

    Concept: IV. A. 3 Competency: 52
    Question Type: *Applied*

56. Charles works hard at maintaining a positive public image. He does a lot of high-profile charity work, and he is careful not to lose his temper in public. He believes that other parents see him as a role model for their children. His views of what he thinks others believe about him are known as:
    a. reflected appraisals
    b. basked glory
    c. the collective self
    d. the minimal self

    Concept: IV. B. 1. a Competency: 53
    Question Type: *Applied*

57. In the context of sociometer theory, if a person was a hermit who lived alone, how would their self-esteem be affected?

    ____

    ____

    ____

    ____

    Concept: IV. B. 2 Competency: 54
    Question Type: *Conceptual*

58. Desean has a tendency to see himself in overly positive ways. In fact, he believes that everyone around him should treat him with an extra level of respect. He also has no qualms about manipulating others to get what he wants. Desean's feelings suggest that he has:
    a. high reflected appraisals
    b. a high degree of narcissism
    c. a slightly above average self-esteem
    d. a positive sociometer

    Concept: IV. B. 4 Competency: 55
    Question Type: *Applied*

59. Raymond says to his brother Charlie, "I'm a very good driver," despite the fact that he is totally inept and has never driven before. This inflated view of the self is often referred to as:
    a. delusional cognitions
    b. the better-than-average effect
    c. self-evaluative maintenance
    d. downward social comparison

    Concept: IV. C. 1 Competency: 56
    Question Type: *Applied*

60. Which of the following is NOT one of the domains of positive illusions?
    a. overestimate one's skills, abilities, and competencies
    b. unrealistic perception of one's personal control over events
    c. unrealistically optimistic about one's personal future
    d. unconditional acceptance of others' misfortunes

    Concept: IV. C. 1 Competency: 56
    Question Type: *Applied*

61. Tara and Lynn just finished a difficult psychology exam. Lynn is upset and expresses concern over several questions on which she felt she might have done poorly. Although Tara is mildly apprehensive about a couple of questions, she feels much better after hearing Lynn moan about her test disaster. Tara's reaction illustrates the working of:
    a. upward social comparison
    b. counterfactual thinking
    c. downward social comparison
    d. self-serving bias

    Concept: IV. C. 3 Competency: 57
    Question Type: *Applied*

62. Jodie got her results for her two exams on the same day. She got an A on her psychology exam but received a D on her anthropology exam. She attributed her psychology grade to her hard work, but stated that her poor performance in anthropology was because her professor is a "stupid jerk who tested irrelevant information." Assuming the tests were roughly equal in difficulty, her attributions are an example of:
    a. upward social comparison
    b. the better-than-average effect
    c. downward social comparison
    d. self-serving bias

    Concept: IV. C. 4 Competency: 58
    Question Type: *Applied*

63. Brandy has been encouraged by her parents to attend soccer camp. They want her to develop her skills enough that she will be selected for competitive leagues, even though it will mean leaving her friends behind on the community teams. Because of this influence, Brandy's self-concept will likely be characterized by:
    a. independent self-construals
    b. interdependent self-construals
    c. collectivism
    d. self-discrepancy

    Concept: IV. D. 1 Competency: 59
    Question Type: *Factual*

ANSWER KEY

Item	Answer
1.	organization; dynamic; psychophysical systems; characteristic
2.	a
3.	instinct; pleasure principle; libido
4.	conscious; preconscious; unconscious
5.	d
6.	d
7.	b
8.	a
9.	Id; Ego; Superego
10.	b
11.	Without a superego, the id would have much more influence. Personality would likely be more animalistic where individuals focused indiscriminately on fulfilling their wishes. The pleasure principle would guide most behaviour. Also, without a superego, the role of the ego would be less certain because the ego serves to balance the needs of the id and superego.
12.	b
13.	d
14.	c
15.	c
16.	a
17.	d
18.	b

19. b
20. a
21. personality trait
22. c
23. c
24. Introversion-Extroversion; Emotional Stability; Psychoticism (Constraint)
25. Openness to Experience; Conscientiousness; Extroversion; Agreeableness; Neuroticism
26. a
27. d
28. c
29. a
30. a
31. b
32. a
33. b
34. d
35. b
36. c
37. d
38. a
39. c
40. d
41. there is little correspondence between stereotypes and self-reports of people in those countries.
42. c
43. a
44. d
45. Activity Level; Emotionality; Sociability
46. d
47. c
48. girls; boys
49. a
50. c
51. b
52. d
53. b
54. Many examples are possible, but here are two. This concept is often implemented in stores. When customers first walk in there is a video camera pointed at the door with a monitor showing what it is recording. This is meant to show that customers are being watched and lets customers see themselves (both with the goal of reducing shoplifting). Mirrors are also often seen in bars, perhaps as a means of getting patrons to act in more socially acceptable ways.
55. d
56. a
57. The sociometer theory suggests that self-esteem is an indication of acceptance or rejection. Thus, if the person lived alone because of rejection their self-esteem should be quite low. However, the theory is also based on a fundamental need to belong so it is likely that in a case where the hermit doesn't feel rejected, self-esteem would still suffer due to the lack of other people around and a low sense of belongingness.
58. b
59. b
60. d
61. c
62. d
63. a

KEY TERM EXERCISES

behavioural approach system (BAS)

Textbook Definition:
Your Own Definition:
Your Own Example:

behavioural inhibition system (BIS)

Textbook Definition:
Your Own Definition:
Your Own Example:

defence mechanisms

Textbook Definition:
Your Own Definition:
Your Own Example:

ego

Textbook Definition:
Your Own Definition:
Your Own Example:

five-factor theory

Textbook Definition:

Your Own Definition:

Your Own Example:

humanistic approaches

Textbook Definition:

Your Own Definition:

Your Own Example:

id

Textbook Definition:

Your Own Definition:

Your Own Example:

idiographic approaches

Textbook Definition:

Your Own Definition:

Your Own Example:

interactionists

Textbook Definition:

Your Own Definition:

Your Own Example:

nomothetic approaches

Textbook Definition:

Your Own Definition:

Your Own Example:

objective measures

Textbook Definition:

Your Own Definition:

Your Own Example:

personality

Textbook Definition:

Your Own Definition:

Your Own Example:

personality trait

Textbook Definition:

Your Own Definition:

Your Own Example:

personality types

Textbook Definition:

Your Own Definition:

Your Own Example:

projective measures

Textbook Definition:
Your Own Definition:
Your Own Example:

psychodynamic theory

Textbook Definition:
Your Own Definition:
Your Own Example:

psychosexual stage

Textbook Definition:
Your Own Definition:
Your Own Example:

self-serving bias

Textbook Definition:
Your Own Definition:
Your Own Example:

situationism

Textbook Definition:
Your Own Definition:
Your Own Example:

sociometer

Textbook Definition:
Your Own Definition:
Your Own Example:

superego

Textbook Definition:
Your Own Definition:
Your Own Example:

temperaments

Textbook Definition:
Your Own Definition:
Your Own Example:

trait approach

Textbook Definition:
Your Own Definition:
Your Own Example:

CHAPTER 14 Psychological Disorders

CONCEPT MAP

I. How Are Psychological Disorders Conceptualized and Classified?
   A. Psychopathology
      1. Prevalence
   B. Criteria for Psychopathology
      1. Does the Behaviour Deviate from Cultural Norms?
      2. Is the Behaviour Maladaptive?
      3. Is the Behaviour Causing the Individual Personal Distress?
   C. Psychological Disorders Are Classified into Categories
      1. *Diagnostic and Statistical Manual of Mental Disorders* (*DSM*)
         a. Multiaxial System
            1. Clinical Disorders
            2. Mental Retardation or Personality Disorders
            3. Medical Conditions
            4. Psychosocial Problems
            5. Global Assessment of Functioning
   D. Psychological Disorders Must Be Assessed
      1. Assessment
         a. Diagnosis
         b. Prognosis
         c. Mental Status Exams
         d. Clinical Interview
      2. Structured vs. Unstructured Interviews
      3. Types of Testing
         a. Observed Behaviour
         b. Psychological Testing
            1. Minnesota Multiphasic Personality Inventory (MMPI)
         c. Neuropsychological Testing
      4. Evidence-Based Assessment
   E. Dissociative Identity Disorder Is a Controversial Diagnosis
      1. Assessment
   F. Psychological Disorders Have Many Causes
      1. Diathesis-Stress Model
      2. Biological Factors
         a. Genetics
         b. Brain
      3. Psychological Factors
         a. Family Systems Model
         b. Socio-cultural Model
      4. Cognitive-Behavioural Factors
      5. Sex Differences in Mental Disorders
      6. Culture and Mental Disorders

II. Can Anxiety Be the Root of Seemingly Different Disorders?
   A. Anxiety Disorders
      1. Phobic Disorder
         a. Specific Phobia
      2. Generalized Anxiety Disorder
      3. Panic Disorder
         a. Agoraphobia
      4. Obsessive-Compulsive Disorder
         a. Obsessions
         b. Compulsions
   B. Anxiety Disorders Have Cognitive, Situational, and Biological Components
      1. Cognitive Component
      2. Situational Component
      3. Biological Component

III. Are Mood Disorders Extreme Manifestations of Normal Moods?
    A. Mood Disorders
        1. Depressive Disorders
            a. Major Depression
                1. Dysthymia
            b. Prevalence
            c. Gender
        2. Bipolar Disorders
            a. Manic Episodes
            b. Hypomanic Episodes
    B. Mood Disorders Have Cognitive, Situational, and Biological Components
        1. Cognitive Component
            a. Cognitive Triad
                1. Errors in Logic
            b. Learned Helplessness Model
        2. Situational Component
        3. Biological Component
            a. Biological Rhythms
                1. Seasonal Affective Disorder (SAD)

IV. What Is Schizophrenia?
    A. Schizophrenia
    B. Positive and Negative Symptoms
        1. Positive Symptoms of Schizophrenia
            a. Delusions
                1. Paranoid
                2. Grandeur
                3. Persecution
            b. Hallucinations
                1. Auditory
                2. Visual
                3. Olfactory
                4. Somatosensory
            c. Loosening of Associations
                1. Clang Associations
            d. Disorganized and Inappropriate Behaviour
                1. Echolalia
        2. Negative Symptoms of Schizophrenia
            a. Catatonic Schizophrenia
    C. Schizophrenia Is Primarily a Brain Disorder
        1. Genetics
        2. Brain
            a. Timing
    D. Environmental Factors Influence Schizophrenia
        1. Schizovirus

V. Are Personality Disorders Truly Mental Disorders?
    A. Personality Disorders
        1. Three Groups
            a. Odd and Eccentric Behaviour
                1. Paranoid, Schizoid, and Schizotypal
            b. Dramatic and Emotional Behaviour
                1. Histrionic, Narcissistic, Borderline, and Anti-social
            c. Anxious and Fearful Behaviour
                1. Avoidant, Dependent, and Obsessive-Compulsive
                2. Controversial Aspects
    B. Types of Personality Disorders
        1. Borderline Personality Disorder
        2. Anti-social Personality Disorder
            a. Causes
                1. Brain
                2. Genetics and Environment

VI. Should Childhood Disorders Be Considered a Unique Category?
    A. Autism
        1. Asperger's Syndrome
        2. Core Symptoms of Autism
            a. Unaware of Others
            b. Deficits in Communication
                1. Echolalia
                2. Pronoun Reversal
            c. Restricted Activities and Interests
        3. Autism Is Primarily a Biological Disorder
            a. Overgrowth-Undergrowth
            b. Oxytocin
            c. Blood Proteins
            d. Antibodies
    B. Attention Deficit Hyperactivity Disorder Is a Disruptive Impulse Control Disorder
        1. Etiology of ADHD
        2. ADHD across the Life Span

CHAPTER SUMMARY

How Are Psychological Disorders Conceptualized and Classified?

• Psychological Disorders Are Classified into Categories: The *Diagnostic and Statistical Manual of Mental Disorders* is a multiaxial system for diagnosing groups of symptoms in the contexts of related factors.

• Psychological Disorders Must Be Assessed: Assessment is the process of examining a person's mental functions and psychological health to make a diagnosis. Assessment is accomplished through interviews, behavioural evaluations, and psychological testing.

• Dissociative Identity Disorder Is a Controversial Diagnosis: Also called multiple personality disorder, dissociative identity disorder involves two or more distinct identities within one person. It is a controversial diagnosis because people may fake its symptoms.

• Psychological Disorders Have Many Causes: Disorders may arise from psychological factors, such as family dynamics or socio-cultural context. They may be the result of learned, maladaptive cognitions. Biological factors also underlie mental illness. The diathesis-stress model looks at mental disorders as an interaction among multiple factors. In this model, stressful circumstances may trigger a disorder in an individual with underlying vulnerabilities.

Can Anxiety Be the Root of Seemingly Different Disorders?

• There Are Different Types of Anxiety Disorders: Phobias are exaggerated fears of specific stimuli. Generalized anxiety disorder is diffuse and omnipresent. Panic attacks cause sudden overwhelming terror and may lead to agoraphobia. Obsessive-compulsive disorders involve anxiety-related thoughts and behaviours.

• Anxiety Disorders Have Cognitive, Situational, and Biological Components: The etiology of OCD involves genetics as well as brain dysfunction. The irrational thoughts that accompany panic attacks may lead to agoraphobia through cognitive-behavioural connections.

Are Mood Disorders Extreme Manifestations of Normal Moods?

• There Are Different Types of Mood Disorders: Depressive disorders may be major or bipolar and are more severe than dysthymia.

• Mood Disorders Have Cognitive, Situational, and Biological Components: The biological factors of depression include genetics, frontal-lobe functioning, and serotonin modulation, as well as biological rhythms. Negative thinking and poor interpersonal relations also contribute to depression.

What Is Schizophrenia?

• Schizophrenia Has Positive and Negative Symptoms: Positive symptoms include excesses, such as delusions and hallucinations. Negative symptoms are deficits in functioning, such as social withdrawal and reduced bodily movement.

• Schizophrenia Is Primarily a Brain Disorder: The brains of people with schizophrenia have larger ventricles and less brain mass, with reduced frontal- and temporal-lobe activation. A variety of neurochemical and neural structural abnormalities exist as well.

• Environmental Factors Influence Schizophrenia: Urban environments may trigger the onset of schizophrenia. Trauma or pathogens encountered by pregnant women may increase the likelihood of the disorder in their children.

Are Personality Disorders Truly Mental Disorders?

• Personality Disorders Are Maladaptive Ways of Relating to the World: Odd behaviours, extreme emotions, and fearful behaviours are characteristic of personality disorders. Whether some of these extremes are true psychopathologies is controversial.

• Borderline Personality Disorder Is Associated with Poor Self-Control: Borderline personality disorder involves disturbances in identity, in affect, and in impulse control. A strong relationship exists between the disorder and both trauma and abuse.

• Anti-social Personality Disorder Is Associated with a Lack of Empathy: Anti-social personality disorder is marked by a lack of both empathy and remorse and by a tendency to be manipulative. Both genetics and environment seem to be contributing factors.

Should Childhood Disorders Be Considered a Unique Category?

• Autism Is a Lack of Awareness of Others: Autism, a biological disorder, emerges in infancy and is marked by avoidance of eye contact and impairment in verbal and nonverbal communication. Asperger's syndrome is a high-functioning variation of autism. The biological factors involved in autism may include abnormalities in oxytocin, in brain growth, and in blood proteins.

• Attention Deficit Hyperactivity Disorder Is a Disruptive Impulse Control Disorder: Children with ADHD are restless, inattentive, and impulsive. Its causes may include environmental factors such as poor parenting and social disadvantages; genetic factors; and brain abnormalities, particularly with regard to activation of the frontal lobes and subcortical basal ganglia. ADHD continues into adulthood, presenting challenges to academic work and to career pursuits.

COMPETENCY MAP

How Are Psychological Disorders Conceptualized and Classified?

Psychopathology

1. What is psychopathology?
2. How prevalent is psychopathology?

Criteria for Psychopathology

3. Identify the criteria for psychopathology.

Mental Disorders Are Classified into Categories

4. What is the DSM?
5. Explain the meaning of multiaxial.

6. Identify the five components of the multiaxial system.

Psychological Disorders Must Be Assessed

7. Distinguish between diagnosis and prognosis.
8. What are mental status exams and clinical interviews?
9. Distinguish between structured and unstructured interviews.
10. Describe the pros and cons of different types of testing for psychopathology.
11. What is evidence-based assessment?

Dissociative Identity Disorder Is a Controversial Diagnosis

12. Why is dissociative identity disorder controversial?

Psychological Disorders Have Many Causes

13 Explain the diathesis-stress model.
14. Describe biological factors in psychological disorders.
15. Describe the family systems and sociocultural approaches to psychological disorders.
16. Identify cognitive-behavioural factors in psychological disorders.
17. What are the sex differences in psychological disorders?

Can Anxiety Be the Root of Seemingly Different Disorders?

Anxiety Disorders

18. Identify characteristics of a specific phobia.
19. Identify characteristics of generalized anxiety disorder.
20. Identify characteristics of panic disorder.
21. Identify characteristics of agoraphobia.
22. Identify characteristics of obsessive-compulsive disorder.
23. Distinguish between obsessions and compulsions.

Anxiety Disorders Have Cognitive, Situational, and Biological Components

24. Explain the cognitive, situational, and biological components of anxiety disorders.

Are Mood Disorders Extreme Manifestations of Normal Moods?

Mood Disorders

25. Identify characteristics of major depression.
26. How does dysthymia differ from major depression?
27. How does depression differ by gender?
28. Identify characteristics of bipolar disorder.
29. Distinguish between manic and hypomanic episodes.

Mood Disorders Have Cognitive, Situational, and Biological Components

30. Explain the cognitive, situational, and biological components of mood disorders.
31. What is the cognitive triad?
32. Explain learned helplessness.
33. Identify characteristics of seasonal affective disorder.

What Is Schizophrenia?

Positive and Negative Symptoms of Schizophrenia

34. Distinguish between positive and negative symptoms.
35. Describe the various types of delusions.
36. Identify the four types of hallucinations.
37. Explain loosening of associations.
38. Explain clang associations.
39. Identify the characteristics of catatonic schizophrenia.

Schizophrenia Is Primarily a Brain Disorder

40. Identify the contribution of the brain to schizophrenia.

Environmental Factors Influence Schizophrenia

41. Identify the contribution of environmental factors to schizophrenia.

Are Personality Disorders Truly Mental Disorders?

42. Explain why personality disorders and mental retardation are grouped together.

Personality Disorders

43. Identify the three groups of personality disorders.

Types of Personality Disorders

44. Identify characteristics of borderline personality disorder.
45. Identify characteristics of anti-social personality disorder.

Should Childhood Disorders Be Considered a Unique Category?

Autism

46. Identify characteristics of autism.
47. How does Asperger's Syndrome differ from autism?

48. Explain deficits in communication associated with autism.

49. Identify the biological components of autism.

Attention Deficit Hyperactivity Disorder Is a Disruptive Impulse Control Disorder

50. Identify characteristics of ADHD.

KNOWLEDGE CHECK

1. ______________________________ is the term for a sickness or disorder of the mind.

   Concept: I. A Competency: 1
   Question Type: *Factual*

2. Gweneth is waiting for her train along with 100 other people. Based on what she knows about the prevalence of psychopathology, approximately how many people waiting with her are seriously affected by a disorder (assuming it is a random sample)?
   a. 30–40
   b. 10–15
   c. 6–8
   d. 1–2

   Concept: I. A. 1 Competency: 2
   Question Type: *Applied*

3. While riding the subway in Toronto you notice an older man looking for something. As he passes he asks, "Do you hear that sound? It's the sound of a kazoo being played by a little wee man. This is so much fun!" He then proceeds to disrobe, laughing all the while. This example BEST describes which characteristic of determining if something is a disorder?
   a. deviates from cultural norms
   b. behaviour is maladaptive
   c. behaviour is causing personal distress
   d. behaviour is dangerous

   Concept: I. B Competency: 3
   Question Type: *Applied*

4. Emil uses the most common psychological text in Canada to diagnose Sybil. The book he is using is known as the:
   a. *Minnesota Multiphasic Personality Inventory* (*MMPI*)
   b. *Diagnostic and Statistical Manual of Mental Disorders* (*DSM*)
   c. *Mental Health Guide Book* (*MHGB*)
   d. *International Classification of Diseases* (*ICD-10*)

   Concept: I. C Competency: 4
   Question Type: *Applied*

5. When Sybil is being diagnosed, she is not given one label but is rated on factors, such as clinical syndromes, personality disorders, and psychosocial stressors. This is the case because the *DSM-IV* employs a ______________ system to classify disorders.
   a. multivariate
   b. cross-cut
   c. multiaxial
   d. diathesis-stress

   Concept: I. C. 1. a Competency: 5
   Question Type: *Applied*

6. Concept: I. C. 1. a Competency: 6
   Question Type: *Factual*

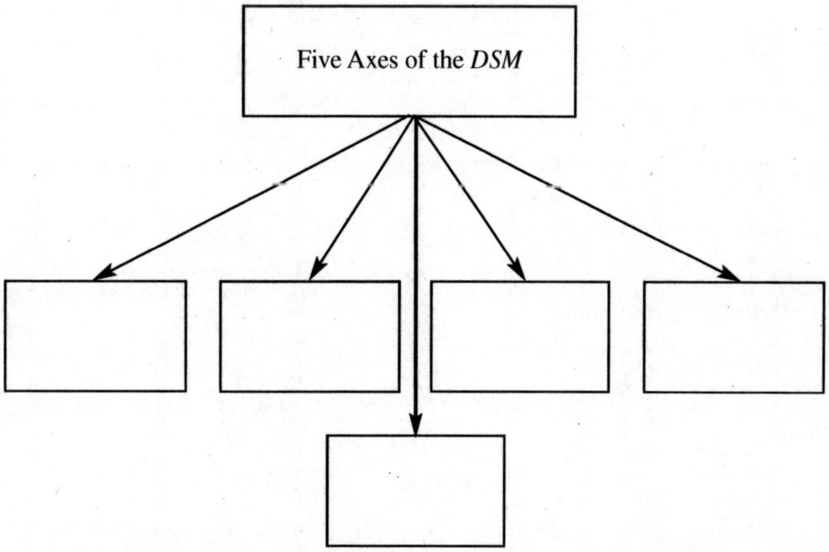

7. Samantha believes that she might have a problem and sees a therapist to determine a _______________ that will help identify appropriate treatment. Based on that she will have an idea of the _______________ or eventual outcome.
   a. prognosis; assessment
   b. diagnosis; assessment
   c. diagnosis; prognosis
   d. diagnosis; diagnosis

   Concept: I. D. 1 Competency: 7
   Question Type: *Applied*

8. Randy is in the emergency room because he stabbed himself, because he "had to kill the bugs." A mental health worker makes a series of observations regarding his mood, speech, appearance, etc. as part of a(n) _______________. Later he will undergo a(n) _______________ with a psychologist during which information will be solicited and used to understand the extent of any potential illness.
   a. mental status exam; clinical interview
   b. clinical interview; mental status exam
   c. intake diagnosis; mental status exam
   d. clinical interview; intake diagnosis

   Concept: I. D. 1 Competency: 8
   Question Type: *Applied*

9. There are two main types of interviews for determining the extent of a client's problems. The first is _______________________________ and follows a standard set of questions. The other is _______________________________ and covers topics as the conversation and therapist dictate.

   Concept: I. A. 2 Competency: 9
   Question Type: *Factual*

10. What are the best means of testing for psychopathology? Provide pros and potential cons of each.

    ____

    ____

    ____

    ____

    Concept: I. A. 3 Competency: 10
    Question Type: *Conceptual*

11. _______________________________ is an approach to clinical evaluation that uses research to guide how psychological disorders are evaluated, including selecting appropriate psychological tests, using appropriate neuropsychological methods, and using critical thinking in making a diagnosis.

    Concept: I. A. 4 Competency: 11
    Question Type: *Factual*

12. Which of the following is NOT a reason that the diagnosis of dissociative identity disorder (DID) is controversial?
    a. Diagnoses of DID often occur after people have been accused of committing crimes.
    b. There has been a sharp rise in reported cases (up to tens of thousands vs. a handful prior to the 1980s).
    c. Those evincing the disorder went from having two or three identities to having several dozen, or even hundreds.
    d. Most of those diagnosed with DID never experienced abuse.

    Concept: I. E. 1 Competency: 12
    Question Type: *Factual*

13. Kramer has a family history of psychotic behaviour. However, he does not exhibit symptoms himself until he goes through an extremely stressful period with his mother and girlfriend. This interaction of factors that causes Kramer's difficulties is representative of the _______________ model of psychological disorders.
    a. synergistic
    b. diathesis-stress
    c. cognitive-behavioural
    d. interactive

    Concept: I. F. 1 Competency: 13
    Question Type: *Applied*

14. Which of the following is NOT true of biological factors in psychological disorders?
    a. The large amount of biological evidence argues against the influence of situational factors.
    b. Identical and fraternal twins show the importance of genetic factors to the development of psychological disorders.
    c. The fetus is particularly vulnerable, and there is evidence that some psychological disorders may arise from prenatal problems such as maternal illness, malnutrition, and exposure to toxins.
    d. The unexpected effects of medications have led to discoveries about the neurotransmitters involved in psychological disorders.

    Concept: I. E. 2 Competency: 14
    Question Type: *Factual*

15. Tron is seeing a therapist for his obsessive-compulsive disorder. The therapist inquires about how much Tron's mother emphasized cleanliness. The therapist is most likely taking which approach?
    a. sociocultural
    b. cognitive-behavioural
    c. family systems
    d. biological

    Concept: I. E. 3 Competency: 15
    Question Type: *Factual*

16. Megan is seeing a therapist for her anxiety disorder. The therapist asks many questions, but determines that the most important information was that Megan was frequently yelled at and punished for the slightest infractions. The therapist is most likely taking which approach?
    a. sociocultural
    b. cognitive-behavioural
    c. family systems
    d. biological

    Concept: I. E. 4 Competency: 16
    Question Type: *Factual*

17. For each of the following, please match each disorder with the sex in which the disorder is more common.

____	Anti-social personality disorders	a) Male b) Female
____	Anorexia	
____	Post-traumatic stress disorder	
____	Childhood attention deficit hyperactivity	
____	Alcohol and drug dependence	
____	Panic disorders	

    Concept: I. E. 5 Competency: 17
    Question Type: *Factual*

18. Ever since Adam fell off the top bunk at camp when he was 12 years old, he has had a fear of heights. Because of this fear, he refuses to go to the top of the CN Tower, go out on his balcony, or sleep on a top bunk again. What type of disorder is he experiencing?
    a. specific phobia
    b. xenophobia
    c. social phobia
    d. agoraphobia

    Concept: II. A. 1. a Competency: 18
    Question Type: *Applied*

19. Rebecca notices that her roommate, Tabitha, freaks out when a professor tells her that she needs to study a little more. Rebecca also notices that Tabitha is constantly worried about her relationship with her boyfriend, even though it is a wonderful, loving one. Because of this constant worry that is not linked to an identifiable source, Rebecca thinks Tabitha suffers from:
    a. phobic disorder
    b. panic disorder
    c. generalized anxiety disorder
    d. obsessive-compulsive disorder

    Concept: II. A. 2 Competency: 19
    Question Type: *Applied*

20. An 18-year-old self-described "worrier" began to experience unexpected intense feelings of dread and impending doom while waiting in line at the food court in the local mall. During this time the patient experienced a feeling of something lodged in his throat and had trouble breathing. Although this only lasted a few minutes, he likely suffers from a(n):
    a. phobic disorder
    b. panic disorder
    c. generalized anxiety disorder
    d. obsessive-compulsive disorder

    Concept: II. A. 3 Competency: 20
    Question Type: *Applied*

21. Amber can't seem to go anywhere and has become a prisoner of her own dorm room. She no longer shops at the mall or goes to the movies, and she is in constant fear of having a panic attack in front of others. Amber's intense fear of public places in which escape would be difficult is referred to as:
    a. agoraphobia
    b. xenophobia
    c. ophidiophobia
    d. generalized anxiety disorder

    Concept: II. A. 3. a Competency: 21
    Question Type: *Applied*

22. Rita has been suffering from ever-increasing panic attacks. She worries about either doing something impulsive or going crazy. Which of the following disorders is she likely to develop if these episodes are not treated?
    a. social phobia
    b. acute stress disorder
    c. agoraphobia
    d. generalized anxiety disorder

    Concept: II. A. 3. a Competency: 21
    Question Type: *Applied*

23. When Monica leaves for work in the morning, she checks three times to see if her curling iron is off and then checks the coffee maker three times. Next she checks the locks to the house three times before finally leaving. Monica is likely suffering from:
 a. somatoform disorder
 b. dissociative disorder
 c. obsessive-compulsive disorder
 d. generalized anxiety disorder

 Concept: II. A. 4 Competency: 22
 Question Type: *Applied*

24. Which of the following choices can be considered an obsession related to obsessive-compulsive disorder?
 a. washing one's hands 15 times before leaving the bathroom after each use
 b. a baseball player banging his shoes in the dirt before hitting
 c. cutting your food into even-numbered amounts before eating
 d. thinking about how you might have left your door unlocked before class

 Concept: II. A. 4. a Competency: 23
 Question Type: *Applied*

25. Tino has developed a fear of sparklers and fireworks because he saw his cousin get burned by one. Now each time he hears fireworks he experiences debilitating panic. This demonstrates the ______________ component of anxiety.
 a. situational
 b. cognitive
 c. cultural
 d. biological

 Concept: II. B Competency: 24
 Question Type: *Applied*

26. Pete, a 58-year-old plumber, goes to the doctor because he feels lethargic throughout the day, largely because of lack of sleep. He also has little motivation to do his job and eats frequently, and has been this way as long as he can remember. Pete likely suffers from which disorder?
 a. major depression
 b. bipolar disorder
 c. generalized anxiety disorder
 d. schizophrenia

 Concept: III. A. 1. a Competency: 25
 Question Type: *Applied*

27. Angelina has been feeling down for the past 2 years. She reports having more sad days than happy days, and during most days is "down" most of the day. She hasn't noticed that her eating and sleeping have been affected and doesn't report feeling worthless. Angelina likely suffers from which disorder?
 a. major depression
 b. bipolar disorder
 c. generalized anxiety disorder
 d. dysthymia

 Concept: III. A. 1. a. 1 Competency: 26
 Question Type: *Applied*

28. Of the genders, ______________________________ are twice as likely to be diagnosed with major depression. One theory is that ______________________________ respond to stressful events by "internalizing" their feelings, which leads to depression and anxiety, whereas ______________________________ "externalize" with alcohol and violence.

 Concept: III. A. 1. c Competency: 27
 Question Type: *Factual*

29. One week, Katy was so happy to be a university student. She excitedly told her entire family how much fun she was having, and she decided that she was going to have as much fun as possible while in university. Now, 2 weeks later, Katy has trouble getting out of bed in the morning and is even thinking about dropping out of school. This drastic change in mood is characteristic of the disorder currently known as:
 a. bipolar disorder
 b. dysthymia
 c. manic depression
 d. schizophrenia

 Concept: III. A. 2 Competency: 28
 Question Type: *Applied*

30. Jewell is experiencing a burst of creativity and productivity that she really enjoys and would like to continue. This episode is best described as:
 a. manic
 b. bipolar
 c. hypomanic
 d. schizophrenic

 Concept: III. A. 2 Competency: 29
 Question Type: *Applied*

31. LeCharles recently had what may be considered a manic episode. His chances of having bipolar disorder are greater because his mom is bipolar. This demonstrates the _______________ component of mood disorders.
   a. situational
   b. cognitive
   c. cultural
   d. biological

   Concept: III. B Competency: 30
   Question Type: *Applied*

32. Which of the following is NOT part of Beck's cognitive triad of depression?
   a. learned helplessness
   b. negative thoughts about the self
   c. negative thoughts about the situation
   d. negative thoughts about the future

   Concept: III. B. 1. a Competency: 31
   Question Type: *Factual*

33. After studying for hours and still failing the first two exams in his anthropology class, Jay has given up studying for the class completely. He feels that he has no control whatsoever when it comes to this class, and he is bound to fail despite his level of studying. Jay's expectation of failure and the resulting apathy and depression are examples of:
   a. dysthymic cognitions
   b. self-perpetuating style
   c. learned helplessness
   d. melancholia

   Concept: III. B. 1. b Competency: 32
   Question Type: *Applied*

34. William lives in Whitehorse. He finds that he becomes depressed every winter when the days become shorter and there is little sunlight. William likely suffers from:
   a. unipolar disorder
   b. seasonal affective disorder
   c. dysthymia
   d. melancholia

   Concept: III. B. 3. a. 1 Competency: 33
   Question Type: *Applied*

35. Matt was diagnosed as having paranoid schizophrenia. He has delusions of the world being taken over by giant lizards and hallucinations of insects crawling over him. Matt's schizophrenic behaviours are an example of which type of symptom?
   a. negative symptoms
   b. positive symptoms
   c. flattened affect
   d. mood disorders

   Concept: IV. B Competency: 34
   Question Type: *Applied*

36. Pete was sitting in his psychology class when he thought he saw an individual staring at him from the outside. He began to notice those around him acting oddly, and he felt he was being watched every place he went. He even checked the phones in his apartment because he believed they were tapped. Pete was having which type of delusion?
   a. somatic
   b. grandeur
   c. reference
   d. persecution

   Concept: IV. B. 1. a Competency: 35
   Question Type: *Applied*

37. Concept: IV. B. 1. b Competency: 36
   Question Type: *Factual*

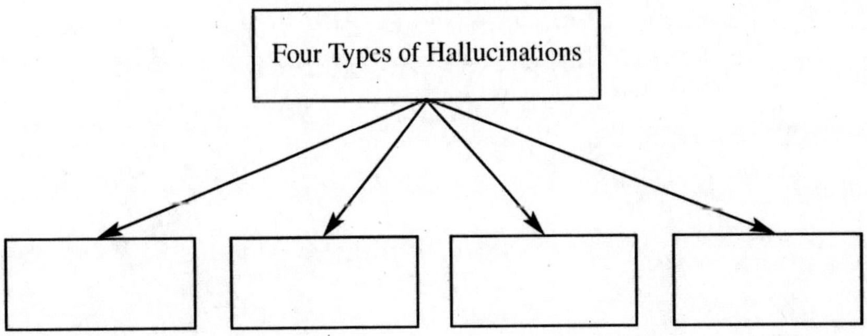

38. The stress of school has pushed Ginger over the edge into exhibiting some schizophrenic symptoms. When asked a question about the Scantron sheet during the exam, she replies, "When a sperm and egg come together, they make a beautiful baby." This represents the category of symptoms known as:
    a. disturbance in thought content
    b. loosening of associations
    c. affective symptoms
    d. perceptual disturbances

    Concept: IV. B. 1. c Competency: 37
    Question Type: *Applied*

39. Amy has been admitted to a prestigious graduate school on the East Coast. However, the housing situation at the school is so bad that Amy deteriorates into speaking in clang association to her professors. Which of the following represents what she most likely said?
    a. How are you today? How are you today? How are you today?
    b. School rule, fool, tool, drool, ghoul, jewel, cool toadstool.
    c. Fred blue hammer Tar Heel Jordan basketball Tobacco Road.
    d. I am so tired of dregling for parsingian apartments.

    Concept: IV. B. 1. c. 1 Competency: 38
    Question Type: *Applied*

40. Mara was highly upset at not being named athlete of the week in the local university newspaper. The stress of this crushing blow caused her to relapse into catatonic schizophrenic behaviour. Which of the following symptoms is Mara most likely to exhibit?
    a. She giggles hebephrenically and smears her feces on the wall of the lobby.
    b. She believes that her coach has talked the newspaper editor into writing bad things about her in the paper.
    c. She curls up in the corner by the candy machine and exhibits mutism.
    d. She shows a lot of prominent schizophrenic symptoms that do not clearly fit any one pattern.

    Concept: IV. B. 2. a Competency: 39
    Question Type: *Applied*

41. Which of the following is NOT true of biological factors that contribute to schizophrenia?
    a. If one twin develops schizophrenia, the likelihood of the others also succumbing is almost 50 percent if the twins are identical.
    b. If one parent has schizophrenia, the risk of a child's developing the disease is 13 percent.
    c. If both parents have schizophrenia, the risk jumps to almost 50 percent.
    d. Children of mothers who were simultaneously accepting and rejecting their children are more likely to have schizophrenia.

    Concept: IV. C Competency: 40
    Question Type: *Factual*

42. All of the following are true of environmental factors that contribute to greater incidence of schizophrenia EXCEPT:
    a. living in a large urban city
    b. living with adopted siblings who were psychologically healthy
    c. exposure to a virus leading to the production of antibodies
    d. being born during the late winter or early spring

    Concept: IV. D Competency: 41
    Question Type: *Factual*

43. Personality disorders and mental retardation are grouped together in the *DSM* for which of the following reasons?
    a. They both are very uncommon, and more likely in men.
    b. They are both genetic disorders.
    c. They are both identified in early childhood.
    d. They both last throughout the life span with no expectation of significant change.

    Concept: V. A Competency: 42
    Question Type: *Factual*

44. For each of the following personality disorders, please match each to its appropriate grouping.

____ Narcissistic	a) Odd and eccentric behaviour
____ Avoidant	
____ Schizoid	b) Dramatic and emotional behaviour
____ Dependent	
____ Paranoid	
____ Anti-social	c) Anxious and fearful behaviour
____ Schizotypal	
____ Borderline	
____ Histrionic	
____ Obsessive-compulsive	

Concept: V. A. 1 Competency: 43
Question Type: *Factual*

45. Tammy is a person who is very unsure of herself. When others aren't around she is very uncomfortable and immediately seeks out other people. Because she fears loneliness, she is often convinced that her friends are going to stop liking her and that everyone will abandon her. This leads her to being very manipulative and lying to people around her in an attempt to control her relationships. Tammy suffers from the disorder currently known as ______________ personality.
   a. histrionic
   b. anti-social
   c. paranoid
   d. borderline

   Concept: V. B. 1 Competency: 44
   Question Type: *Applied*

46. April's personality has begun to closely resemble those of some of the most notorious murderers of the past few decades. She has become very manipulative and self-serving. She feels sorry for nothing and seems to lack a conscience. April suffers from the disorder currently known as ______________ personality.
   a. psychopathic
   b. sociopathic
   c. anti-social
   d. narcissistic

   Concept: V. B. 2 Competency: 45
   Question Type: *Applied*

47. Vinny is 22 months old, and his parents have noticed that he doesn't smile and avoids looking at people. Vinny also seems to have little interest in talking. Instead, he is much more interested in playing with his toy trains, often for several hours a day. Vinny most likely suffers from:
   a. autism
   b. Asperger's Syndrome
   c. ADHD
   d. ADD

   Concept: VI. A Competency: 46
   Question Type: *Applied*

48. ____________________________ is high-functioning autism, in which children of normal intelligence have specific deficits in social interaction, such as having an impoverished theory of mind.

   Concept: VI. A. 1 Competency: 47
   Question Type: *Factual*

49. Heather has shown symptoms of autism since she was a little girl. She now is exhibiting the speech symptom of echolalia. Which of the following represents what she would most likely say?
   a. How are you today? How are you today? How are you today?
   b. School rule, fool, tool, drool, ghoul, jewel, cool toadstool.
   c. Fred blue hammer Tar Heel Jordan basketball Tobacco Road.
   d. I am so tired of dregling for parsingian apartments.

   Concept: VI. A. 2. b. 1 Competency: 48
   Question Type: *Applied*

50. The brains of children with autism grow unusually large during the first 2 years of life, and then growth slows until age 5, while the brain also does not develop normally during adolescence. This demonstrates:
   a. the influence of oxytocin
   b. the overgrowth-undergrowth pattern
   c. the influence of blood proteins
   d. the influence of antibodies

   Concept: VI. A. 3 Competency: 48
   Question Type: *Factual*

51. Although the syndrome of ADHD has been around for quite some time, its prevalence seems to have exploded in recent years. Speculate as to possible biological and cultural reasons for this increase.

   ____

   ____

   ____

   ____

   Concept: VI. B Competency: 50
   Question Type: *Conceptual*

ANSWER KEY

Item	Answer
1.	Psychopathology
2.	c
3.	a
4.	b
5.	c

6. clinical disorders; mental retardation or personality disorders; medical conditions; psychosocial problems; global assessment of functioning
7. c
8. a
9. structured; unstructured
10. The first way is to observe a person's behaviour. Observation is beneficial because it can be done without the person's awareness, thus making it difficult for them to purposefully change behaviour. However, when observing there is always a possibility that what you believe an observed behaviour means is not accurate. Psychological testing can be much more thorough, and gets information directly from the source. However, there is always the possibility that a person could lie or misrepresent the facts. Finally, neurological testing is beneficial because it can't be faked, so if a person has a problem with a part of the brain it can be identified. Unfortunately this does not give much insight into how the disorder happened, and may only identify one contributing factor to the disorder.
11. Evidence-based assessment
12. d
13. b
14. a
15. c
16. b
17. a; b; b; a; a; b
18. a
19. c
20. b
21. a
22. c
23. c
24. d
25. a
26. a
27. d
28. women; women; men
29. a
30. a
31. d
32. a
33. c
34. b
35. b
36. d
37. Auditory; Visual; Olfactory; Somatosensory
38. b
39. b
40. c
41. d
42. b
43. d
44. b; c; a; c; a; b; a; b; b; c
45. d
46. c
47. a
48. Asperger's Syndrome
49. a
50. b
51. Answers will vary but, as with all disorders, greater awareness of it leads to improved diagnosis. In addition, students might consider the North American cultural phenomenon of having both parents in the workforce. More students are being placed in structured day care settings at an earlier age and are expected to follow rules and behave cooperatively with others. Similarly, class sizes in school have increased appreciably so that two or three disruptive children represent a significant problem. Poor parenting has been related to ADHD, and students might relate this to the breakup of the traditional family and high divorce rates. Overall, the pace of life has quickened in society, and exposure to rapid information media (e.g., television versus books) may reduce attention spans. Finally, students might speculate as to biological reasons that contribute to the underarousal of frontal lobes seen in ADHD. Undetected environmental toxins from an industrialized society are a possible culprit.

KEY TERM EXERCISES

agoraphobia

Textbook Definition:
Your Own Definition:
Your Own Example:

anti-social personality disorder (APO)

Textbook Definition:
Your Own Definition:
Your Own Example:

assessment

Textbook Definition:
Your Own Definition:
Your Own Example:

attention deficit hyperactivity disorder (ADHD)

Textbook Definition:
Your Own Definition:
Your Own Example:

autism

Textbook Definition:
Your Own Definition:
Your Own Example:

bipolar disorder

Textbook Definition:
Your Own Definition:
Your Own Example:

borderline personality disorder

Textbook Definition:
Your Own Definition:
Your Own Example:

cognitive-behavioural approach

Textbook Definition:
Your Own Definition:
Your Own Example:

delusions

Textbook Definition:
Your Own Definition:
Your Own Example:

diathesis-stress model

Textbook Definition:
Your Own Definition:
Your Own Example:

disorganized behaviour

Textbook Definition:
Your Own Definition:
Your Own Example:

dissociative identity disorder (DID)

Textbook Definition:
Your Own Definition:
Your Own Example:

dysthymia

Textbook Definition:
Your Own Definition:
Your Own Example:

etiology

Textbook Definition:
Your Own Definition:
Your Own Example:

family systems model

Textbook Definition:
Your Own Definition:
Your Own Example:

generalized anxiety disorder (GAD)

Textbook Definition:
Your Own Definition:
Your Own Example:

hallucinations

Textbook Definition:
Your Own Definition:
Your Own Example:

learned helplessness model

Textbook Definition:
Your Own Definition:
Your Own Example:

loosening of associations

Textbook Definition:
Your Own Definition:
Your Own Example:

major depression

Textbook Definition:
Your Own Definition:
Your Own Example:

multiaxial system

Textbook Definition:
Your Own Definition:
Your Own Example:

negative symptoms

Textbook Definition:
Your Own Definition:
Your Own Example:

obsessive-compulsive disorder (OCD)

Textbook Definition:
Your Own Definition:
Your Own Example:

panic disorder

Textbook Definition:
Your Own Definition:
Your Own Example:

positive symptoms

Textbook Definition:
Your Own Definition:
Your Own Example:

psychopathology

Textbook Definition:
Your Own Definition:
Your Own Example:

schizophrenia

Textbook Definition:
Your Own Definition:
Your Own Example:

socio-cultural model

Textbook Definition:
Your Own Definition:
Your Own Example:

CHAPTER 15 Treatment of Psychological Disorders

CONCEPT MAP

I. How Are Psychological Disorders Treated?
   A. Psychotherapy
      1. Biological Therapies
         a. Psychopharmacology
   B. Psychotherapy Is Based on Psychological Principles
      1. Psychodynamic Therapy
         a. Free Association
         b. Dream Analysis
         c. Insight
         d. Controversy
      2. Humanistic Therapy
         a. Client-Centred Therapy
         b. Reflective Listening
         c. Motivational Interviewing
      3. Cognitive-Behavioural Therapy
         a. Behaviour Modification
         b. Social Skills Training
            1. Modelling
         c. Cognitive Therapy
            1. Cognitive Restructuring
            2. Rational-Emotive Therapy
            3. Interpersonal Therapy
         d. Cognitive-Behavioural Therapy
            1. Exposure
      4. Group Therapy
      5. Family Therapy
         a. Systems Approach
         b. Expressed Emotion
      6. Confession Is Good for the Spirit
   C. Culture Can Affect the Therapeutic Process
   D. Medication Is Effective for Certain Disorders
      1. Psychotropic Medications
      2. Anti-Anxiety Drugs
      3. Antidepressants
         a. MAO Inhibitors
         b. Tricyclic Antidepressants
         c. Selective Serotonin Reuptake Inhibitors (SSRIs)
      4. Antipsychotics
      5. Other Types
         a. Lithium
         b. Anticonvulsants
   E. Alternative Biological Treatments Are Used in Extreme Cases
      1. Trepanning
      2. Prefrontal Lobotomies
      3. Electroconvulsive Therapy
      4. Transcranial Magnetic Stimulation
      5. Deep Brain Stimulation
   F. Therapies Not Supported by Scientific Evidence Can Be Dangerous
      1. Pseudotherapies
      2. Counterproductive Approaches

II. What Are the Most Effective Treatments?
   A. Psychological Treatments vs. Psychotherapy
   B. Behaviour and Cognitive Treatments Are Superior for Anxiety Disorders
      1. Specific Phobias
         a. Fear Hierarchy
            1. Virtual Environments
      2. Panic Disorder
      3. Obsessive-Compulsive Disorder (OCD)
         a. Cognitive-Behavioural Therapy vs. Medication
   C. Many Effective Treatments Are Available for Depression
      1. Pharmacological Treatment

a. MAO Inhibitors
b. Tricyclics
c. Prozac (an SSRI)
d. Effectiveness
2. Cognitive-Behavioural Treatment of Depression
a. Effectiveness
3. Alternative Treatments
a. Light
b. Exercise
c. Electroconvulsive Therapy (ECT)
d. Transcranial Magnetic Stimulation (TMS)
4. Deep Brain Stimulation
5. Gender Issues in Treating Depression
D. Lithium Is Most Effective for Bipolar Disorder
1. Effectiveness
E. Pharmacological Treatments Are Superior for Schizophrenia
1. Pharmacological Treatment
a. Reserpine
b. Chlorpromazine
c. Haloperidol
d. Tardive Dyskinesia
e. Clozapine
2. Psychosocial Treatments
3. Prognosis in Schizophrenia
F. On Ethics: Involuntary Treatment for Mental Disorders
G. There Are Important Considerations in Selecting a Psychotherapist
1. Major Types of Specialized Practitioners
a. Clinical Psychologists
b. Psychiatrists
c. Counselling Psychologists
d. Psychiatric Social Workers
e. Psychiatric Nurses
f. Paraprofessionals

III. Can Personality Disorders Be Treated?
A. Dialectical Behaviour Therapy Is Most Successful for Borderline Personality Disorder
1. Dialectical Behaviour Therapy
a. Borderline Personality Disorder
B. Anti-social Personality Disorder Is Difficult to Treat
1. Therapeutic Approaches for Anti-social Personality Disorder
2. Prognosis for Anti-social Personality Disorder

IV. How Should Childhood and Adolescent Disorders Be Treated?
A. The Use of Medication to Treat Adolescent Depression is Controversial
1. Effectiveness for Young People
2. Suicidal Feelings
3. Treatment vs. Nontreatment
B. Children with ADHD Can Benefit from a Variety of Approaches
1. Pharmacological Treatment of ADHD
a. Ritalin
2. Behavioural Treatment of ADHD
C. Children with Autism Benefit from a Structured Treatment Approach
1. Behavioural Treatment of Autism
a. Applied Behavioural Analysis
2. Biological Treatment for Autism
3. Prognosis for Children with Autism

CHAPTER SUMMARY

How Are Psychological Disorders Treated?

• Psychotherapy Is Based on Psychological Principles: Psychotherapeutic treatments focus on insights. Psychodynamic forms focus on uncovering the unconscious. Humanistic approaches focus on clarifying feelings and motives. Behavioural approaches focus on modifying maladaptive behaviours. Cognitive approaches restructure thinking. Group therapy provides support, and a systems approach is part of family therapy. Common factors across treatments include both the value of confession and expectations that things will get better.

• Culture Can Affect the Therapeutic Process: The dominant culture in any country defines psychological health and psychological disorders; it also determines who needs psychotherapy and what type of therapy should be made available. Psychologists need to have multicultural knowledge if they are to provide competent psychotherapy to people from different backgrounds and with different belief systems.

• Medication Is Effective for Certain Disorders: Psychotropic medications change neurochemistry. Anti-anxiety drugs increase GABA activity. Antidepressants affect serotonin availability. Antipsychotics reduce positive symptoms.

• Alternative Biological Treatments Are Used in Extreme Cases: When traditional treatments are not successful, alternative treatments are used. These include psychosurgery, electroconvulsive therapy, transcranial magnetic stimulation, and deep brain stimulation.

• Therapies Not Supported by Scientific Evidence Can Be Dangerous: Increasingly, psychologists are turning to evidence-based practices. Some treatment approaches that have no credible evidence to support their use have proved lethal, and all may prevent or delay a patient from seeking help through an evidence-based therapy.

What Are the Most Effective Treatments?

• Treatments That Focus on Behaviour and on Cognition Are Superior for Anxiety Disorders: Behavioural methods alleviate specific phobias. Cognitive restructuring is effective in treating panic disorders. Obsessive-compulsive disorder (OCD) responds to medications that block serotonin reuptake and to cognitive-behavioural therapy.

• Many Effective Treatments Are Available for Depression: Pharmacological treatments include MAO inhibitors, tricyclics, and SSRIs. Cognitive-behavioural treatments are most effective when combined with antidepressants. Alternative therapies include phototherapy for seasonal affective disorder (SAD) and both electroconvulsive therapy and transcranial magnetic stimulation for severe depression.

• Lithium Is Most Effective for Bipolar Disorder: The psychotropic medication lithium has been the most effective in stabilizing mood in bipolar patients but has considerable side effects. Psychological therapy can help support compliance with drug treatment.

• Pharmacological Treatments Are Superior for Schizophrenia: Antipsychotic medications are most effective for reducing the positive symptoms of schizophrenia. Tardive dyskinesia and other side effects are common with the older antipsychotic drugs. Clozapine acts specifically on dopamine receptors and reduces positive and negative symptoms, with fewer side effects. The prognosis for patients depends on factors including age of onset, gender, and culture.

• There Are Important Considerations in Selecting a Psychotherapist: Many types of education and training exist for psychotherapists. In selecting a psychotherapist, it is important to find someone with whom the client can establish a good relationship and who the patient believes is committed to his or her improvement.

Can Personality Disorders Be Treated?

• Dialectical Behaviour Therapy Is Most Successful for Borderline Personality Disorder: DBT combines elements of behavioural, cognitive, and psychodynamic therapy. Therapy proceeds in three stages. First, the most extreme behaviours are targeted and replaced with more appropriate behaviours. Next, the therapist explores past traumatic events. Finally, the therapist helps the patient develop self-respect and independence.

• Anti-social Personality Disorder Is Difficult to Treat: Psychotherapeutic approaches have not proved effective for treating anti-social personality disorder. Behavioural and cognitive approaches have been more effective, primarily in a controlled residential treatment environment. Generally, the prognosis is poor. Focusing on prevention by addressing conduct disorder in childhood may be the best strategy.

How Should Childhood and Adolescent Disorders Be Treated?

• The Use of Medication to Treat Adolescent Depression Is Controversial: The use of medication, such as Prozac, is increasing as a treatment for adolescent depression. Such medications may lead to increased suicidality, but the available evidence indicates that medications may have more benefits than costs. Cognitive-behavioural treatment is also beneficial and may be preferred because its effects are long-lasting.

• Children with ADHD Can Benefit from Various Approaches: Ritalin, despite its side effects, is an effective pharmacological treatment and works best as part of an overall treatment plan including psychotherapy, particularly behavioural treatment.

• Children with Autism Benefit from a Structured Treatment Approach: Behavioural approaches have been effective in improving language and social behaviour. The treatment strategy is very time intensive and extends for years. In general, the long-term prognosis is poor.

COMPETENCY MAP

How Are Psychological Disorders Treated?

Psychotherapy

1. Describe the common characteristics of all forms of psychotherapy.
2. What is the basis for biological therapies?

Psychotherapy Is Based on Psychological Principles

3. Know how many approaches to psychotherapy exist.
4. What does it mean to take an eclectic approach?
5. What is the goal of psychoanalysis?
6. Describe free association and dream analysis.
7. Explain the concept of insight.
8. What does client-centred therapy encourage?
9. What does reflective listening involve?
10. What is the premise of focusing on behaviour in cognitive-behavioural therapy?
11. How can social skill training help?
12. Explain the basis for cognitive therapy.
13. What is the goal of cognitive restructuring?
14. Distinguish between rational-emotive and interpersonal therapy.

15. How is exposure used in therapy?
16. Be able to identify helpful aspects of group therapy.
17. What is the basic idea behind a systems approach?
18. Explain the role of expressed emotion.
19. Describe Freud's notion of catharsis.
20. Describe the usefulness of talking about problems.

Medication Is Effective for Certain Disorders

21. Be able to match medications with the type of disorder they treat.
22. Describe how anti-anxiety drugs work and potential side effects.
23. Identify types of antidepressants.
24. Identify how the major types of antidepressants work.
25. Describe how antipsychotic drugs work.
26. Identify the type of medication used to treat bipolar disorder.

Alternative Biological Treatments Are Used in Extreme Cases

27. What is trepanning?
28. Describe the goal of prefrontal lobotomies and their use today.
29. Describe the goal of electroconvulsive therapy and its use today.
30. Describe the goal of transcranial magnetic stimulation and its use today.
31. Describe the goal of deep brain stimulation and its use today.

Therapies Not Supported by Scientific Evidence Can Be Dangerous

32. Identify types of treatment that have little or no scientific basis for support.

What Are the Most Effective Treatments?

Psychological Treatments vs. Psychotherapy

33. What do we know about the effectiveness of psychotherapy?
34. Distinguish between psychological treatments and psychotherapy.

Behaviour and Cognitive Treatments Are Superior for Anxiety Disorders

35. Explain the concept of fear hierarchies in systematic desensitization.
36. Describe how virtual environments are used in therapy.
37. Describe the most effective treatment for panic disorder.
38. Explain the two most important components of behavioural therapy for OCD.

Many Effective Treatments Are Available for Depression

39. Describe the effectiveness of cognitive-behavioural treatments for depression.
40. Describe how alternative treatments for depression work.
41. For what disorder is ECT most effective?
42. Explain the effectiveness of TMS for treating types of depression.
43. Be able to identify the gender issues in treatments for depression.

Pharmacological Treatments Are Superior for Schizophrenia

44. Identify the different pharmacological treatments for schizophrenia.
45. What is the prognosis for schizophrenia?

On Ethics: Involuntary Treatment for Mental Disorders

46. Identify the ethical issues associated with involuntary treatment of psychological disorders.

There Are Important Considerations in Selecting a Psychotherapist

47. Distinguish between the types of specialized practitioners.
48. Identify which types of practitioners can prescribe medication.
49. Distinguish between Psy.D. and Ph.D. training.

Can Personality Disorders Be Treated?

Dialectical Behaviour Therapy Is Most Successful for Borderline Personality Disorder

50. What is dialectical behaviour therapy?

Anti-social Personality Disorder Is Difficult to Treat

51. Identify therapeutic approaches for anti-social personality disorder.

52. What is the prognosis for anti-social personality disorder?

How Should Childhood and Adolescent Disorders Be Treated?

The Use of Medication to Treat Adolescent Depression Is Controversial

53. Explain the controversial aspects of using medication for adolescent depression.

Children with ADHD Can Benefit from a Variety of Approaches

54. Describe the effectiveness of pharmacological treatment of ADHD.

55. What are the effects of using Ritalin?

Children with Autism Benefit from a Structured Treatment Approach

56. Identify effective therapies for autism.

57. What is the prognosis for children with autism?

KNOWLEDGE CHECK

1. Although the particular techniques and methods used may depend on the training of the practitioner, all forms of psychotherapy involve ______________________________

   Concept: I. A Competency: 1
   Question Type: *Factual*

2. Ashanti is a therapist who follows a medical approach to illness and disease. She views psychological disorders as the result of abnormalities in neural and bodily processes. What type of therapy is she most likely a proponent of?
   a. psychodynamic therapy
   b. client-centred
   c. biological therapy
   d. eclectic therapy

   Concept: I. A. 1 Competency: 2
   Question Type: *Applied*

3. According to a recent study, there are approximately ______________ approaches to psychotherapy.
   a. 5
   b. 50
   c. 100
   d. 400

   Concept: I. B. 1 Competency: 3
   Question Type: *Factual*

4. While Joann is therapist shopping, she tries a clinical psychologist who describes herself as eclectic. This means that her therapist:
   a. uses a mix of techniques based on what she believes is best for the client's particular condition
   b. does not use techniques from any of the major approaches
   c. uses a combination of cognitive and behavioural approaches
   d. tries mostly new experimental techniques that have been supported by empirical research

   Concept: I. B. 1 Competency: 4
   Question Type: *Applied*

5. Marika is a therapist who specializes in the techniques of psychoanalysis. What is her goal for psychotherapy sessions?
   a. Identify problem areas that are amenable to psychopharmacology.
   b. Uncover unconscious feelings and drives that give rise to maladaptive thoughts and behaviours.
   c. Relearn maladaptive behaviours that were acquired through improper learning.
   d. Facilitate personal growth and self-actualization through reflective listening and unconditional positive regard.

   Concept: I. B. 1 Competency: 5
   Question Type: *Applied*

6. Samantha has been feeling quite depressed lately and decides to go see a psychoanalyst. When she goes to her first session, she is told to say whatever comes to mind, no matter how crazy or embarrassing it may seem. This basic technique of psychoanalysis is known as:
   a. word association
   b. systematic desensitization
   c. free association
   d. transference

   Concept: I. B. 1. a Competency: 6
   Question Type: *Applied*

7. Raul is a therapist who tries to help patients achieve a personal understanding of their own psychological processes. This, he believes, will free patients from unconscious influences, leading to a reduction in symptoms. Raul is focusing on:
   a. insight
   b. systematic desensitization
   c. free association
   d. transference

   Concept: I. B. 1. c Competency: 7
   Question Type: *Applied*

8. Carmella is a therapist who specializes in client-centred therapy. What is her goal for psychotherapy sessions?
   a. Identify problem areas that are amenable to psychopharmacology.
   b. Uncover unconscious feelings and drives that give rise to maladaptive thoughts and behaviours.
   c. Relearn maladaptive behaviours that were acquired through improper learning.
   d. Facilitate personal growth and self-actualization through reflective listening and unconditional positive regard.

   Concept: I. B. 2. a Competency: 8
   Question Type: *Applied*

9. Shelby goes into her therapist's office and spills all her current troubles. At the end of her monologue, the therapist says, "It sounds like you have a lot going on right now. You are having problems with your parents, your boyfriend, and at school, and you are unsure how to proceed." This is an example of the client-centred therapy technique of:
   a. analysis of resistance
   b. reflective listening
   c. unconditional positive regard
   d. confronting irrational beliefs

   Concept: I. B. 2. b Competency: 9
   Question Type: *Applied*

10. Jerry is suffering from obsessions about germs and cleanliness and decides to seek out behavioural therapy. From his choice, it is obvious that Jerry believes his problem can be alleviated through:
    a. uncovering unconscious feelings and drives that give rise to maladaptive thoughts and behaviours
    b. facilitating personal growth and self-actualization through reflective listening and unconditional positive regard
    c. unlearning maladaptive behaviours by the use of classical and operant conditioning
    d. identifying problem areas that are amenable to psychopharmacology

    Concept: I. B. 3 Competency: 10
    Question Type: *Applied*

11. Zachariah is having difficulty making friends so his mom takes him to a therapist for help. At their sessions, the therapist shows Zachariah how to interact with other kids, then has Zachariah imitate the behaviour. This technique is known as:
    a. modelling therapy
    b. social skills training
    c. behaviour modification
    d. unconditional positive regard

    Concept: I. A. 3. b Competency: 11
    Question Type: *Applied*

12. Katie has been suffering from frequent panic attacks, so she goes to see a psychologist. The psychologist instructs her to hyperventilate, which causes her to panic. Then she teaches her to respond calmly to her panicked feelings. Soon Katie is able to calm herself when she feels the onset of panic. What type of therapy is the psychologist using to treat Katie?
    a. modelling therapy
    b. client-centred therapy
    c. psychoanalytic therapy
    d. cognitive therapy

    Concept: I. B. 3. c Competency: 12
    Question Type: *Applied*

13. Nerissa is depressed because she feels like absolutely everything she does is a failure and that no one likes her. Her therapist knows this can't be true and proceeds to ask questions designed to get her view of the world to more closely match the true state of affairs. This technique is known as:
    a. cognitive restructuring
    b. social skills training
    c. behaviour modification
    d. unconditional positive regard

    Concept: I. B. 3. c. 1 Competency: 13
    Question Type: *Applied*

14. In ______________________________, therapists act as teachers who explain and demonstrate more adaptive ways of thinking and behaving. ______________________________ focuses on relationships that the patient attempts to avoid.

    Concept: I. B. 3. c Competency: 14
    Question Type: *Factual*

15. The therapy technique of exposure involves repeatedly exposing a person directly to the anxiety-producing stimulus or situation. The goal of this therapy is most similar to which concept from classical conditioning?
    a. unconditioned responses
    b. acquisition
    c. extinction
    d. spontaneous recovery

    Concept: I. B. 3. d. 1 Competency: 15
    Question Type: *Conceptual*

16. Curly, Moe, Larry, and Shemp are in treatment to reduce their aggressive behaviours. The group setting provides an opportunity for members to improve their social skills, support one another, and learn from each others' experiences. The generic term for this treatment approach is:
    a. supportive therapy
    b. transpersonal therapy
    c. interpersonal therapy
    d. group therapy

    Concept: I. B. 4 Competency: 16
    Question Type: *Applied*

17. Carly and Gus are in therapy with the Whitaker family. They notice that as one child begins to improve her behaviour, the other child becomes more disruptive. When both children are better, the mother and father begin to fight. Carly and Gus are trying to get the entire family to communicate and behave better. They are taking a(n) _______________ approach to psychotherapy.
    a. dynamic
    b. systems
    c. integrative
    d. supportive

    Concept: I. B. 5. a Competency: 17
    Question Type: *Applied*

18. Kaliegh is in therapy and mentions to her therapist that her mom is overprotective and routinely cries because "her daughter is mentally ill." This is an example of:
    a. expressed emotions
    b. systems
    c. reflective listening
    d. unconditional positive regard

    Concept: I. A. 5. b Competency: 18
    Question Type: *Applied*

19. Dr. Freud is counselling a woman who has difficulty trusting men. She thinks they are all out to get her and will use her and toss her aside if she gives them the chance. Her therapist encourages her to open up to him and talk freely about her past experiences with men, including her father. What is Dr. Freud hoping to achieve by advising his patient to open up?
    a. eclecticism
    b. conditional positive regard
    c. catharsis
    d. reciprocal determinism

    Concept: I. B. 6 Competency: 19
    Question Type: *Applied*

20. Which of the following is NOT a finding of research on simply writing about one's problems?
    a. Writing leads to better performance in work and school and improved memory and cognition.
    b. Writing about emotional events improves immune function.
    c. Writing reduces blood pressure, muscle tension, and skin conduction during the disclosure and immediately after.
    d. Talking about problems produces immediate positive feelings and relief.

    Concept: I. B. 6 Competency: 20
    Question Type: *Applied*

21. For each of the following medications, please match each to its most appropriate classification.

____	MAO Inhibitors	a) Anti-anxiety
____	Xanax	b) Antidepressants
____	Ativan	c) Antipsychotic
____	Clozapine	
____	Buspirone	
____	Selective Serotonin Reuptake Inhibitors (SSRIs)	
____	Risperdal	
____	Prozac	

    Concept: I. D. 1 Competency: 21
    Question Type: *Factual*

22. Violet is frequently anxious. Her psychiatrist puts her on benzodiazepines that help Violet feel more relaxed. Which of the following is NOT true of this type of medication?
    a. They are highly addictive.
    b. They must be taken every day.
    c. They may cause drowsiness.
    d. They increase GABA activity.

    Concept: I. D. 2 Competency: 22
    Question Type: *Applied*

23. Christine's semester has been going downhill steadily. She is behind on all her course assignments and is having difficulty concentrating. Her physician decides to put her on antidepressants. Which of the following classes of medications is NOT a choice for her?
    a. MAO inhibitors
    b. Tricyclics
    c. Neuroleptics
    d. SSRIs

    Concept: I. D. 3 Competency: 23
    Question Type: *Applied*

24. Carla has been depressed lately. Her boyfriend just broke up with her, and she is failing two of her classes. Her psychiatrist puts her on MAO inhibitors. Now Carla feels a lot better about herself and is starting to pull up her grades. How do these pills work to improve Carla's mood?
    a. They increase the supply of melatonin and diethylamide.
    b. They increase her metabolism.
    c. They increase the supply of norepinephrine, serotonin, and dopamine.
    d. They increase the supply of GABA and endorphins.

    Concept: I. D. 3 Competency: 24
    Question Type: *Applied*

25. Donny is a client at a day treatment facility for schizophrenics. When he takes his traditional antipsychotic medication (specifically chlorpromazine) his hallucinations are greatly reduced. This drug acts by:
    a. blocking serotonin
    b. releasing serotonin
    c. blocking dopamine
    d. releasing dopamine

    Concept: I. D. 4 Competency: 25
    Question Type: *Applied*

26. Most of the time Eileen is laughing, but she also has periods of wild mood swings that range from mania to depression. As she is diagnosed with bipolar disorder, which of the following medications is she most likely taking?
    a. Tofranil
    b. Prozac
    c. Librium
    d. Lithium

    Concept: I. D. 5 Competency: 26
    Question Type: *Applied*

27. Lorn is hearing voices and is convinced he has evil spirits in his head. To remedy this, he goes to an unlicensed therapist who illegally performs a procedure where he cuts holes in Lorn's head. It isn't effective. This procedure is known as:
    a. trepanning
    b. prefrontal lobotomy
    c. phrenology
    d. ECT

    Concept: I. E. 1 Competency: 27
    Question Type: *Applied*

28. Shevon is a therapist specializing in alternative techniques. Today she is conducting a procedure that involves severing nerve-fibre pathways. This is known as ______________ and is used ______________.
    a. trepanning; for most personality disorders
    b. a prefrontal lobotomy; for most personality disorders
    c. a prefrontal lobotomy; as a last resort
    d. deep brain stimulation; as a last resort

    Concept: I. E. 1 Competency: 28
    Question Type: *Applied*

29. Shevon is a therapist specializing in alternative techniques. Today she is conducting a procedure that involves purposefully creating a seizure while the patient is under anesthesia and muscle relaxants. This is known as:
    a. transcranial magnetic stimulation
    b. electroconvulsive therapy
    c. a prefrontal lobotomy
    d. deep brain stimulation

    Concept: I. E. 3 Competency: 29
    Question Type: *Applied*

30. Shevon is a therapist specializing in alternative techniques. Today she is conducting a procedure that involves inducing an electrical current over a specific region of the brain in order to disrupt brain activity. This is known as:
    a. transcranial magnetic stimulation
    b. electroconvulsive therapy
    c. a prefrontal lobotomy
    d. deep brain stimulation

    Concept: I. E. 4 Competency: 30
    Question Type: *Applied*

31. Shevon is a therapist specializing in alternative techniques. Today she is conducting a procedure that involves implanting electrodes in the brain that are regulated with a pacemaker-like device. This is known as:
   a. transcranial magnetic stimulation
   b. electroconvulsive therapy
   c. a prefrontal lobotomy
   d. deep brain stimulation

   Concept: I. E. 5 Competency: 31
   Question Type: *Applied*

32. Which of the following popular treatments is not counterproductive?
   a. encouraging people to describe their experiences following major trauma
   b. writing about problems over email
   c. scared straight
   d. using hypnosis to recover painful memories

   Concept: I. F. 2 Competency: 32
   Question Type: *Factual*

33. Kevin is worried about whether he will be wasting his money by seeking psychotherapy. Connie tells him that a recent study on psychotherapy found all EXCEPT which of the following?
   a. Cognitive therapy was found superior to behavioural therapy as well as psychoanalysis.
   b. The majority of respondents felt that intervention had helped them.
   c. Those who sought help from mental health professionals reported more positive results than those who consulted with a family doctor.
   d. The longer the therapy, the greater was the reduction of psychiatric symptoms.

   Concept: II. A Competency: 33
   Question Type: *Applied*

34. There is a need to treat disorders in ways that scientific research has shown to be effective. As such, ________________________ refer to techniques that are evidence-based, while ________________________ is a generic term that refers to any form of talk therapy.

   Concept: II. A Competency: 34
   Question Type: *Factual*

35. Joey is horrified by the idea of being in public. His therapist teaches him to pair relaxation with being in public. At first, Joey thinks about public places and relaxes. Then he steps outside and relaxes. Then he steps off his porch and relaxes. This goes on until Joey is able to go to the mall and stay without panicking. This treatment technique is called:
   a. systematic desensitization
   b. flooding
   c. implosion
   d. cathartic submersion

   Concept: II. B. 1 Competency: 35
   Question Type: *Applied*

36. Manuel is afraid of heights. Because he lives in a small town, it is not easy to find a tall building to expose him to his fears. His therapist uses a computer to simulate for Manuel the experience of standing on the edge of a really tall building. His therapist has effectively created an exposure technique through the use of:
   a. systematic desensitization
   b. in vivo environments
   c. split reality
   d. virtual environments

   Concept: II. B. 1. a. 1 Competency: 36
   Question Type: *Applied*

37. Which of the following is the MOST effective treatment for panic disorder with agoraphobia?
   a. structured supportive therapy
   b. cognitive-behavioural therapy (CBT)
   c. cognitive-behavioural therapy (CBT) and medication
   d. medication (e.g., imipramine)

   Concept: II. B. 2 Competency: 37
   Question Type: *Applied*

38. Steve decides to pursue behavioural therapy to treat his obsessive-compulsive disorder. From reading about empirically validated treatments, Steve knows that the two most important components of behavioural therapy for OCD are:
   a. exposure and response prevention
   b. contingency and reinforcement
   c. insight and action
   d. relaxation and confrontation

   Concept: II. B. 3. a Competency: 38
   Question Type: *Applied*

39. Harding is experiencing major depression and has many distorted cognitions. According to Aaron Beck's cognitive triad, he will experience distorted thoughts in which area?
    a. oneself
    b. the situation
    c. future
    d. oneself, the situation, and the future

    Concept: II. C. 2. a Competency: 39
    Question Type: *Applied*

40. Brynn wants to relieve her symptoms of depression and has decided to engage in aerobic exercise. This has been shown to be effective due to:
    a. the blocking of endorphins
    b. the release of endorphins
    c. the blocking of norepinephrine
    d. decreased levels of acetylcholine

    Concept: II. C. 3. b Competency: 40
    Question Type: *Applied*

41. For which of the following disorders is electroconvulsive therapy (ECT) most effective?
    a. schizophrenia
    b. depression
    c. dissociative identity disorder
    d. obsessive-compulsive disorder

    Concept: II. C. 3. c Competency: 41
    Question Type: *Factual*

42. TMS seems to be more effective for ______________ depression, whereas ECT seems to be more effective for ______________ depression.
    a. nonpsychotic; psychotic
    b. manic; unipolar
    c. unipolar; bipolar
    d. dysthymic; bipolar

    Concept: II. C. 3. d Competency: 42
    Question Type: *Factual*

43. For each of the following statements, please match the sex that the statement describes.

____ Reluctant to admit to being depressed	a) Male
____ Have the additional burden of how work and family interact	b) Female
____ Primary consumers of psychotherapy	
____ Manifest depression as isolation and irritability	

    Concept: II. C. 5 Competency: 43
    Question Type: *Factual*

44. Jacki has been experiencing hallucinations lately and believes that everyone in her dorm is out to get her. Her physician decides to put her on medication to treat schizophrenia. Which of the following medications is NOT a choice for her?
    a. MAO inhibitors
    b. Reserpine
    c. Chlorpromazine
    d. Haloperidol

    Concept: II. D. 1 Competency: 44
    Question Type: *Applied*

45. Which of the following statements is TRUE regarding the prognosis for schizophrenia?
    a. Those diagnosed with schizophrenia later in life tend to have a poorer prognosis than those who experience their first symptoms during childhood or adolescence.
    b. Men tend to have a better prognosis than women.
    c. Schizophrenia in developing countries is often not as severe as in developed countries.
    d. Supportive family networks tend to interfere with improvement in individuals with schizophrenia.

    Concept: II. D. 4 Competency: 45
    Question Type: *Applied*

46. Suppose a close friend or family member has an obvious psychological problem (e.g., eating disorder, drug/alcohol, personality disorder) yet refuses to seek psychological treatment. What would you do? What can you do?

    ____

    ____

    ____

    ____

    Concept: II. E Competency: 46
    Question Type: *Conceptual*

47. Kevin is having some psychological problems, but he is picky about the qualifications of his therapist. He looks in the yellow pages under the term *psychiatrists.* From our knowledge of therapist training we can tell him that:
   a. we know nothing about these therapists' qualifications
   b. we know that these therapists have at least a master's degree in a mental health field
   c. we know that the therapists have a medical degree and a supervised residency
   d. we know that these therapists have a graduate degree and a 1-year internship in a mental health setting

Concept: II. F Competency: 47
Question Type: *Applied*

48. Jerry, George, Elaine, and Kramer are seeing a psychologist in group therapy during their stay in prison. What are their chances of receiving medication from him to deal with their mental health issues?
   a. None—psychiatrists are the only mental health professionals allowed to prescribe medication.
   b. None—nurses and medical social workers are the only mental health professionals allowed to prescribe medication.
   c. Slim—some U.S. states have passed legislation to allow clinical psychologists to prescribe medication, provided they receive appropriate training.
   d. Fair—recently graduated psychologists in all 50 states have completed special training programs and are allowed to prescribe medication.

Concept: II. F. 1 Competency: 48
Question Type: *Applied*

49. Sandi is interested in becoming a clinical psychologist. She is looking into graduate schools and notices that some offer a Ph.D. and some offer a Psy.D. What is the difference between the two clinical psychology degrees?
   a. Both degrees have training in psychotherapy; however, the Ph.D. degree has more training in psychological research.
   b. The Ph.D. offers training in prescribing medication; the Psy.D. offers more traditional psychotherapy training.
   c. The Ph.D. has more of an environmental focus; the Psy.D. has more of a medical/biological focus.
   d. Although the degrees have a different history, they are virtually identical in everyday practice.

Concept: II. F. 1 Competency: 49
Question Type: *Applied*

50. Which of the following is NOT one of the stages of dialectical behaviour therapy?
   a. The therapist targets the client's most extreme and dysfunctional behaviours.
   b. The therapist confronts the client's manipulations.
   c. The therapist helps the client explore past traumatic experiences that may be at the root of emotional problems.
   d. The therapist helps the patient develop self-respect and independent problem solving.

Concept: III. A. 1 Competency: 50
Question Type: *Applied*

51. Which of the following statements about treatment of anti-social personality disorder is NOT true?
   a. Psychotropic medications have not been effective in treating this disorder.
   b. Traditional psychotherapeutic approaches seem to be of little use in treating anti-social personality disorder.
   c. Cognitive approaches encounter barriers because these clients don't care that they are doing something wrong.
   d. A behavioural approach is effective when implemented on an outpatient basis.

Concept: III. B. 1 Competency: 51
Question Type: *Factual*

52. Keith is a 30-year-old male who is in prison for embezzlement. He has a lengthy criminal history and is diagnosed with anti-social personality disorder. The prognosis for Keith's improvement is:
   a. poor
   b. fair
   c. guarded
   d. good

Concept: III. B. 2 Competency: 52
Question Type: *Applied*

53. Evidence from the treatment of adolescent depression has NOT demonstrated that:
   a. the group receiving both Prozac and CBT had the best outcomes
   b. participants in the Prozac group were twice as likely to have serious suicidal thoughts or intentions compared with those undergoing other treatments
   c. suicide attempts for those on antidepressants were common
   d. improvement with CBT alone was similar to Prozac alone

Concept: IV. A Competency: 53
Question Type: *Factual*

54. Which of the following therapies is most effective in the treatment of attention-deficit/hyperactivity disorder?
    a. play therapy
    b. stimulant medication (e.g., Ritalin)
    c. behaviour modification
    d. stimulant medication plus behavioural therapy

    Concept: IV. B Competency: 54
    Question Type: *Factual*

55. Hoa has been diagnosed with ADHD and has been prescribed Ritalin. According to research, she will experience all of the following EXCEPT:
    a. She will be happier, more socially adept, and more academically successful.
    b. She has a greater chance of developing a substance abuse problem.
    c. She will interact more positively with her parents.
    d. She may experience sleep problems, reduced appetite, bodily twitches, and temporary growth suppression.

    Concept: IV. B. 1. a Competency: 55
    Question Type: *Applied*

56. Which of the following therapies is most effective for children with autism?
    a. supportive therapies
    b. structured therapies
    c. play therapy
    d. unstructured therapies

    Concept: IV. C. 1 Competency: 56
    Question Type: *Factual*

57. The long-term prognosis for children with autism is
    a. poor
    b. fair
    c. guarded
    d. good

    Concept: IV. C. 3 Competency: 57
    Question Type: *Factual*

ANSWER KEY

Item **Answer**

1. interactions between the practitioner and client aimed at helping clients understand their symptoms and problems and providing solutions for them.
2. c
3. d
4. a
5. b
6. c
7. a
8. d
9. b
10. c
11. b
12. d
13. a
14. rational-emotive therapy; Interpersonal therapy
15. c
16. d
17. b
18. b
19. c
20. d
21. b; a; a; c; a; b; c; b
22. b
23. c
24. c
25. c
26. d
27. a
28. c
29. b
30. a
31. d
32. b
33. a
34. psychological treatments; psychotherapy
35. a
36. d
37. c
38. a
39. d
40. b
41. b
42. a
43. a; b; b; a
44. a
45. c

46. Answers will vary, but this is a common problem individuals face. On the whole, psychotherapy is based on a client who is in distress and is willing to make changes to alleviate that distress. This is much more difficult when the individual either does not recognize the issue or is unwilling to take steps to correct it. As an interested bystander, you can tactfully express your concerns to your friend or family member. If this does not work, you should consider involving other friends and family members both for feedback and support. You will want to be diplomatic about this because you want to continue to keep the lines of communication open and be available when needed. Immediately alienating the person generally is not beneficial. If the behaviour continues or becomes more dangerous or life-threatening, then you and the other members of this person's social circle might consider an intervention where everyone gets together at one time in one place and expresses their concern. Again, be sure this is done in a caring rather than punitive fashion, and have some concrete sources available for help. If the person becomes a danger to self or others, you can go to your local hospital to get him or her committed against his or her will. If you are totally stuck and afraid, call your local police and they will help you with options.

    Remember that going through psychological problems with a friend or family member can be stressful for you. Consider getting your own sources of help including friend and family support groups. Research the disorder and support groups to see what is available in your community. You can also go to the sites for the Canadian Mental Health Association (www.cmha.ca) and Health Canada (www.hc-sc.gc.ca/hl-vs/mental) for further information.
47. c
48. a
49. a
50. c
51. d
52. a
53. c
54. d
55. b
56. b
57. a

KEY TERM EXERCISES

anti-anxiety drugs

Textbook Definition:
Your Own Definition:
Your Own Example:

antidepressants

Textbook Definition:
Your Own Definition:
Your Own Example:

antipsychotics

Textbook Definition:
Your Own Definition:
Your Own Example:

applied behavioural analysis (ABA)

Textbook Definition:
Your Own Definition:
Your Own Example:

biological therapies

Textbook Definition:
Your Own Definition:
Your Own Example:

client-centred therapy

Textbook Definition:
Your Own Definition:
Your Own Example:

cognitive-behavioural therapy (CBT)

Textbook Definition:
Your Own Definition:
Your Own Example:

cognitive restructuring

Textbook Definition:
Your Own Definition:
Your Own Example:

cognitive therapy

Textbook Definition:
Your Own Definition:
Your Own Example:

dialectical behaviour therapy (DBT)

Textbook Definition:
Your Own Definition:
Your Own Example:

electroconvulsive therapy (ECT)

Textbook Definition:
Your Own Definition:
Your Own Example:

exposure

Textbook Definition:
Your Own Definition:
Your Own Example:

expressed emotion

Textbook Definition:
Your Own Definition:
Your Own Example:

insight

Textbook Definition:
Your Own Definition:
Your Own Example:

psychotherapy

Textbook Definition:
Your Own Definition:
Your Own Example:

psychotropic medications

Textbook Definition:
Your Own Definition:
Your Own Example:

CHAPTER 16 Cultural Psychology

CONCEPT MAP

I. What Is Culture?
  A. Information Transmitted through Learning
    1. Imitative or Social Learning
  B. Shared and Unique Aspects of Culture
    1. Cultural Learning in Other Species
    2. Human Cultural Learning
  C. Accumulating Cultural Information
    1. Ratio of Cerebral Cortex to Brain Volume
      a. Group Dynamics
      b. Social Learning
      c. Communication Skills
      d. Theory of Mind
      e. Development of Tools

II. What Is Cultural Psychology?
  A. The Study of How Culture Shapes Psychological Processes
    1. Interaction Between People and Information
    2. Individuality and Belongingness
    3. Universal and Culturally Specific Psychologies
    4. Generalizability of Research Findings

III. How Does Culture Affect the Mind?
  A. Universal Behaviours, Reactions, and Institutions
    1. Sex, Gender, and the Family
    2. Social Differentiation
    3. Social Customs
    4. Emotion
    5. Cognition
  B. Culture and Mind Are Inextricably Bound
    1. Interaction of the Mind and the Individual
      a. Interaction of Mind and Culture
        1. Culture and Education
  C. Sensitive Period for Learning Culture
    1. Language Development
    2. Acculturation
  D. Aging and Cultural Differences in Psychological Processes
    1. Cultural Differences Increase with Age
      a. Correspondence Bias/Fundamental Attribution Error
      b. Dispositional and Situational Attribution
  E. Culture and Variation in Self-Concept
    1. Self-Concept in Individualistic and Collectivistic Cultures
      a. Cultural Variation in Brain Activity
      b. Interdependent and Independent Self-Construal
        1. Postdecisional Dissonance

IV. What Are the Psychological Consequences of Moving to a Different Culture?
  A. Acculturation Requires Significant Adjustment
    1. Acculturation
      a. Psychological Adjustment
        1. U-Shaped Curve
        2. Honeymoon Stage
        3. Culture Shock/Crisis Stage
        4. Adjustment Stage
        5. Cultural Distance
        6. Cultural Fit
  B. Discrimination and Minority Cultural Backgrounds
    1. Stereotype Threat

C. Multicultural People Can Switch between Different Selves
  1. Frame-switching
D. On Ethics: Multicultural vs. Culture-Blind Workplaces
E. Multicultural People May Be More Creative
  1. Creativity and Adapting to Different Cultures

V. How Does Culture Affect How We Think and Behave?
  A. Cultures Differ in Analytic and Holistic Thinking
    1. Taxonomic Categorization
    2. Thematic Categorization
    3. Analytic Thinking
    4. Holistic Thinking
  B. Cultures Differ in Motivations for Control and Choice
    1. Primary Control
    2. Secondary Control
    3. The Role of Culture in Choice
  C. Cultures Differ in the Bases of Relationships
    1. Arranged Marriage
    2. Love Marriage
    3. Physical Attractiveness
  D. Cultures Vary in Perceptions of Happiness
  E. Cultures Differ in Group Performance
    1. Social Loafing
    2. Social Striving
  F. Cultures Differ in Moral Reasoning
    1. Culture and Kohlberg's Moral Reasoning Model
    2. Shweder's Codes of Ethics
      a. Ethic of Autonomy
      b. Ethic of Community
      c. Ethic of Divinity
  G. The Influence of Language on Thought
    1. Whorfian Hypothesis
      a. Language Does Not Determine Thought
      b. Language Influences Thought

VI. How Does Culture Influence Mental Health?
  A. Culture-Bound Disorders Largely Limited to Cultural Contexts
    1. Culture-Bound Disorders
      a. *Dhat* Syndrome
      b. Hysteria
  B. Universal Mental Disorders in Cultural Contexts
    1. Depression
      a. Somatic Symptoms
    2. Social Phobia
      a. *Taijinkyoufushou* (TKS)
    3. Anorexia Nervosa
    4. Schizophrenia

CHAPTER SUMMARY

What Is Culture?

• Information Transmitted Through Learning: Beliefs, values, rules and customs are passed from one generation to the next. More broadly, culture is information acquired by imitative or social learning.

• Shared and Unique Aspects of Culture: Culture is not unique to humans. Monkeys show evidence of imitative learning and dolphins demonstrate cultural learning. Nonetheless, human cultural information is learned quickly, learned by almost all members of a culture group, and it is pervasive in all aspects of our life.

• Accumulating Cultural Information: Culture is adaptive. In humans and other primate species, living in a larger group is associated with having a larger cerebral cortex allowing for greater cognitive capacity in social living. The human brain has evolved to navigate the dynamics of group living, to facilitate social learning, to communicate through language, to attribute the intentions of others, and to develop complex tools.

What Is Cultural Psychology?

• The Study of How Culture Shapes Psychological Processes: The interaction between people and information gives rise to cultural environments. The importance of individuality and seeking belongingness differs across cultures. To account for shared life experiences as well as cultural variation there are universal and culturally specific psychologies. People with different cultural experiences differ in their psychological processes; thus, research findings are not always generalizable.

How Does Culture Affect the Mind?

• Universal Behaviours, Reactions, and Institutions: Cultures can vary in many aspects, but at the same time, many of the psychological experiences of humans are similar.

• Culture and Mind Are Inextricably Bound: Culture is shaped by the mind and in turn culture influences the thoughts of the mind.

• Sensitive Period for Learning Culture: Infants are born with the ability to recognize all 150 language phonemes but with time can only discern phonemes in their own language. Younger children are able to acclimate to new cultures more easily.

• Aging and Cultural Differences in Psychological Processes: The influence of culture increases with age. Cultural differences are more pronounced in adults than in children or even teenagers.

• Culture and Variation in Self-Concept: In individualistic cultures people tend see themselves as independent. In collectivist cultures people tend to see themselves as interdependent. This cultural variation is mirrored in neural imaging studies. Variation in self construal across contexts is influenced by culture. Postdecisional dissonance is evident in some cultures but absent in others.

What Are the Psychological Consequences of Moving to a Different Culture?

• Acculturation Requires Significant Adjustment: Acculturation is a process whereby members of one cultural group adopt the cultural beliefs of another group after moving into contact with the new group. Acculturation involves a long pattern of psychological adjustment.

• Discrimination and Minority Cultural Backgrounds: Prejudice and discrimination against ethnic groups can lead to stereotype threat if members of that group act consistently with an existing negative stereotype.

• Multicultural People Can Switch between Different Selves: Individuals with experience in more than one culture can change how they interpret the world in response to changes in context.

• Multicultural People May Be More Creative: Adapting to a new cultural environment can lead to creative insight. Learning to adjust may give people a new perspective.

How Does Culture Affect How We Think and Behave?

• Cultures Differ in Analytic and Holistic Thinking: Taxonomic categorization is a strategy for grouping objects based on perceived similar attributes. Thematic categorization is a strategy for grouping objects based on the relationship between objects. Analytic thinking involves breaking down an object into its constituent parts in order to understand how they work together. Holistic thinking involves considering the object in relation to the context and to other objects.

• Cultures Differ in Motivations for Control and Choice: Primary control is the belief that one can influence existing realities to fit one's goals and objectives. Secondary control is the belief that one can change oneself to fit with existing realities. Primary control is more common in individualistic cultures while secondary control is more common in collectivist cultures. Culture determines the amount of freedom individuals feel they have to make a choice.

• Cultures Differ in the Bases of Relationships: Arranged marriages are still common in many cultures and studies indicate that they are no less satisfying than marriages based on love. Cultural variation also determines the value assigned to physical attractiveness.

• Cultures Vary in Perceptions of Happiness: Poverty, the importance of positive emotion, and the importance of a balanced life are all factors that can influence people's overall levels of happiness across cultures. Preferred forms of happiness differ across cultures.

• Cultures Differ in Group Performance: Some cultures will work harder as individuals than in a group whereas other cultures work harder in a group than as individuals.

• Cultures Differ in Moral Reasoning: Lawrence Kohlberg developed a model of moral reasoning, but his third stage, the postconventional level, is not universally found across cultures. This level of moral reasoning may represent one of three codes of ethics that guide moral judgments of cultures to varying degrees. Ethic of autonomy emphasizes the right and freedoms of the individual. Ethic of community emphasizes the collective group. Ethic of divinity is concerned with protecting sanctity of God's creation.

• The Influence of Language on Thought: The Whorfian hypothesis has been stated in both a strong form and weak form. The strong form states that language is not only the voice for thought, but determines thought. The weak form states that language does not determine, but rather influences thought.

How Does Culture Influence Mental Health?

• Culture-Bound Disorders Largely Limited to Cultural Contexts: Some psychological disorders are limited to specific cultural contexts. Dhat syndrome, found in South Asian cultures, is characterized by a belief in male patients that they are leaking semen. Hysteria was reported in women in mid-nineteenth-century Europe who displayed symptoms such as faintness, insomnia, paralysis, loss of appetite for food and sex, and disruptive behaviour.

• Universal Mental Disorders in Cultural Contexts: Some psychological disorders are universal but present differently depending on the cultural context. In China symptoms are more likely to be somatic whereas in North America they are likely to be psychological. Social phobia is more common in collectivist cultures where the emphasis on fitting in is strong. *Taijinkyoufushou,* a phobia identified in Japan, is a fear of confronting others that is distinct from social anxiety. Anorexia may be more common in North America than other cultures with the number of diagnosed cases increasing over the last 40 years. In other cultures self-starvation may be motivated by factors other than the fear of gaining weight and the desire to be thin. Schizophrenia is found across cultures but there is cultural variation in how the disorder presents.

COMPETENCY MODEL

What Is Culture?

Information Transmitted through Learning

1. Explain that culture is acquired through imitative or social learning.

Shared and Unique Aspects of Culture

2. Describe instances of cultural learning in other species.
3. How is human cultural learning different from that of other species?

Accumulating Cultural Information

4. How has the social character of humans been important in the evolution of our brains?
5. Describe the cerebral cortex to brain volume ratio.
6. How is human social learning more advanced than other primates?
7. What is the importance of language communication?
8. Describe theory of mind and its importance in the accumulation of cultural information.
9. Why have humans developed increasingly sophisticated tools while other animals have not?

What Is Cultural Psychology?

The Study of How Culture Shapes Psychological Processes

10. Describe cultural environments and how they differ from social environments.
11. Know that individuality and belongingness are emphasized differently across cultures.
12. Know that there are both universal and culturally specific psychologies.
13. What is a major limitation of psychological research with respect to culture?

How Does Culture Affect the Mind?

Universal Behaviours, Reactions, and Institutions

14. Know there are universal psychological experiences.
15. How are universal psychological experiences expressed differently across cultures?

Culture and Mind are Inextricably Bound

16. Describe the interaction between mind and culture.
17. How does culture influence education?

Sensitive Period for Learning Culture

18. How does culture influence language development?
19. What is the sensitive period for acculturation?

Aging and Cultural Differences in Psychological Processes

20. Why do cultural differences in psychological processes increase with age?
21. What is the correspondence bias?
22. What is the fundamental attribution error?
23. Know that dispositional and situational attributions vary across cultures.

Culture and Variation in Self-Concept

24. How does self-concept differ between individualistic and collectivist cultures?
25. Describe cultural variation in brain activity.
26. Explain independent vs. interdependent self-construal.
27. Why does interdependent self-construal vary across contexts?
28. What is postdecisional dissonance?
29. How does postdecisional dissonance differ between cultures?

What Are the Psychological Consequences of Moving to a Different Culture?

Acculturation Requires Significant Adjustment

30. Describe acculturation.
31. What is the common pattern of adjustment in acculturation?
32. Describe the honeymoon stage.
33. Describe the culture shock or crisis stage.
34. Describe the adjustment stage.
35. How does cultural distance predict acculturative success?
36. What is cultural fit?

Discrimination and Minority Cultural Backgrounds

37. What is stereotype threat?
38. What factors play a role in determining the stereotyped groups?
39. What is the colour-blind approach?
40. Describe the multicultural approach.

Multicultural People Can Switch between Different Selves

41. What is frame-switching?

42. What is the role of context in frame-switching?

Multicultural People May Be More Creative

43. Explain why multicultural people may be more creative.

How Does Culture Affect How We Think and Behave?

Cultures Differ in Analytic and Holistic Thinking

44. What is a taxonomic categorization strategy?

45. What is a thematic categorization strategy?

46. How is analytic thinking characterized?

47. How is holistic thinking characterized?

48. Describe cultural differences in analytic and holistic thinking.

Cultures Differ in Motivations for Control and Choice

49. How do people achieve primary control?

50. How do people achieve secondary control?

51. Identify which type of culture might be more likely to exercise primary control.

52. Describe why the freedom of choice is more valued in some cultures than others.

Cultures Differ in the Bases of Relationships

53. Explain the difference between arranged marriage and love marriage.

54. Describe relational mobility.

55. Why is physical attractiveness valued in some cultures but not in others?

Cultures Vary in Perceptions of Happiness

56. Describe why different cultures vary in their level of happiness.

57. Identify the preferred kind of happiness of some cultures.

Cultures Differ in Group Performance

58. Which cultures are more likely to demonstrate social loafing?

59. Which cultures are more likely to demonstrate social striving?

60. Which cultures have higher rates of conformity?

Cultures Differ in Moral Reasoning

61. Know the levels of Kohlberg's moral reasoning model.

62. Describe the ethic of autonomy.

63. Describe the ethic of community.

64. Describe the ethic of divinity.

65. Explain how different cultures assign greater value to one ethic over another.

The Influence of Language on Thought

66. Describe the two forms of the Whorfian hypothesis.

How Does Culture Influence Mental Health?

Culture-Bound Disorders Largely Limited to Cultural Contexts

67. Describe *dhat* syndrome.

68. Explain why hysteria was a culture-bound disorder.

Universal Mental Disorders in Cultural Contexts

69. Explain how depression presents differently in different cultural contexts.

70. Which cultures report more social phobia?

71. Describe *taijinkyoufushou.*

72. Explain why anorexia nervosa may be culturally universal.

73. Explain how environmental factors play a role in the development of schizophrenia.

KNOWLEDGE CHECK

1. While culture commonly refers to the beliefs, values, rules, and customs of a group of people who share an environment, psychologists also refer to culture as information acquired through ____________________________.

   Concept: I. A. 1 Competency: 1
   Question Type: *Factual*

2. The human capacity for culture has an evolutionary basis rooted in all of the following EXCEPT:
   a. the development of social learning
   b. the cerebral cortex to brain ratio
   c. the use of simple tools
   d. the development of theory of mind

   Concept: I. C. 1 Competency: 4
   Question Type: *Factual*

3. Clifford Geertz once said "we all begin with the natural equipment to live a thousand kinds of life but end in the end having lived only one." According to this statement:
   a. regardless of their genes or physical appearance, people can learn any cultural tradition
   b. culture is transmitted unconsciously
   c. culture is genetically programmed
   d. people develop similar cultural systems to make judgments and shape their behaviour

   Concept: III. A Competency: 8
   Question Type: *Applied*

4. Both of 4-month-old Yuriko's parents are Japanese. While they have difficulty distinguishing between the "ra" and "la" sounds in English, Yuriko has no problem. She is able to make this distinction because she:
   a. has a preference for phonemes from other cultures
   b. can still recognize all 150 phonemes
   c. has a preference for morphemes from other cultures
   d. has not begun to "babble" yet

   Concept: III. C. 1 Competency: 9
   Question Type: *Applied*

5. Which of the following statements about cross-cultural differences in attribution is true?
   a. The factors leading to internal or external attributions are the same all over the world.
   b. Attributional differences between two cultures are generally not due to cultural experiences.
   c. Experimental results from Western cultures tend to generalize to all cultures.
   d. Differences in attribution may be more pronounced as people age.

   Concept: III. D. 1 Competency: 20
   Question Type: *Factual*

6. Cross-cultural research has demonstrated that:
   a. people from Western cultures have a more interdependent self-construal
   b. people from Asian cultures have a more interdependent self-construal
   c. people who have a more independent self-construal vary a lot across contexts
   d. people who have a more interdependent self-construal show little variation across contexts

   Concept: III. E. 1 Competency: 24
   Question Type: *Factual*

7 Jill has just moved from Victoria, B.C., to Quebec City to study. Despite being unable to speak French, she has fallen in love with the winter Carnival and fairytale feel of the old buildings. Jill is in which stage of acculturation?
   a. culture shock
   b. adjustment
   c. honeymoon
   d. crisis

   Concept: IV. A. 1. a Competency: 32
   Question Type: *Applied*

8. Kelvin is concerned that if he does poorly on his Graduate Record Examination he will confirm the stereotype that black students do not perform as well on the exam as white students. Kelvin is likely to :
   a. do well on the exam because of stereotype threat
   b. do poorly on the exam because of stereotype threat
   c. do well on the exam because of the self-serving bias
   d. do poorly on the exam because of the self-serving bias

   Concept: IV. B. 1 Competency: 37
   Question Type: *Applied*

9. Ming was born in China but has lived in Canada for half her life. Her main competitor in class, Debra, does better than she does on a test. At school, Ming tells her friends it is because Debra is the teacher's pet. If she were at home, she would tell her parents it is because Debra is very smart. This is an example of:
   a. the fundamental attribution error
   b. frame-switching
   c. stereotyping
   d. prejudice

   Concept: IV. C. 1 Competency: 42
   Question Type: *Applied*

10. Martin moved his successful art studio to Nicaragua in an effort to escape the bleak Canadian winters. His most brilliant works have all been completed since his arrival in the new country. This is likely because: __________________________________.

    Concept: IV. E. 1 Competency: 43
    Question Type: *Applied*

11. Kira was asked to group two of the following three objects: chicken, cow, grass. Kira groups cow and grass together. This is an example of:
    a. taxonomic categorization
    b. thematic categorization
    c. object categorization
    d. elemental categorization

    Concept: V. A. 2 Competency: 44
    Question Type: *Applied*

12. ___________ thinking is characterized by understanding the system as a whole.
    a. Holistic
    b. Parallel
    c. Analog
    d. Analytic

    Concept: V. A   Competency: 47
    Question Type: *Factual*

13. Which of the following forms of control is less common among East Asian cultures?
    a. primary control
    b. secondary control
    c. illusory control
    d. predictive control

    Concept: V. B   Competency: 51
    Question Type: *Factual*

14. Simone, a French exchange student, is trying to choose a cereal at the grocery store but is faced with too many options. Simone cannot understand why anyone would want to choose from fifty cereals rather than just five. This is because she:
    a. values her freedom of choice
    b. gets overwhelmed in big stores
    c. places less value on the freedom of choice
    d. resents the influence of the ingroup

    Concept: V. B. 3   Competency: 52
    Question Type: *Applied*

15. People in arranged marriages are:
    a. more likely to report being unfaithful
    b. likely to report that they have fallen in love
    c. less satisfied than people in love marriages
    d. are more satisfied than people in love marriages

    Concept: V. C. 1   Competency: 53
    Question Type: *Factual*

16. Physical attractiveness is less valued in some cultures because:
    a. there is low relational mobility
    b. there is high relational mobility
    c. there is an emphasis on deindividuation
    d. there is an emphasis on appearing unique

    Concept: V. C. 3   Competency: 55
    Question Type: *Factual*

17. The presence of others would be most likely to improve performance for someone from:
    a. Canada working in a highly valued group
    b. Canada working in a less valued group
    c. China working in a highly valued group
    d. China working in a less valued group

    Concept: V. E. 2   Competency: 59
    Question Type: *Factual*

18. The ethic of ___________ which emphasizes an individual's duties and place in the social hierarchy, represents a level of moral reasoning akin to Kohlberg's ___________ level.
    a. divinity; postconventional
    b. autonomy; preconventional
    c. autonomy; postconventional
    d. community; postconventional

    Concept: V. F. 1   Competency: 61
    Question Type: *Factual*

19. In the last federal election, Jordan voted for the Conservative party. He strongly identifies with the Conservatives and is dedicated to his church community. Which ethic(s) might Jordan primarily use to guide his moral judgments?
    a. ethic of autonomy
    b. ethic of community
    c. ethic of divinity
    d. all of the above to the same extent

    Concept: V. F. 2   Competency: 64
    Question Type: *Applied*

20. The idea that suggests that the words we select and use actually influence the world we perceive is referred to as the:
    a. Whorfian hypothesis
    b. social learning theory
    c. linguistic proximity hypothesis
    d. symbolic interaction theory

    Concept: G. 1   Competency: 66
    Question Type: *Applied*

21. Symptoms of psychological disorders that are observable in a select few cultures are called:
    a. central
    b. universal
    c. culture-bound
    d. somatic

    Concept: VI. A. 1   Competency: 67
    Question Type: *Factual*

22. Nahid is working at a medical clinic in India. A patient arrives displaying highly neurotic symptoms which he blames on his belief that he is losing semen. Nahid diagnoses the patient with:
    a. neurasthenia
    b. schizophrenia
    c. *dhat* syndrome
    d. psychsomatic disorder

    Concept: VI. A. 1. a   Competency: 67
    Question Type: *Applied*

23. Patients in China suffering from depression are more likely to present with ____________ symptoms, whereas Canadian patients suffering from depression are likely to present with ____________ symptoms.
    a. somatic; psychological
    b. psychological; somatic
    c. somatic; catatonic
    d. psychological; neurotic

    Concept: VI. B. 1 Competency: 69
    Question Type: *Factual*

24. *Taijinkyoufushou* differs from social anxiety disorder in that it is characterized by:
    a. extreme self-consciousness
    b. a fear of having an offensive body odour
    c. heart palpitations
    d. avoidance of social situations

    Concept: VI. B. 2. a Competency: 71
    Question Type: *Factual*

25. Which psychological disorder is not culture bound?
    a. *dhat* syndrome
    b. amok
    c. schizophrenia
    d. hysteria

    Concept: VI. B. 4 Competency: 73
    Question Type: *Factual*

ANSWER KEY

Item	Answer
1.	Imitative and social learning
2.	c
3.	a
4.	b
5.	d
6.	b
7.	c
8.	b
9.	b
10.	Multicultural people are more creative. Adapting to a new culture may give people more creative insight.
11.	b
12.	a
13.	a
14.	c
15.	b
16.	a
17.	c
18.	d
19.	d
20.	a
21.	c
22.	c
23.	a
24.	b
25.	c